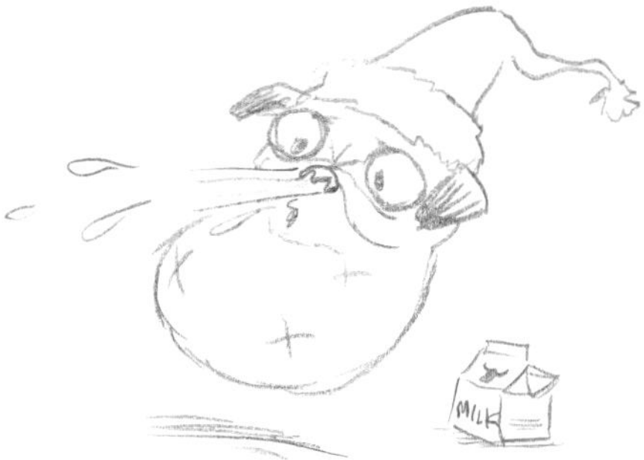

SARAH,

I HO[illegible]
MAKE YOU LAUGH SO HARD THAT
MILK COMES OUT YOUR NOSES!

— JAKE BARLOW
12/29/2011

Dedicated to my mother, Clara. I know she would have laughed at a few of these...

Foreword

Puddin' is a lot of things, but, more than anything else, Puddin' is pure pug without any of the extraneous bits that usually get in the way.

What Puddin' lacks in limbs he makes up for it in freedom. Not so much a "freedom to" as a "freedom from." Indeed, this is such an innate part of his nature that the book is named after this disinclination: Puddin' Don't.

Puddin' don't sit back and watch idly.
Puddin' don't avoid getting in over his head.
Puddin' don't suffer fools kindly.
And Puddin' don't withhold judgment.

Can you blame him?

Puddin' may lack limbs, yet still he overcomes adversity on a daily basis. Such is his ongoing struggle the struggle we all share. So let the following serve as scenes from an ongoing cautionary tale. Where Puddin' is concerned, all that is possible is inevitable, if you just wait long enough.

The real lesson is to handle everything with grace.

Don't worry so much.

Puddin' don't.

- Jeff "Scamper" Robinson

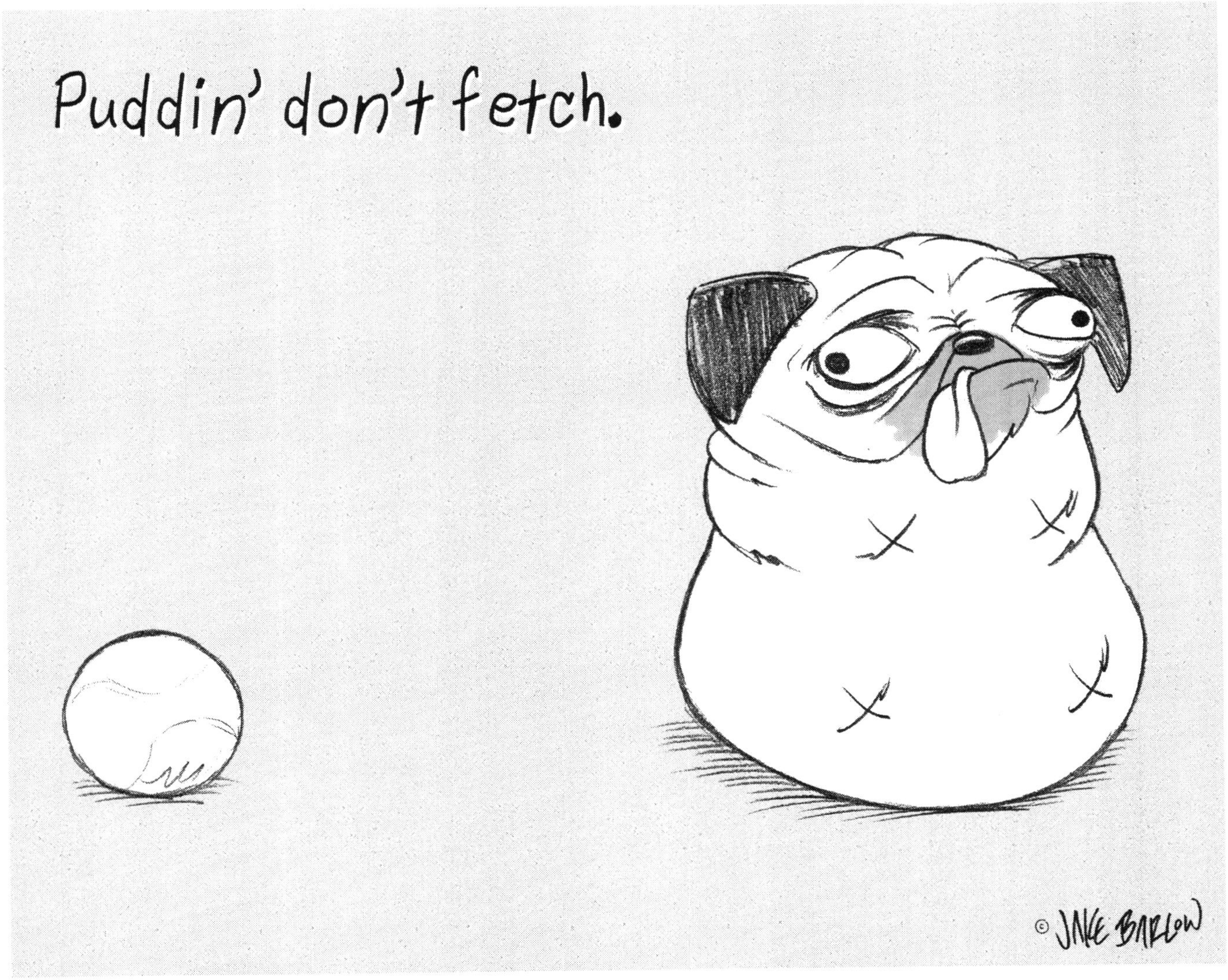
Puddin' don't fetch.
© JAKE BARLOW

Yes, this was the first published 'Puddin' Don't'.

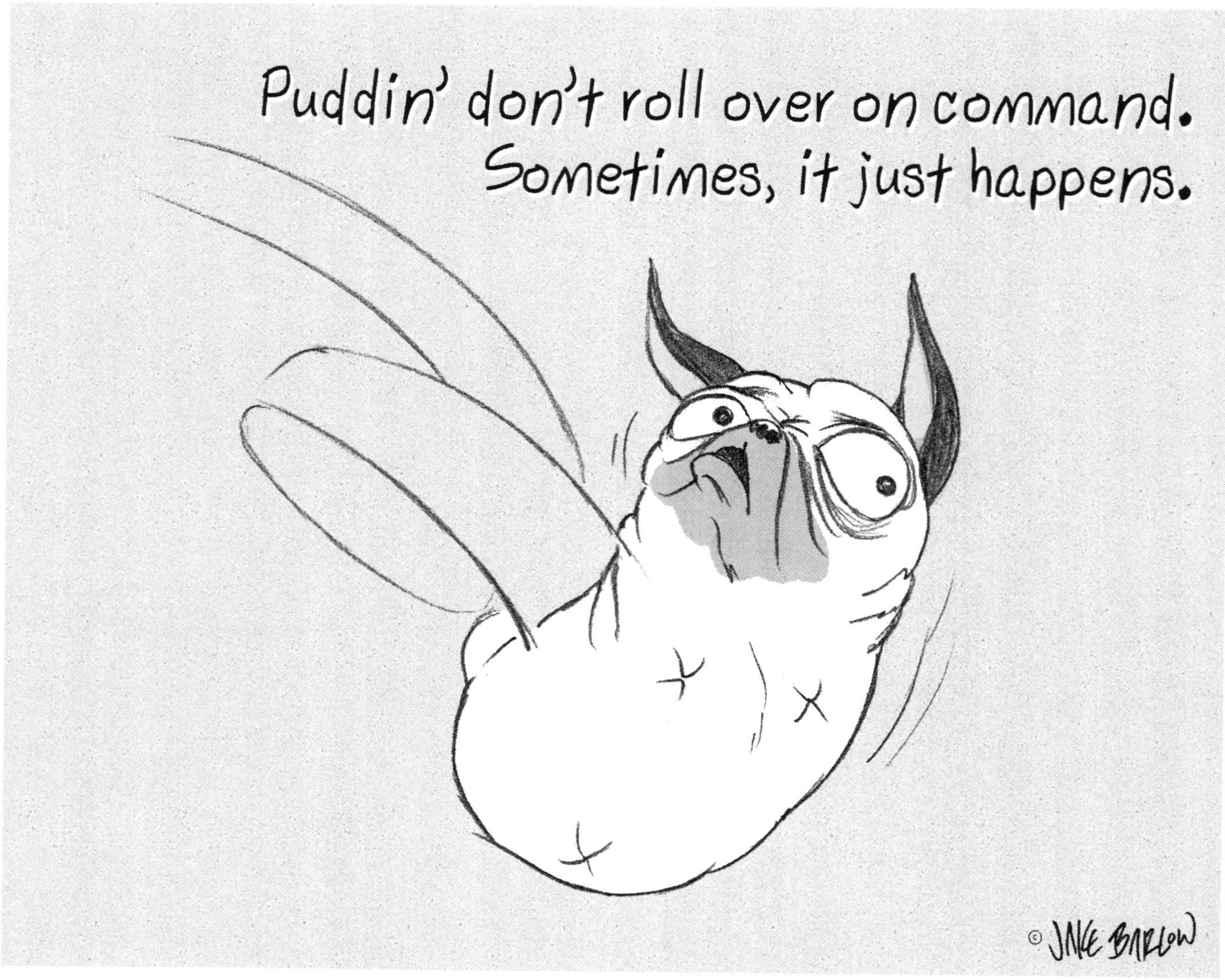
Puddin' don't roll over on command.
Sometimes, it just happens.
© JANE BARLOW

Puddin' don't like long walks.

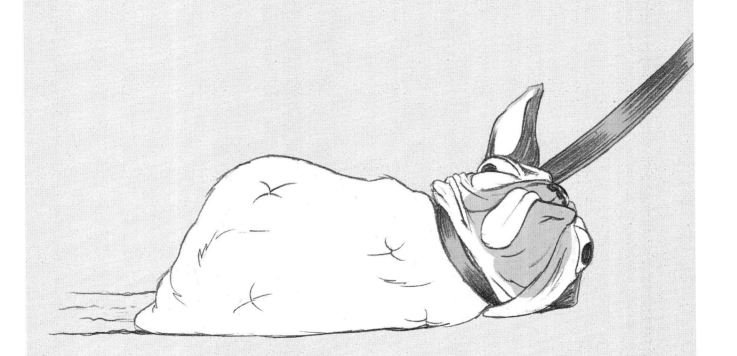

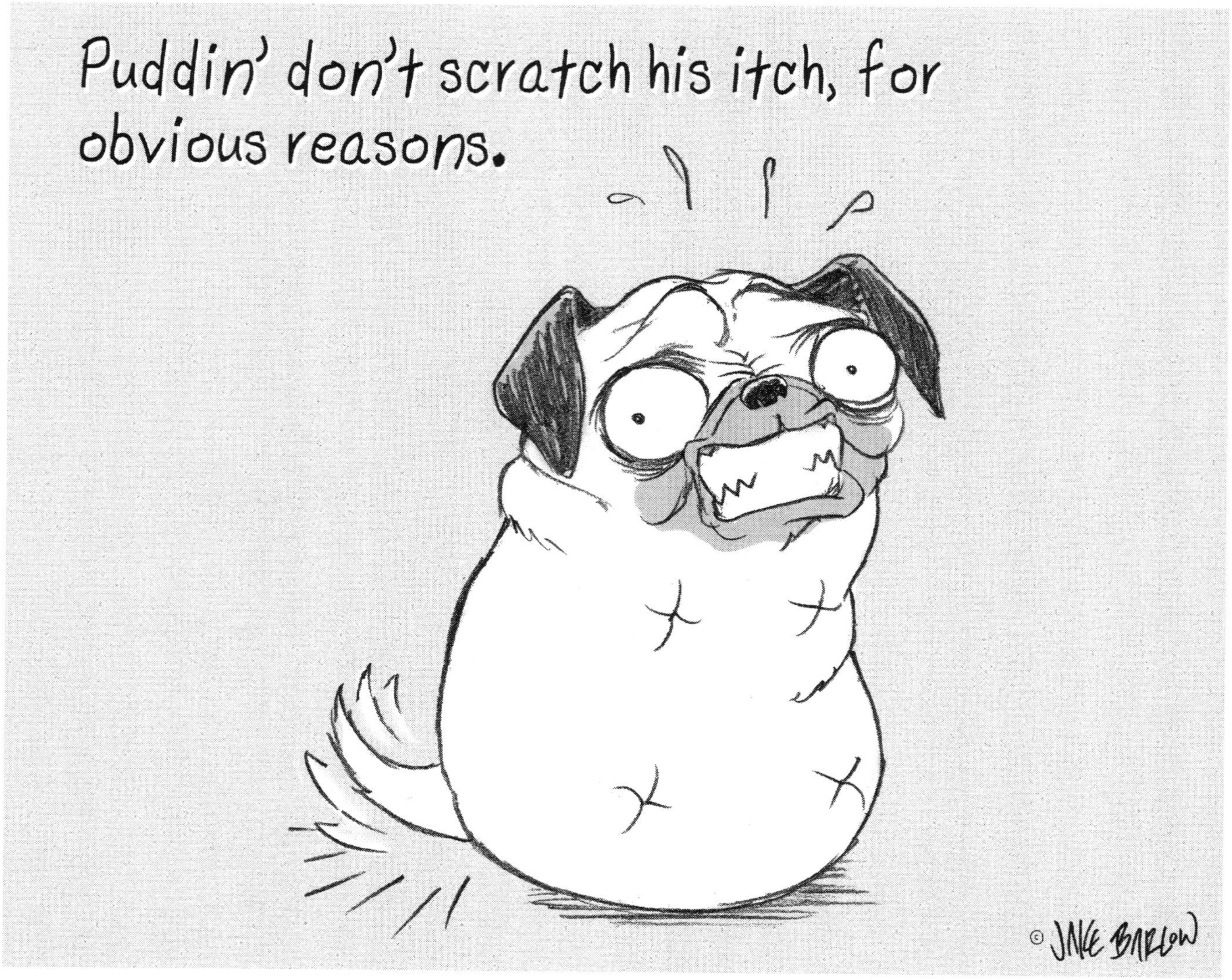
Puddin' don't scratch his itch, for obvious reasons.
© JAKE BARLOW

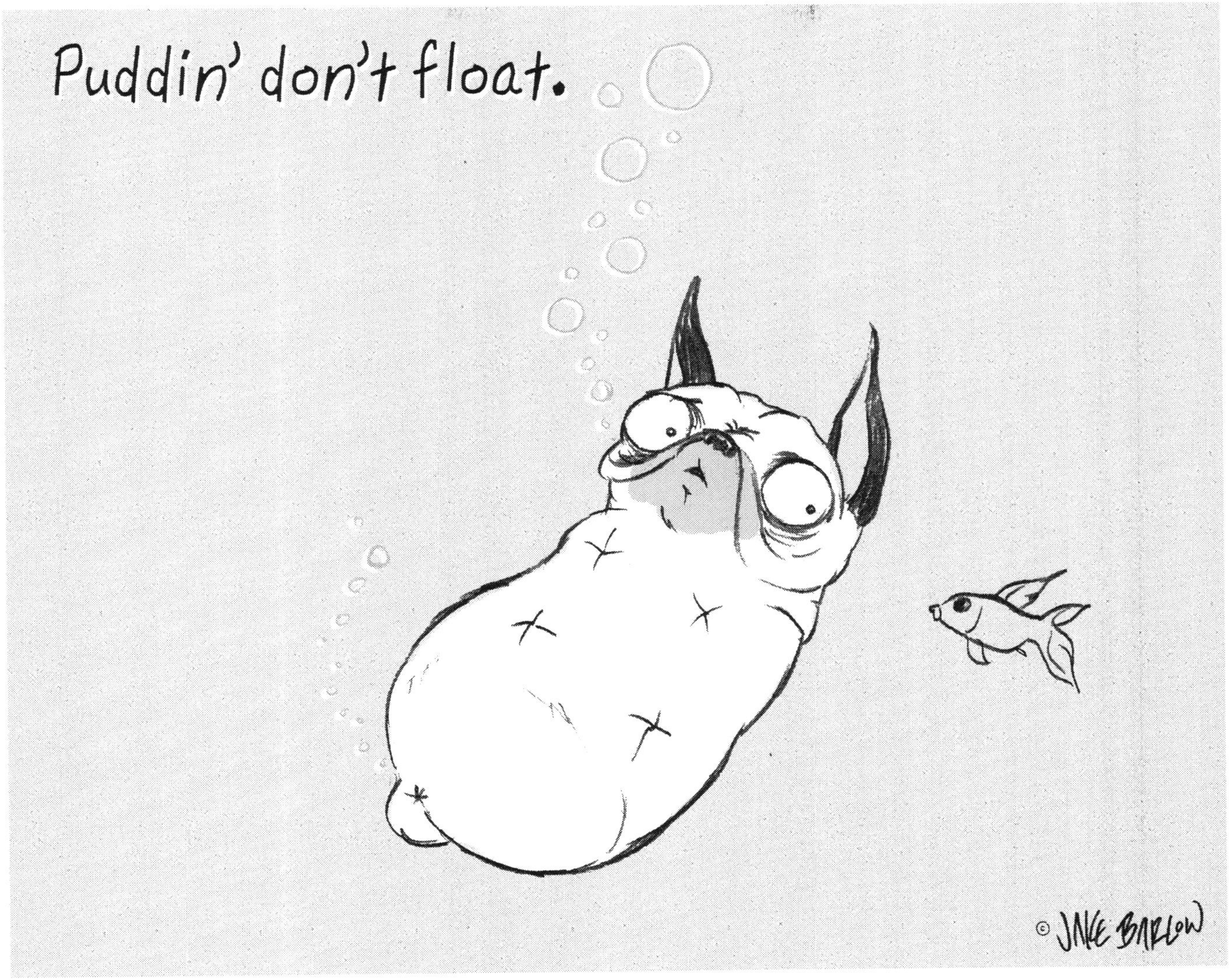
Puddin' don't float.
© JAKE BARLOW

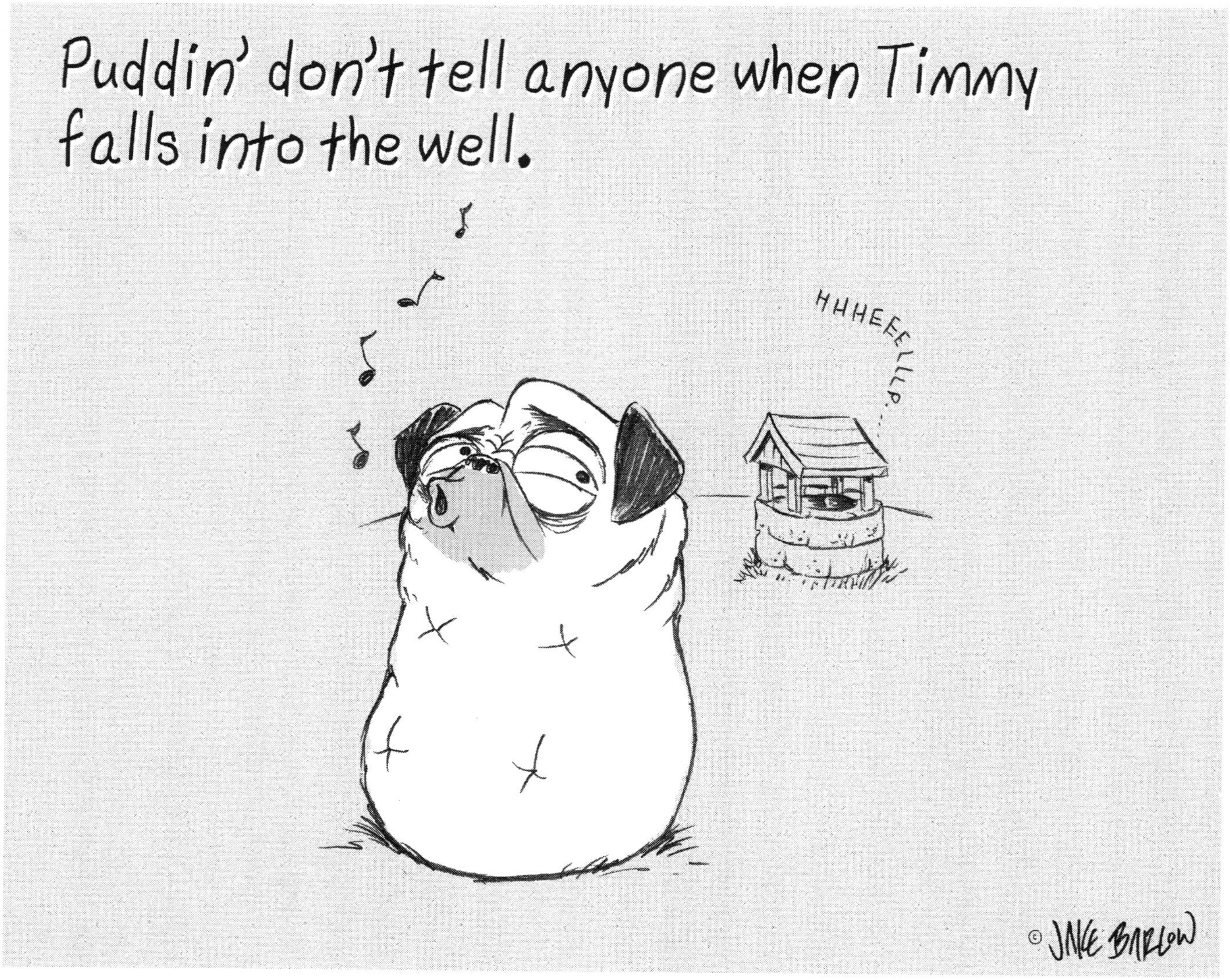
HHHEEELLLP...
© JAKE BARLOW

Puddin' don't tell anyone when Timmy falls into the well.

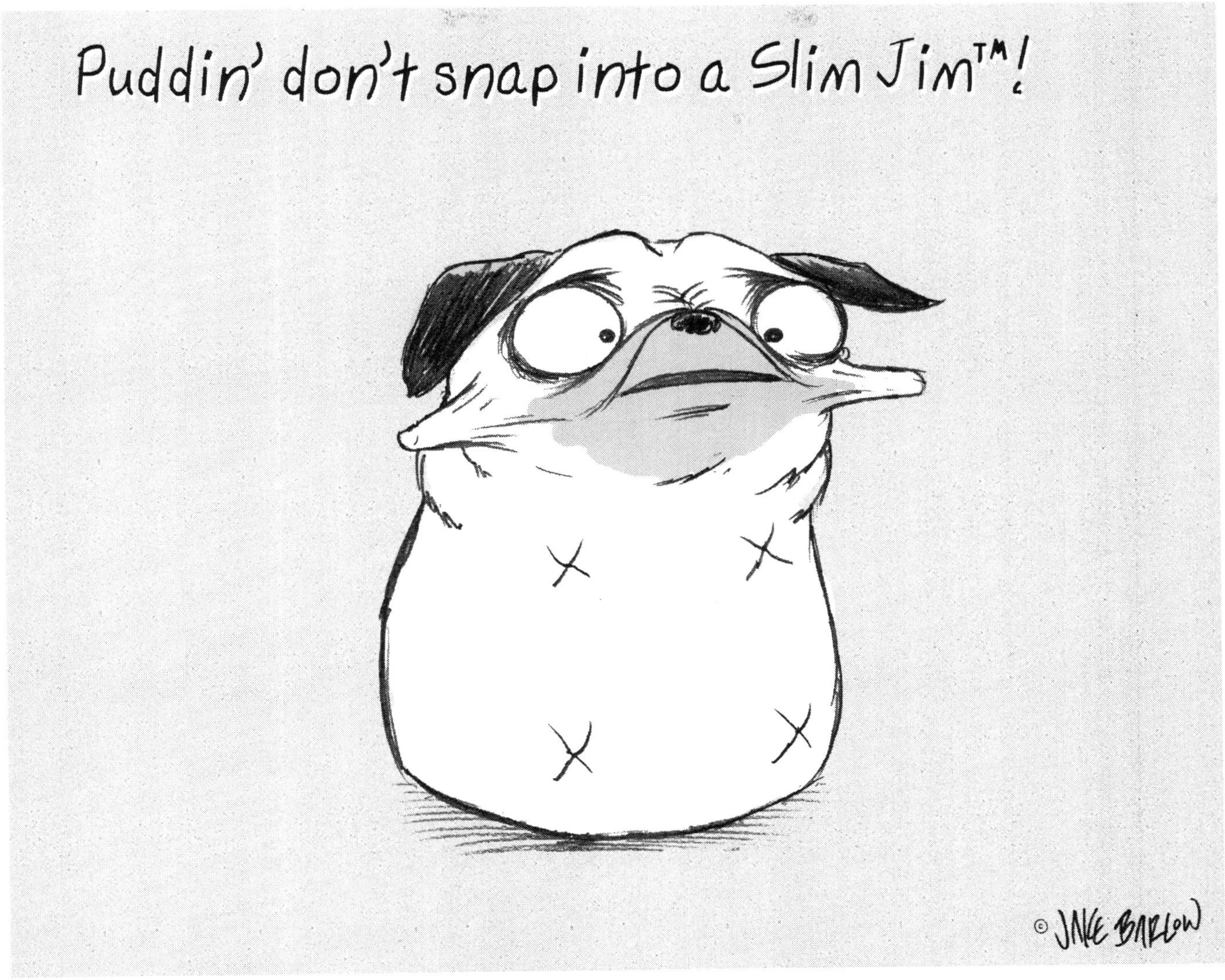
Puddin' don't snap into a Slim Jim™!
© JAKE BARLOW

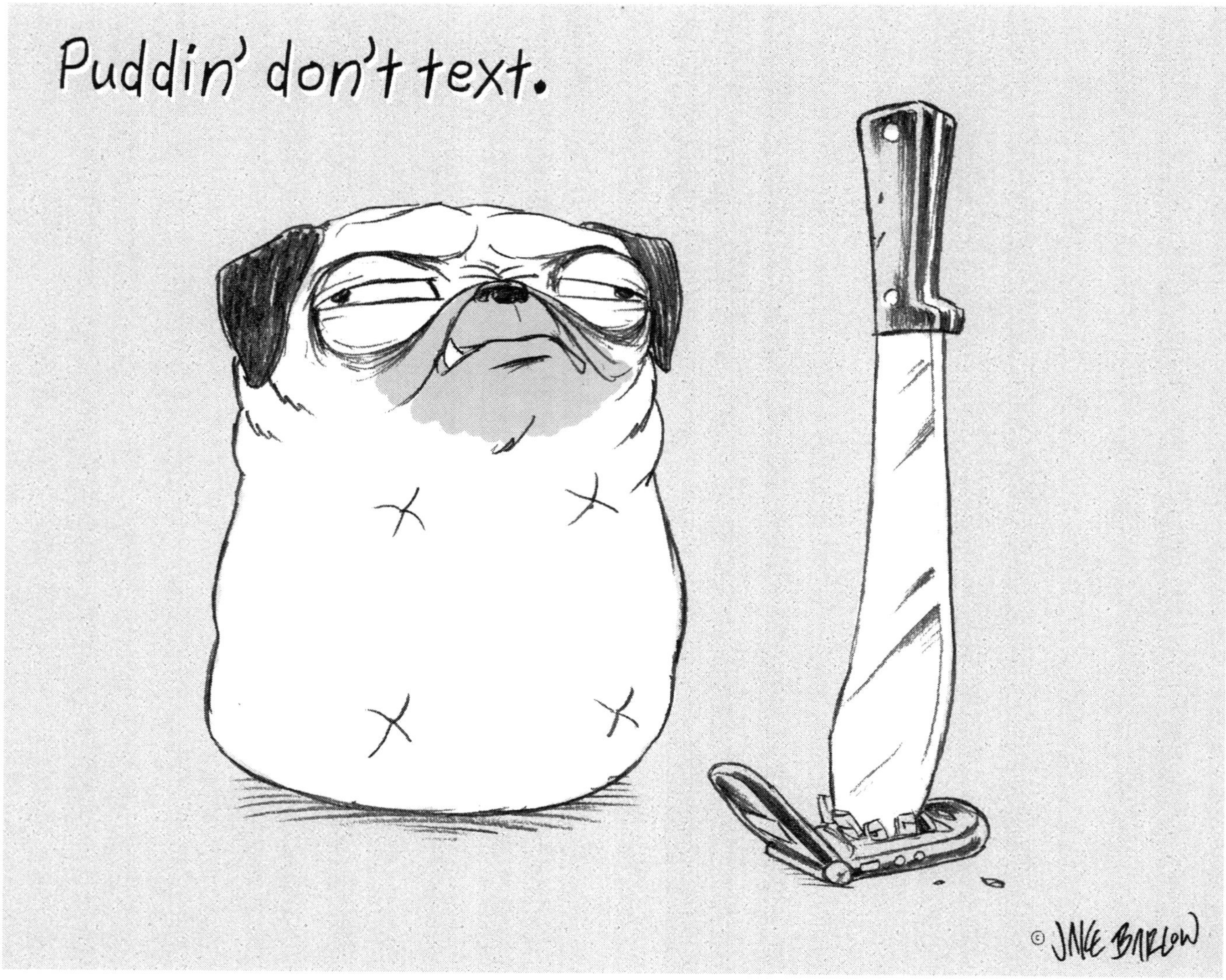
Puddin' don't text.
© JAKE BARLOW

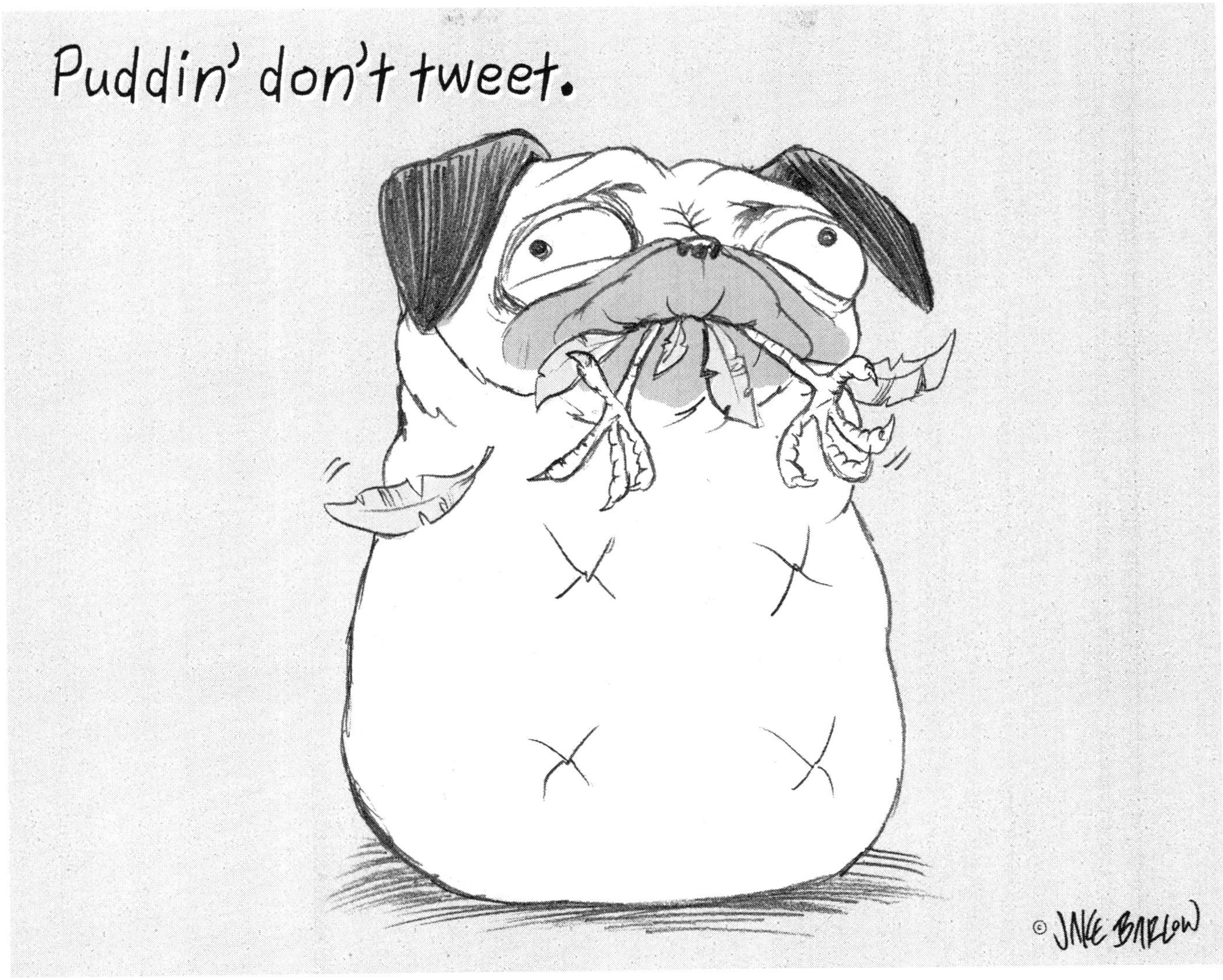
Puddin' don't tweet.
© JAKE BARLOW

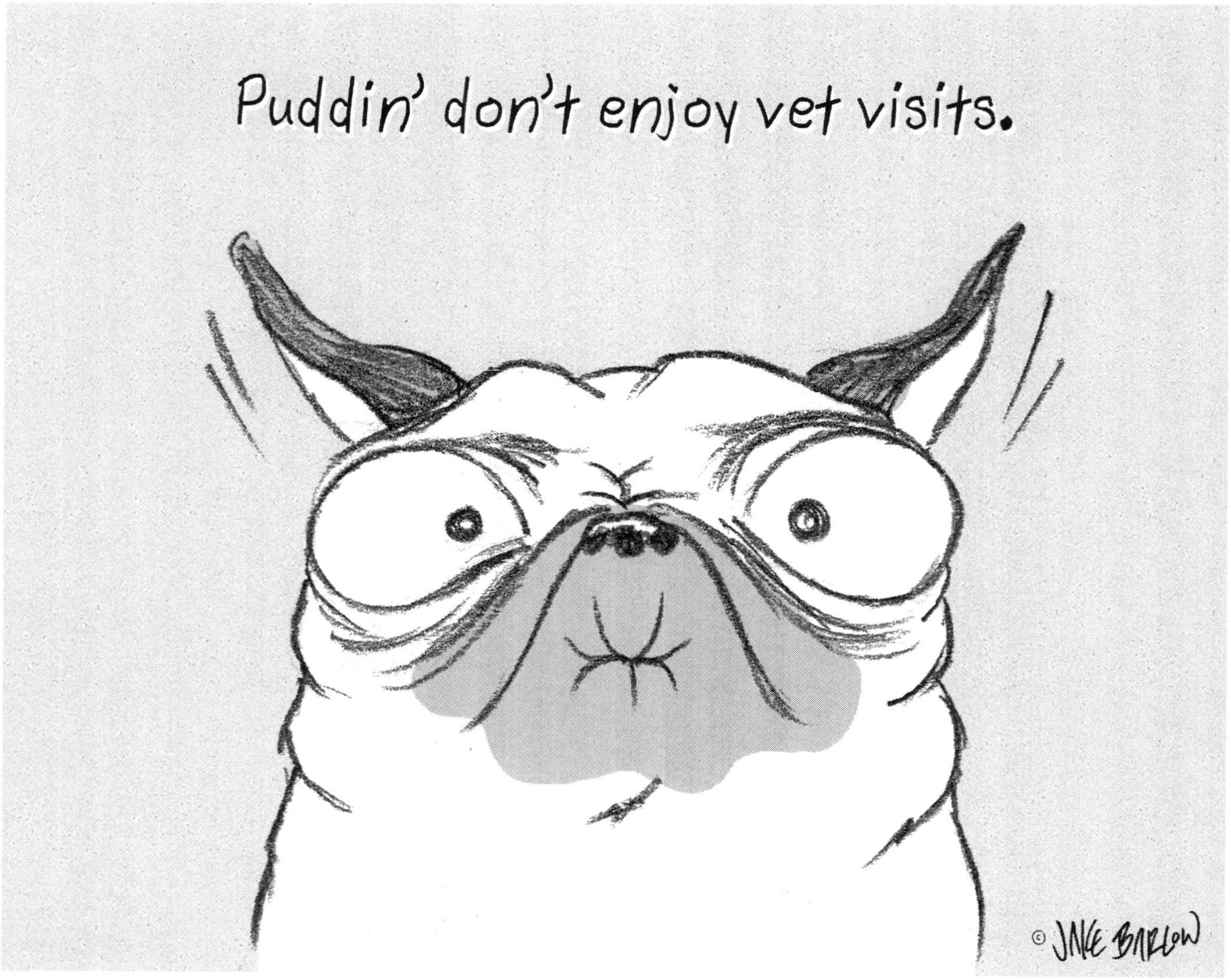
Puddin' don't enjoy vet visits.
© JAKE BARLOW

Puddin' don't pitch – or catch.

© JAKE BARLOW

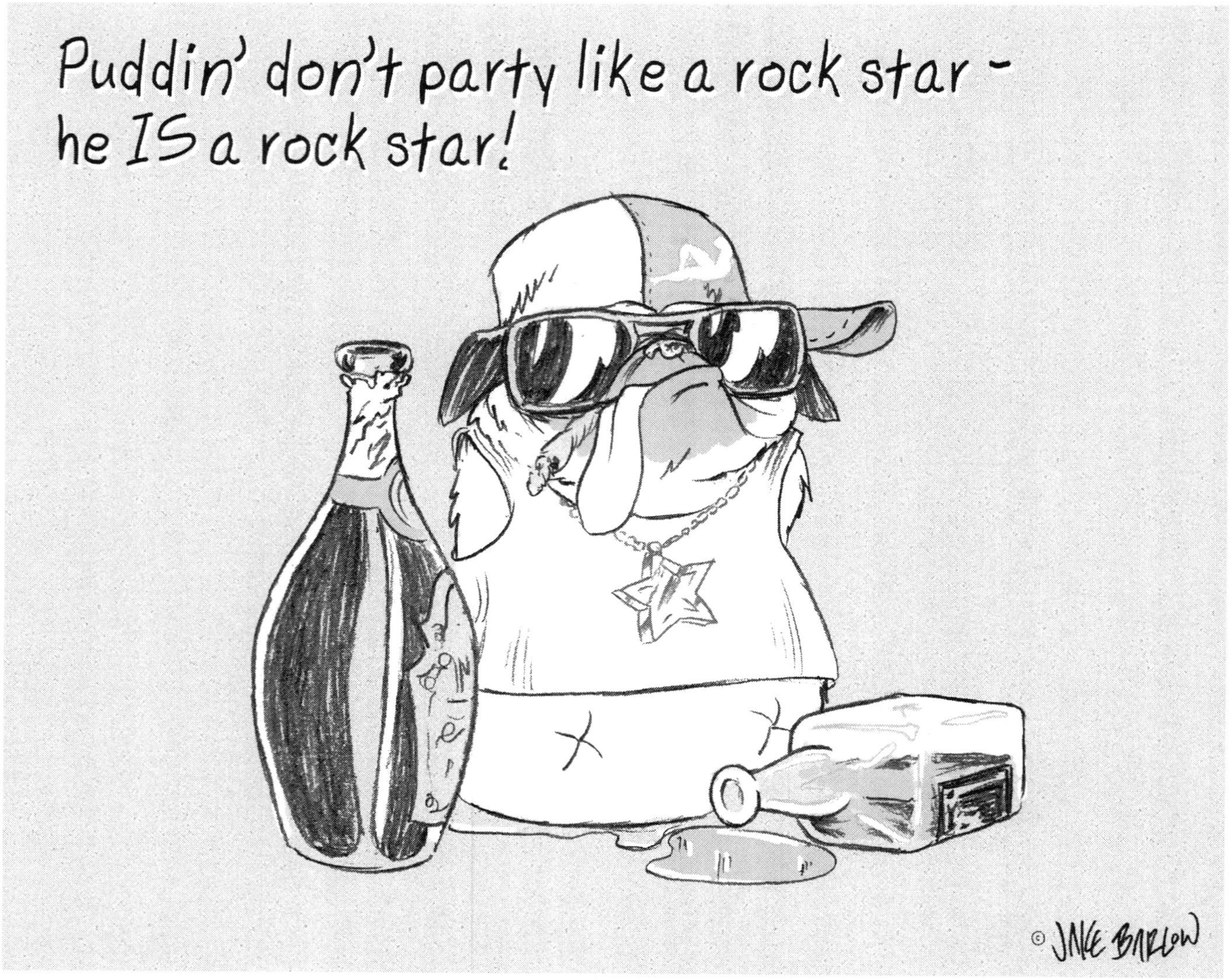
Puddin' don't party like a rock star -
he IS a rock star!
© JAKE BARLOW

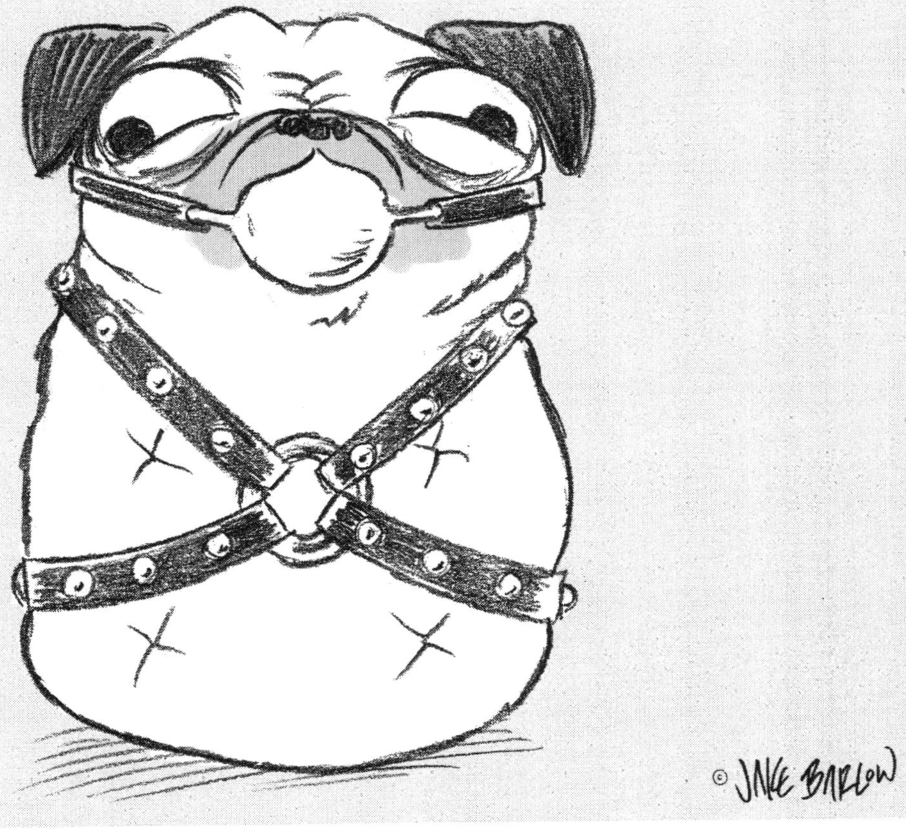
© JAKE BARLOW

Puddin' don't want to talk about it, and he'd appreciate it if you kept this to yourself.

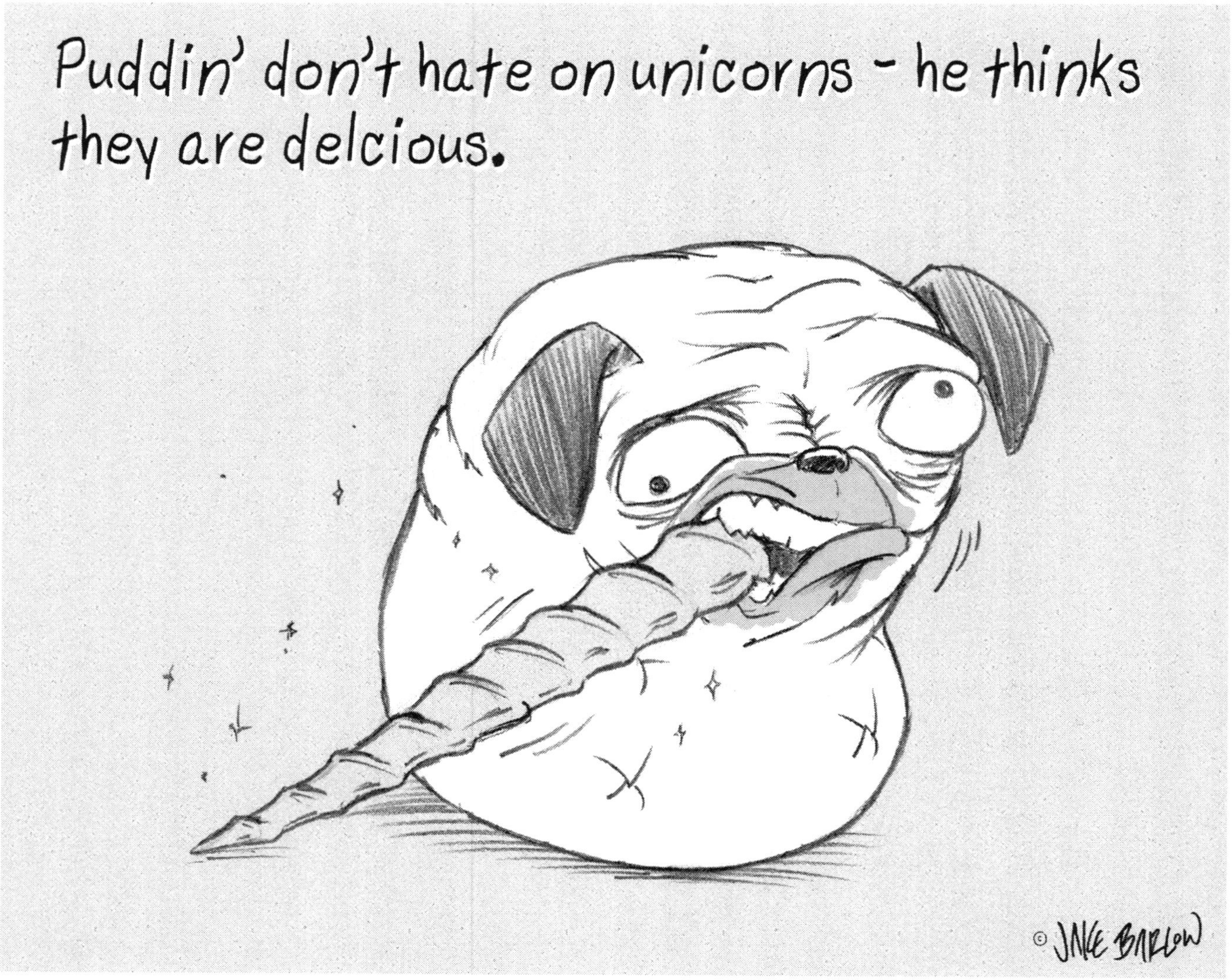
Puddin' don't hate on unicorns - he thinks they are delcious.
© JAKE BARLOW

Puddin' don't go down easy.

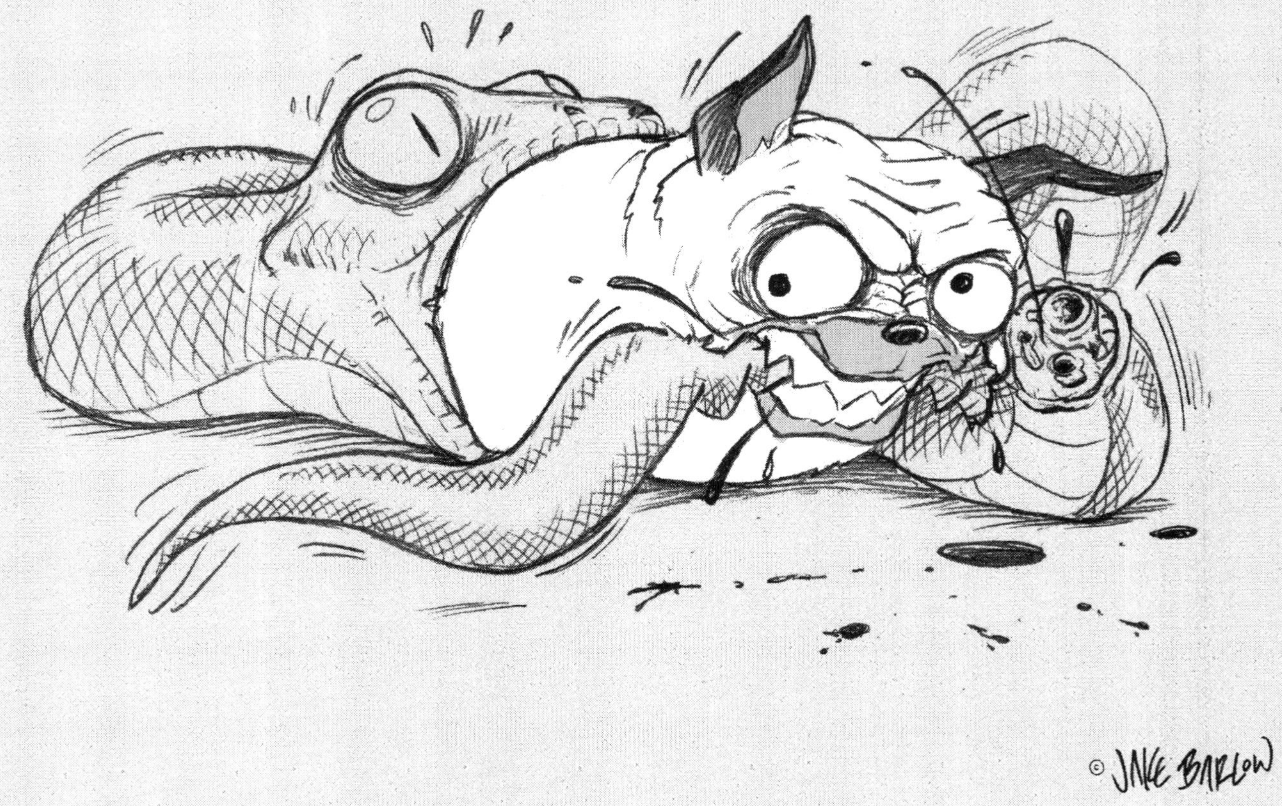
© JAKE BARLOW

Puddin' don't comprehend infinite recursion.

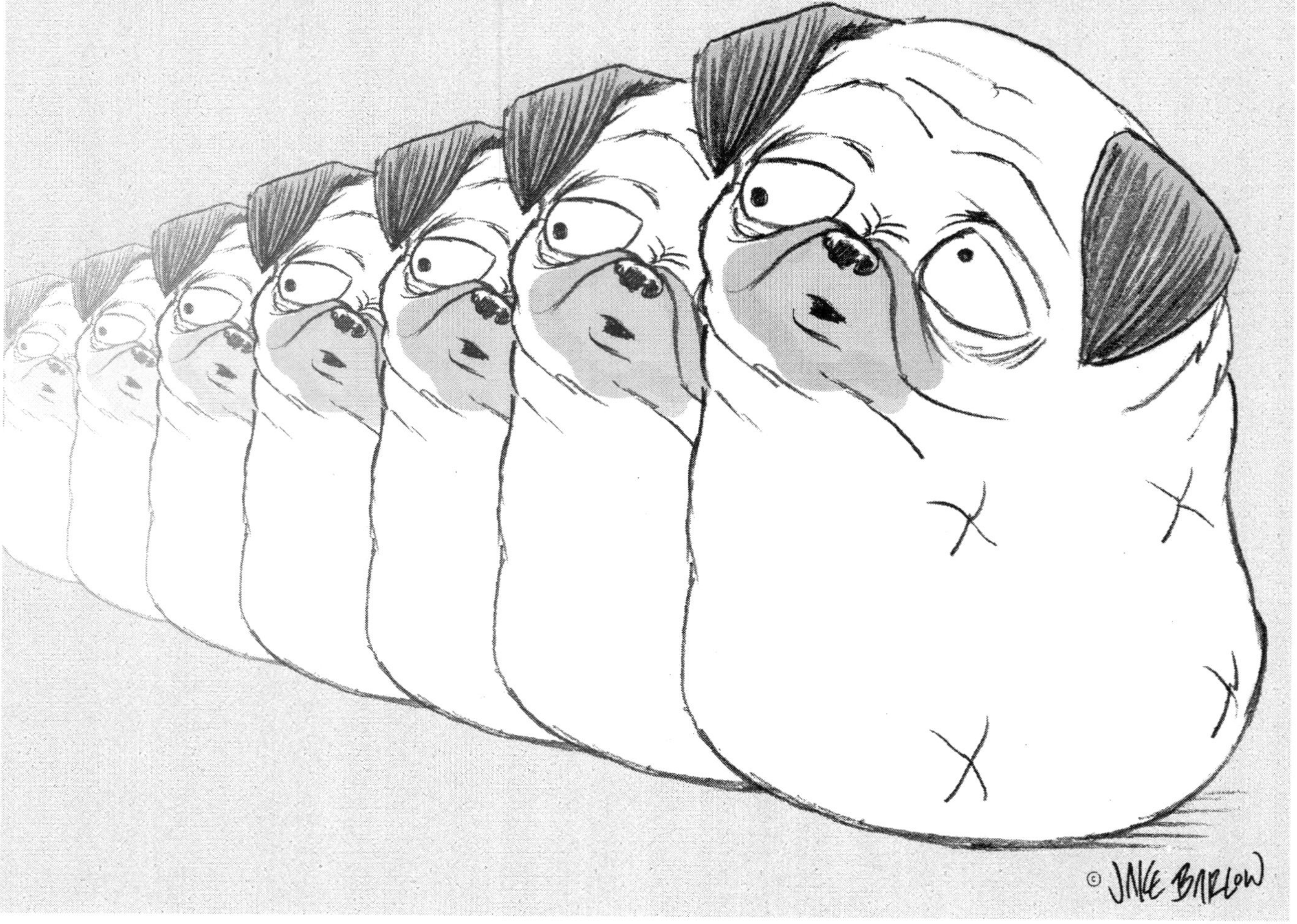
© JAKE BARLOW

Puddin' don't 'high five', not even if he could.

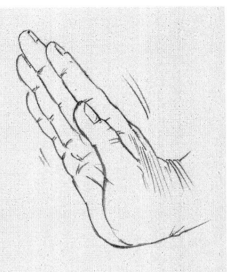

© JAKE BARLOW

Mr. P don't pity the fool.

© JAKE BARLOW

Puddin' don't want to be the chew toy.

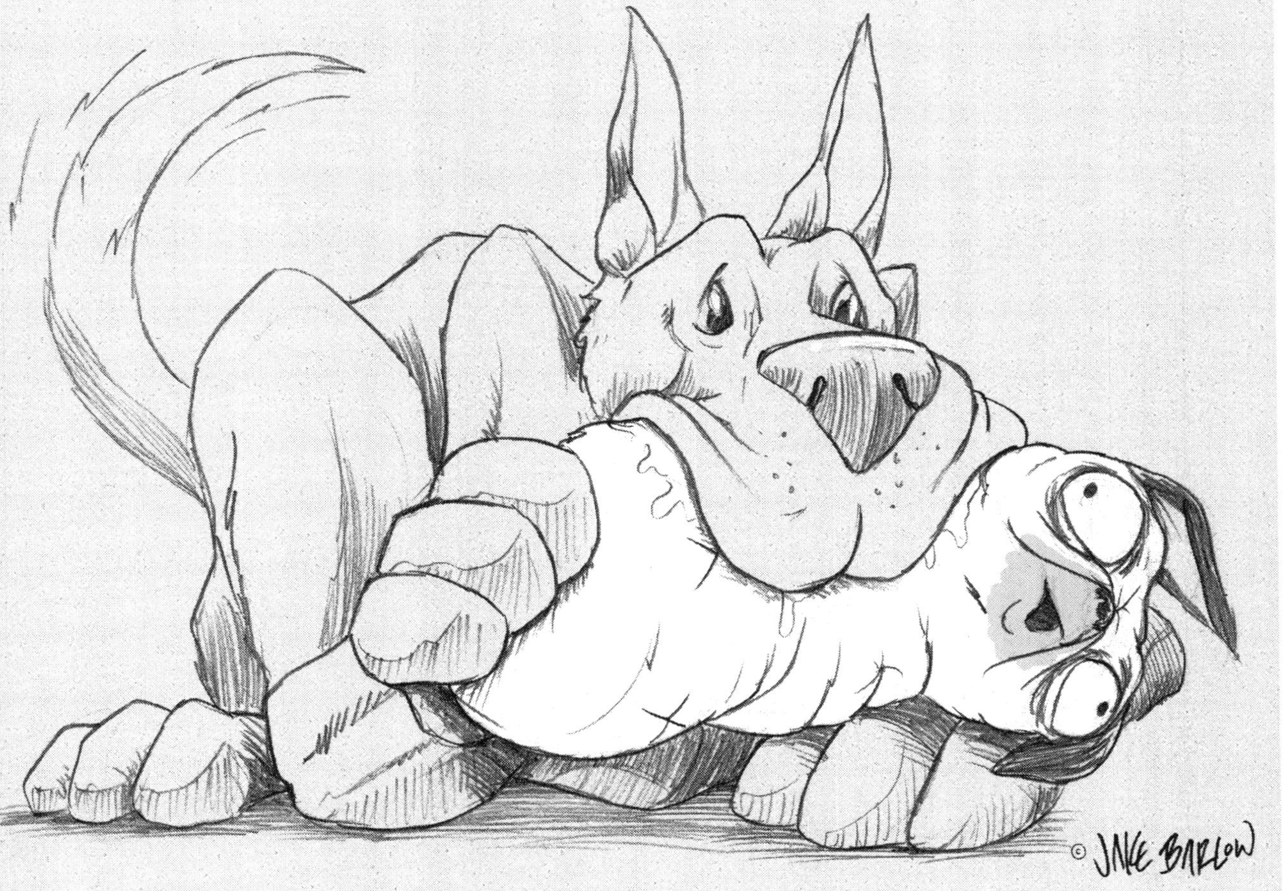
© JAKE BARLOW

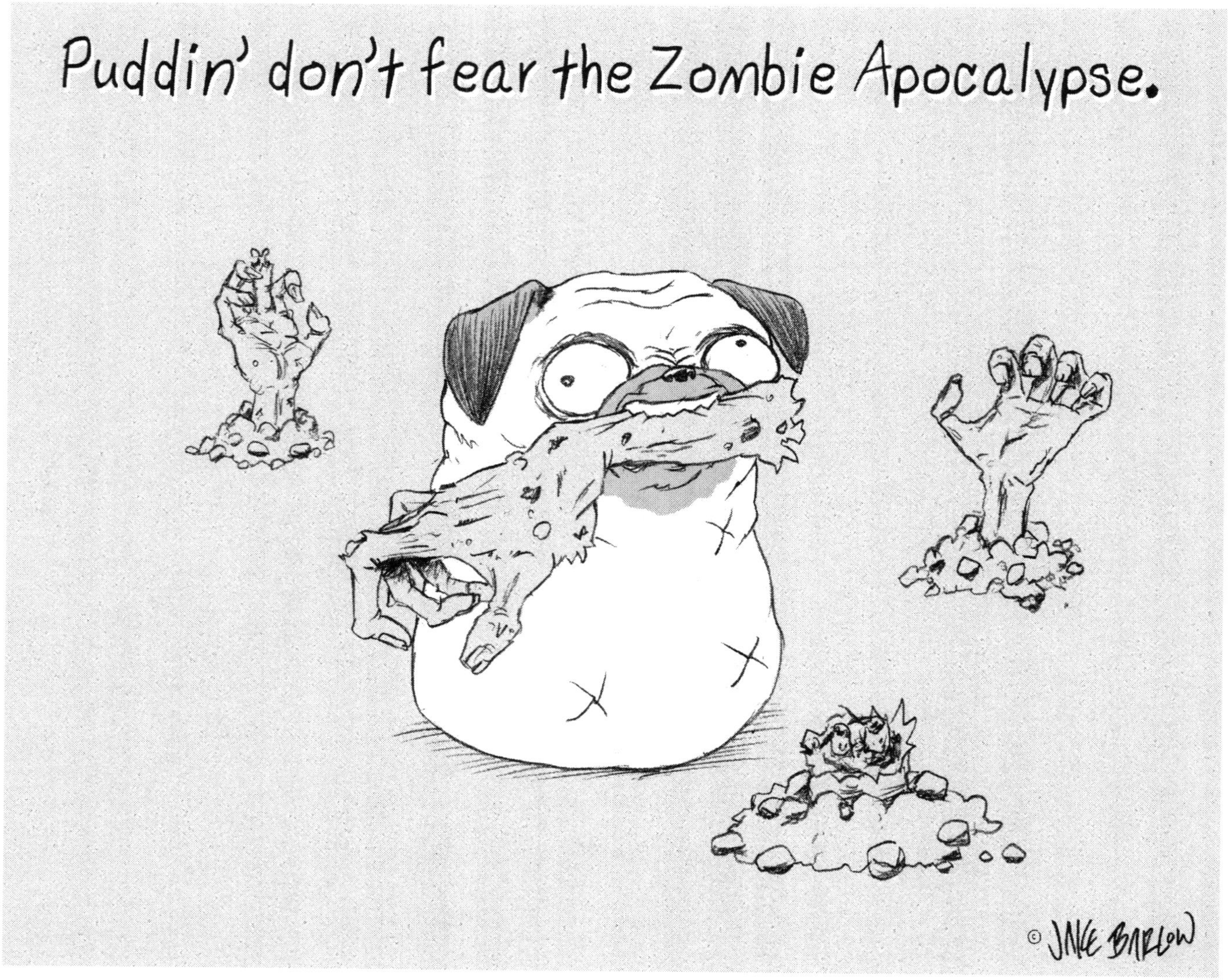
Puddin' don't fear the Zombie Apocalypse.
© JAKE BARLOW

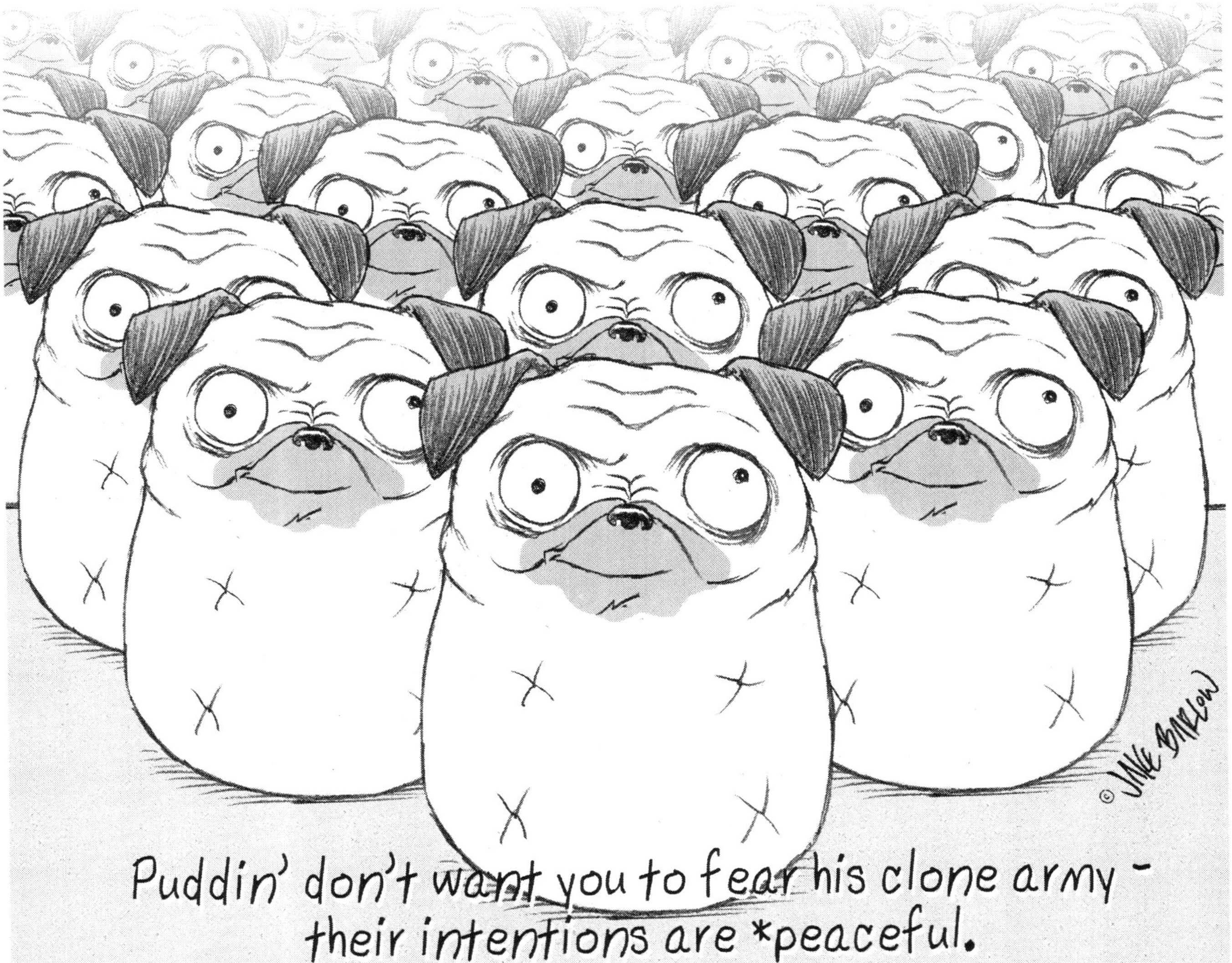
© JAKE BARLOW

Puddin' don't want you to fear his clone army - their intentions are *peaceful.

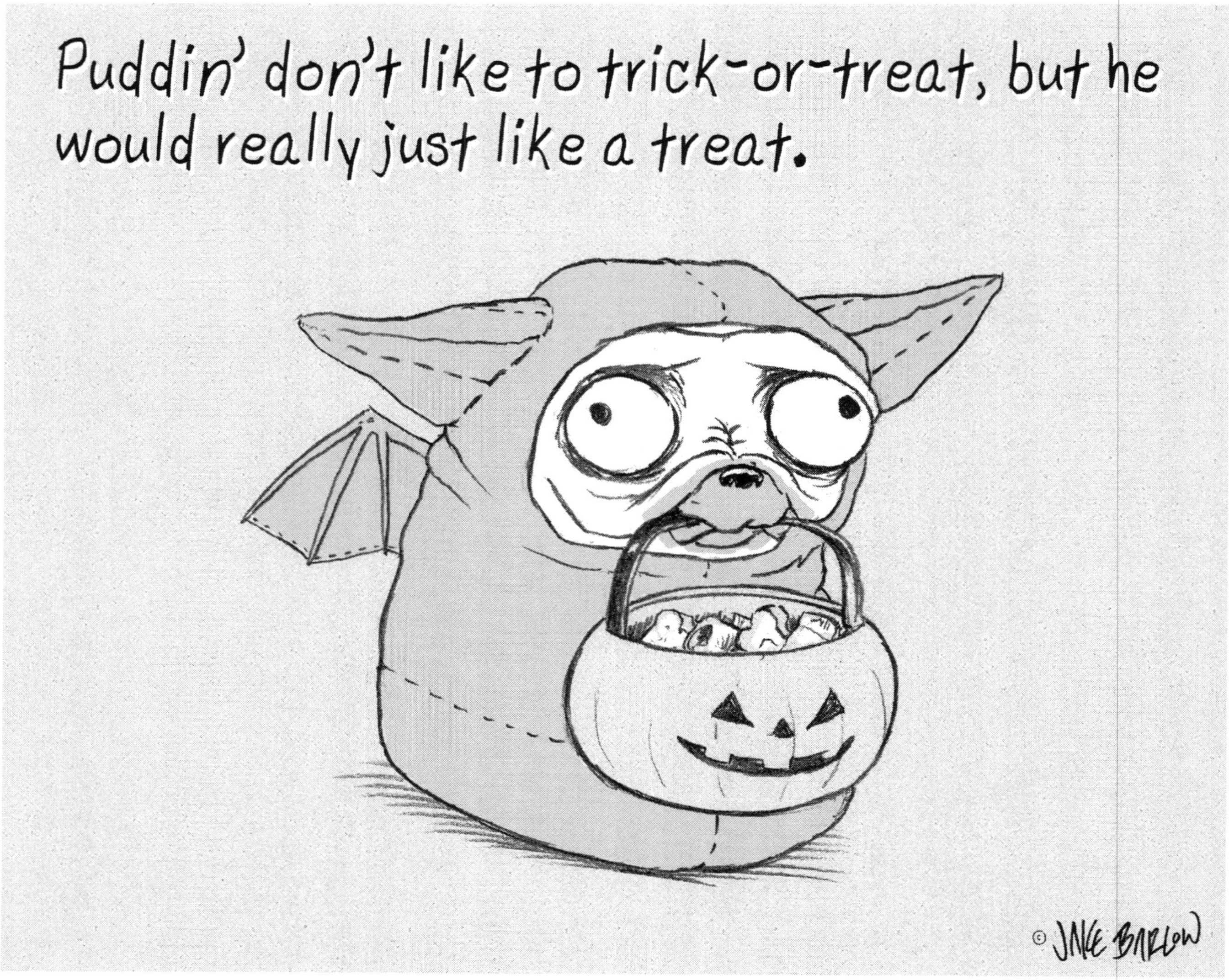
Puddin' don't like to trick-or-treat, but he would really just like a treat.
© JAKE BARLOW

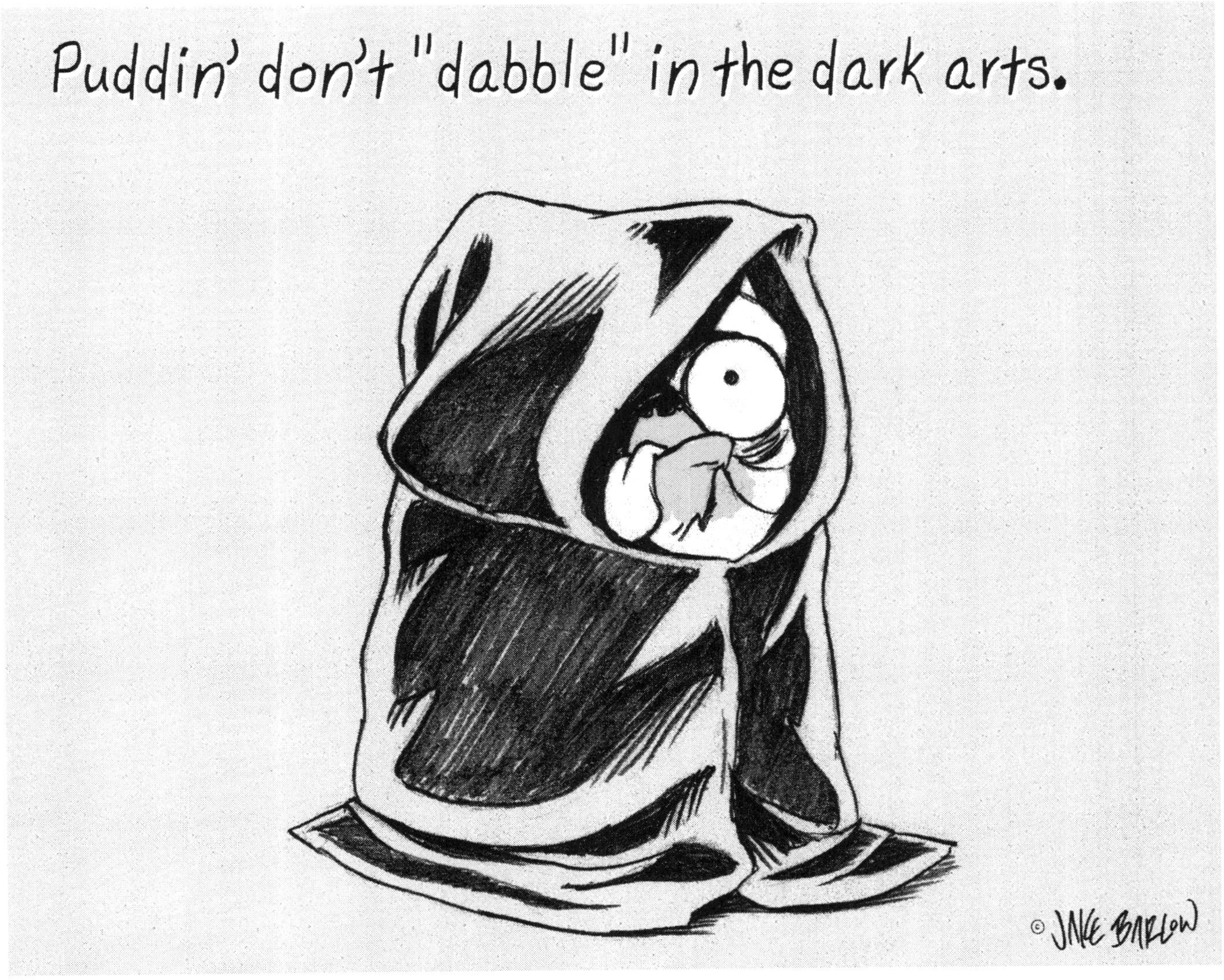
Puddin' don't "dabble" in the dark arts.
© JAKE BARLOW

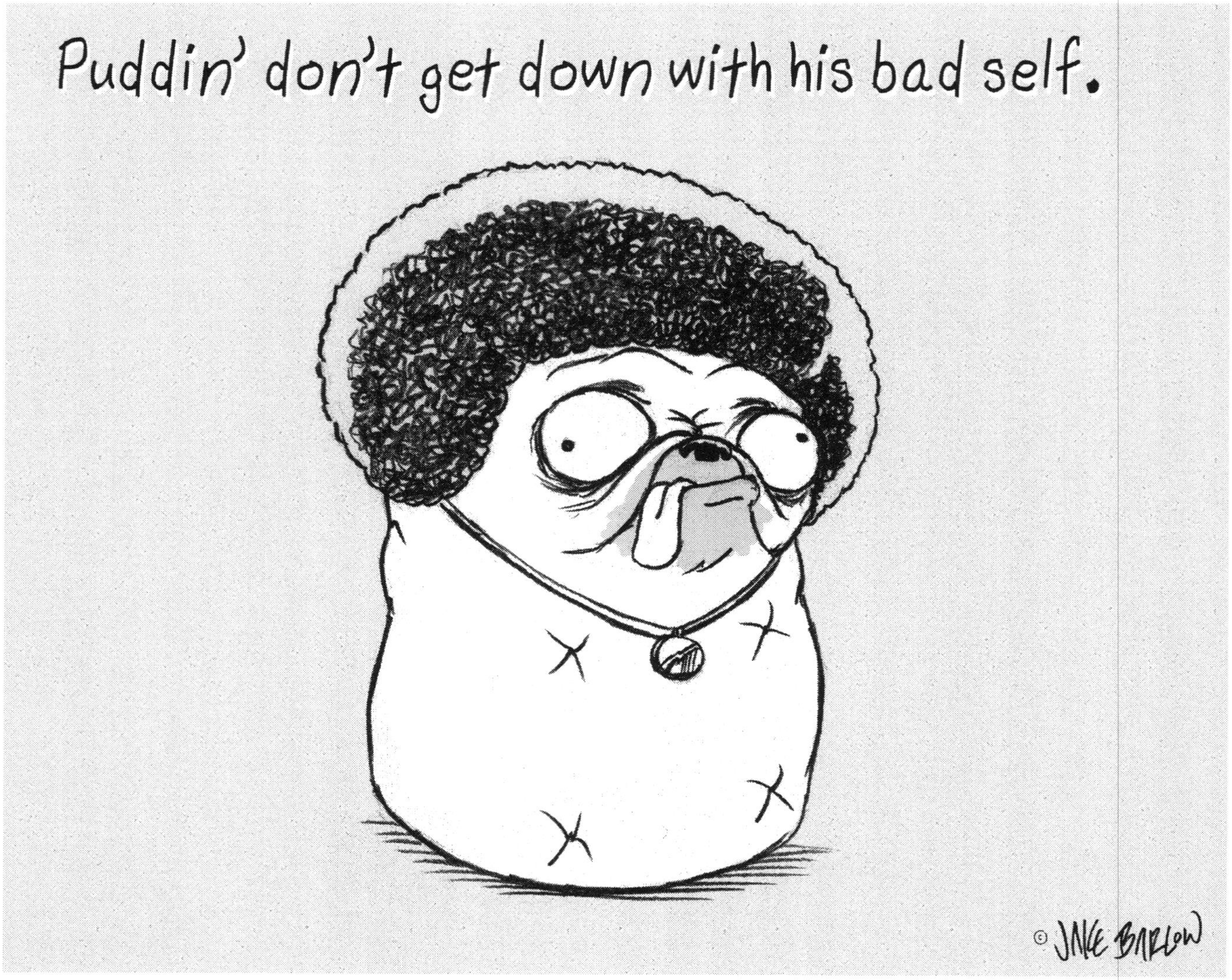
© JAKE BARLOW

Puddin' don't get down with his bad self.

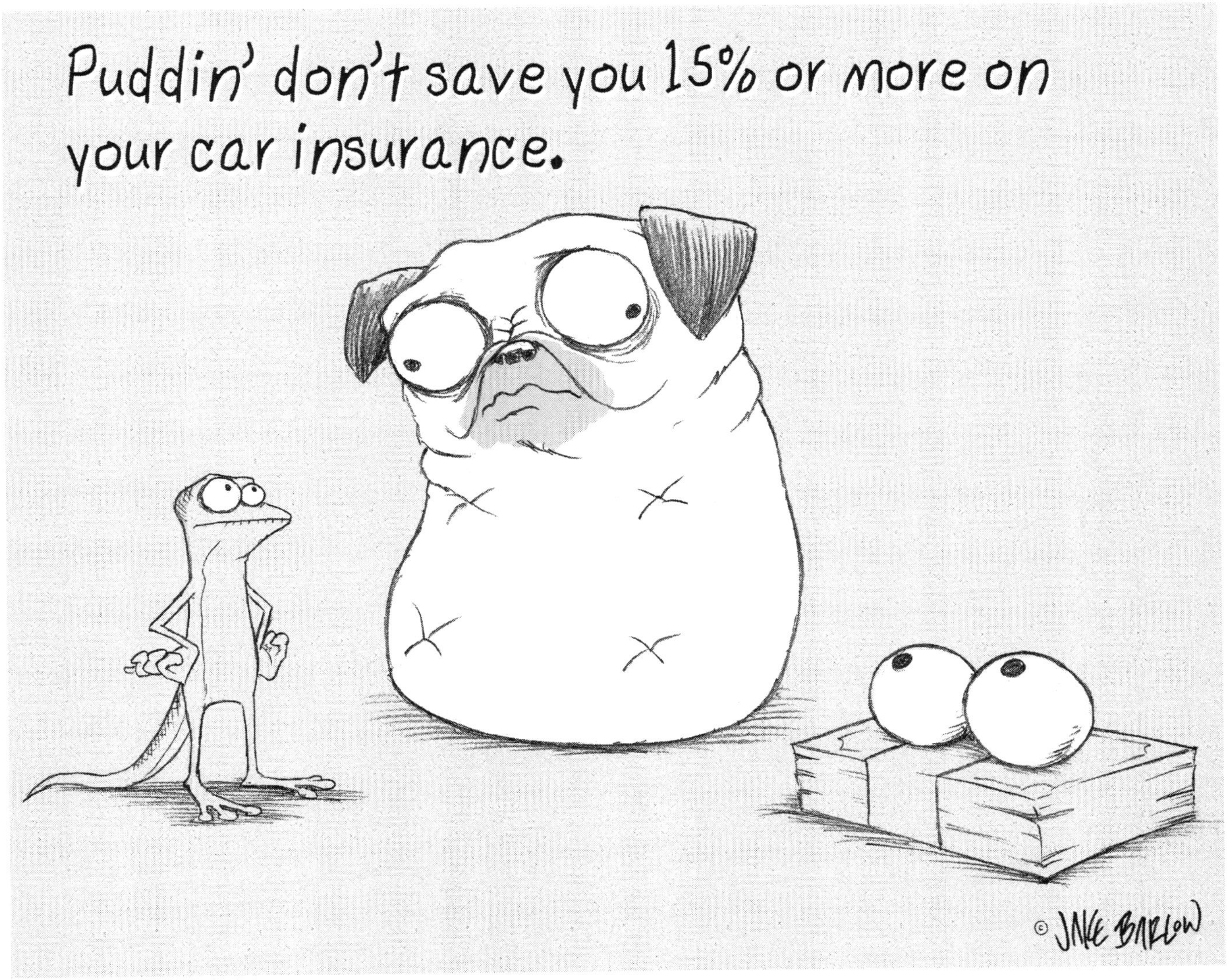
Puddin' don't save you 15% or more on your car insurance.
© JAKE BARLOW

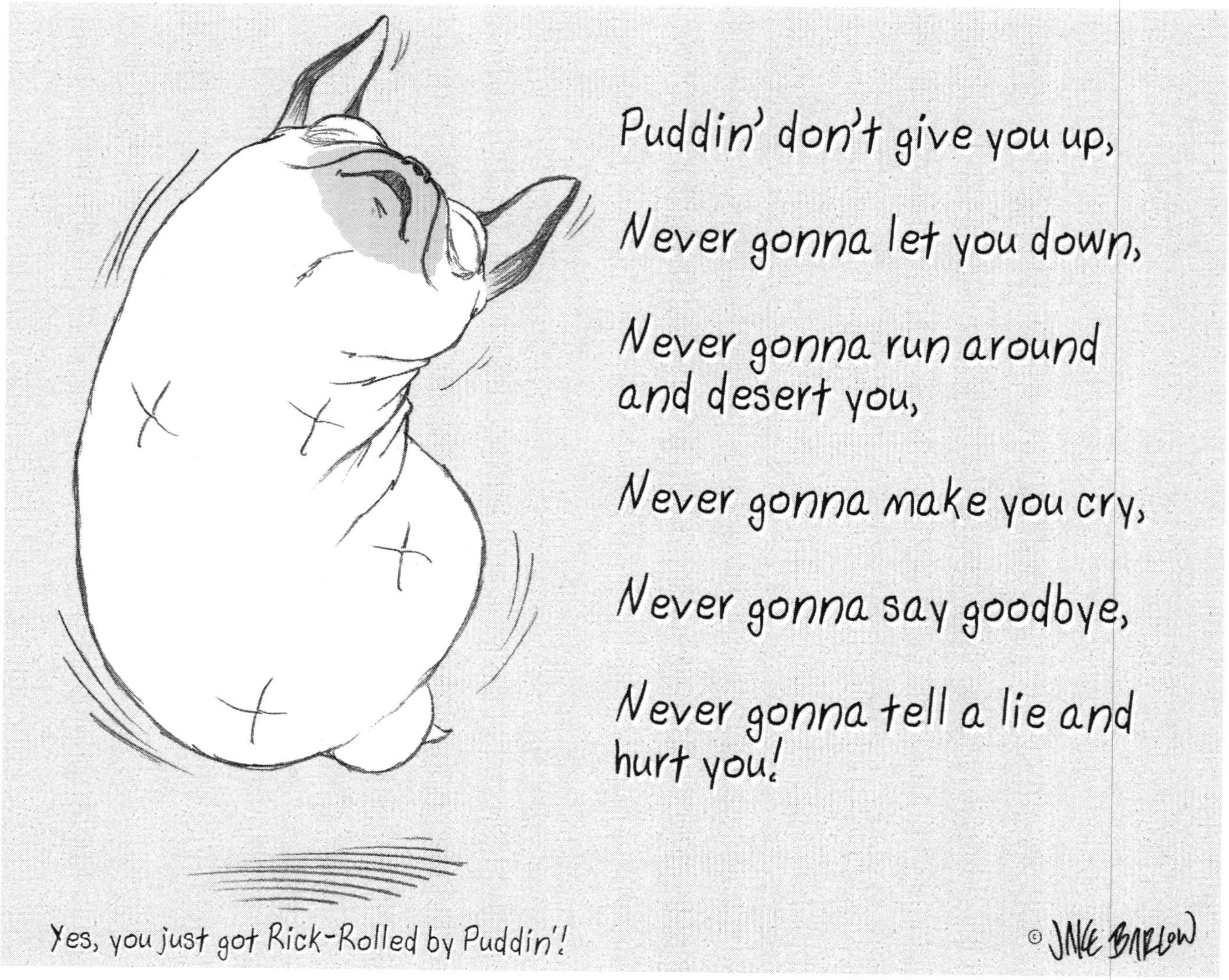
Puddin' don't give you up,
Never gonna let you down,
Never gonna run around and desert you,
Never gonna make you cry,
Never gonna say goodbye,
Never gonna tell a lie and hurt you!
Yes, you just got Rick-Rolled by Puddin'!
© JANE BARLOW

Though it may seem contrary, Puddin' don't Downward Dog, but he does Low Cobra.

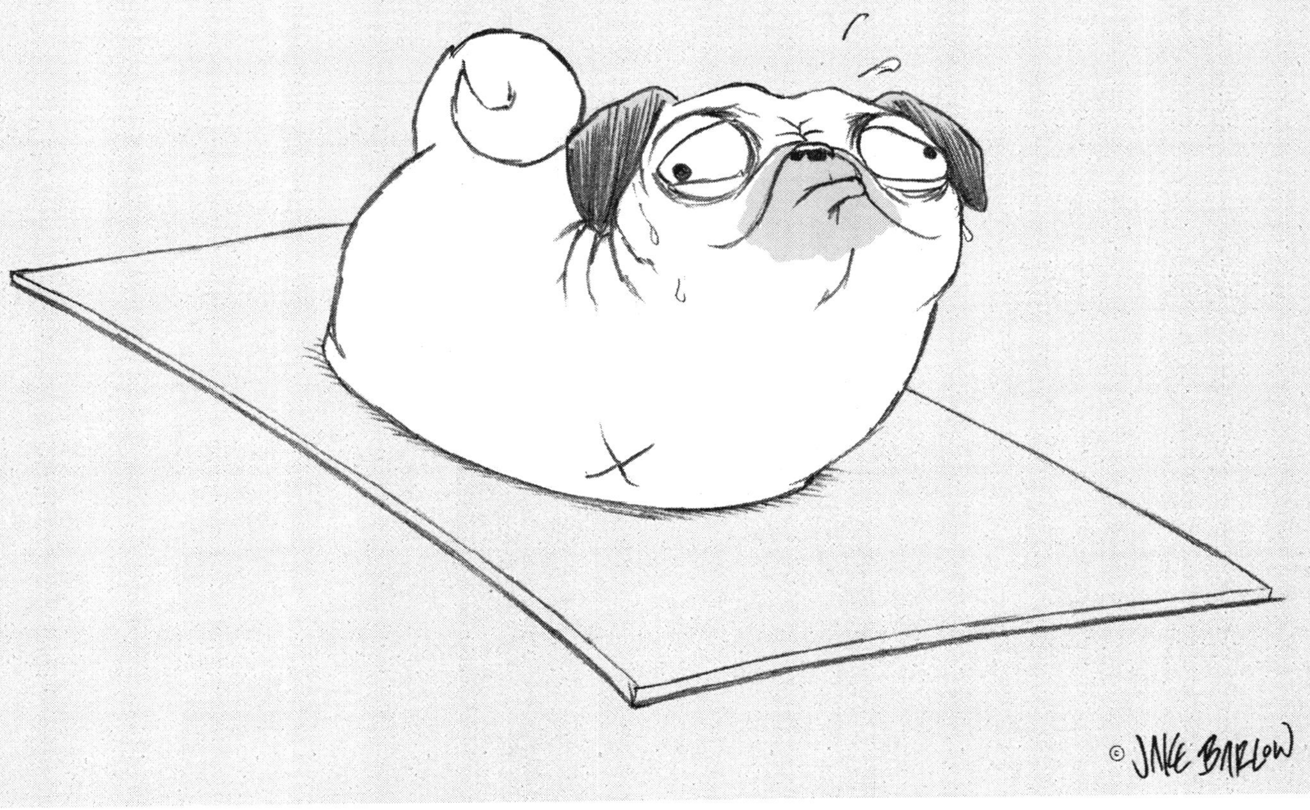
© JAKE BARLOW

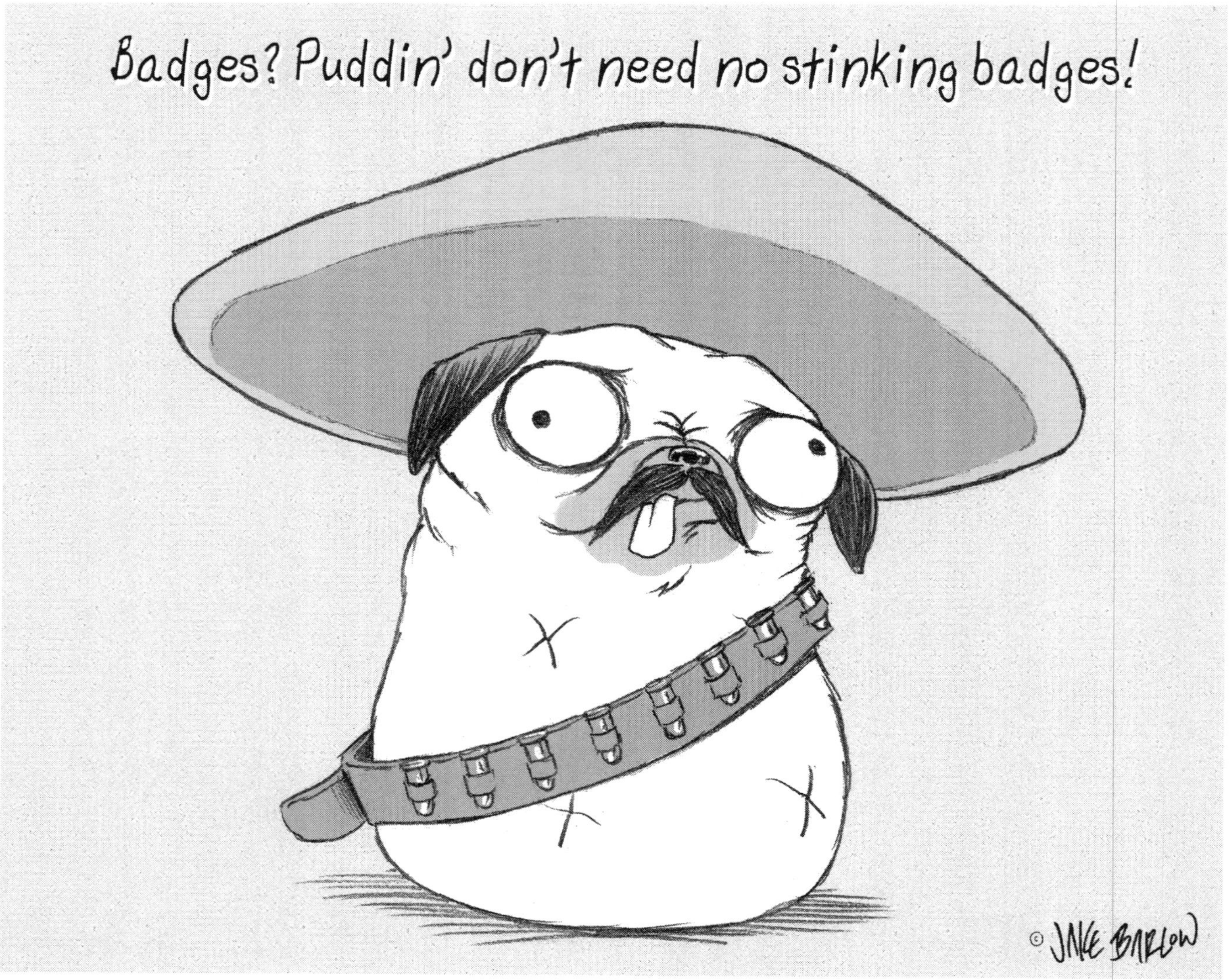
Badges? Puddin' don't need no stinking badges!
© JAKE BARLOW

Puddin' don't like tea parties anymore, thanks to a certain bunch of idiots.

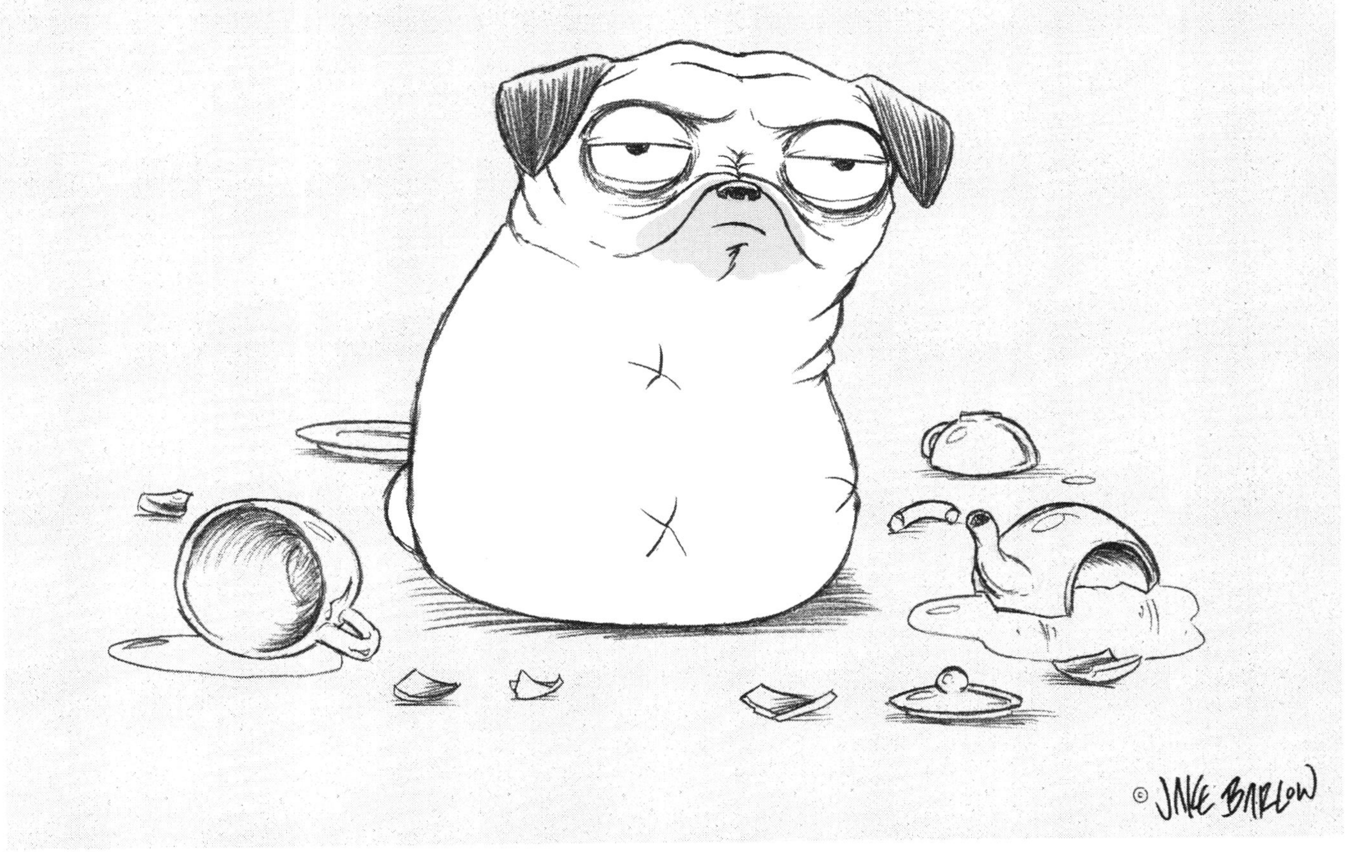
© JAKE BARLOW

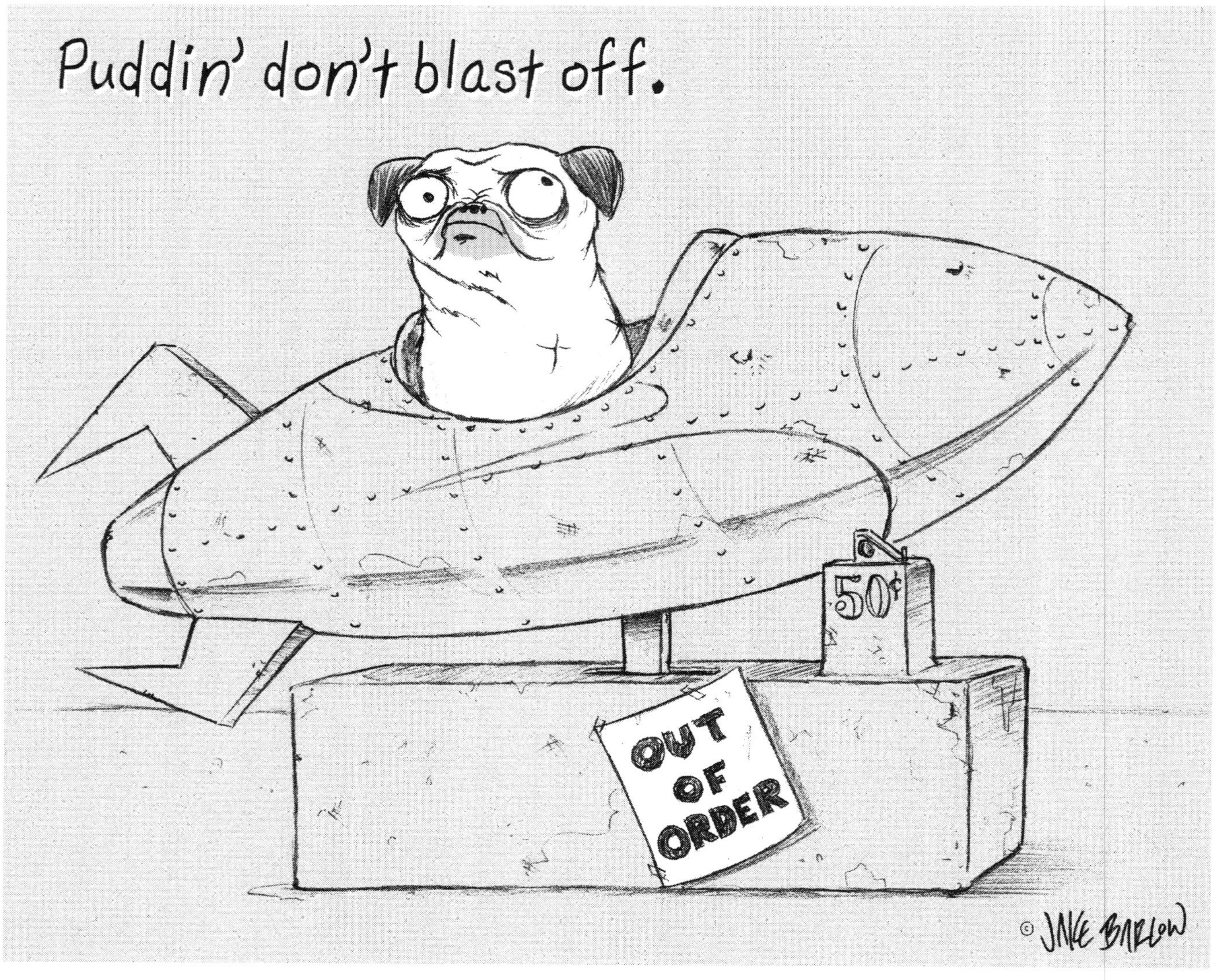
50¢
OUT OF ORDER
© JAKE BARLOW

Puddin' don't blast off.

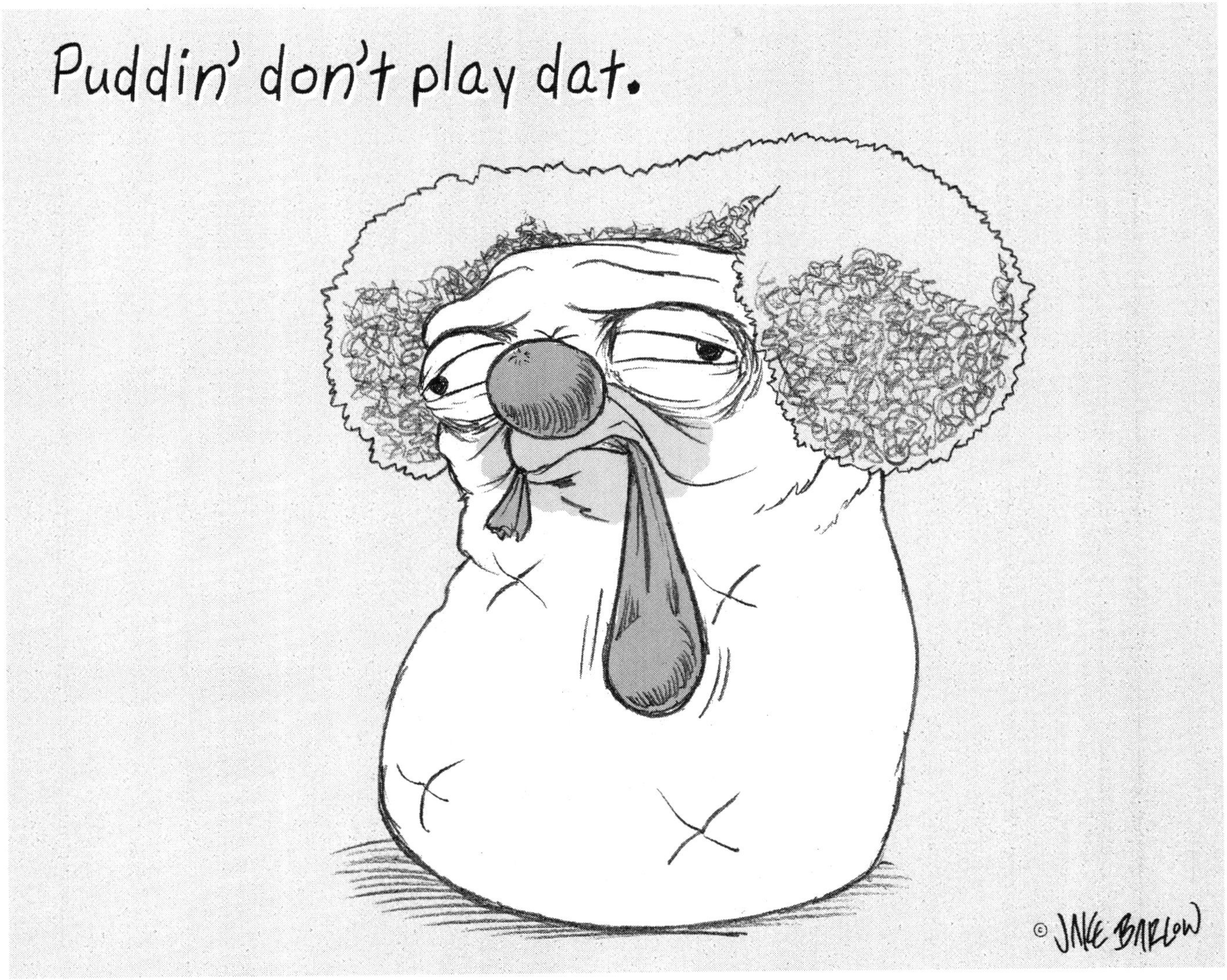
Puddin' don't play dat.
© JAKE BARLOW

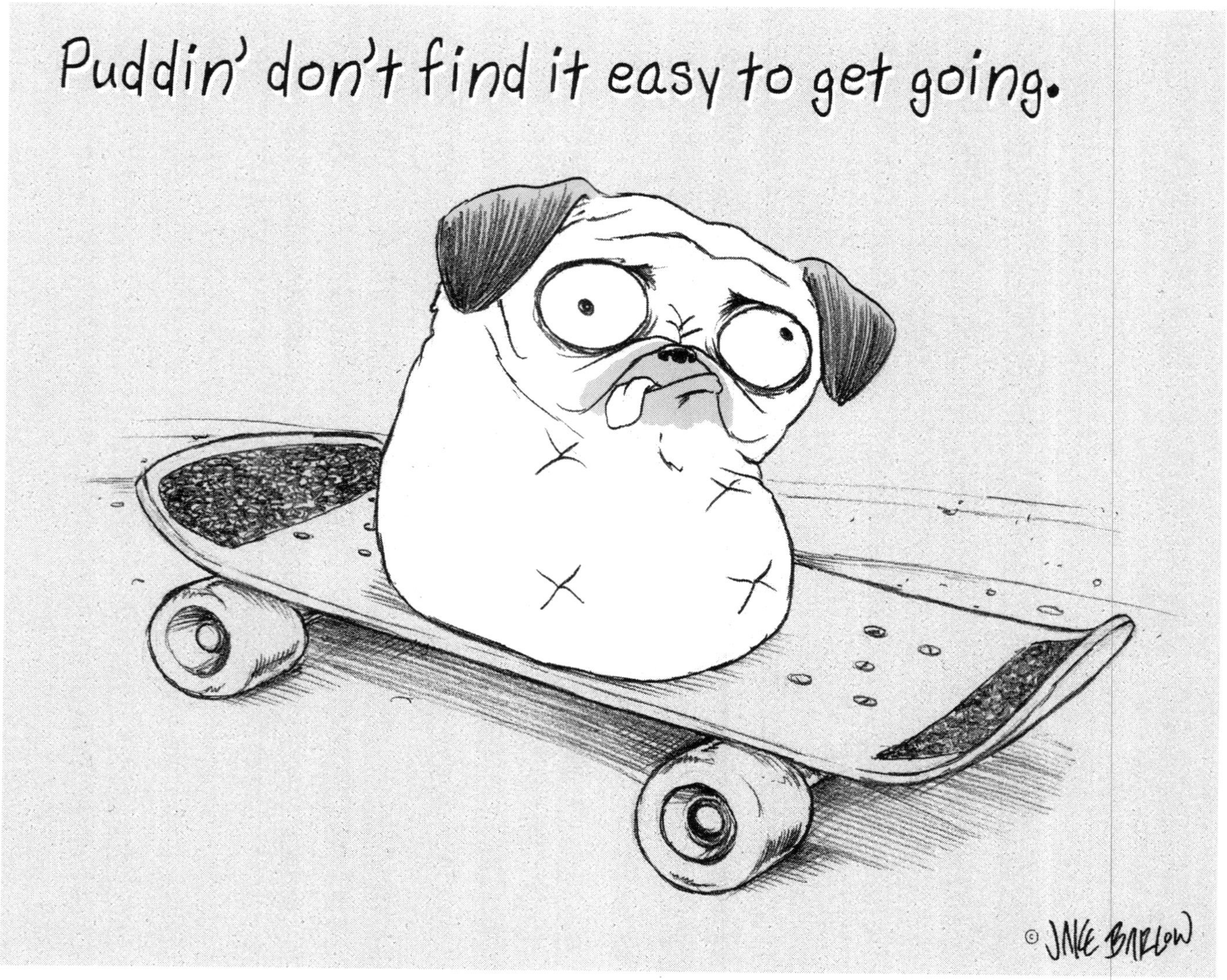
© JAKE BARLOW

Puddin' don't find it easy to get going.

Puddin' don't find it any easier to stop.

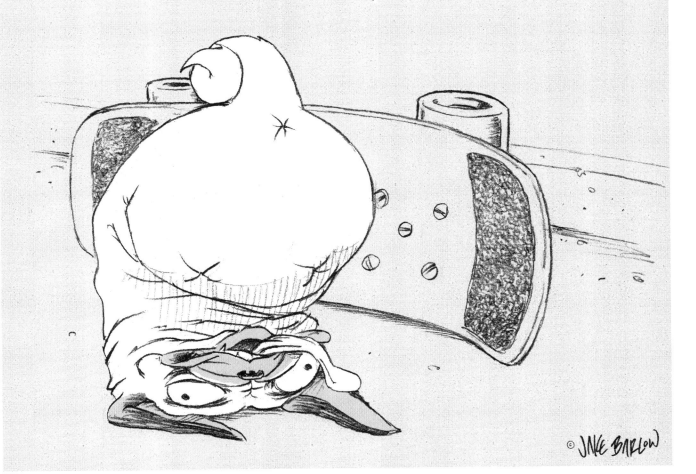

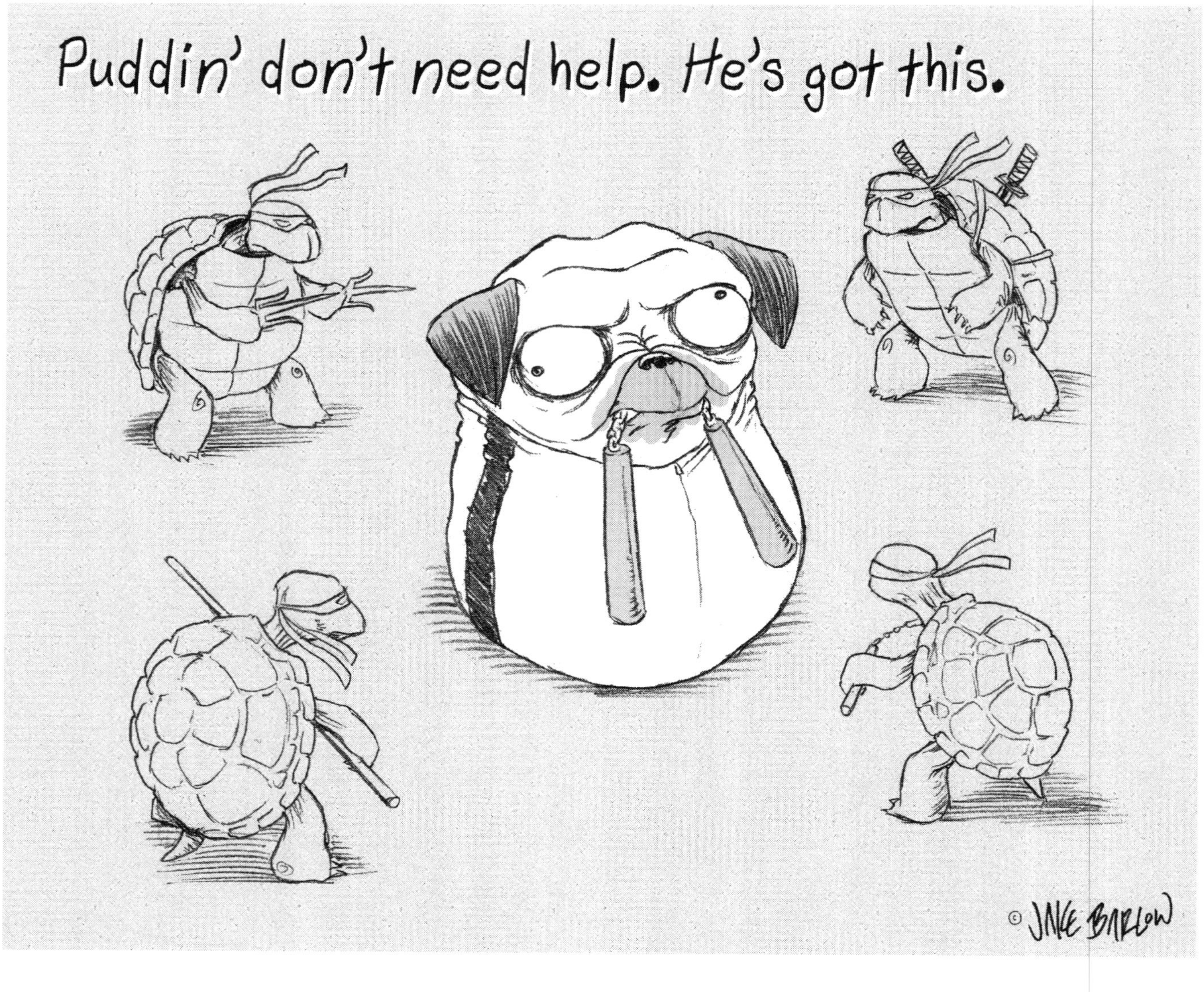
Puddin' don't need help. He's got this.
© JAKE BARLOW

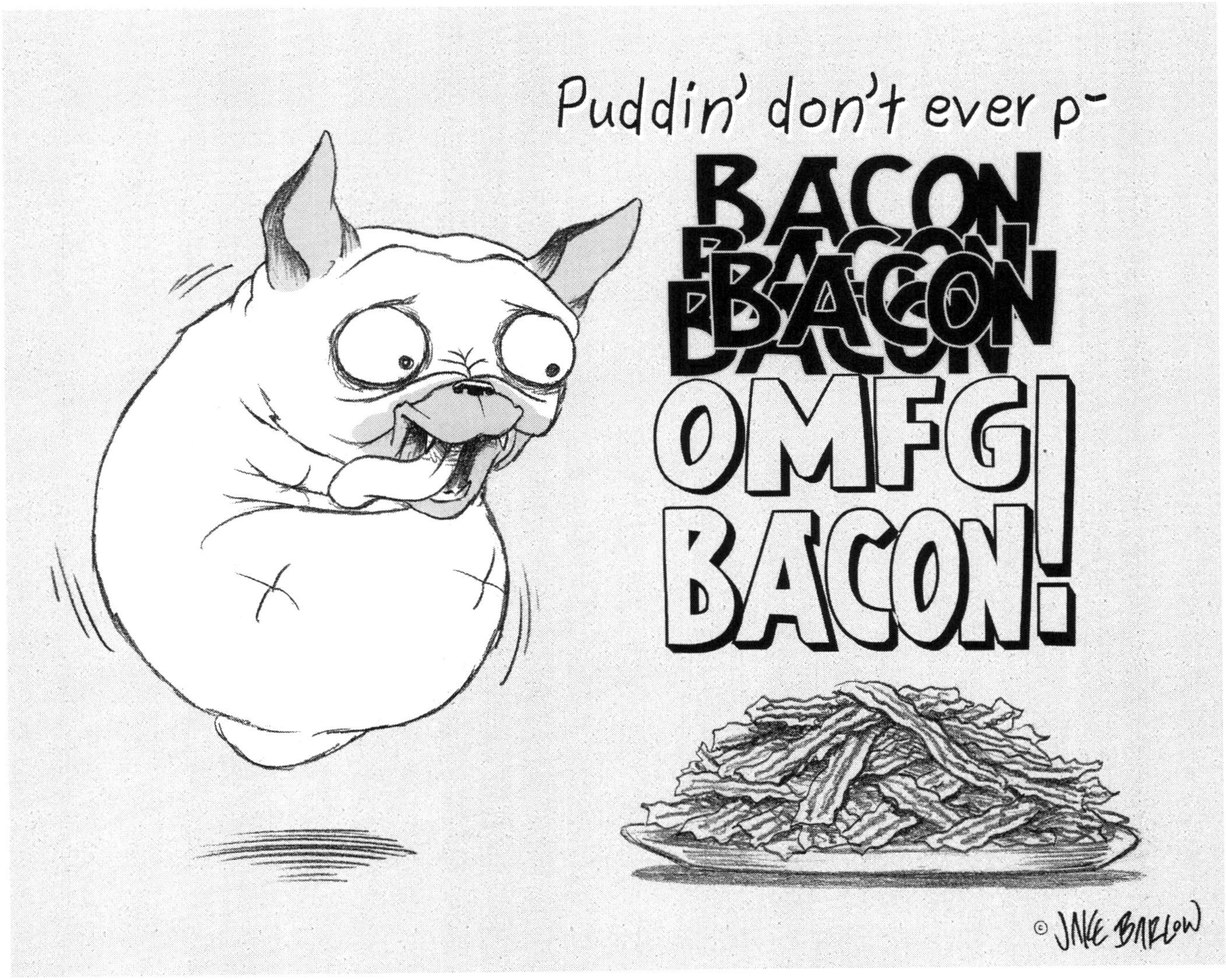
Puddin' don't ever p-
BACON BACON BACON BACON
OMFG!
BACON!
© JAKE BARLOW

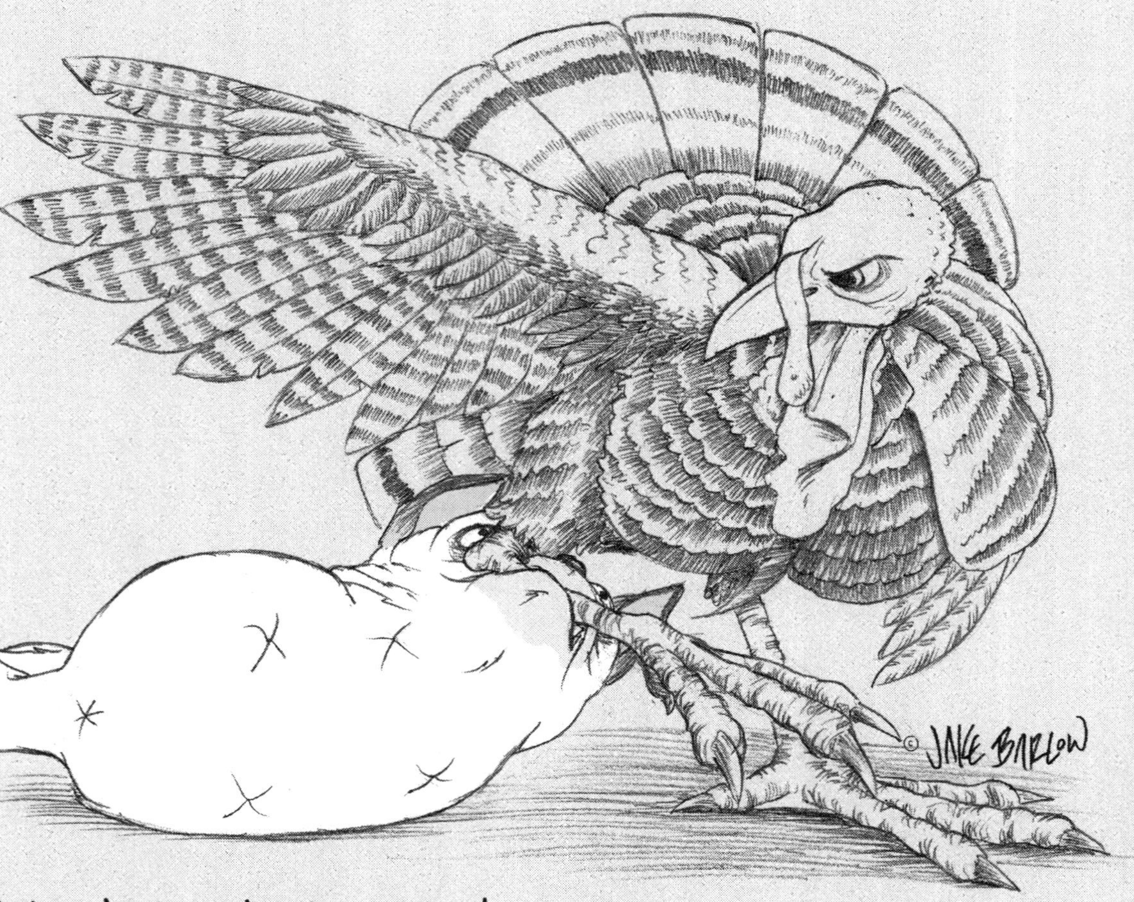
© JAKE BARLOW

Puddin' don't let ANY drumstick get by him.

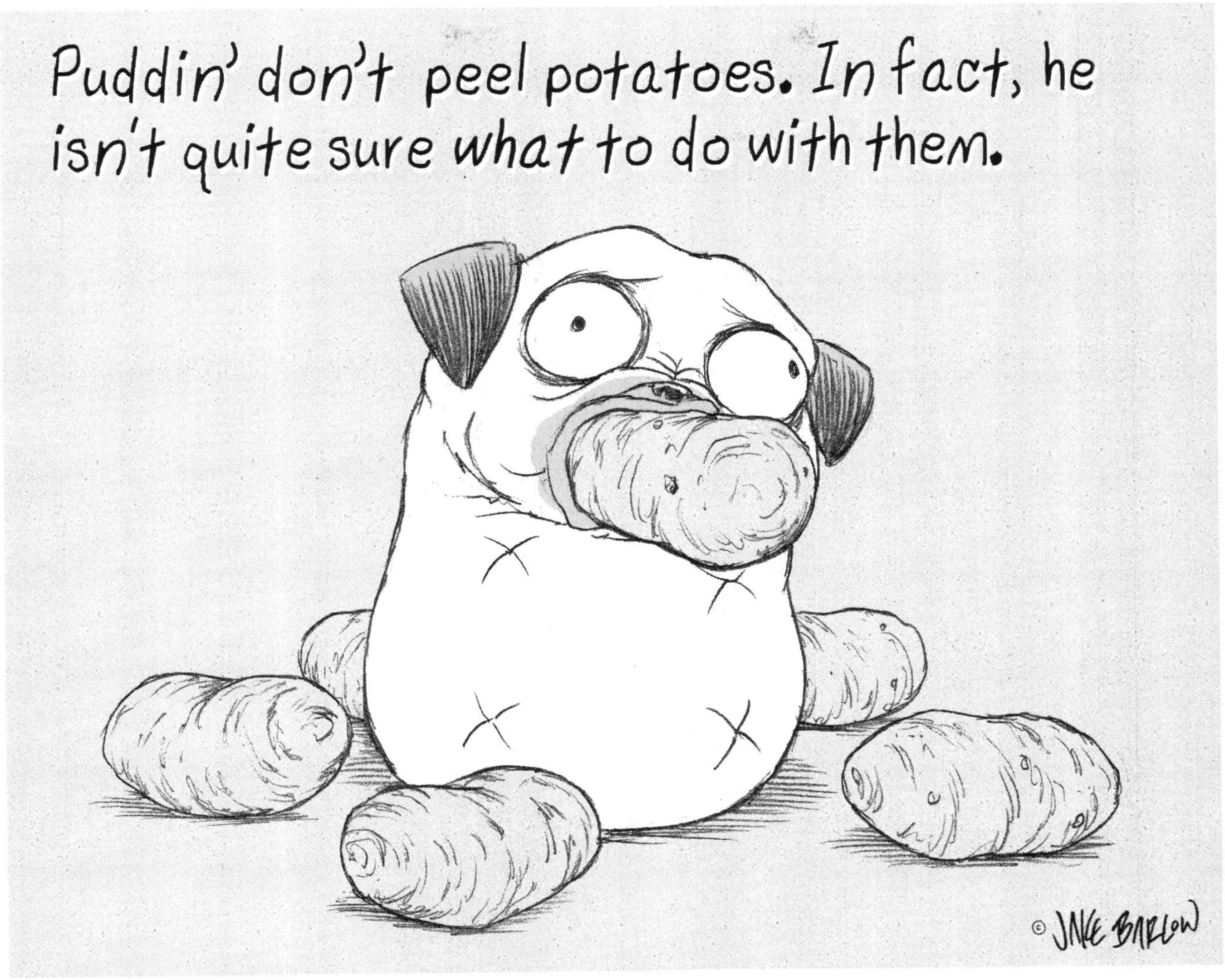
Puddin' don't peel potatoes. In fact, he isn't quite sure what to do with them.
© JAKE BARLOW

Puddin' don't always think things through.

© JAKE BARLOW

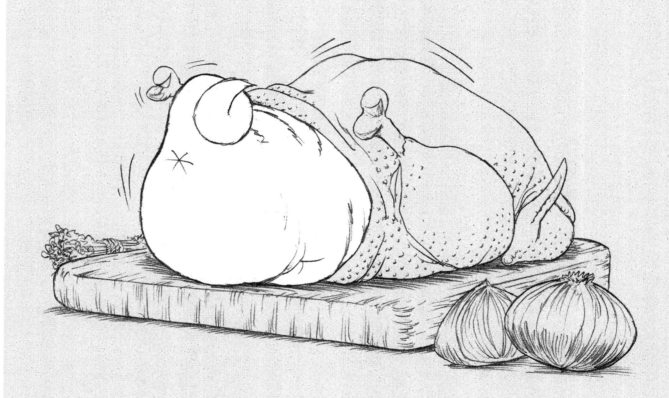

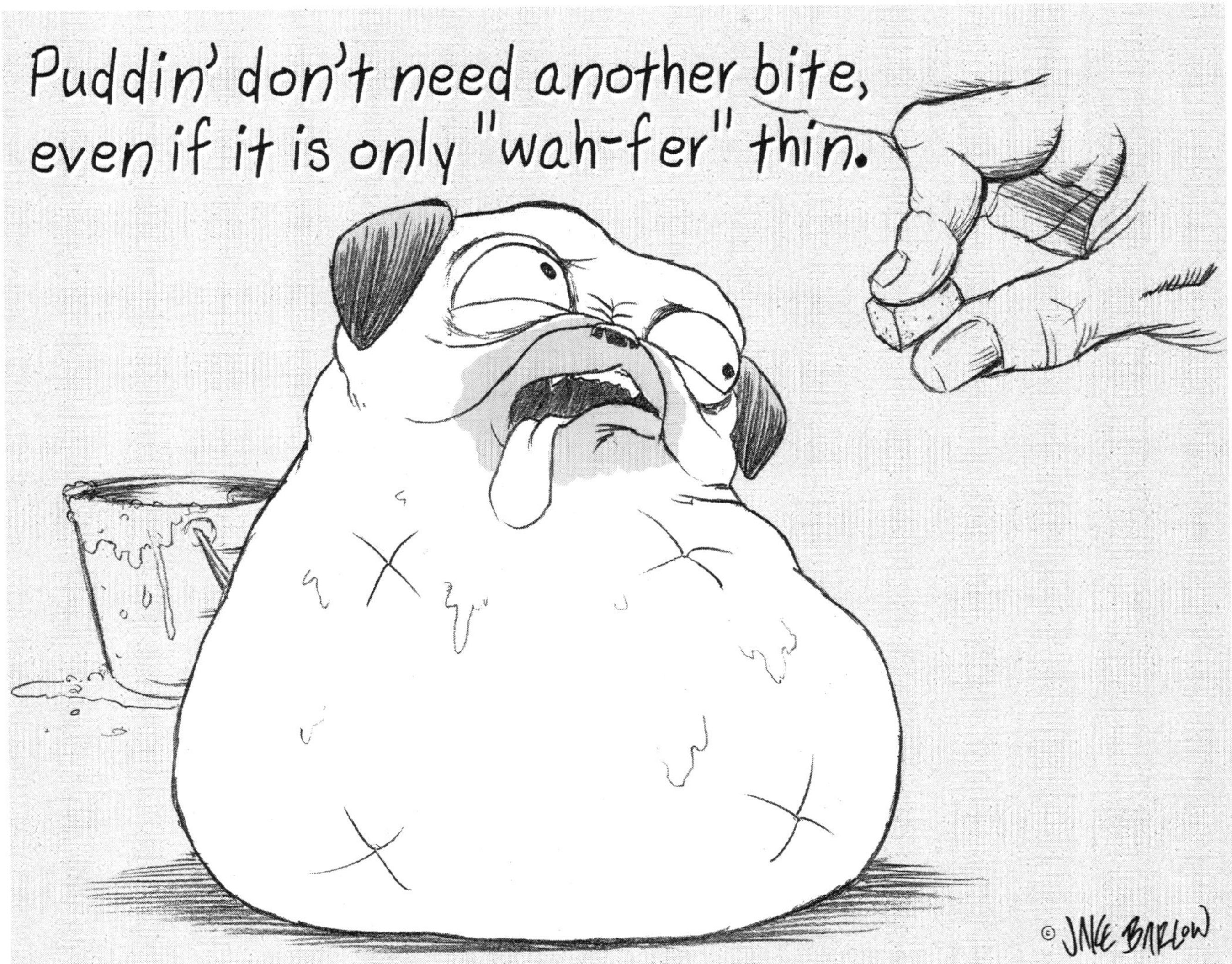
Puddin' don't need another bite,
even if it is only "wah-fer" thin.
© JAKE BARLOW

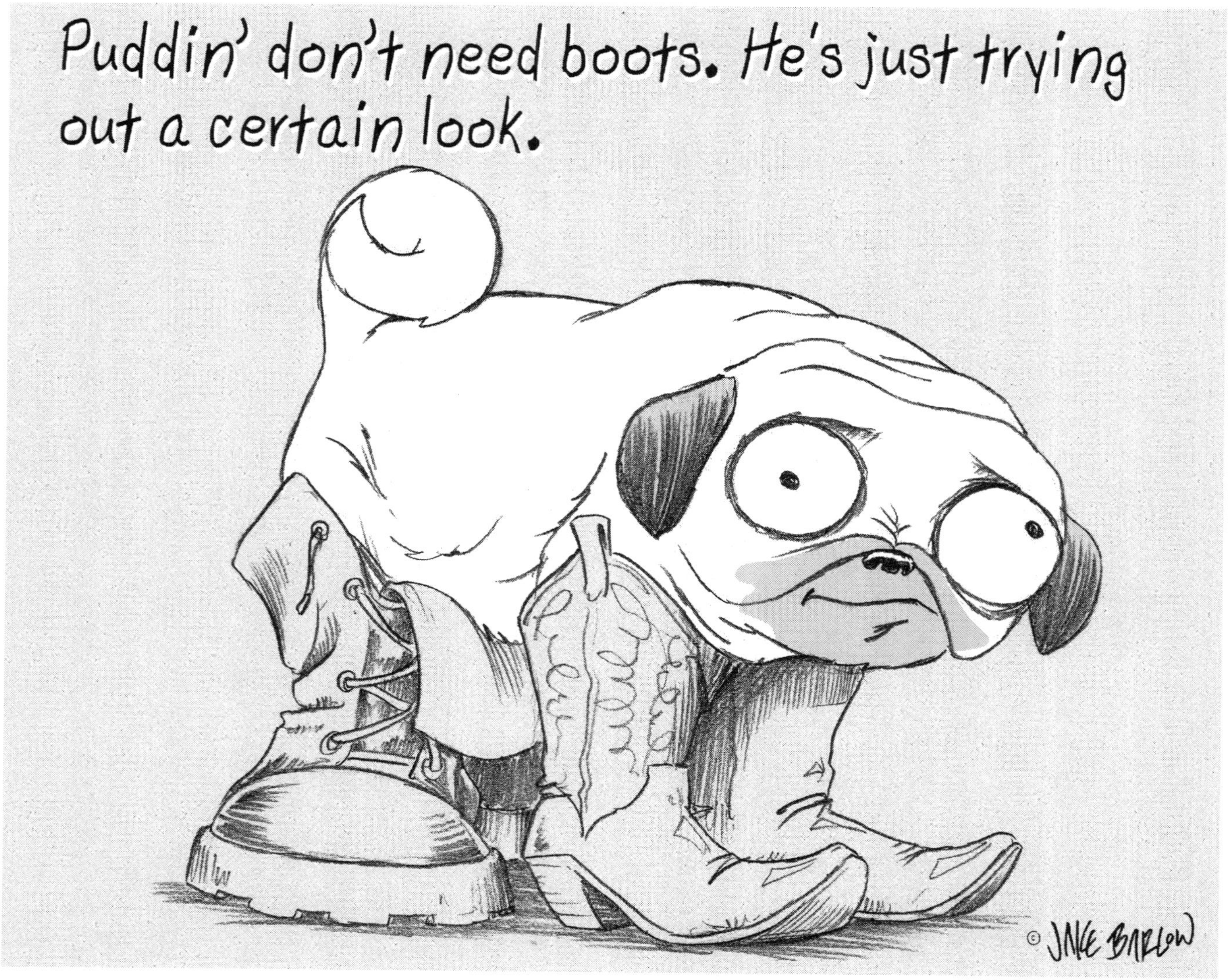
Puddin' don't need boots. He's just trying out a certain look.
© JAKE BARLOW

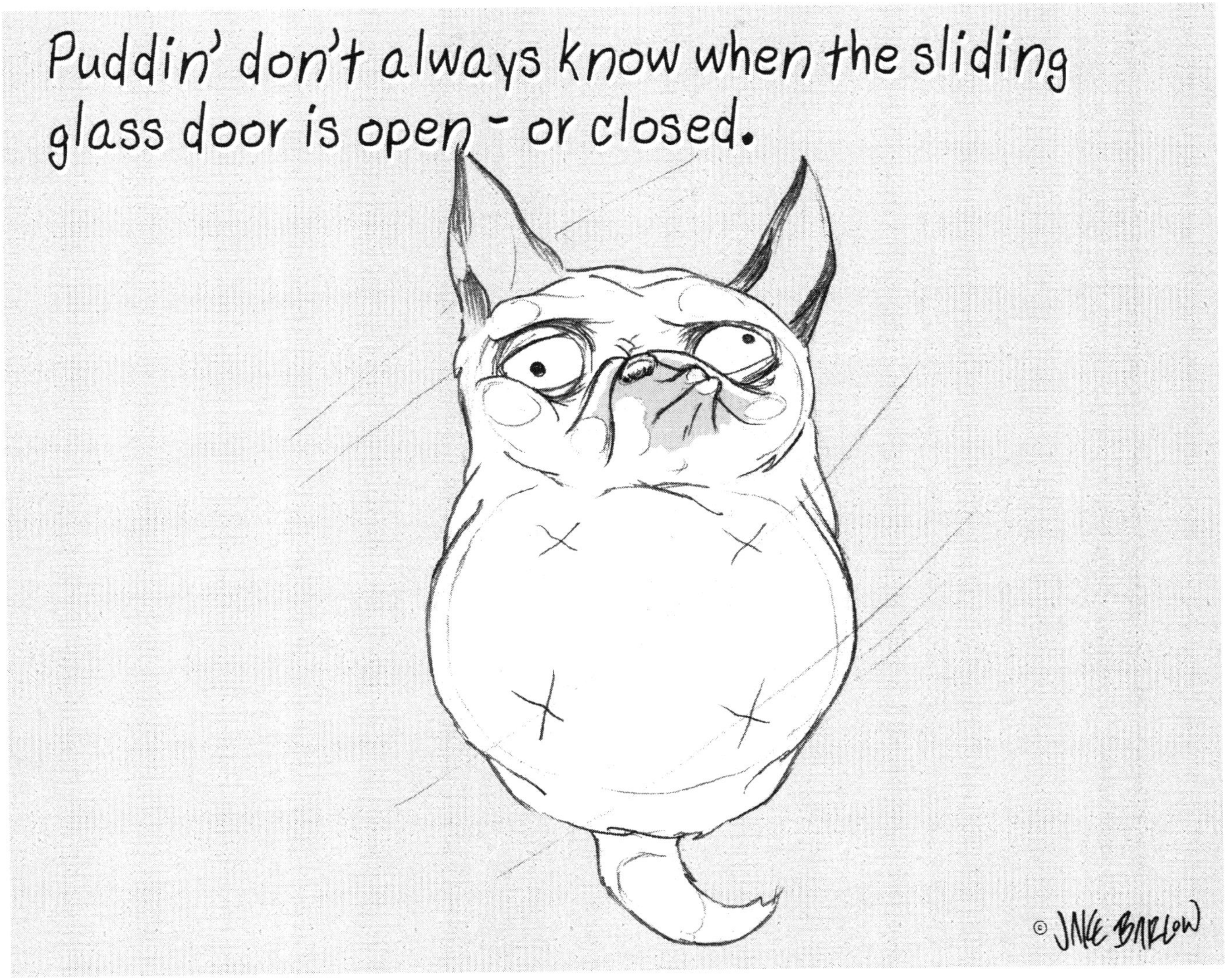
Puddin' don't always know when the sliding glass door is open - or closed.
© JAKE BARLOW

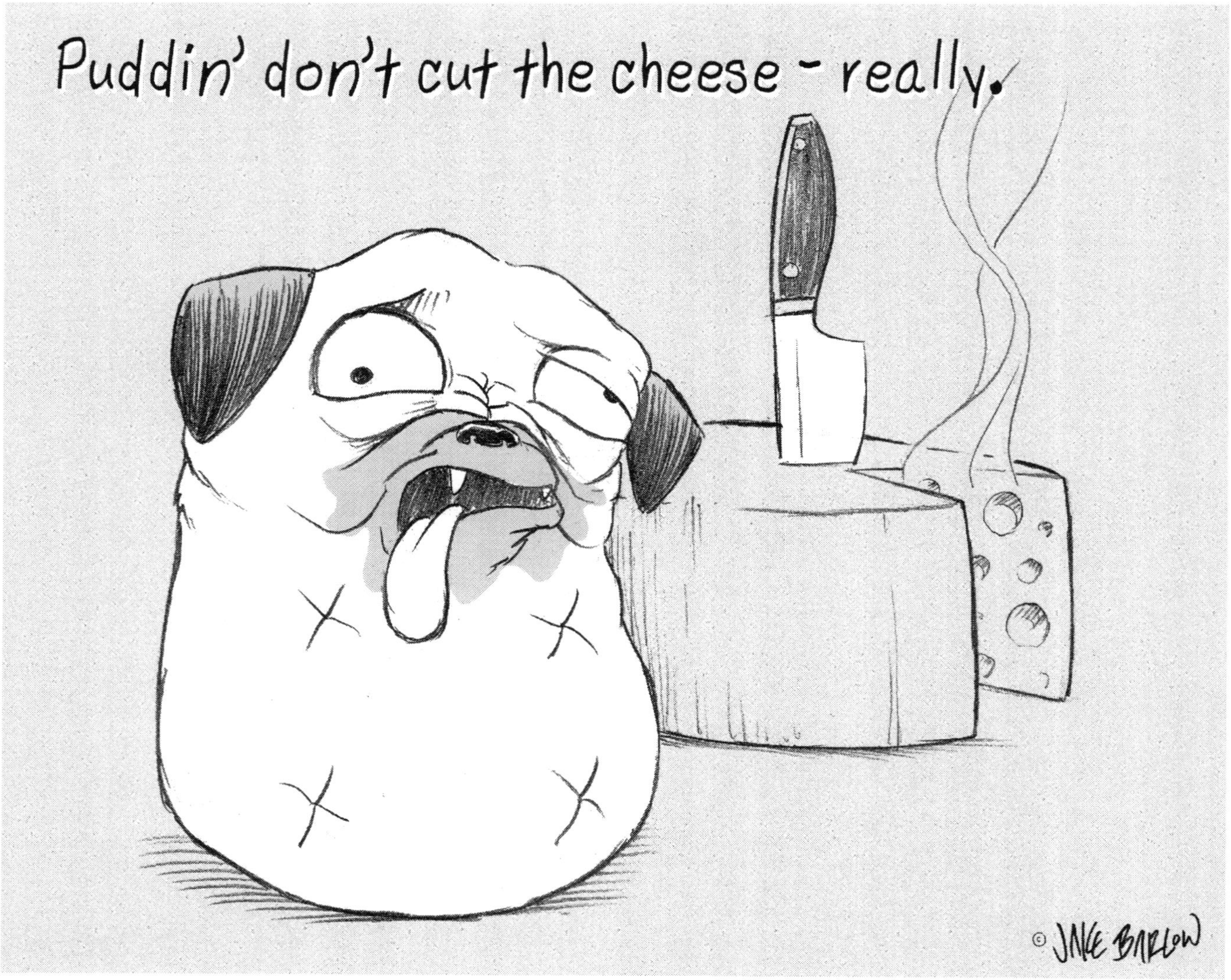
Puddin' don't cut the cheese - really.
© JAKE BARLOW

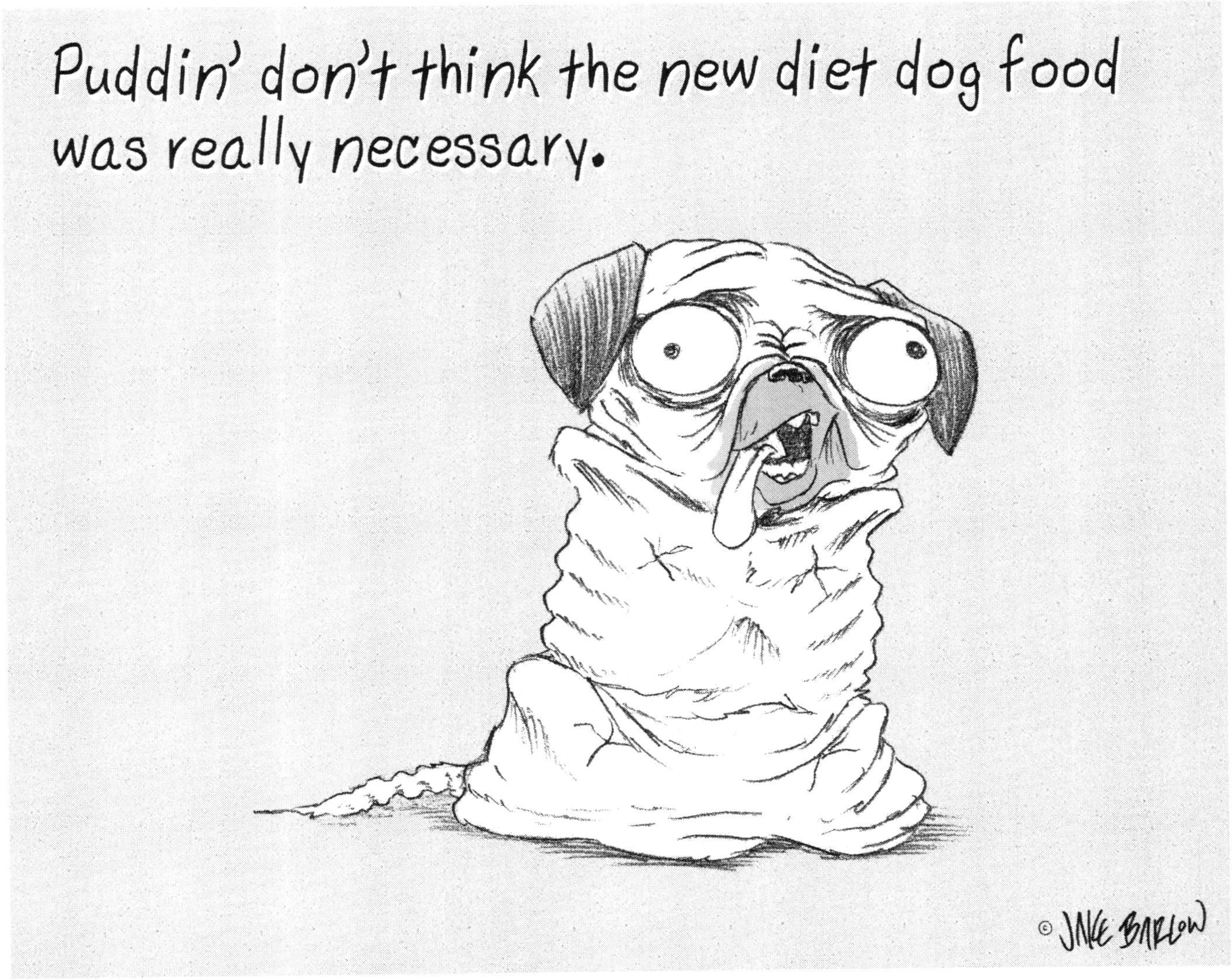
Puddin' don't think the new diet dog food was really necessary.
© JAKE BARLOW

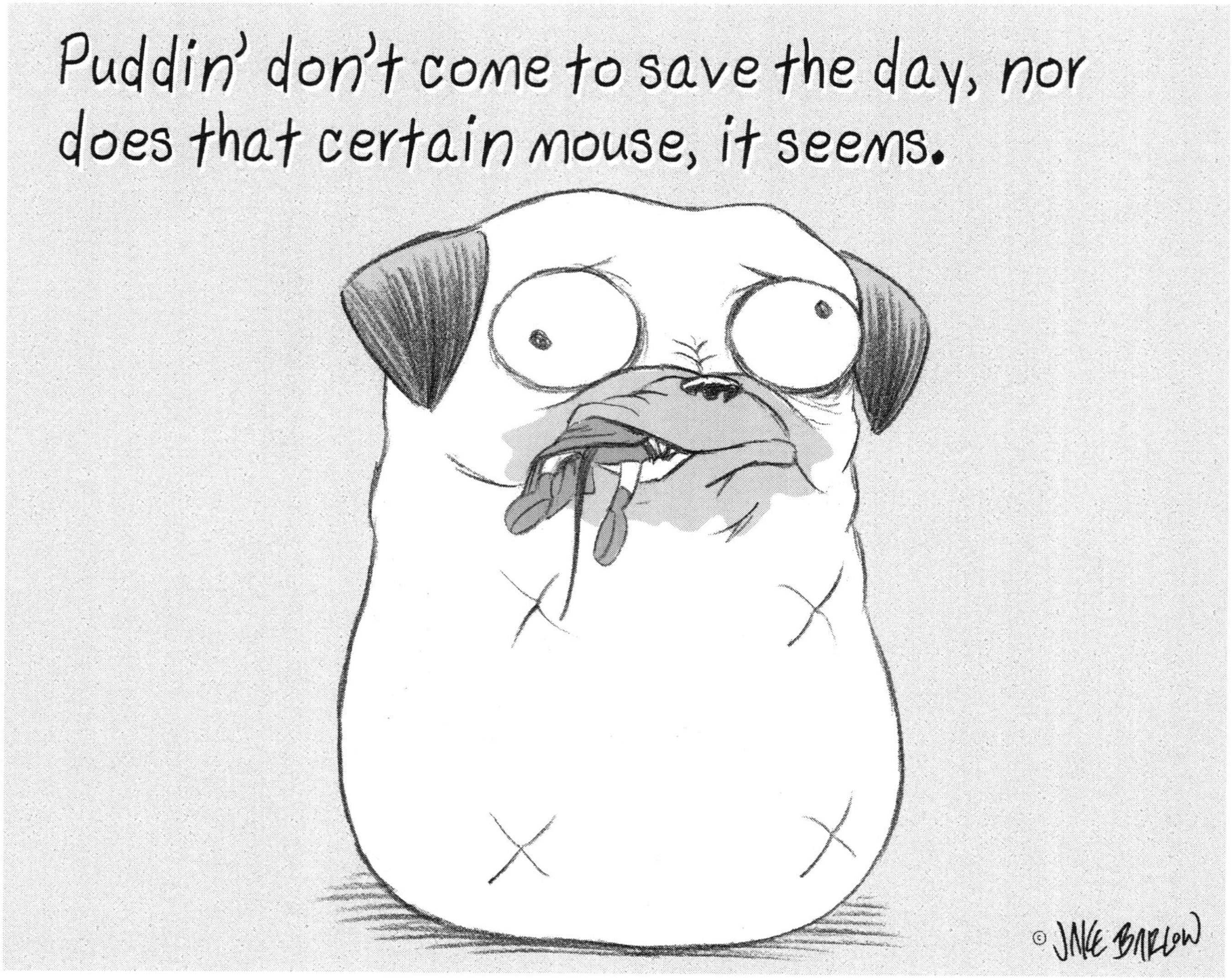
Puddin' don't come to save the day, nor does that certain mouse, it seems.
© JAKE BARLOW

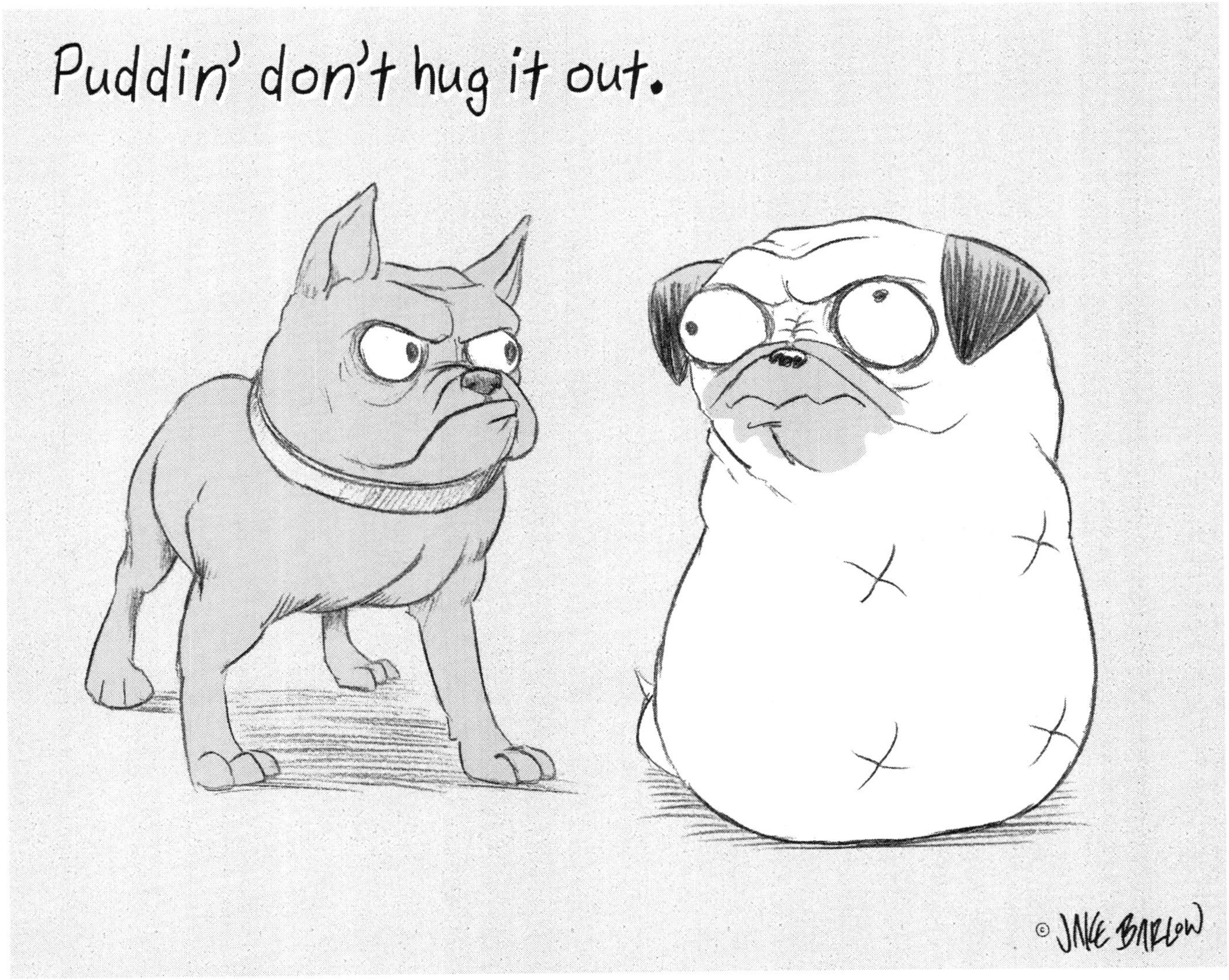
Puddin' don't hug it out.
© JAKE BARLOW

Puddin' don't sneeze without distorting the space-time continuum.

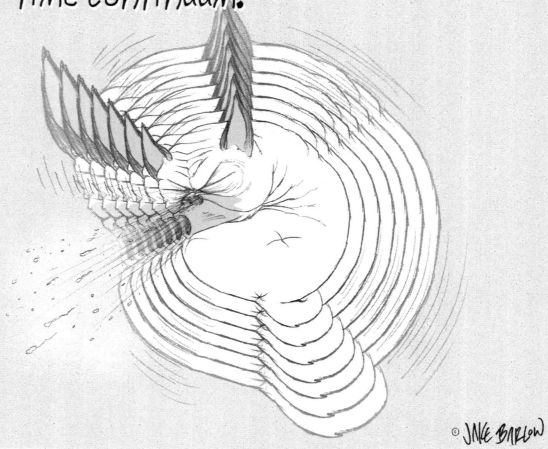

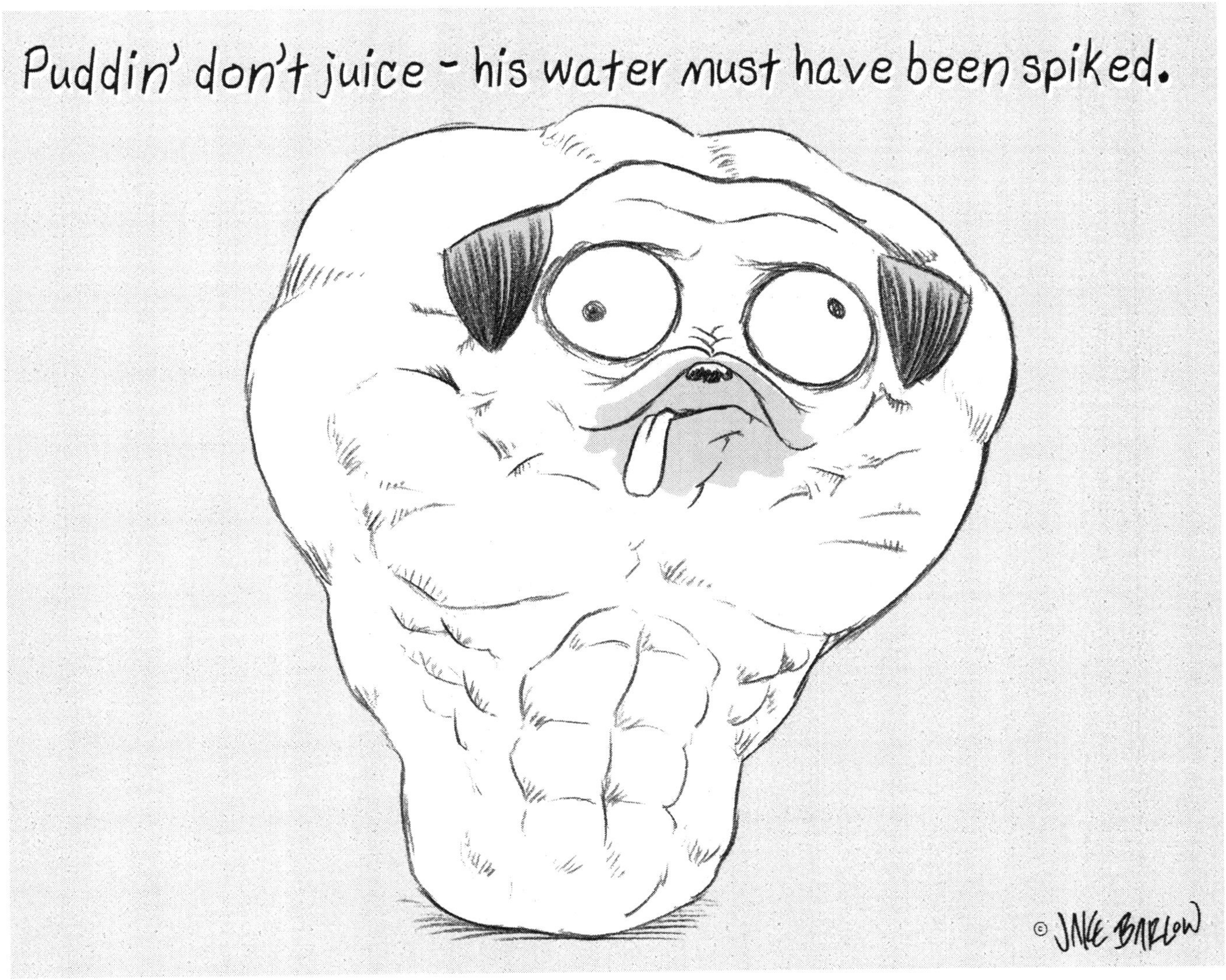
Puddin' don't juice - his water must have been spiked.
© JAKE BARLOW

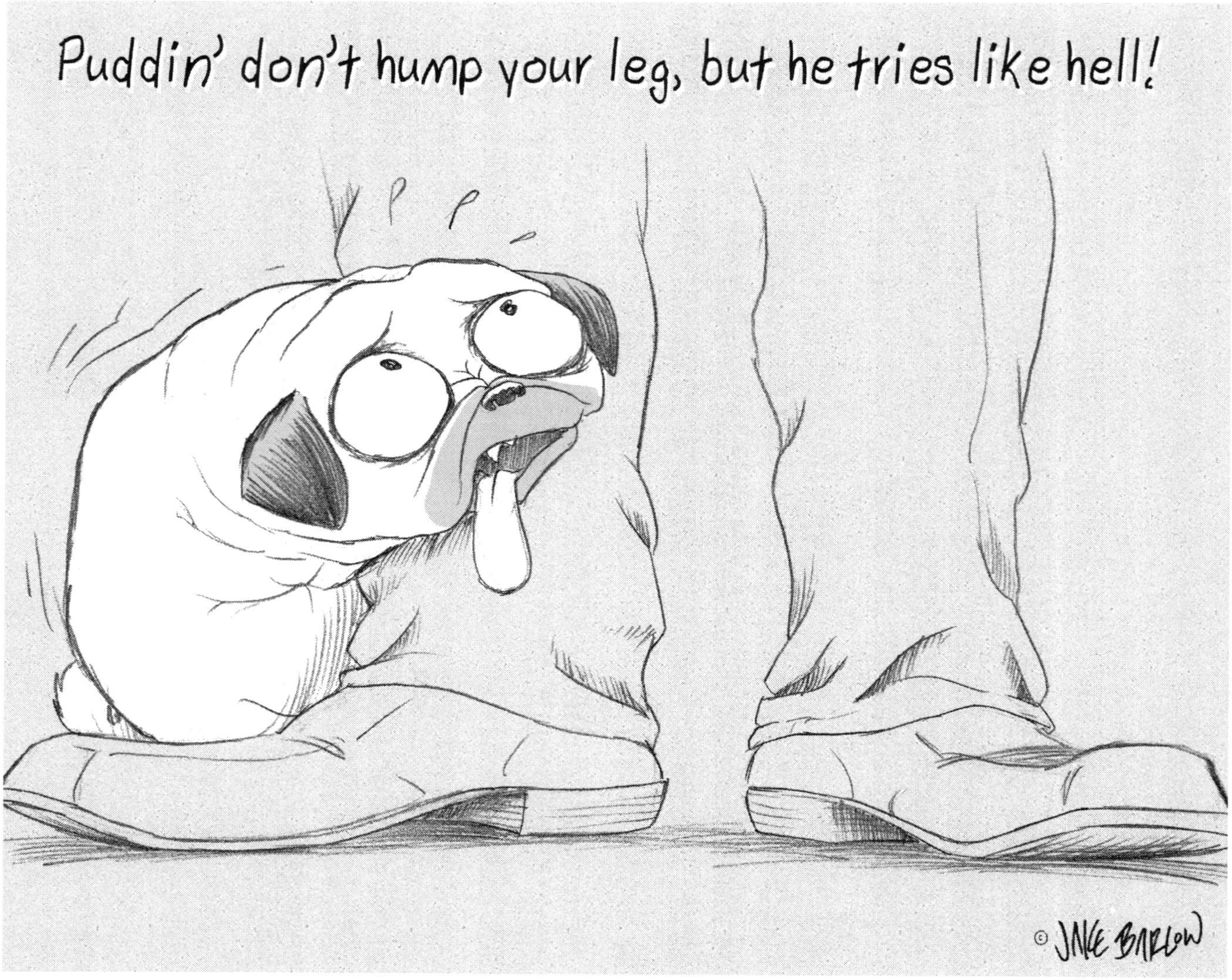
Puddin' don't hump your leg, but he tries like hell!
© JAKE BARLOW

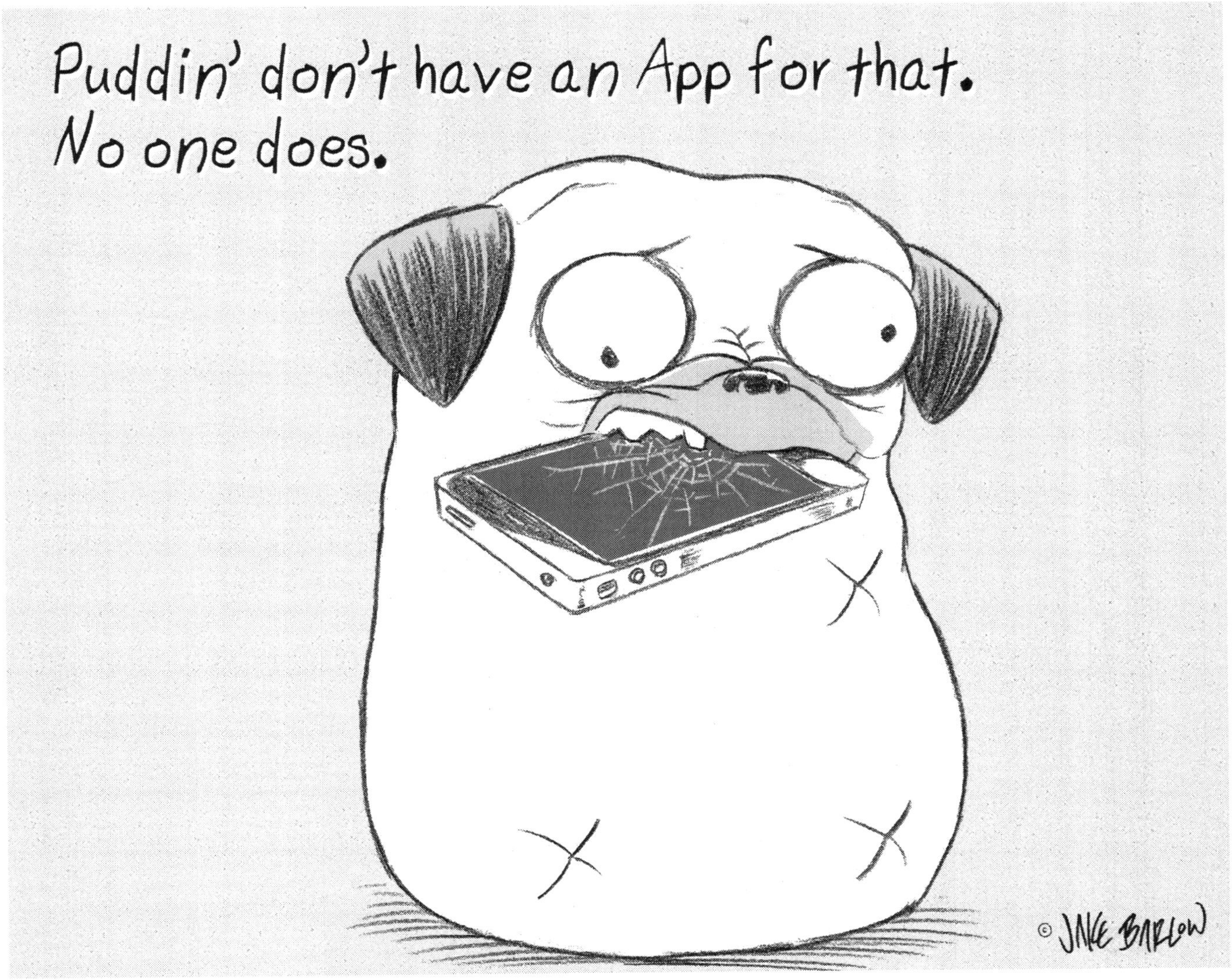
Puddin' don't have an App for that.
No one does.
© JAKE BARLOW

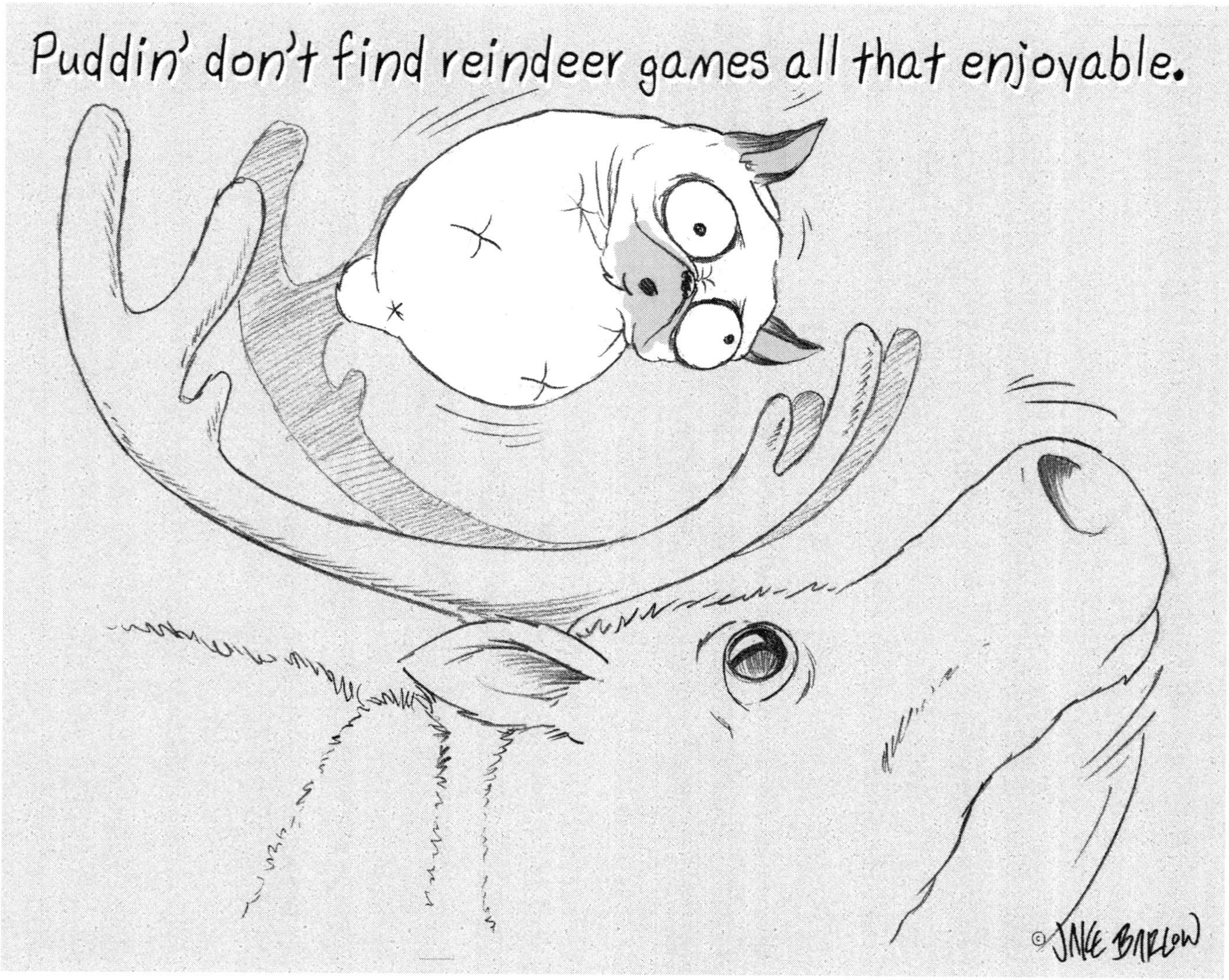
© JAKE BARLOW
Puddin' don't find reindeer games all that enjoyable.

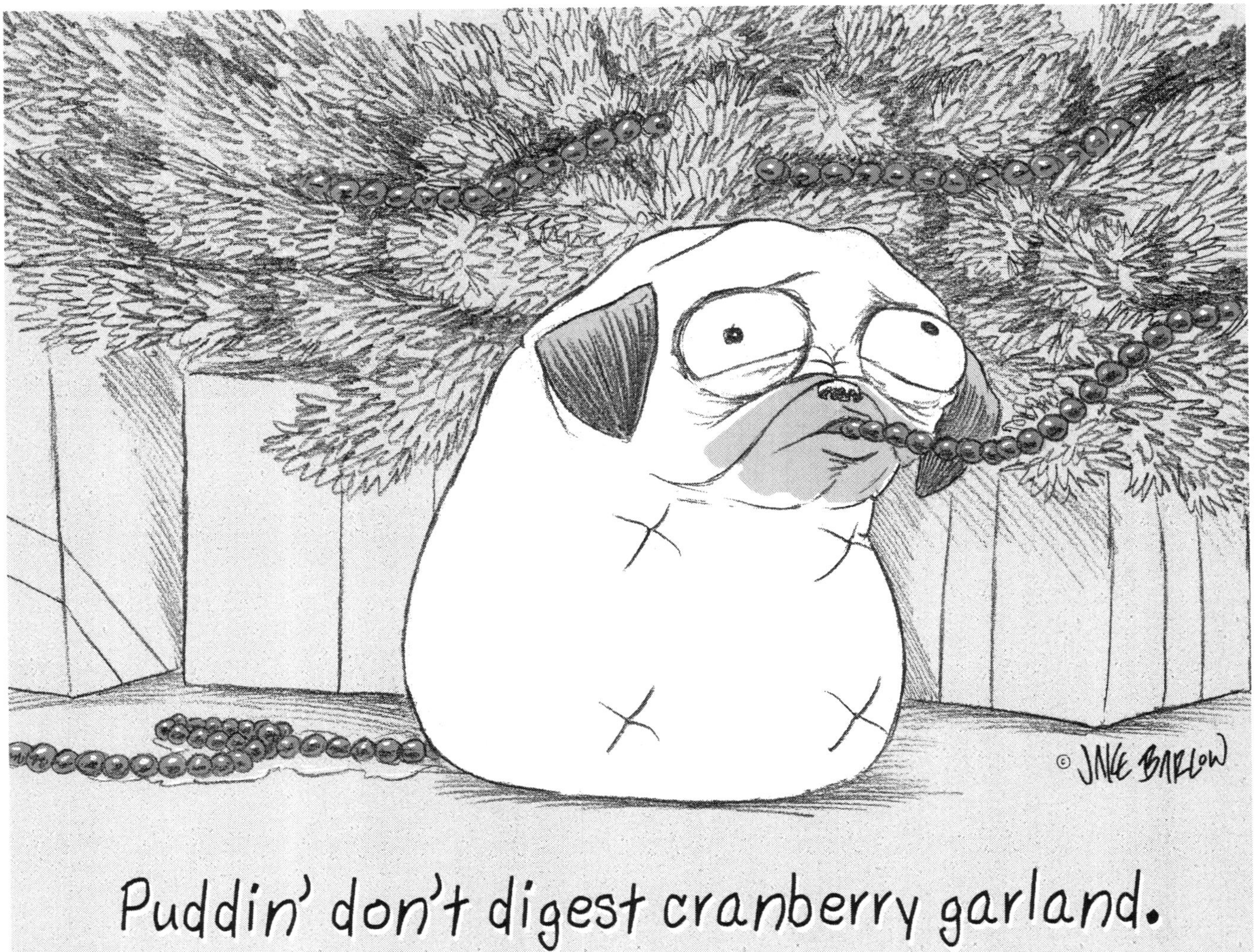
© JAKE BARLOW

Puddin' don't digest cranberry garland.

Puddin' don't 'air his grievances' in the traditional Festivus manner.

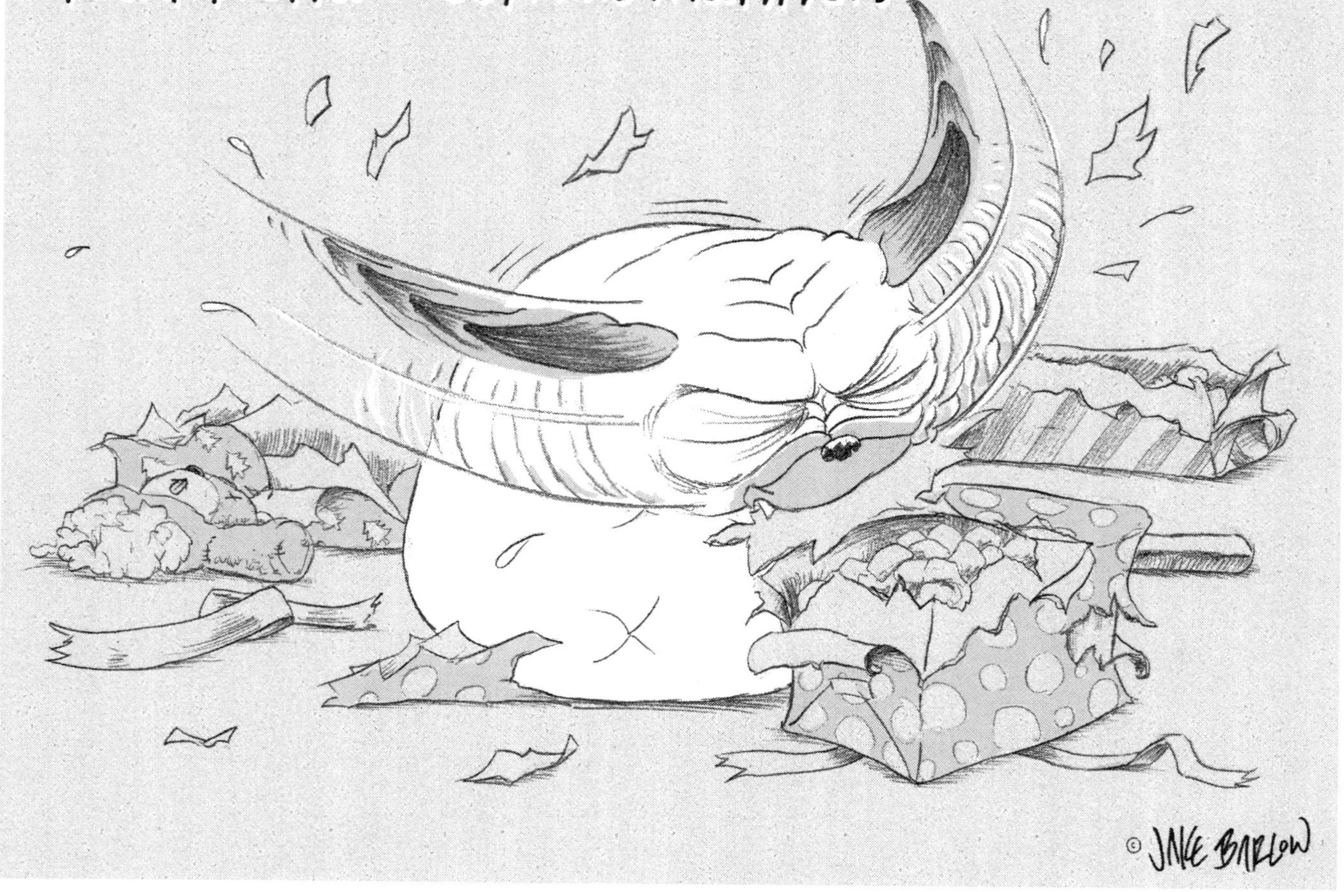
© JAKE BARLOW

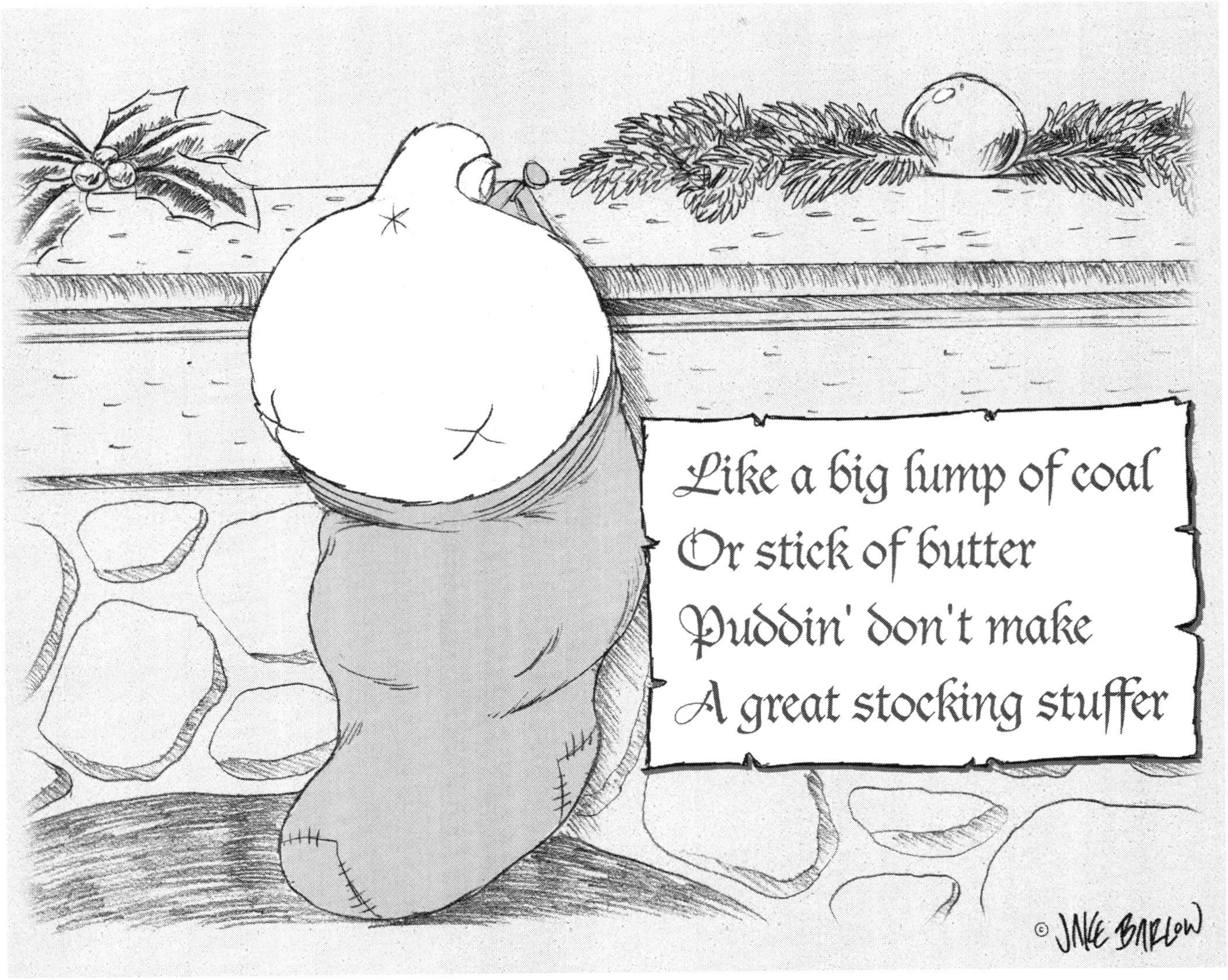
Like a big lump of coal
Or stick of butter
Puddin' don't make
A great stocking stuffer
© JAKE BARLOW

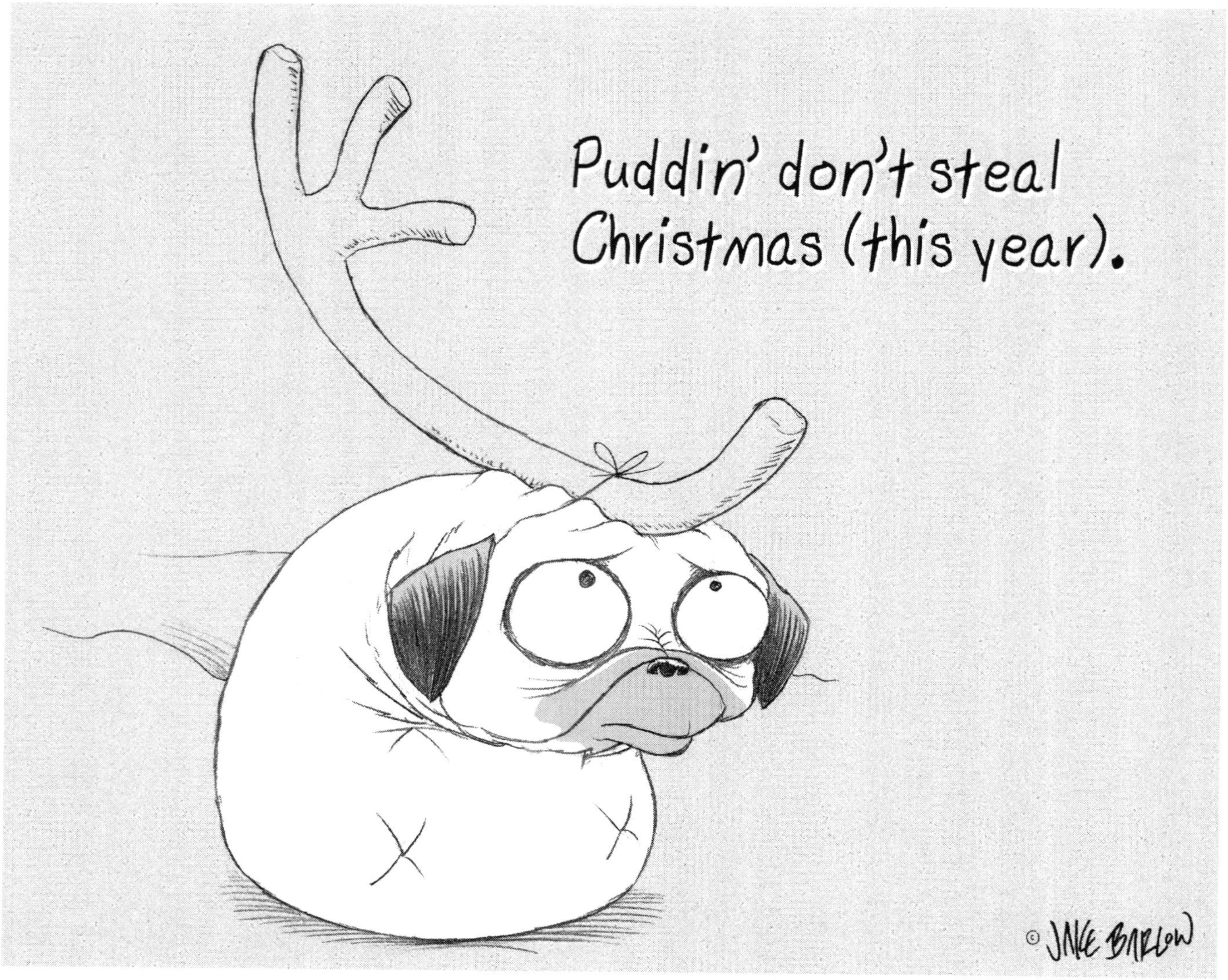
Puddin' don't steal
Christmas (this year).
© JAKE BARLOW

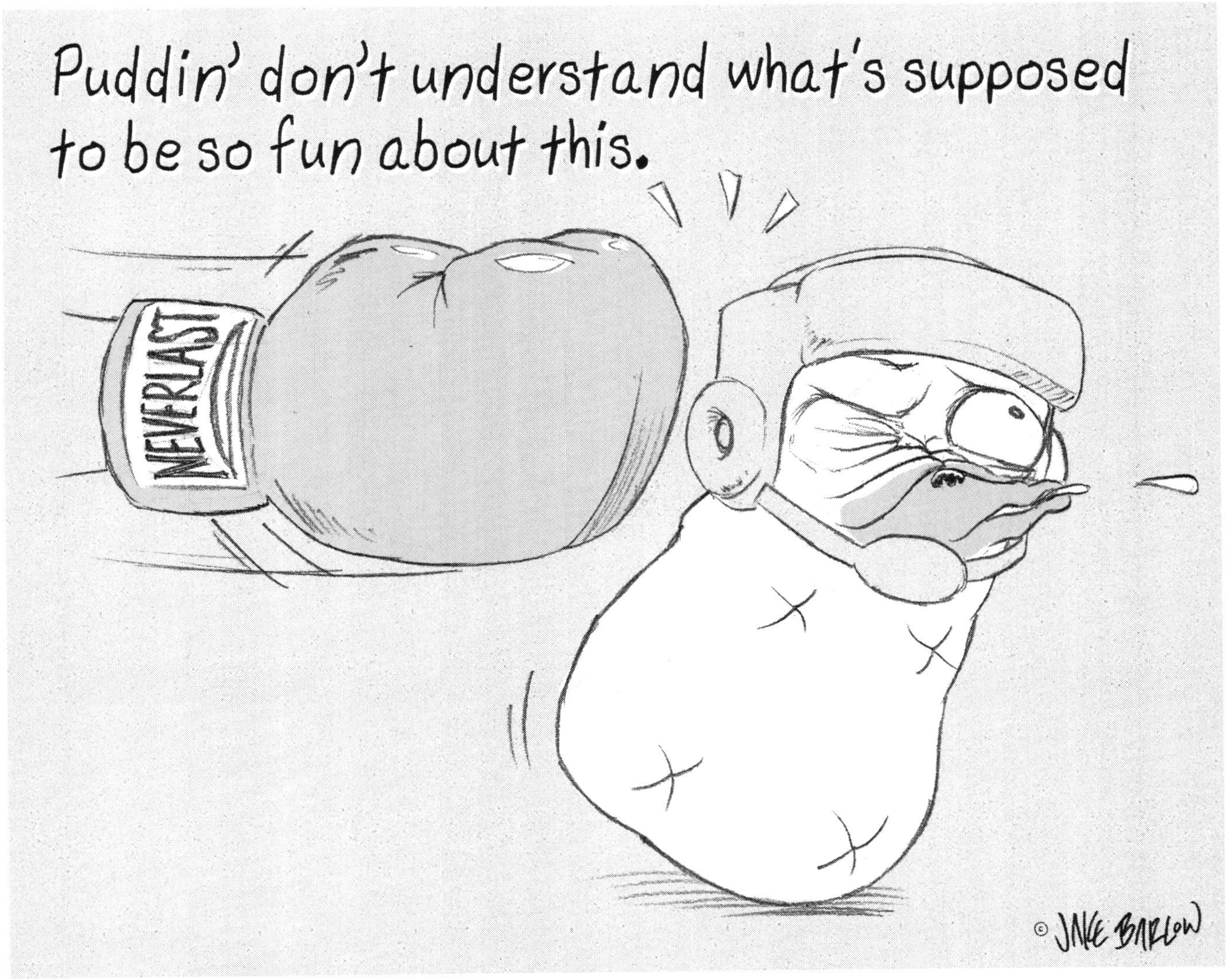
Puddin' don't understand what's supposed to be so fun about this.
EVERLAST
© JAKE BARLOW

Happy Boxing Day!

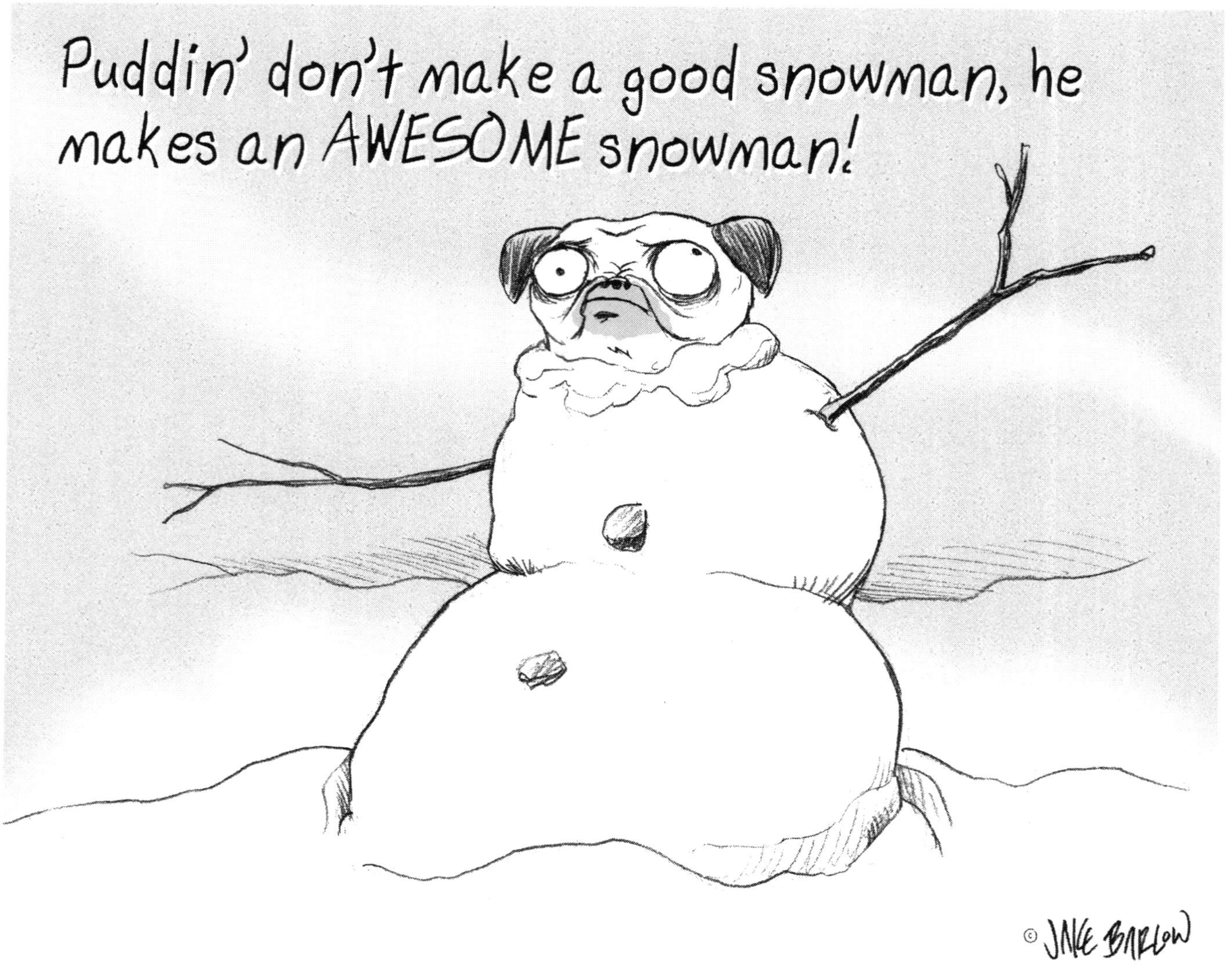
Puddin' don't make a good snowman, he makes an AWESOME snowman!
© JAKE BARLOW

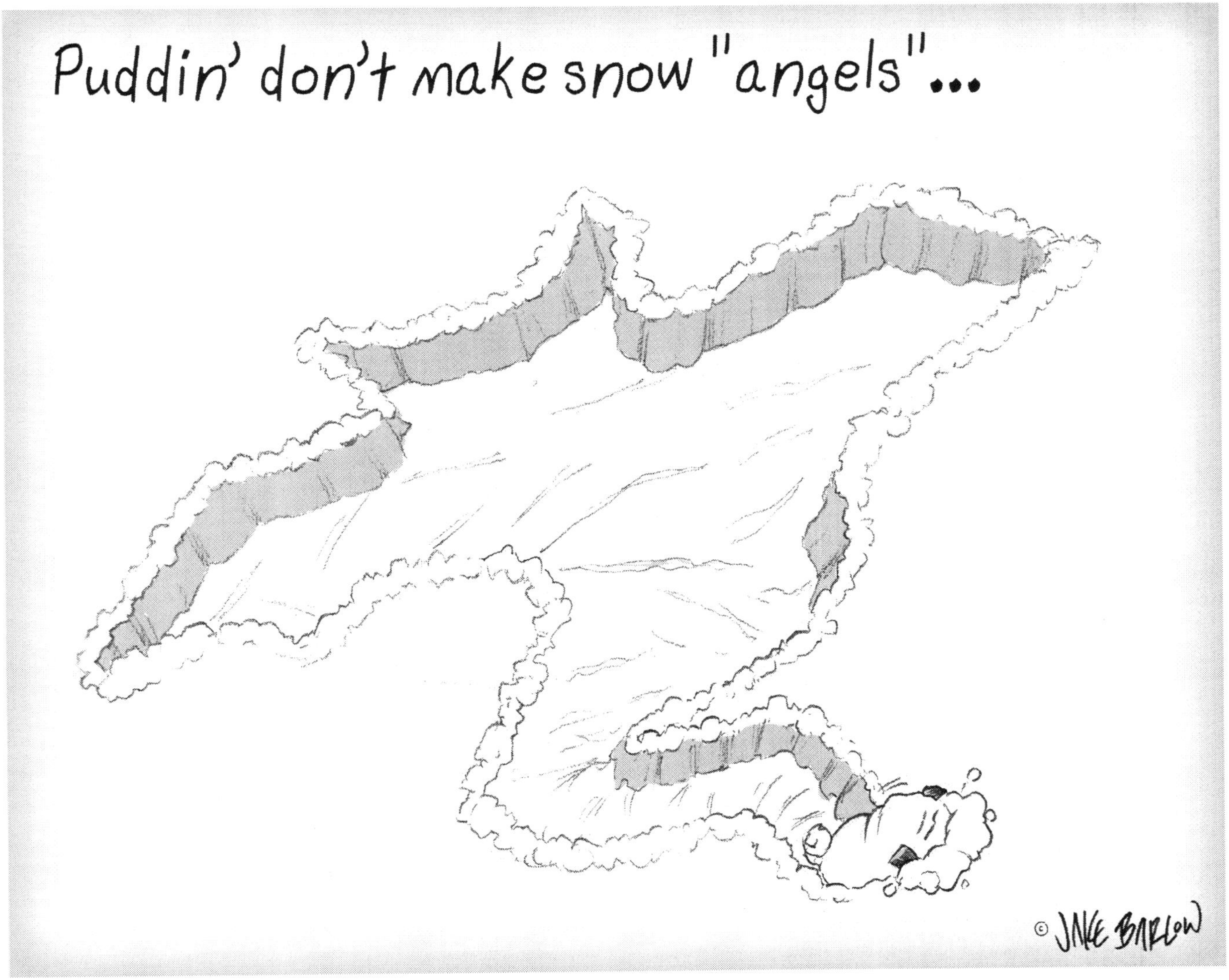
© JAKE BARLOW

Puddin' don't make snow "angels"...

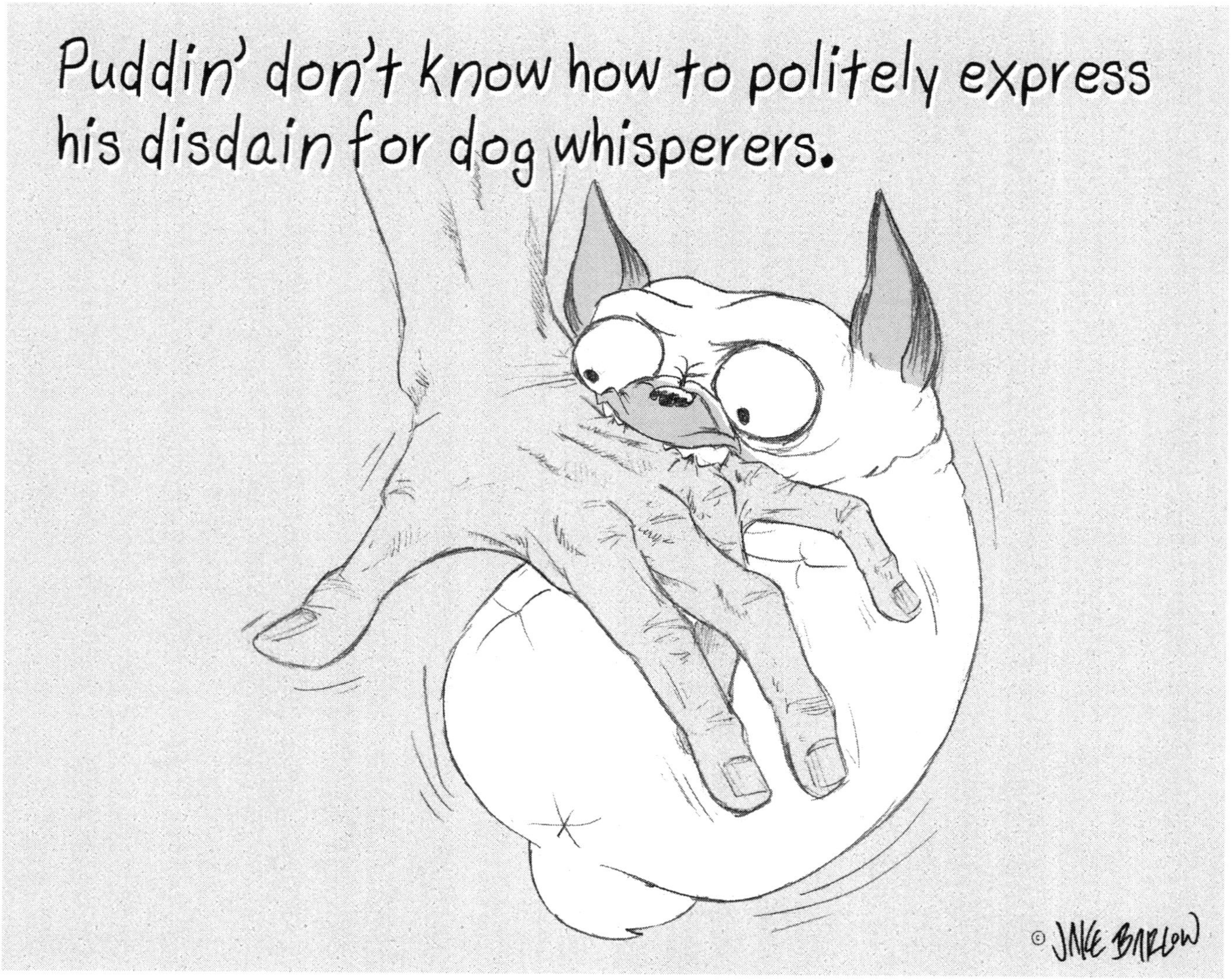
Puddin' don't know how to politely express his disdain for dog whisperers.
© JAKE BARLOW

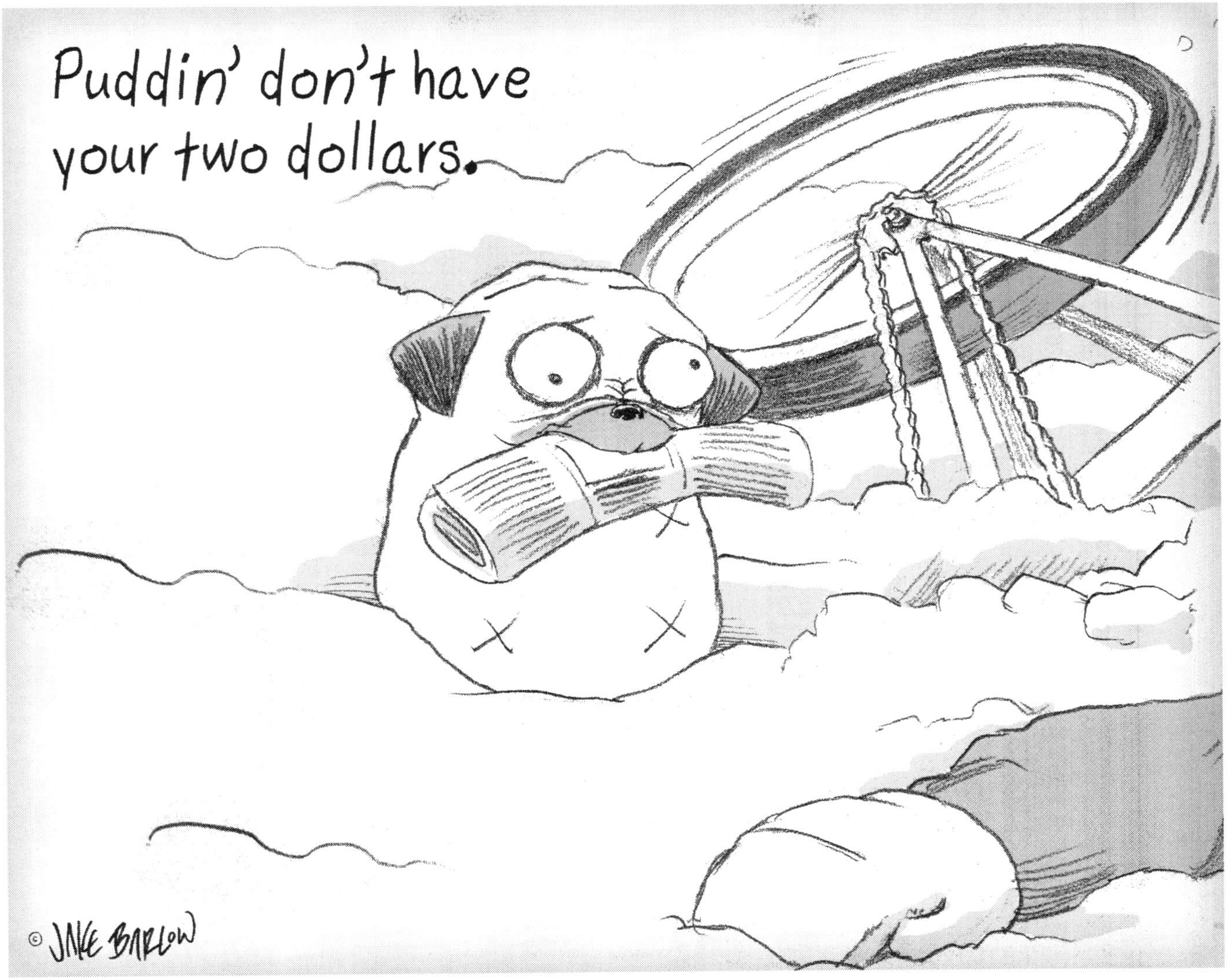
Puddin' don't have
your two dollars.
© JAKE BARLOW

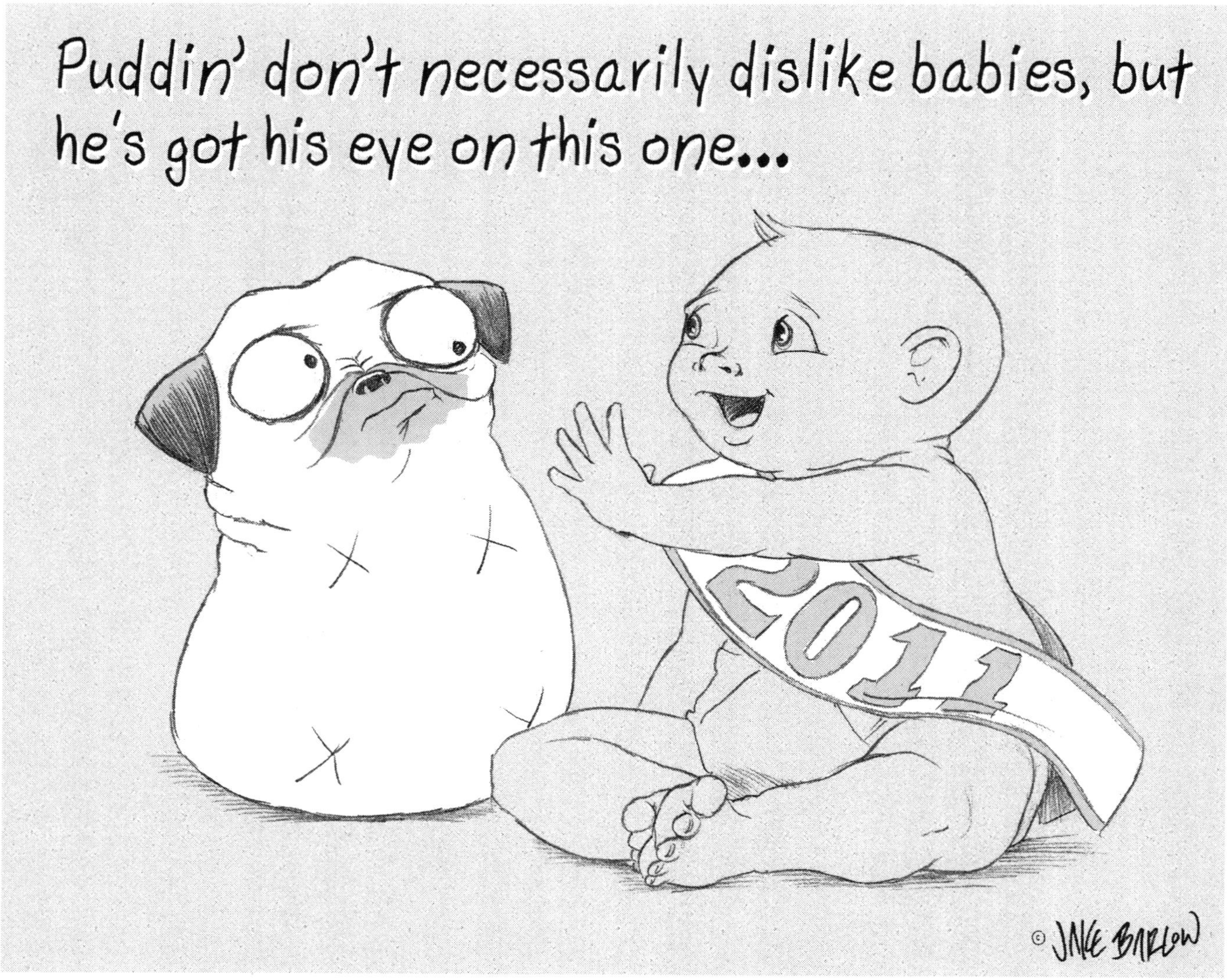
Puddin' don't necessarily dislike babies, but he's got his eye on this one...
2011
© JAKE BARLOW

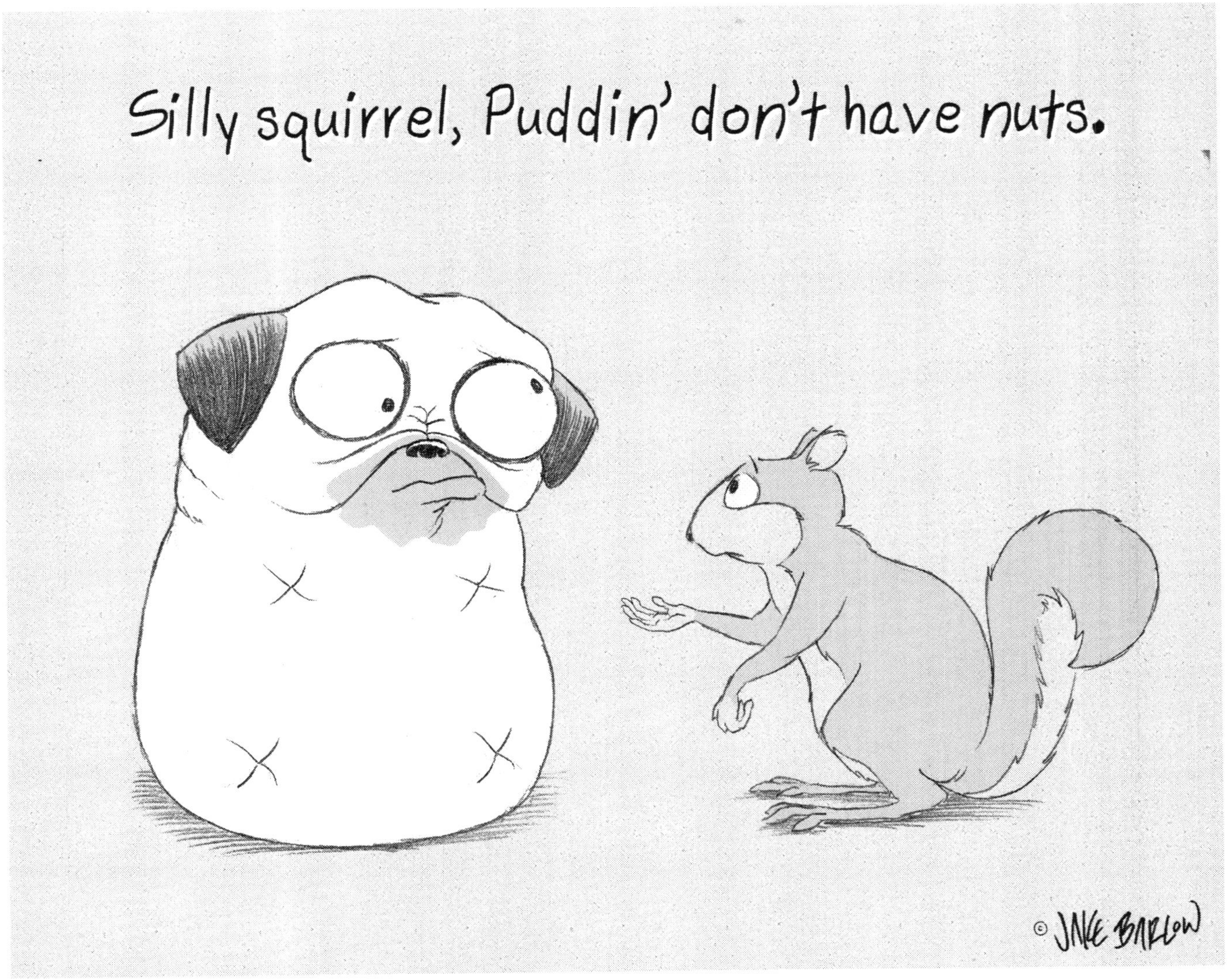
Silly squirrel, Puddin' don't have nuts.
© JAKE BARLOW

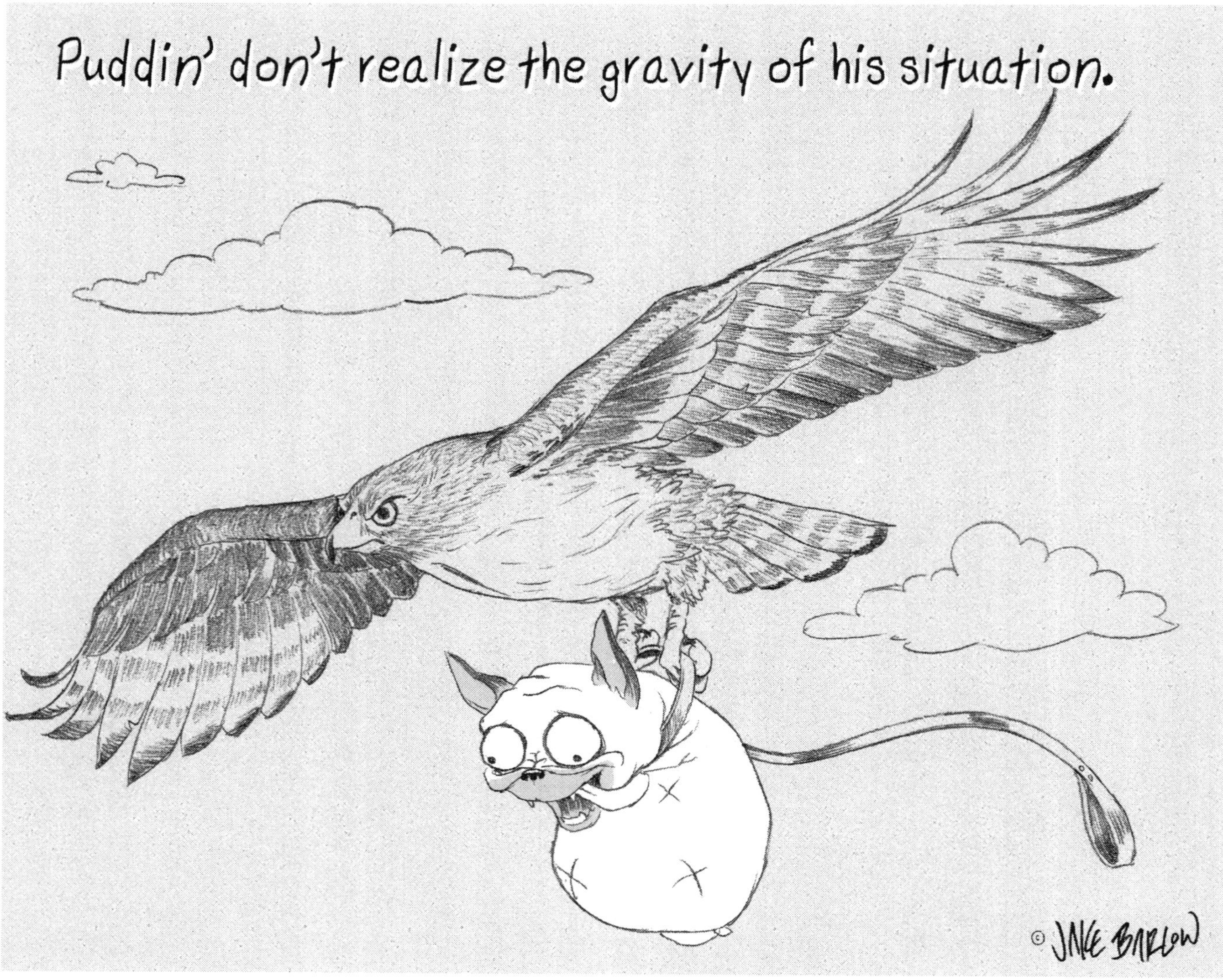
Puddin' don't realize the gravity of his situation.
© JAKE BARLOW

Puddin' don't stay fresh after "Sell By" date.

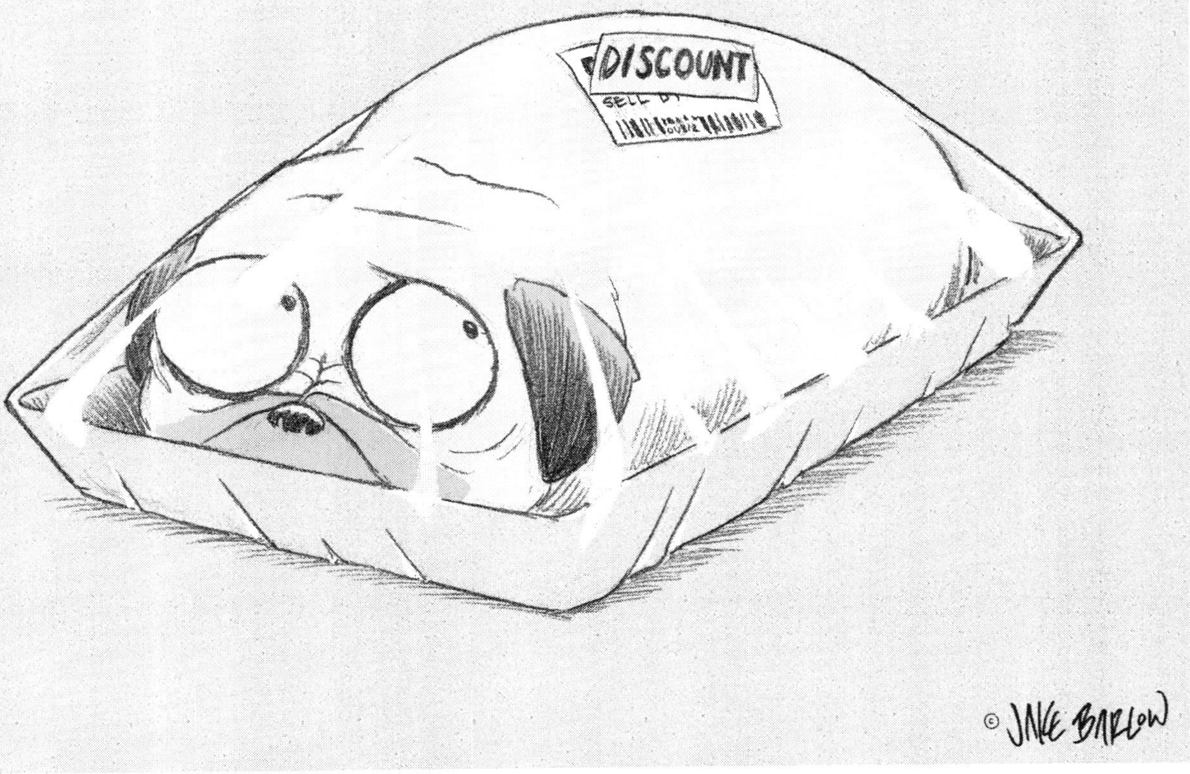
DISCOUNT
SELL BY
© JAKE BARLOW

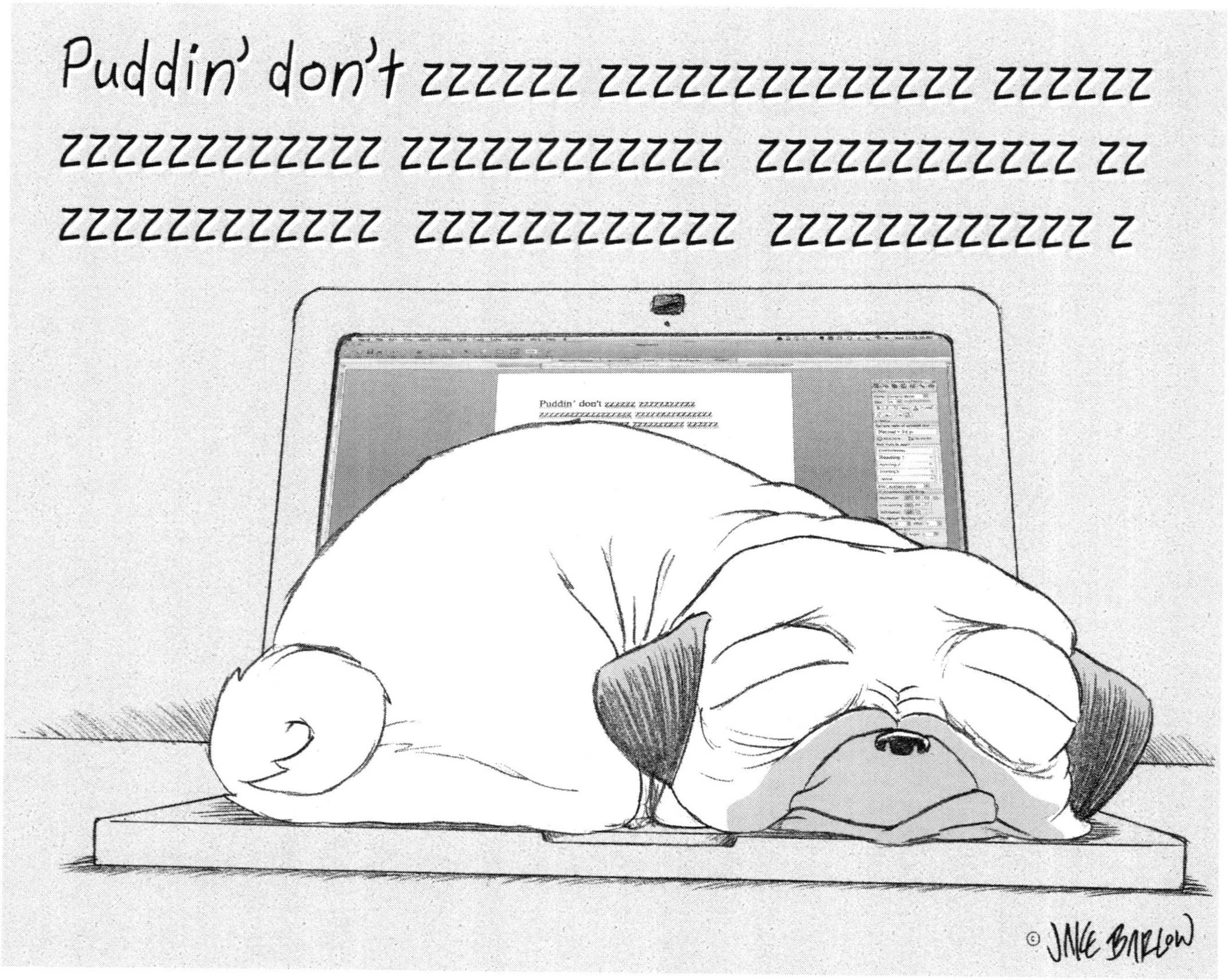
Puddin' don't zzzzzz zzzzzzzzzzzzzzzz zzzzzz
zzzzzzzzzzzzzz zzzzzzzzzzzzzz zzzzzzzzzzzzzz zz
zzzzzzzzzzzzzz zzzzzzzzzzzzzz zzzzzzzzzzzzzz z
© JAKE BARLOW

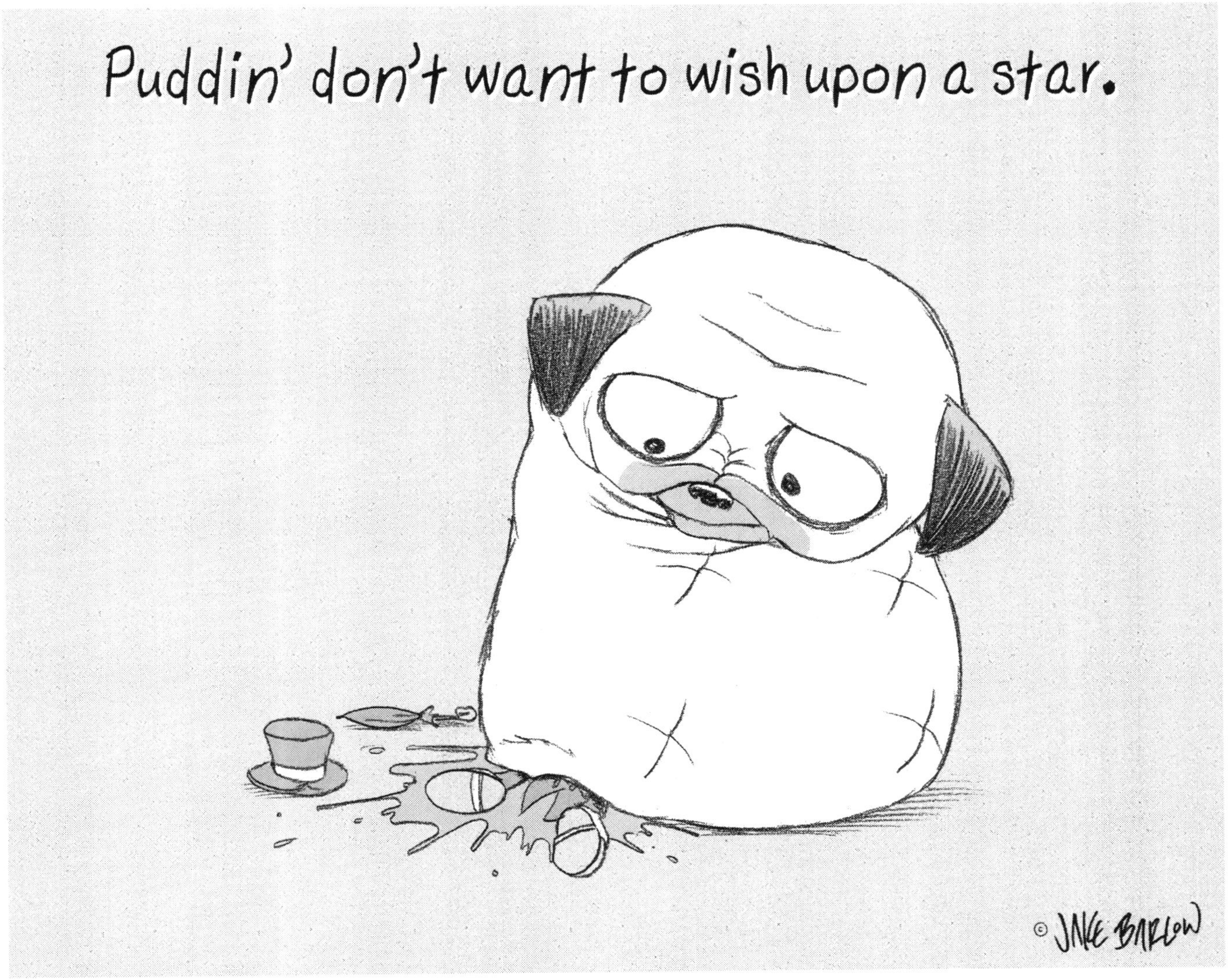
© JAKE BARLOW

Puddin' don't want to wish upon a star.

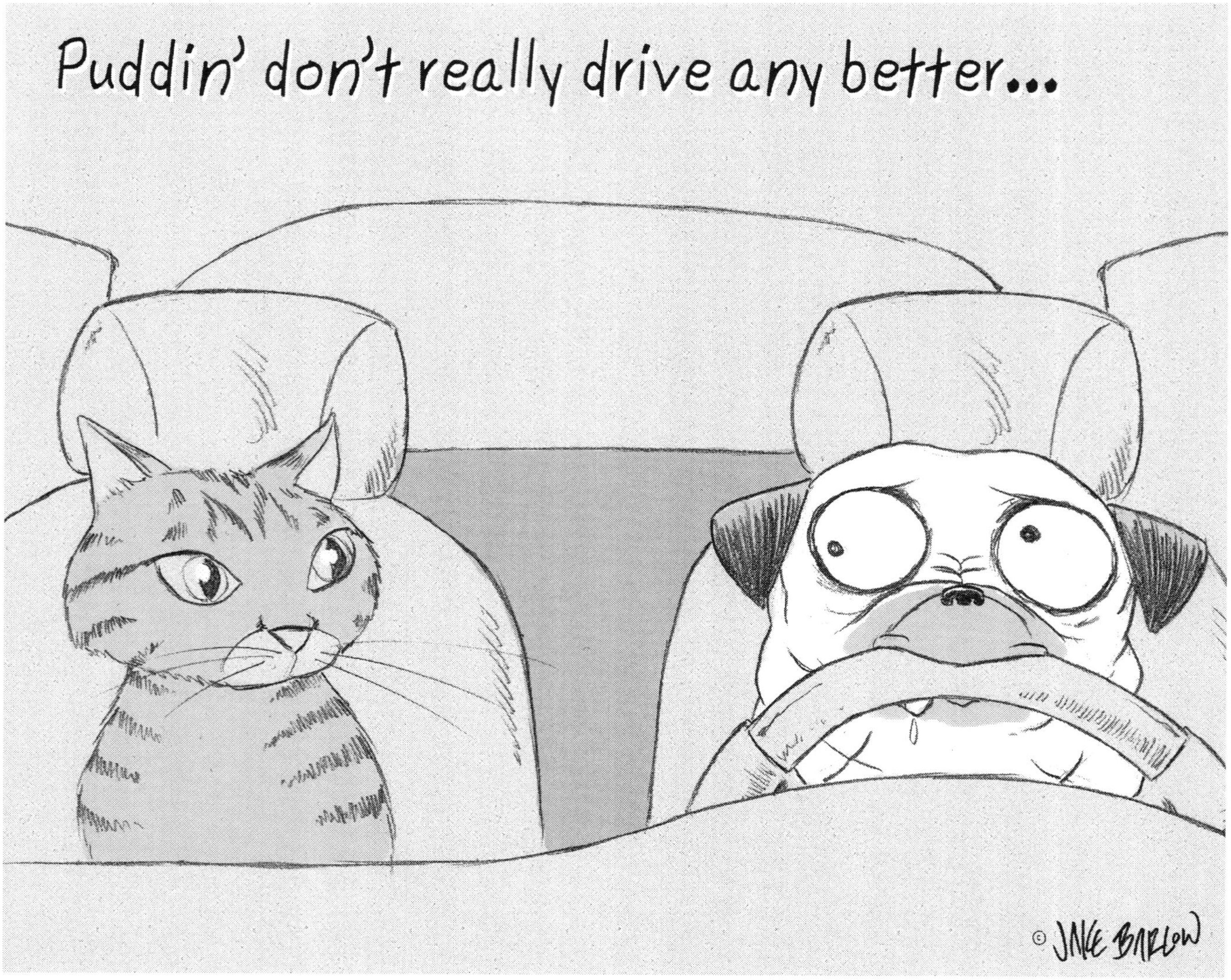
© JAKE BARLOW
Puddin' don't really drive any better...

Puddin' don't let the door hit him on the ass.

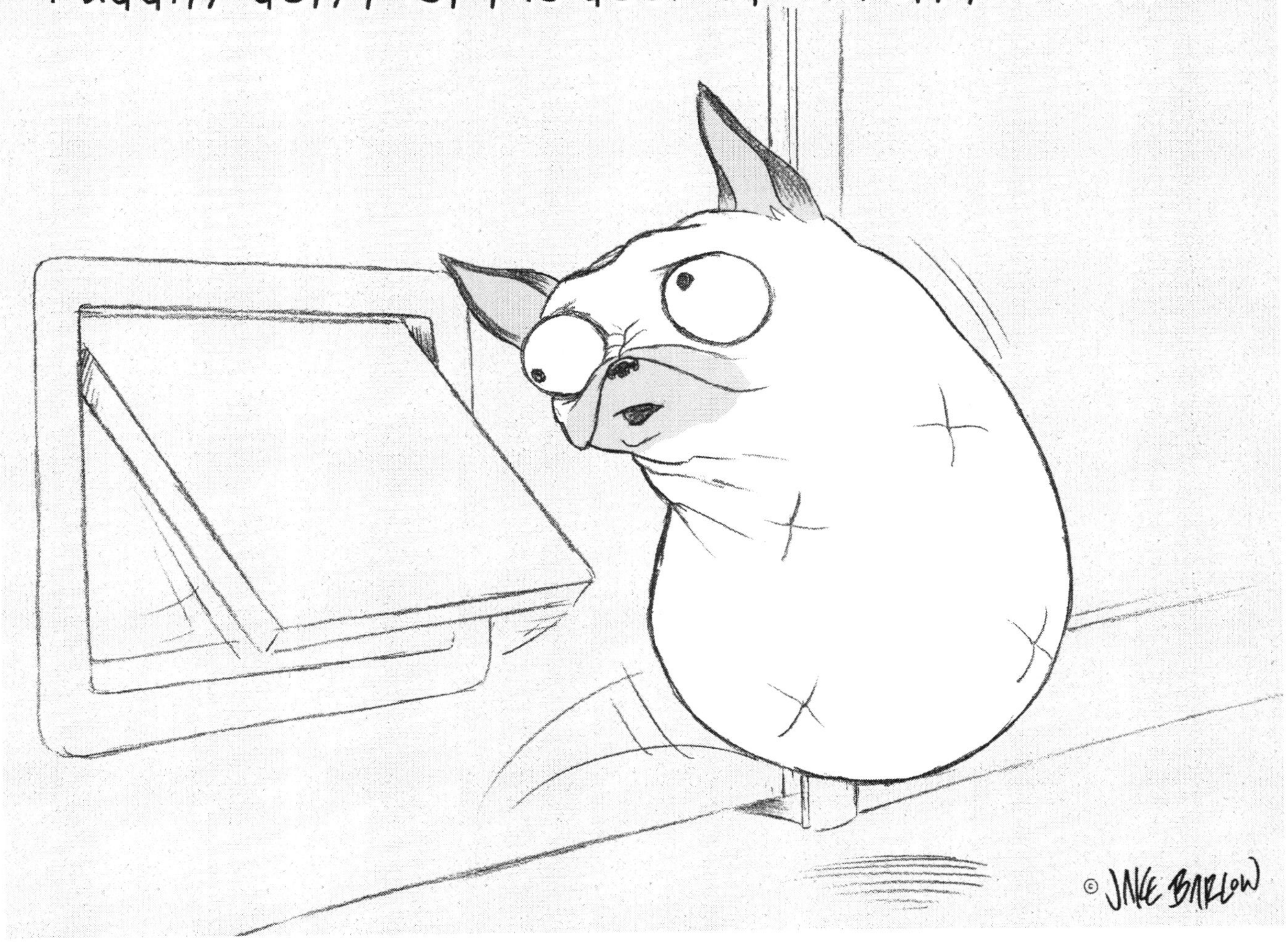
© JAKE BARLOW

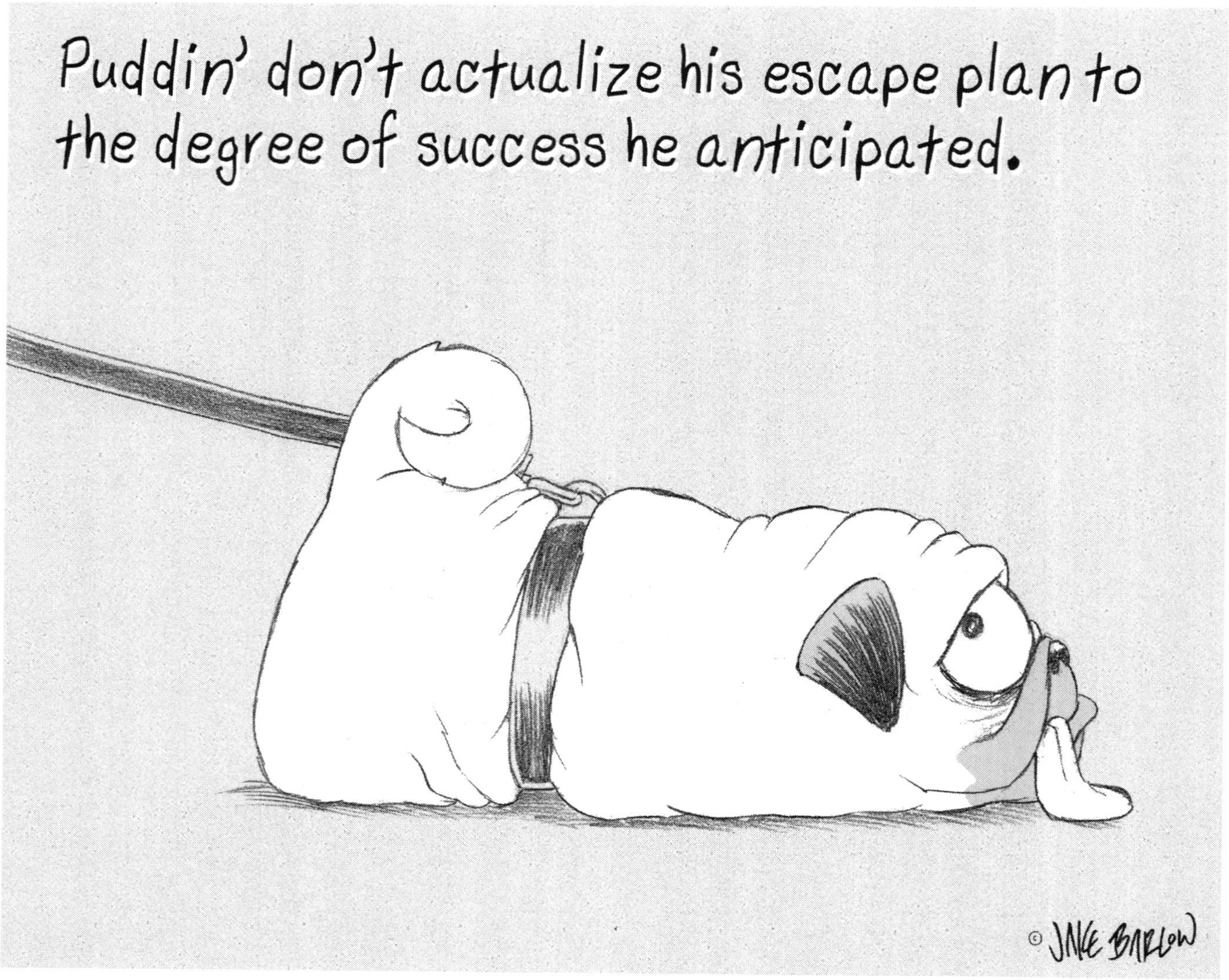
© JAKE BARLOW
Puddin' don't actualize his escape plan to the degree of success he anticipated.

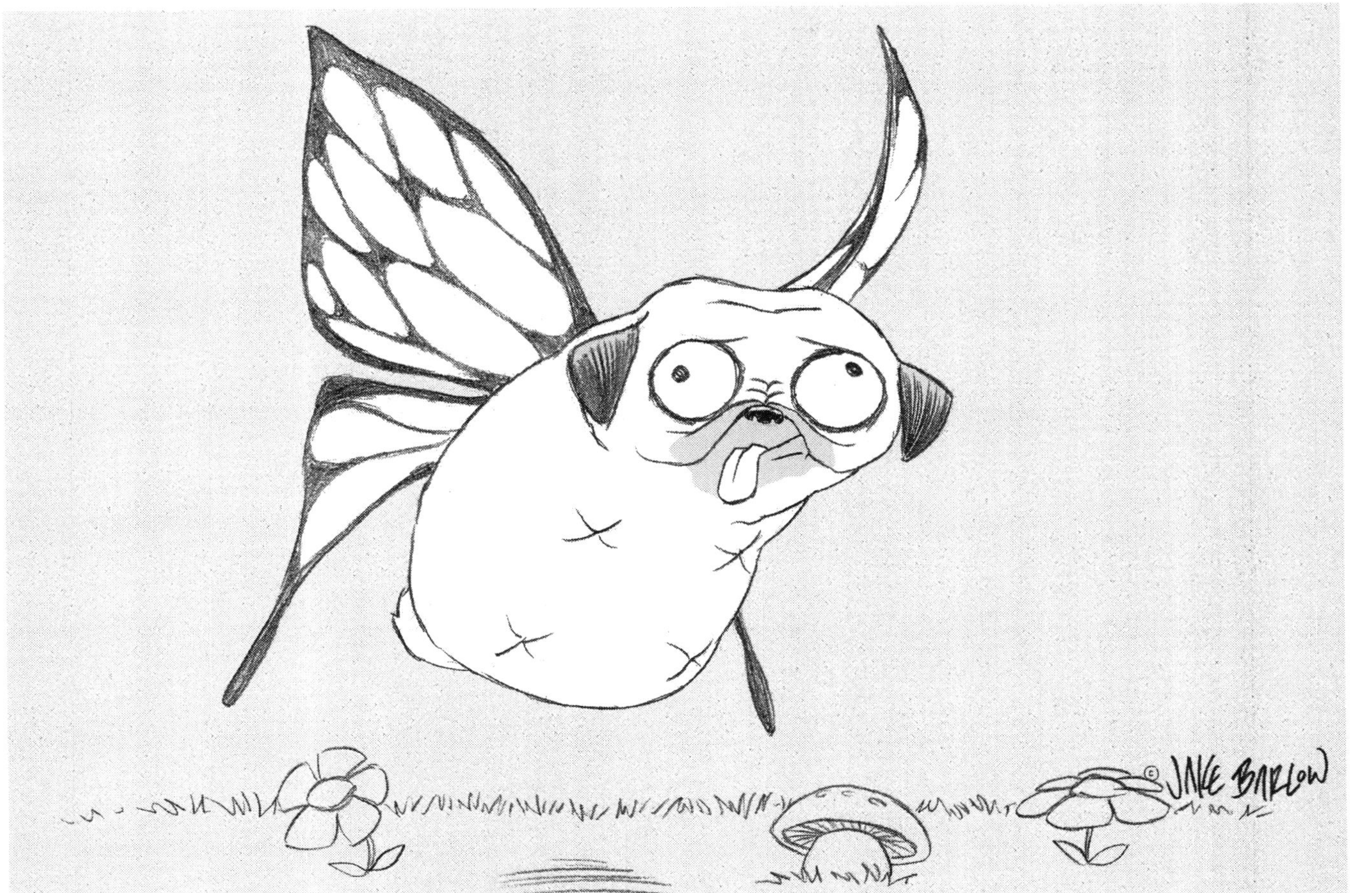
© JAKE BARLOW

Puddin' don't yet realize just how magic those mushrooms really are.

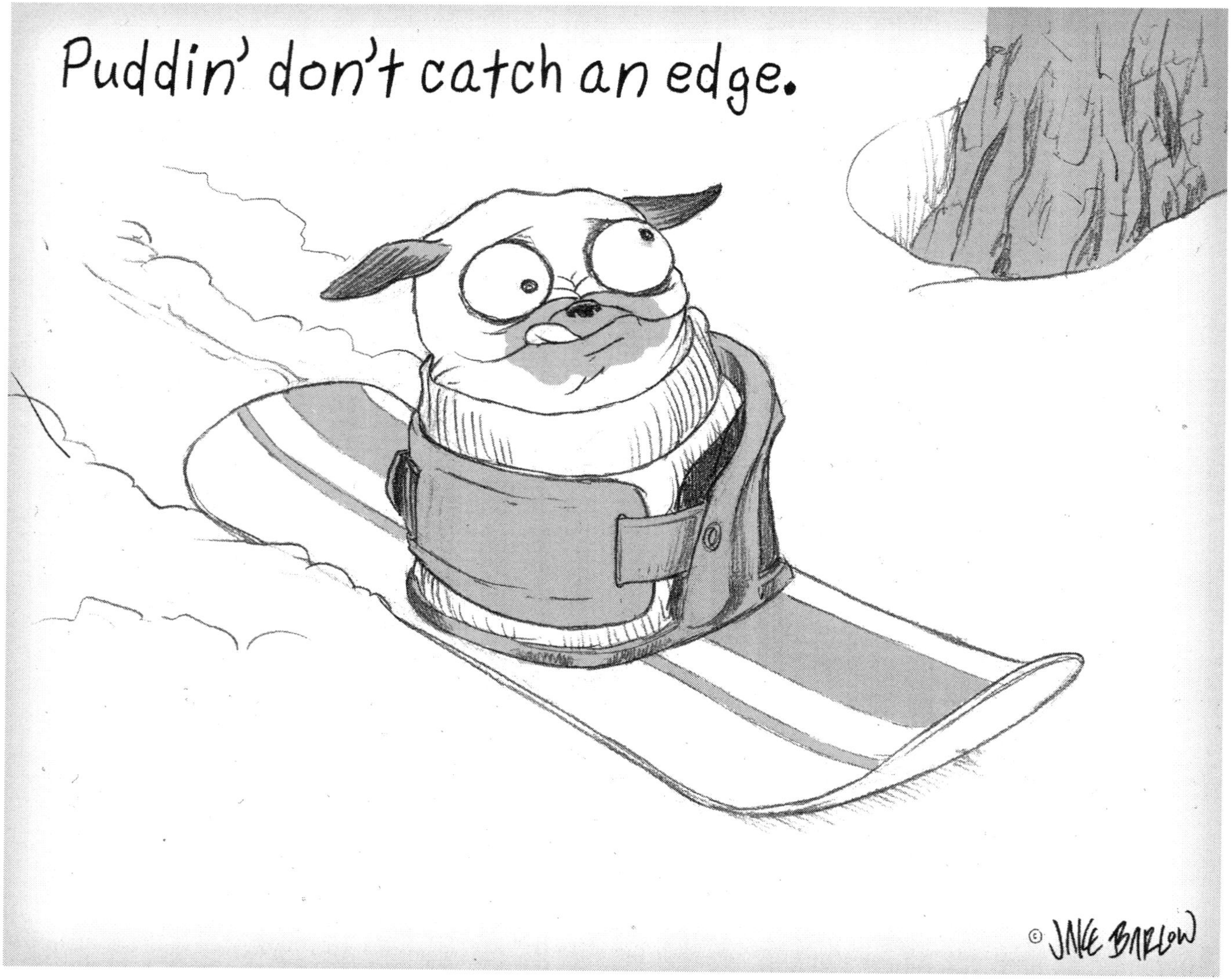
Puddin' don't catch an edge.
© JAKE BARLOW

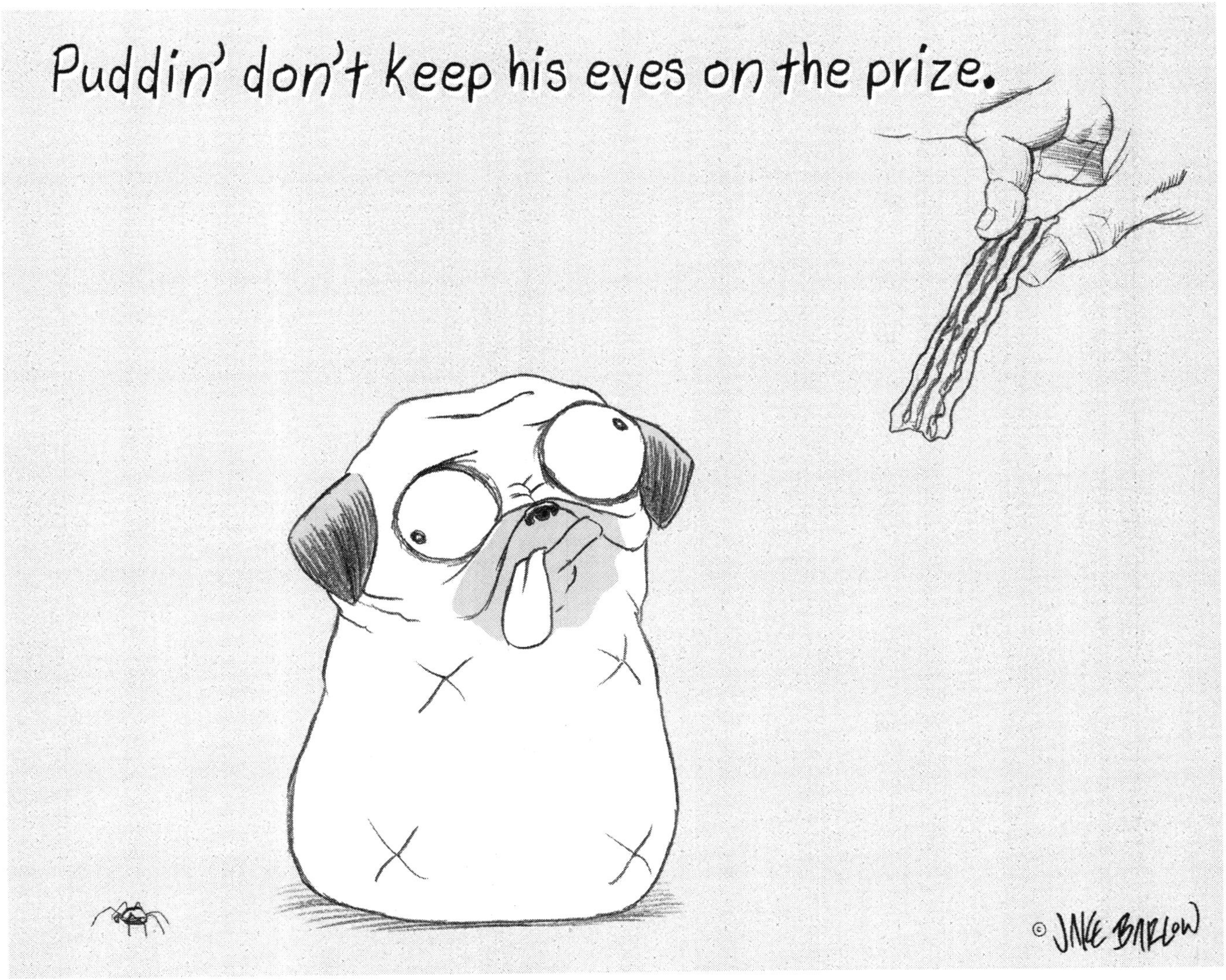
© JAKE BARLOW

Puddin' don't keep his eyes on the prize.

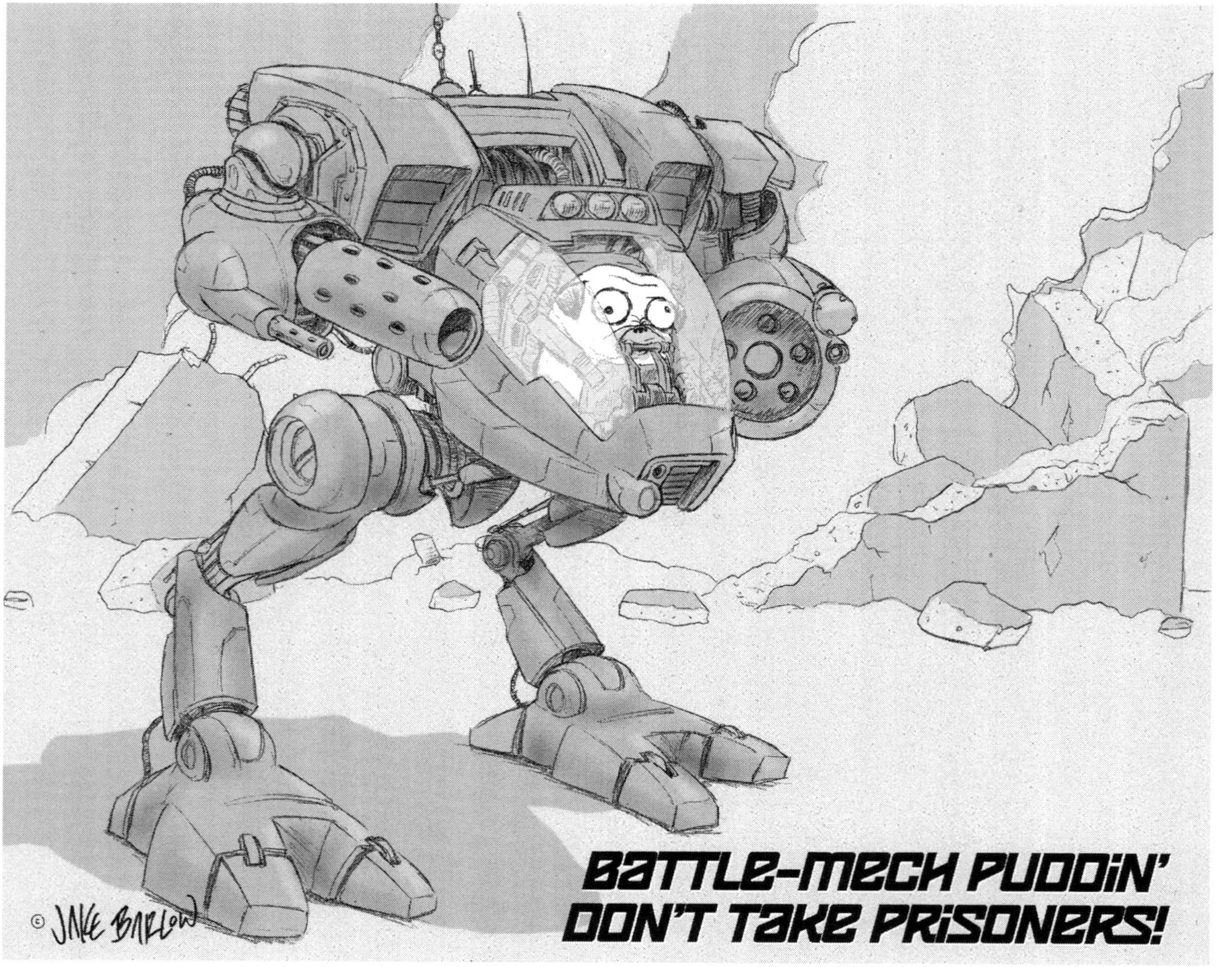
BATTLE-MECH PUDDIN'
DON'T TAKE PRISONERS!
© JAKE BARLOW

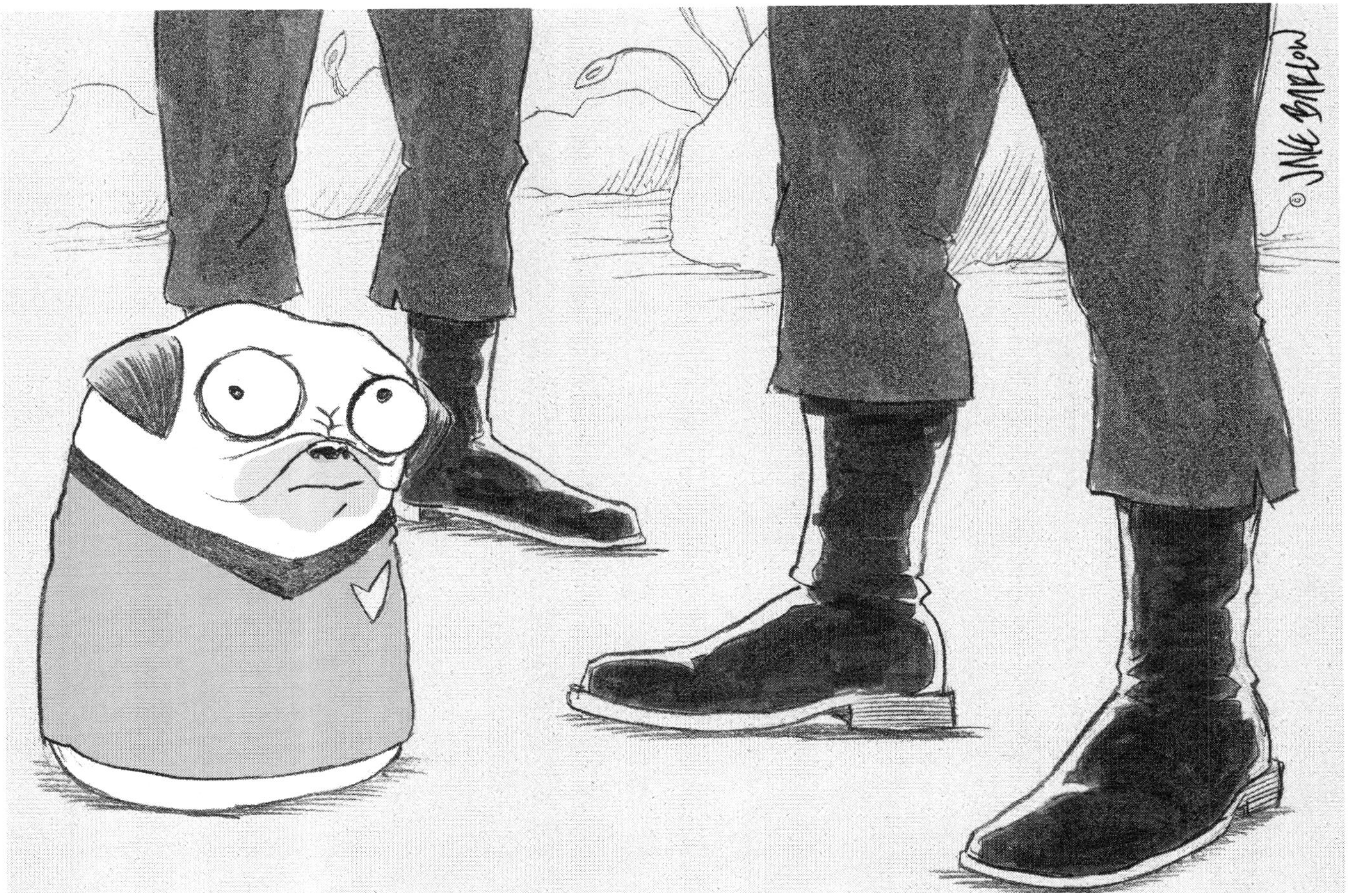
© JAKE BARLOW

Puddin' don't want to be the new guy on this away mission. He knows how this story ends...

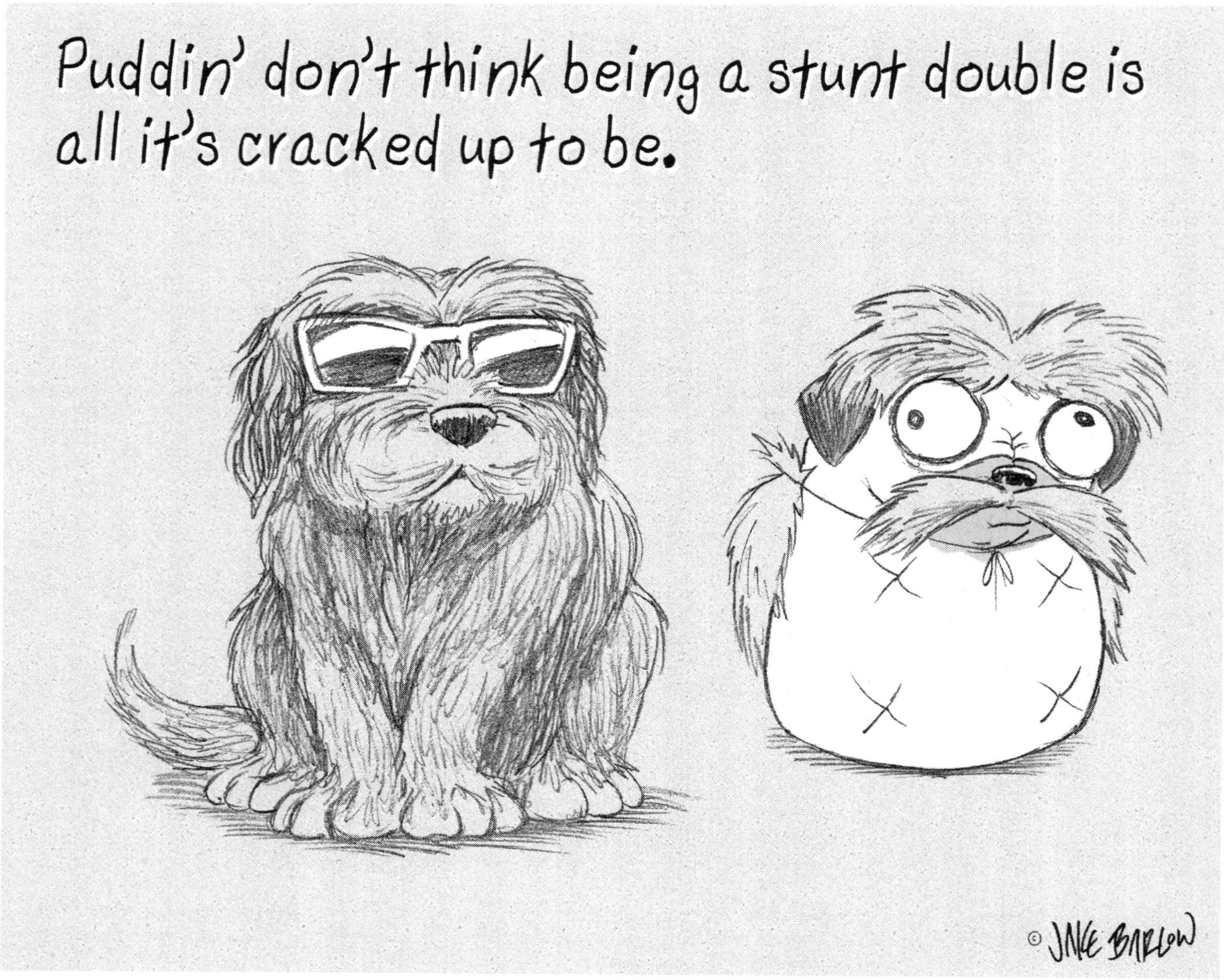
© JAKE BARLOW

Puddin' don't think being a stunt double is all it's cracked up to be.

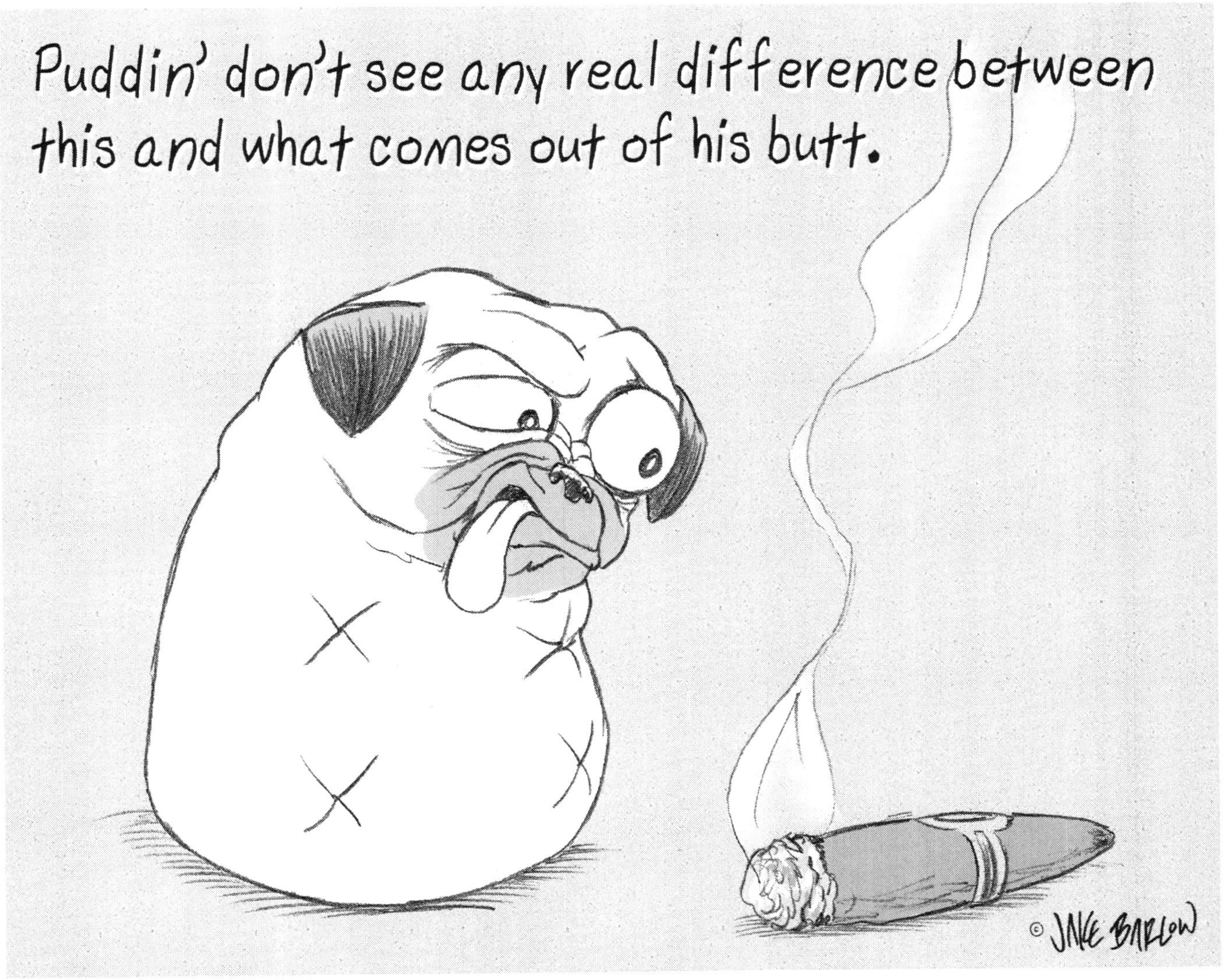
Puddin' don't see any real difference between this and what comes out of his butt.
© JAKE BARLOW

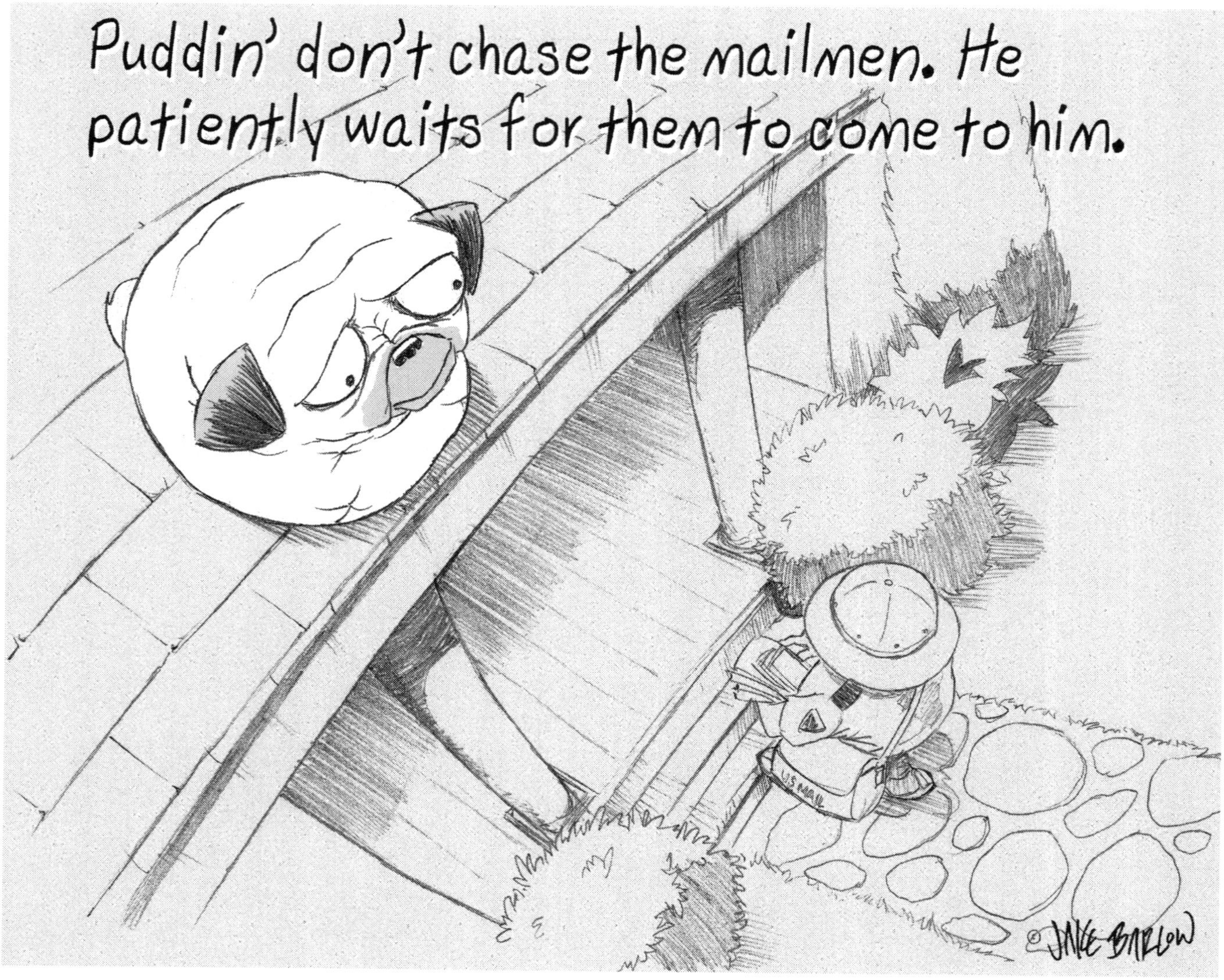
Puddin' don't chase the mailmen. He patiently waits for them to come to him.
©JAKE BARLOW

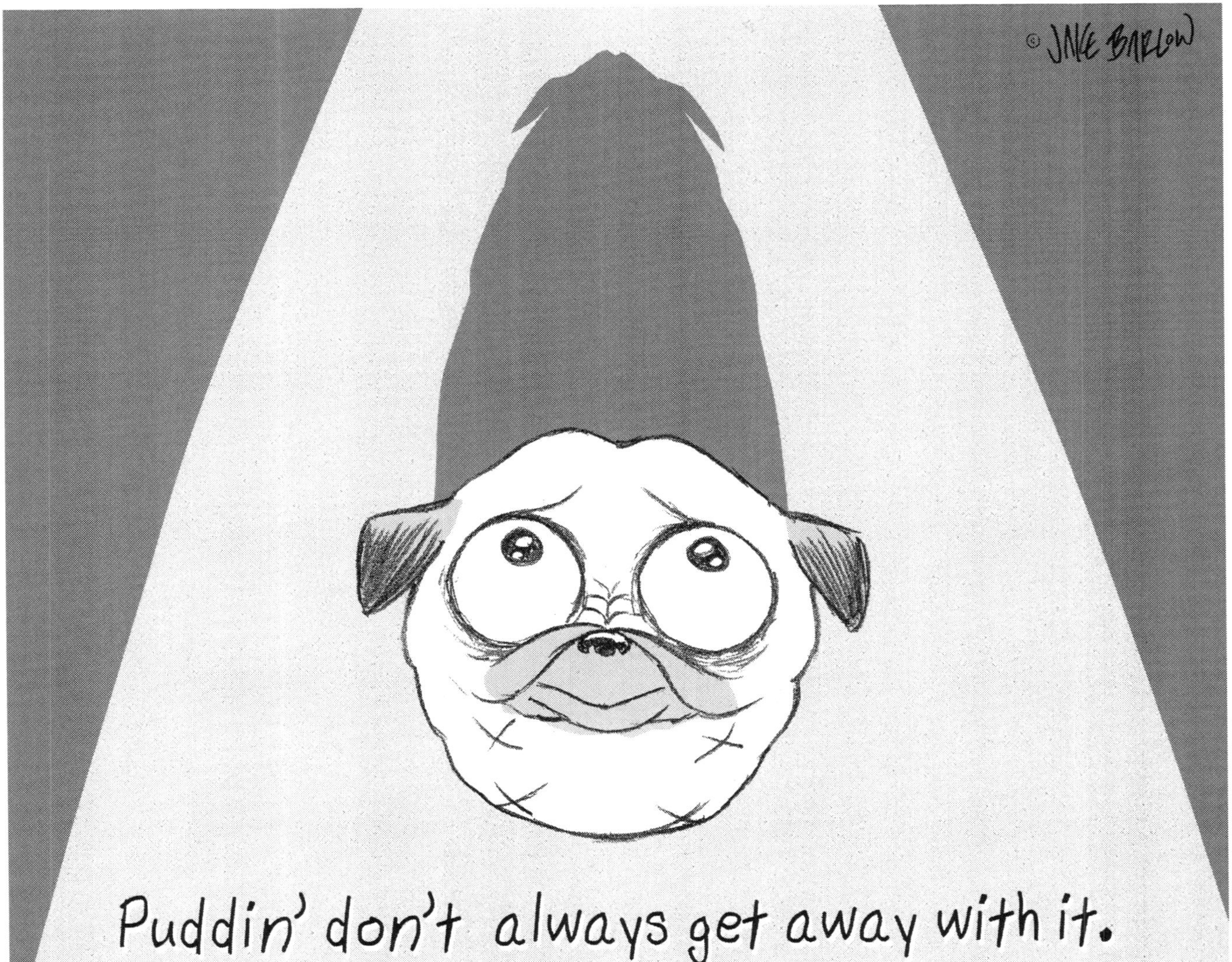
© JAKE BARLOW
Puddin' don't always get away with it.

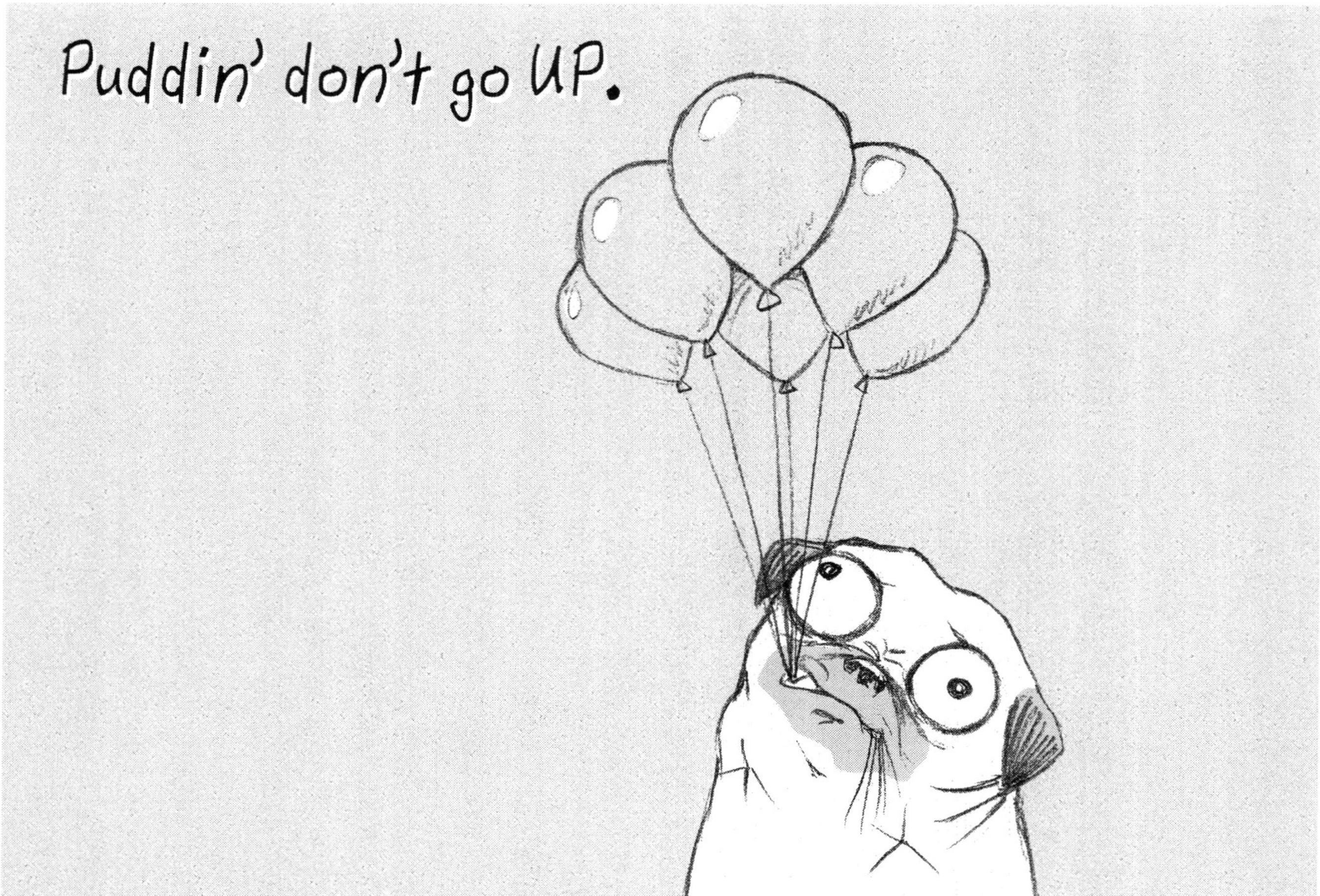
Puddin' don't go UP.
© JAKE BARLOW

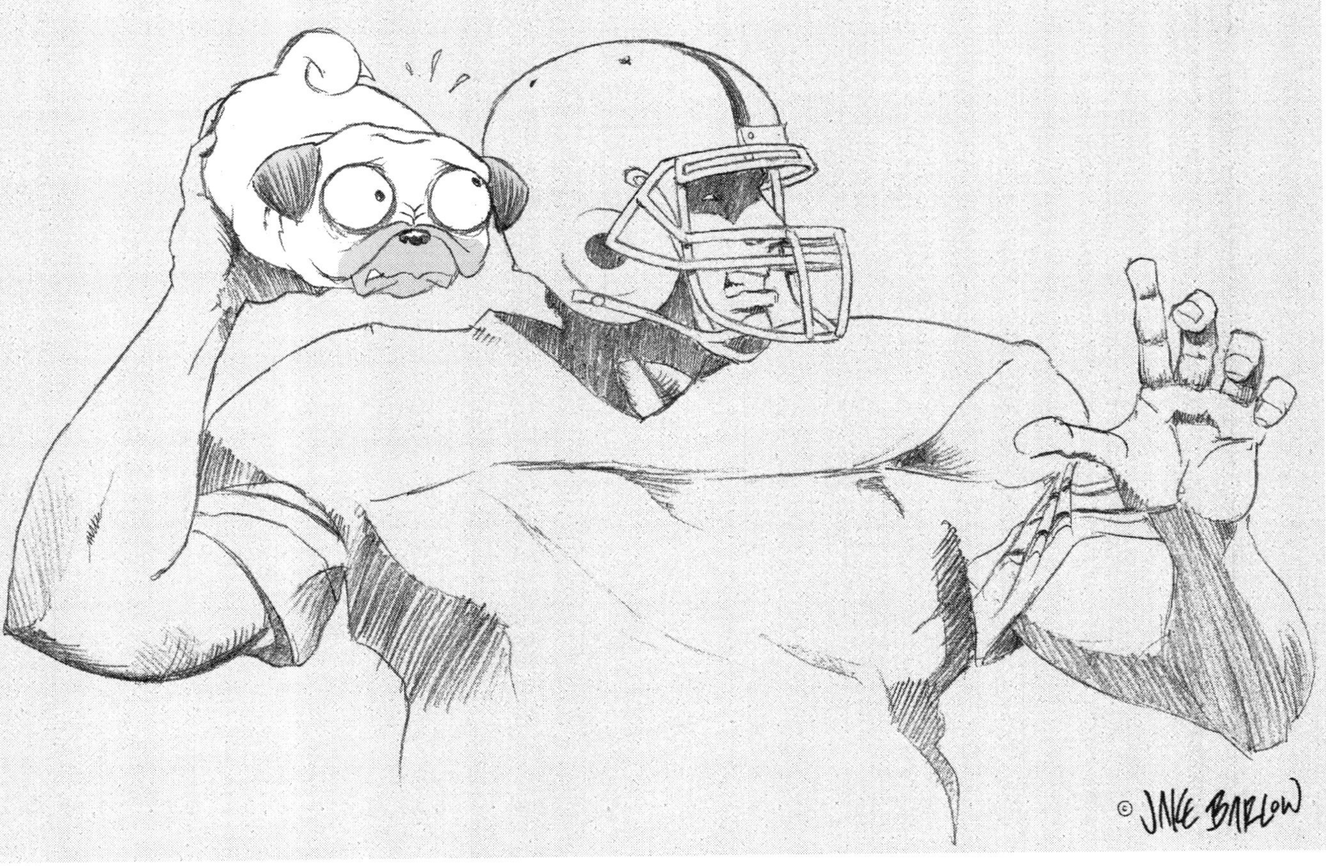
© JAKE BARLOW

Puddin' don't want to go long.

No, Puddin' don't sprout legs from his butt, he just sat on the cat.

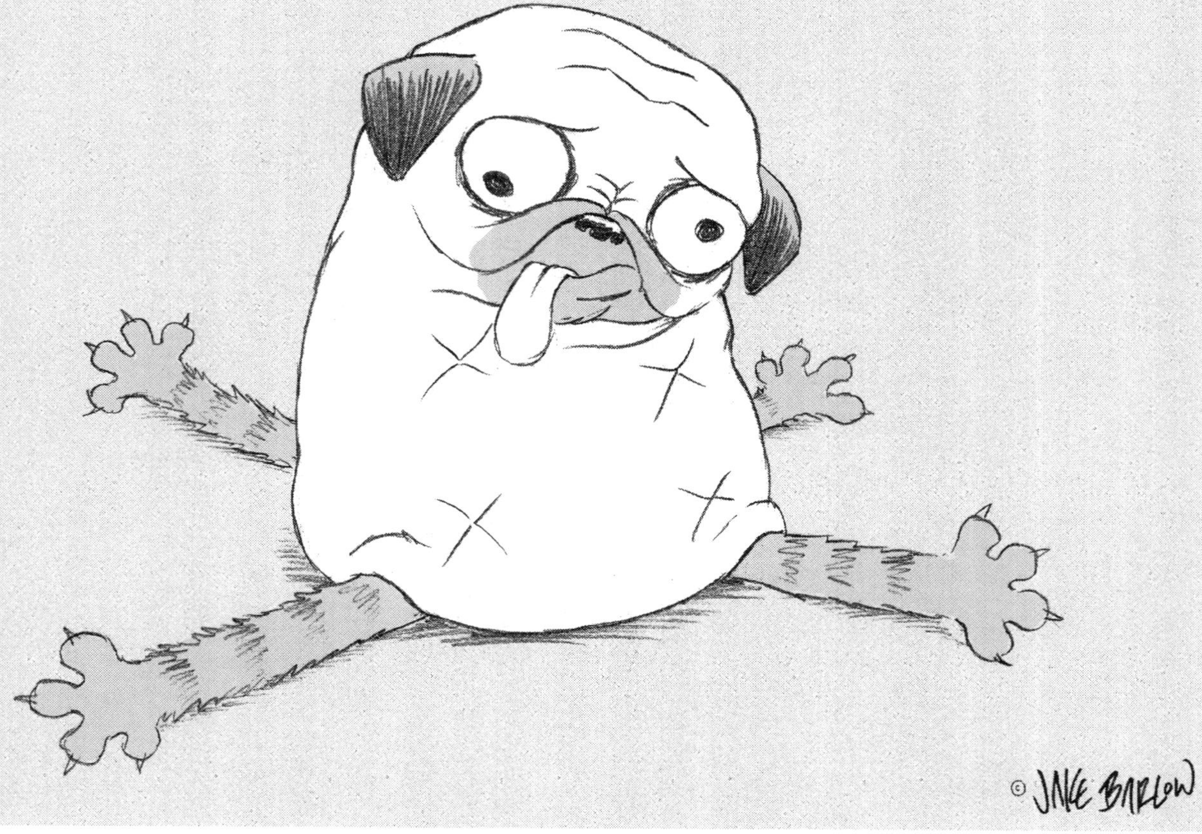
© JAKE BARLOW

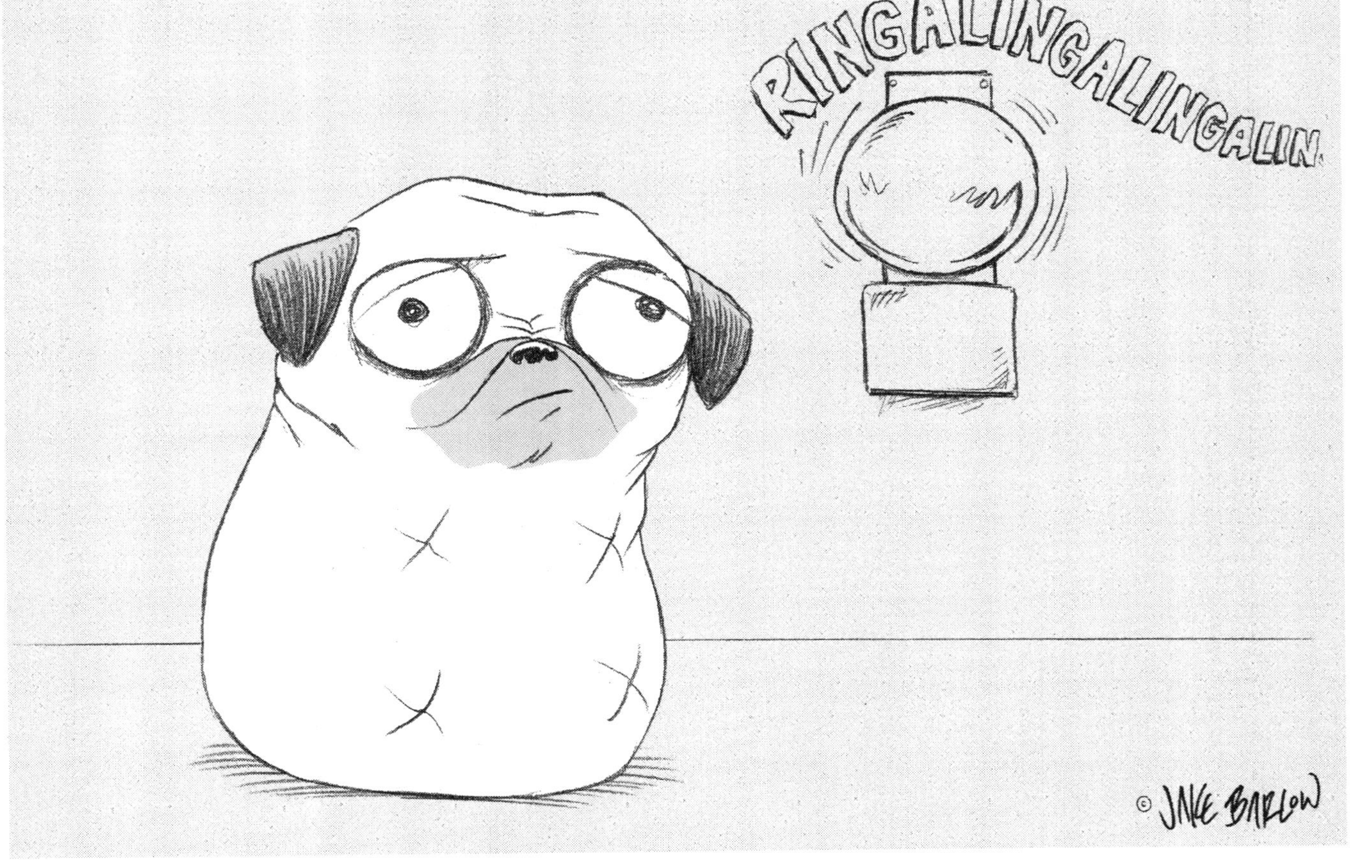
RINGALINGALINGALIN
© JAKE BARLOW

Puddin' don't mean to disappoint you, Pavlov, but he knows the difference between a bell and a biscuit.

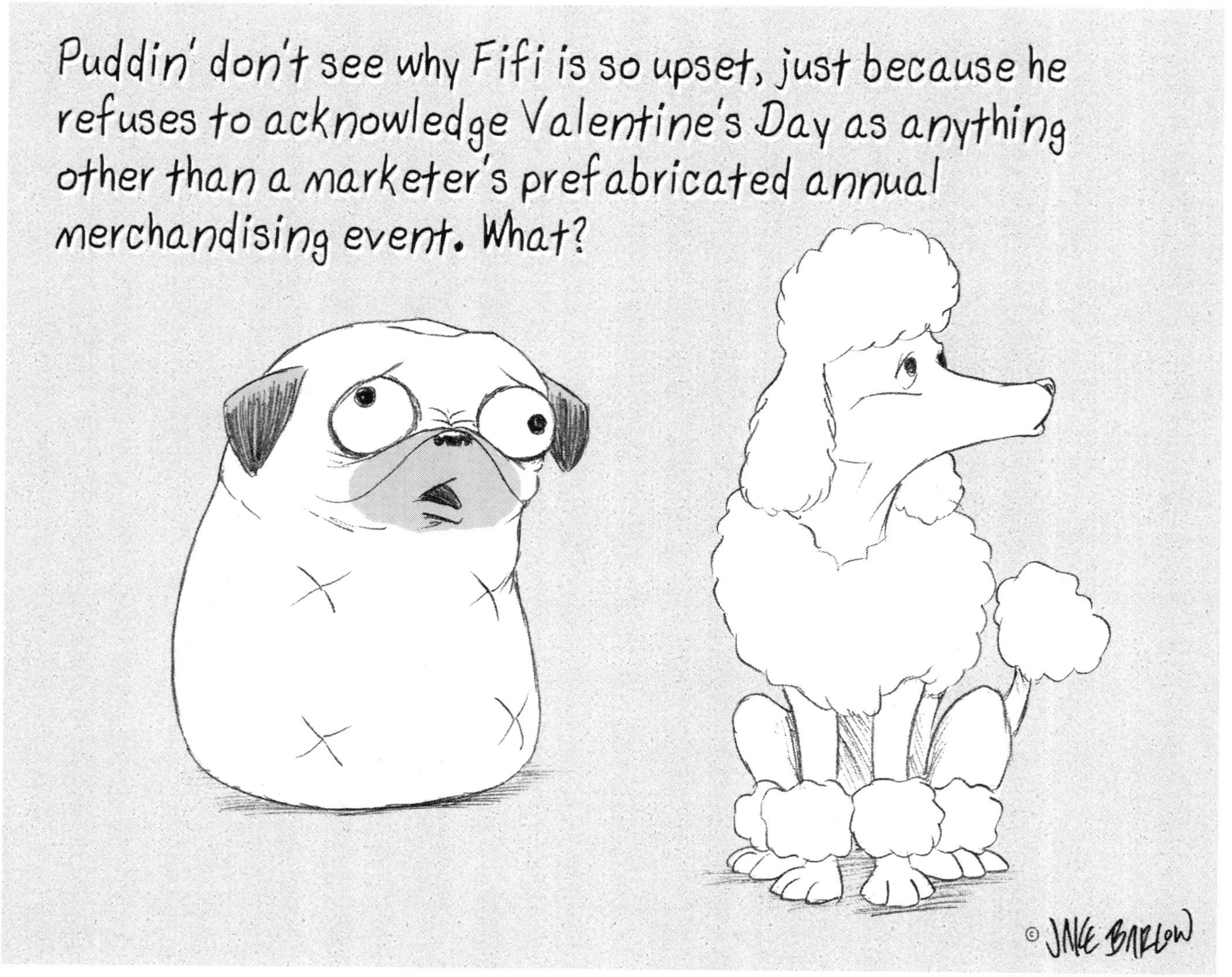
Puddin' don't see why Fifi is so upset, just because he refuses to acknowledge Valentine's Day as anything other than a marketer's prefabricated annual merchandising event. What?
© JAKE BARLOW

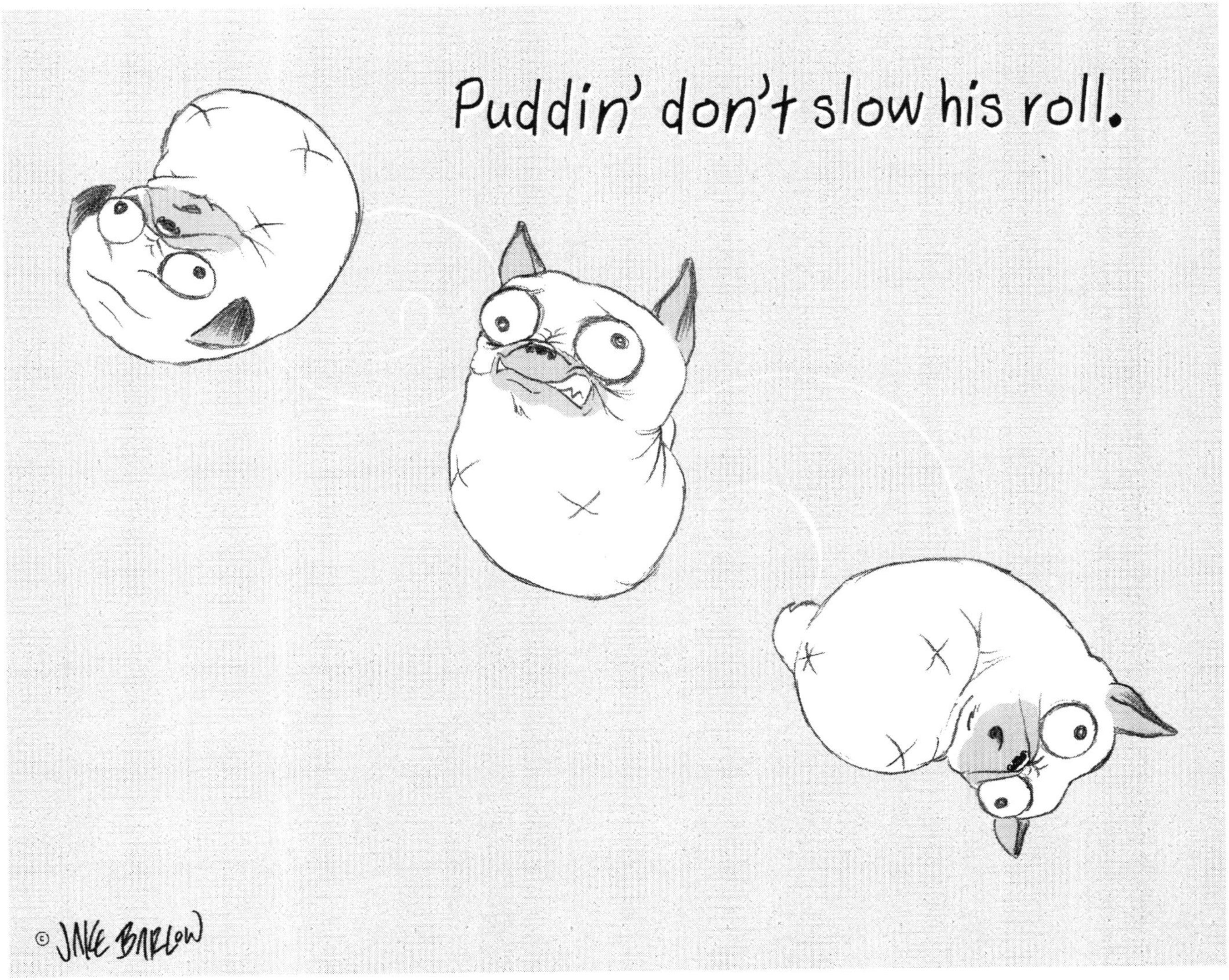
Puddin' don't slow his roll.
© JAKE BARLOW

Puddin' don't know how he got these, and he don't care. But curiously, he now has a problem with spiders...

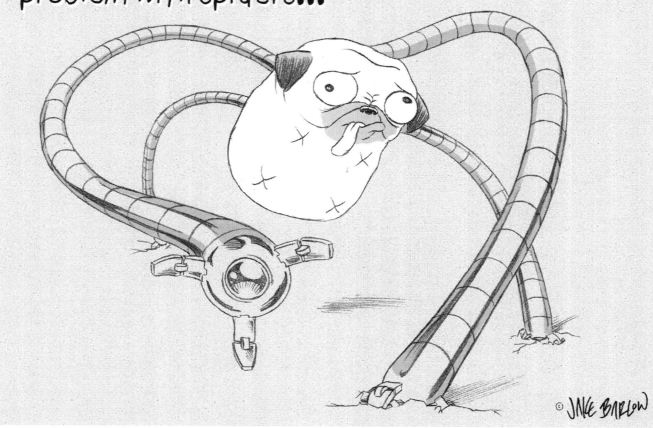

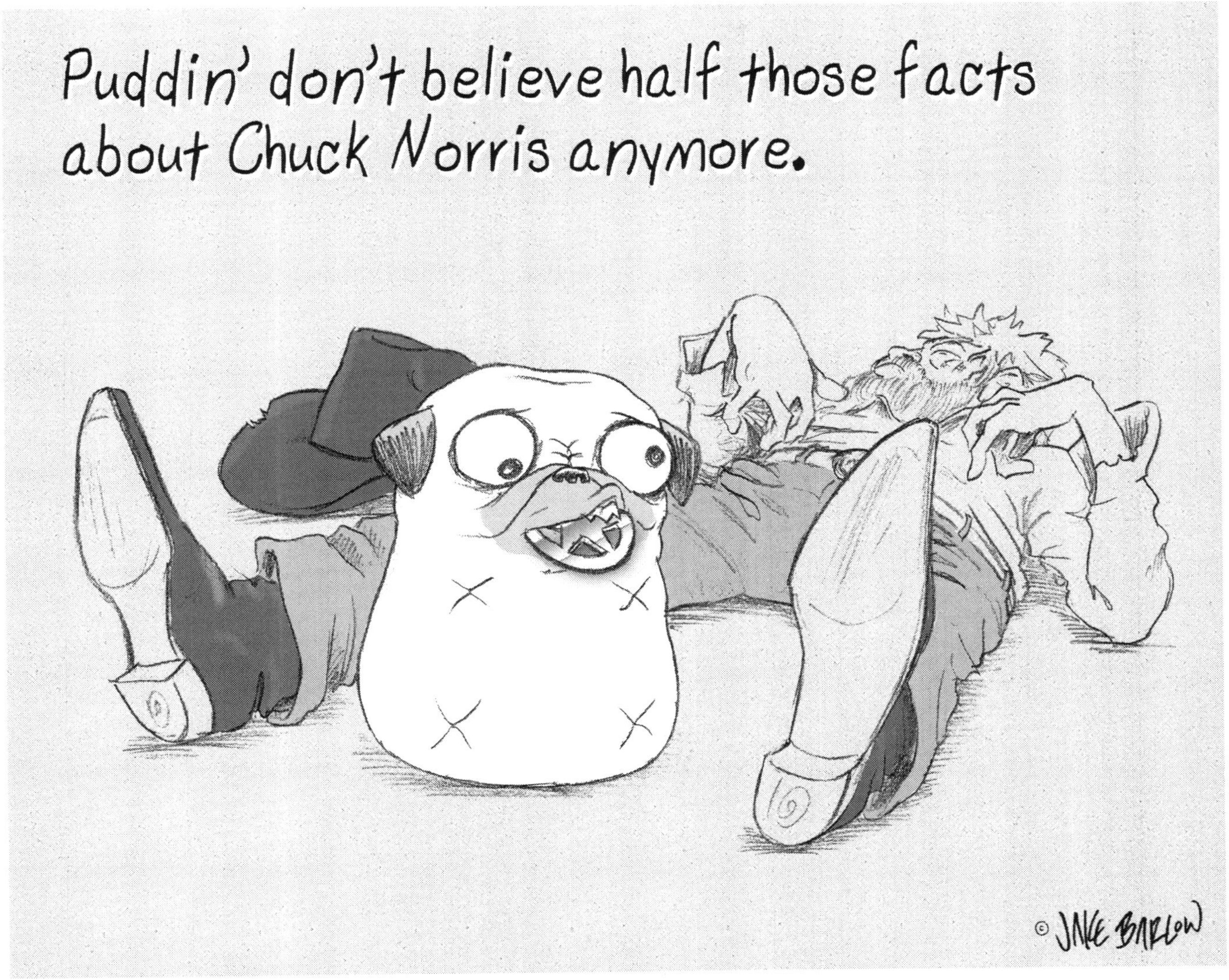
Puddin' don't believe half those facts about Chuck Norris anymore.
© JAKE BARLOW

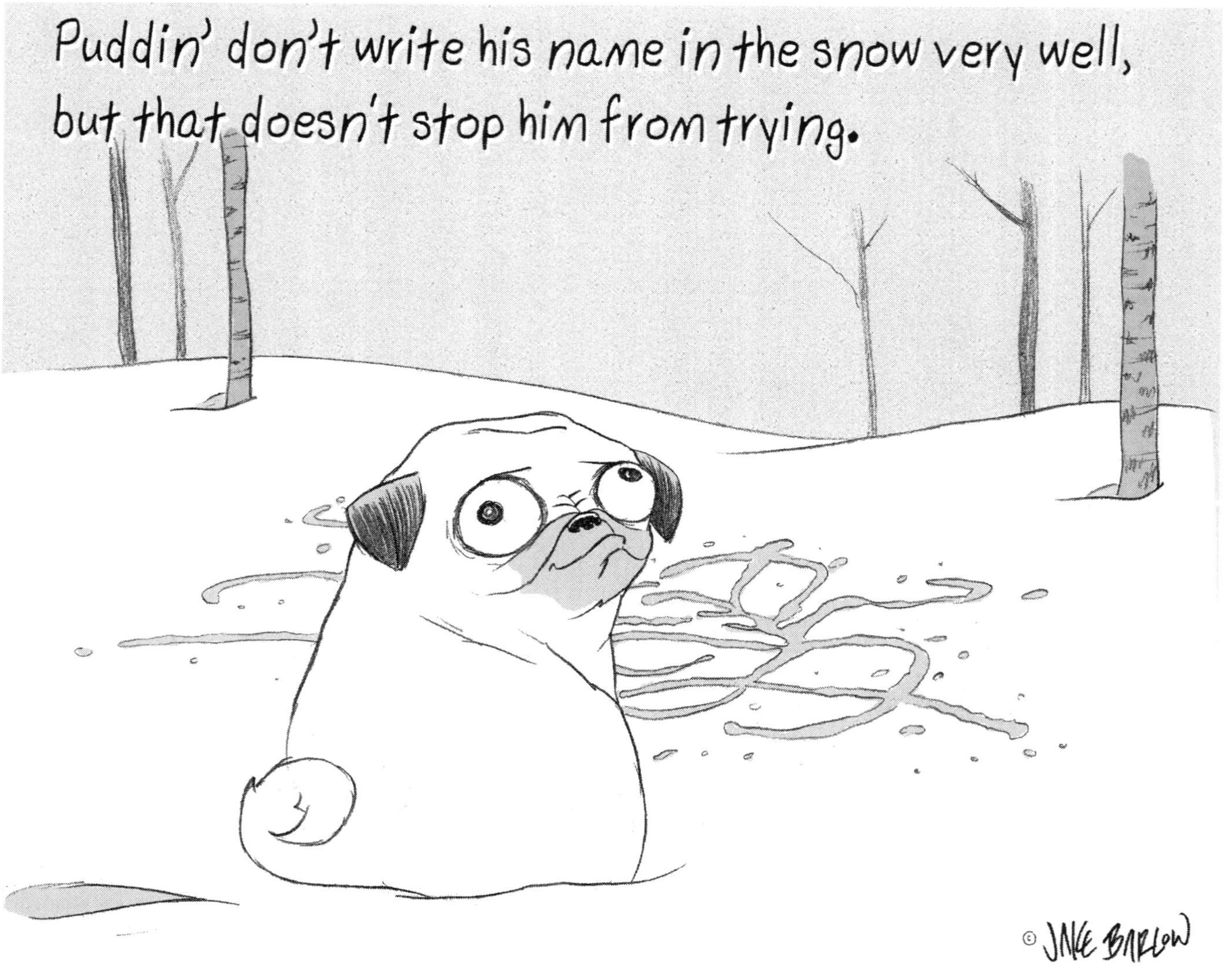
Puddin' don't write his name in the snow very well, but that doesn't stop him from trying.
© JAKE BARLOW

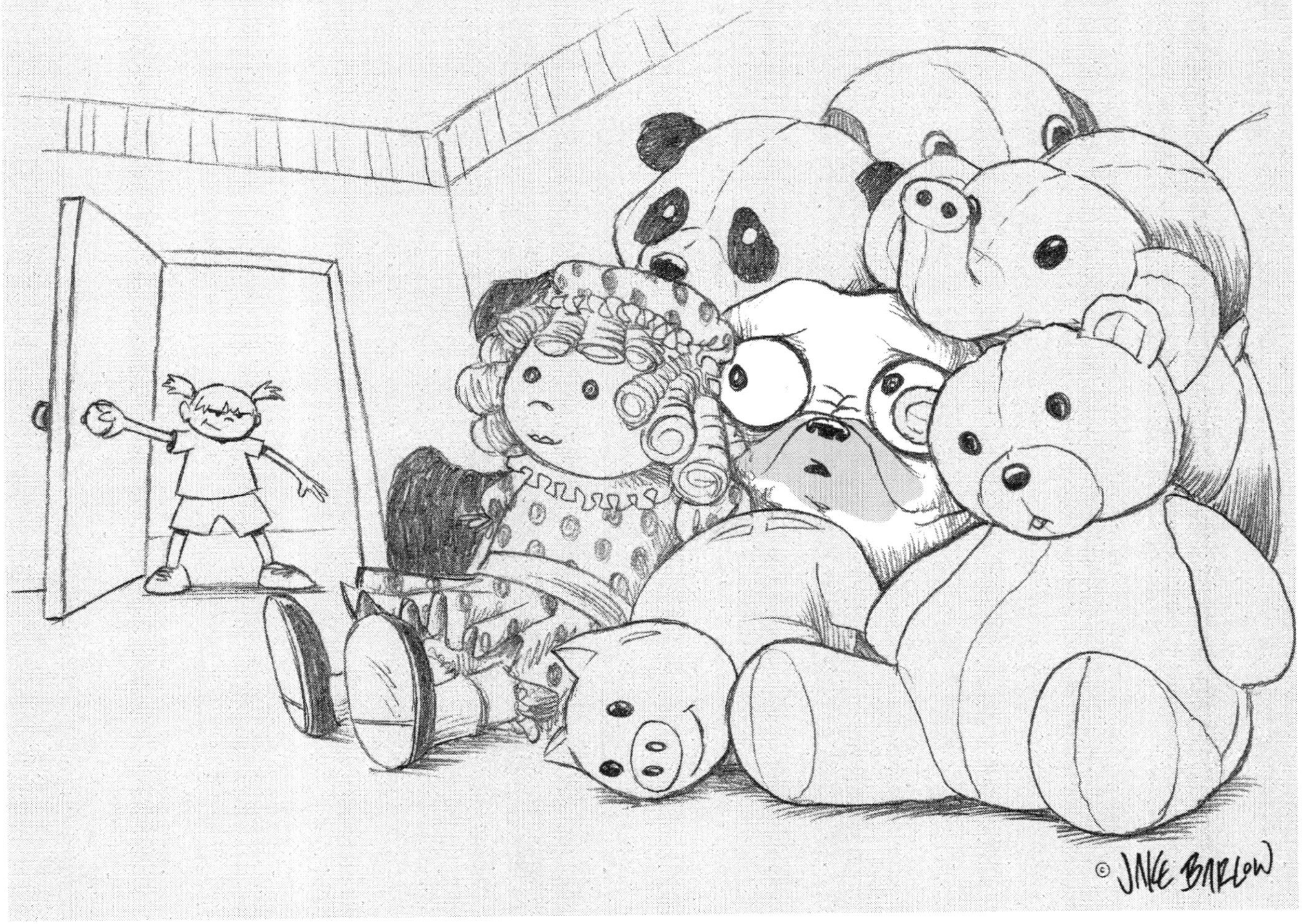
© JAKE BARLOW

Puddin' don't necessarily want to be found.

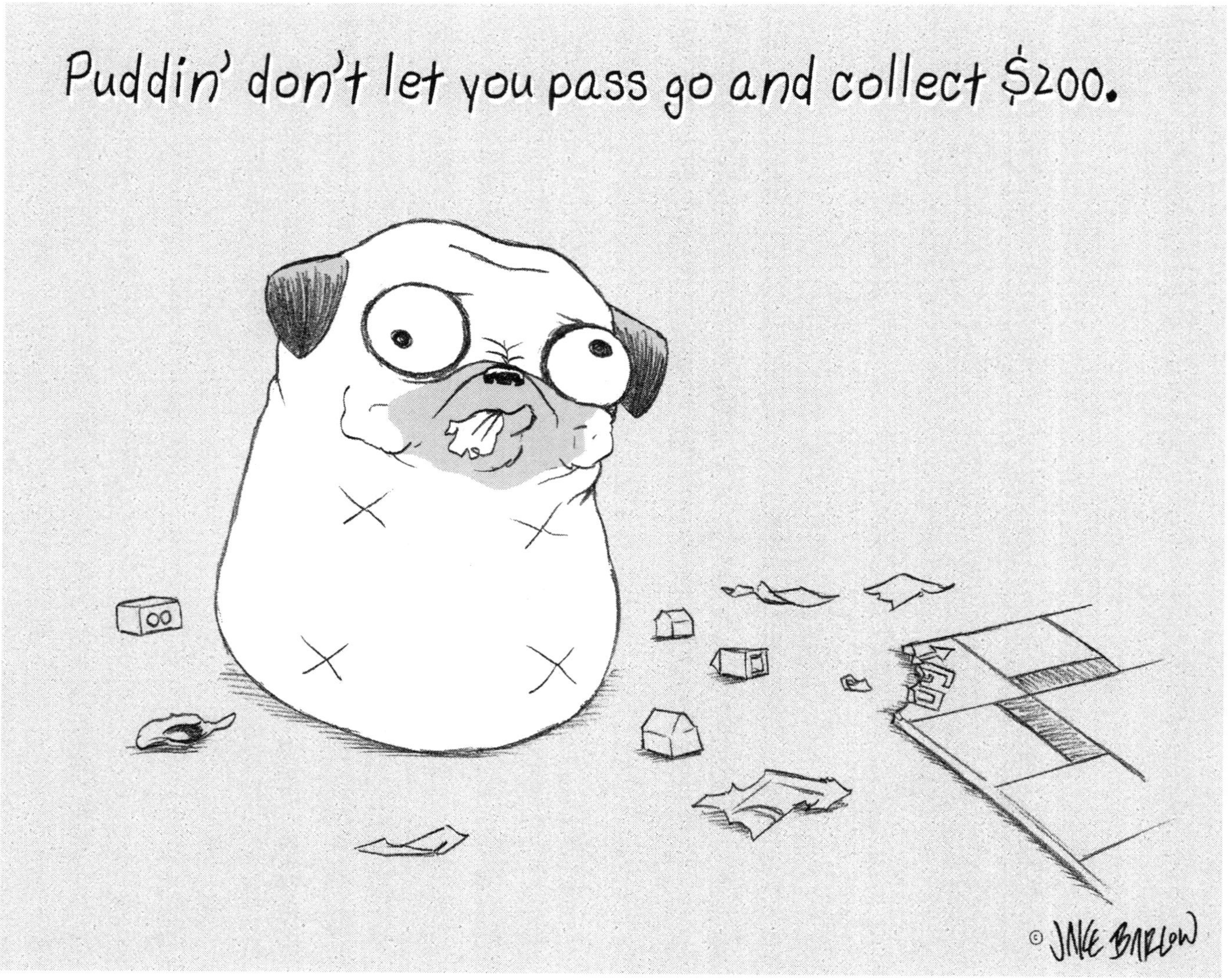
Puddin' don't let you pass go and collect $200.
© JAKE BARLOW

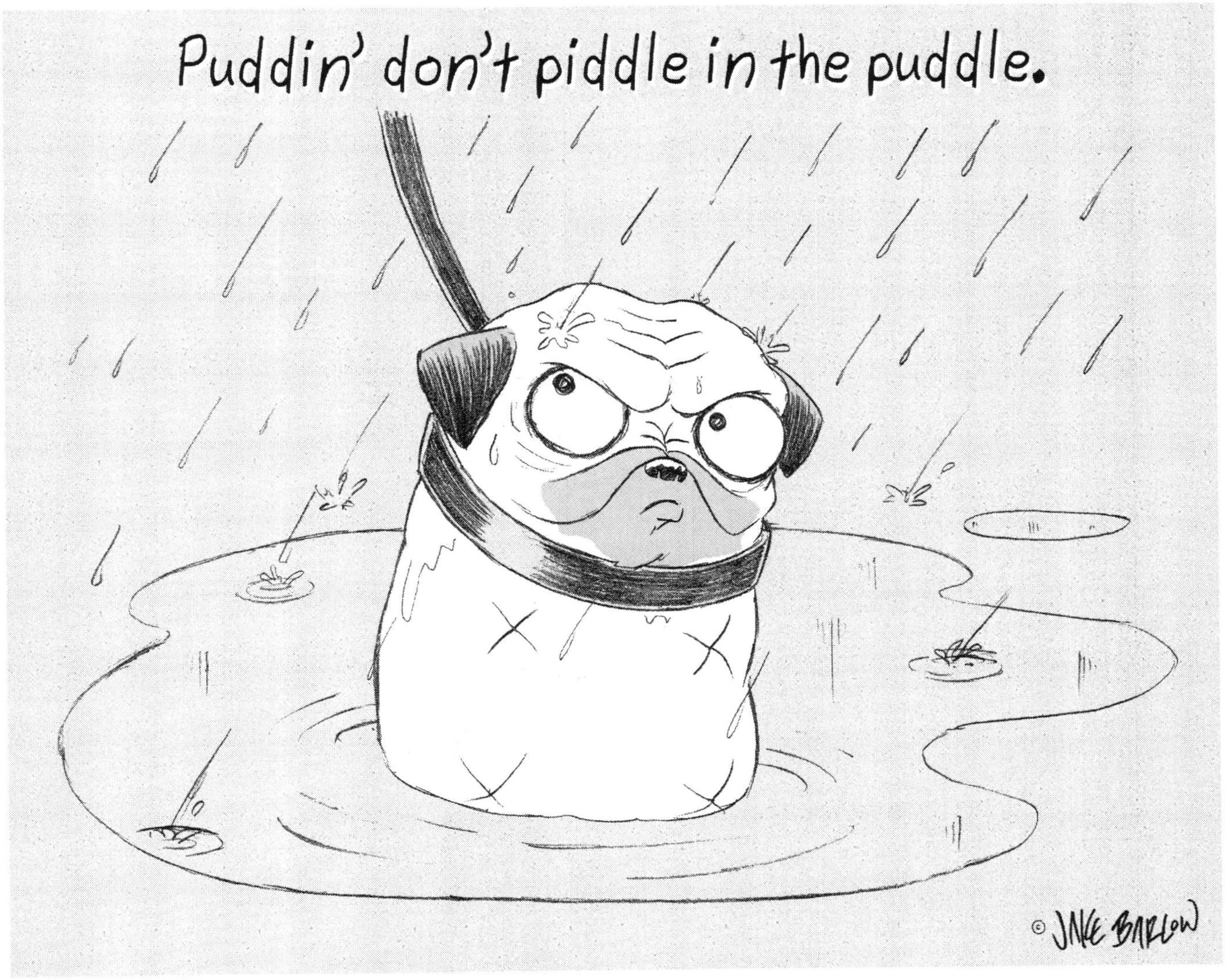
© JAKE BARLOW

Puddin' don't piddle in the puddle.

Puddin' don't see anything wrong here, but he does see a whole lot of right!

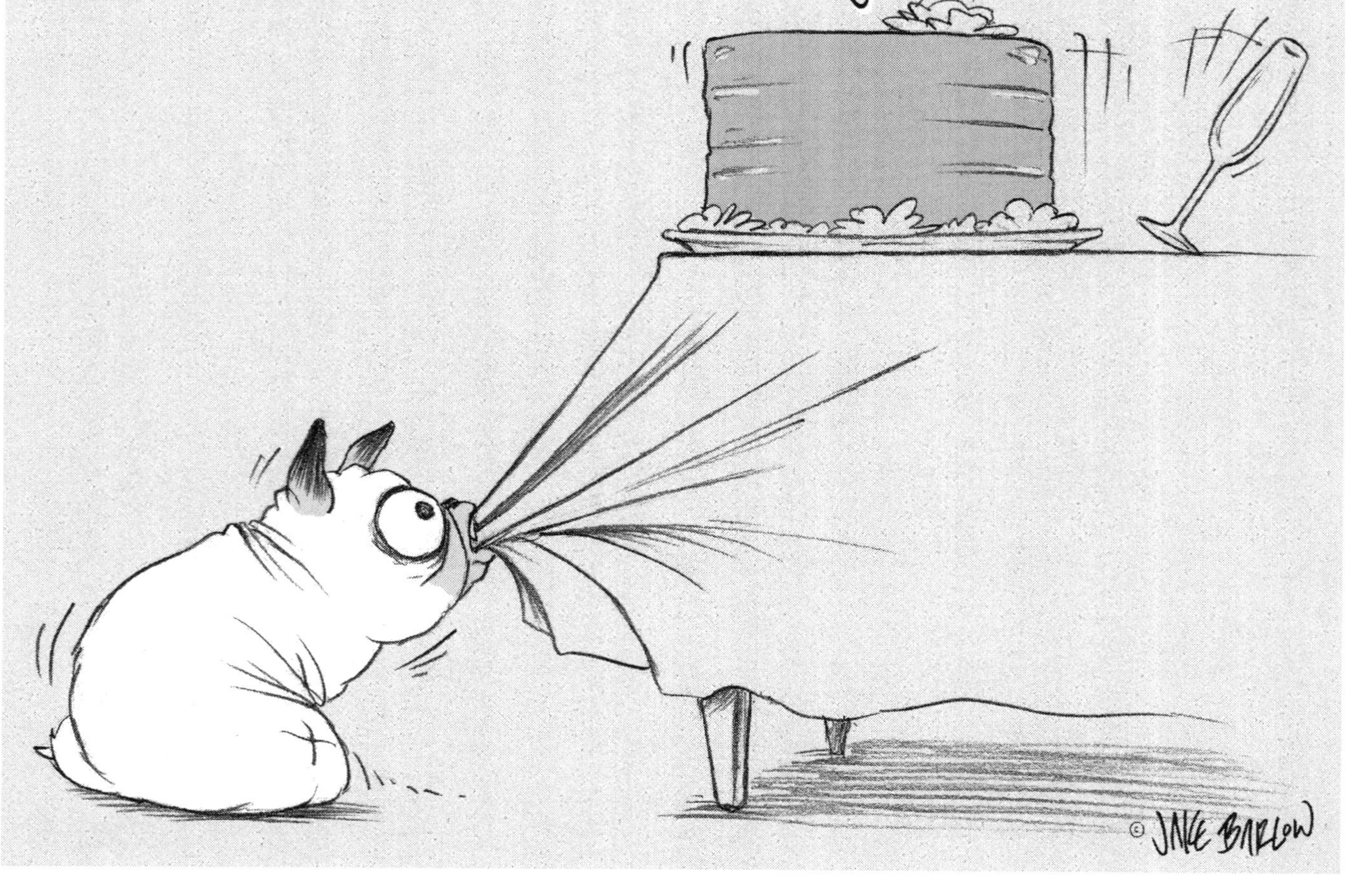
© JAKE BARLOW

Puddin' don't think your expectations are realistic.

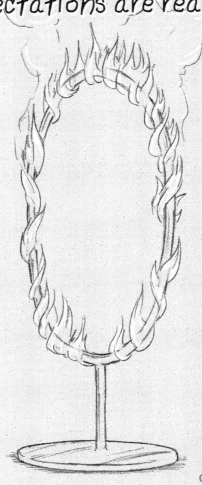

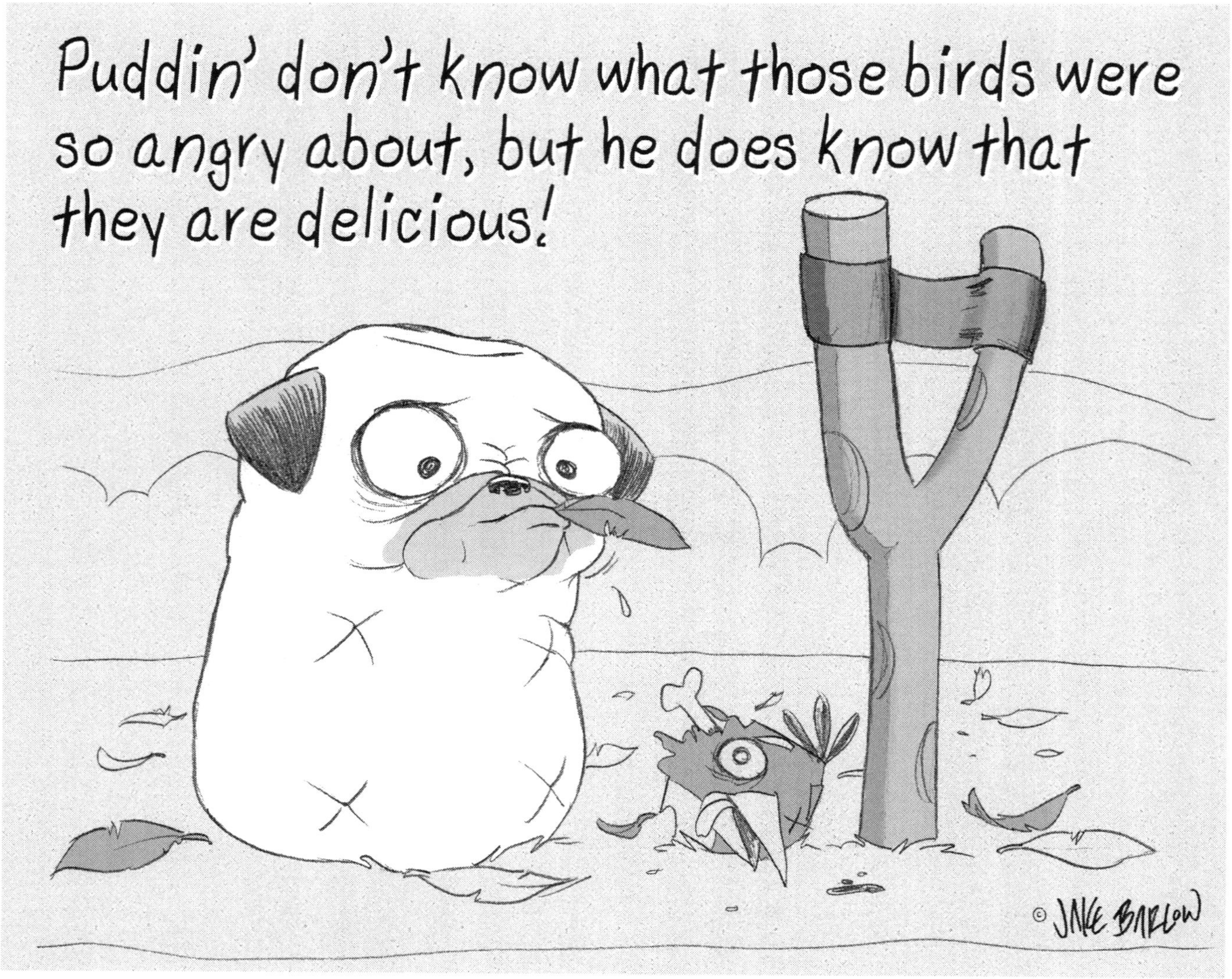
Puddin' don't know what those birds were so angry about, but he does know that they are delicious!
© JAKE BARLOW

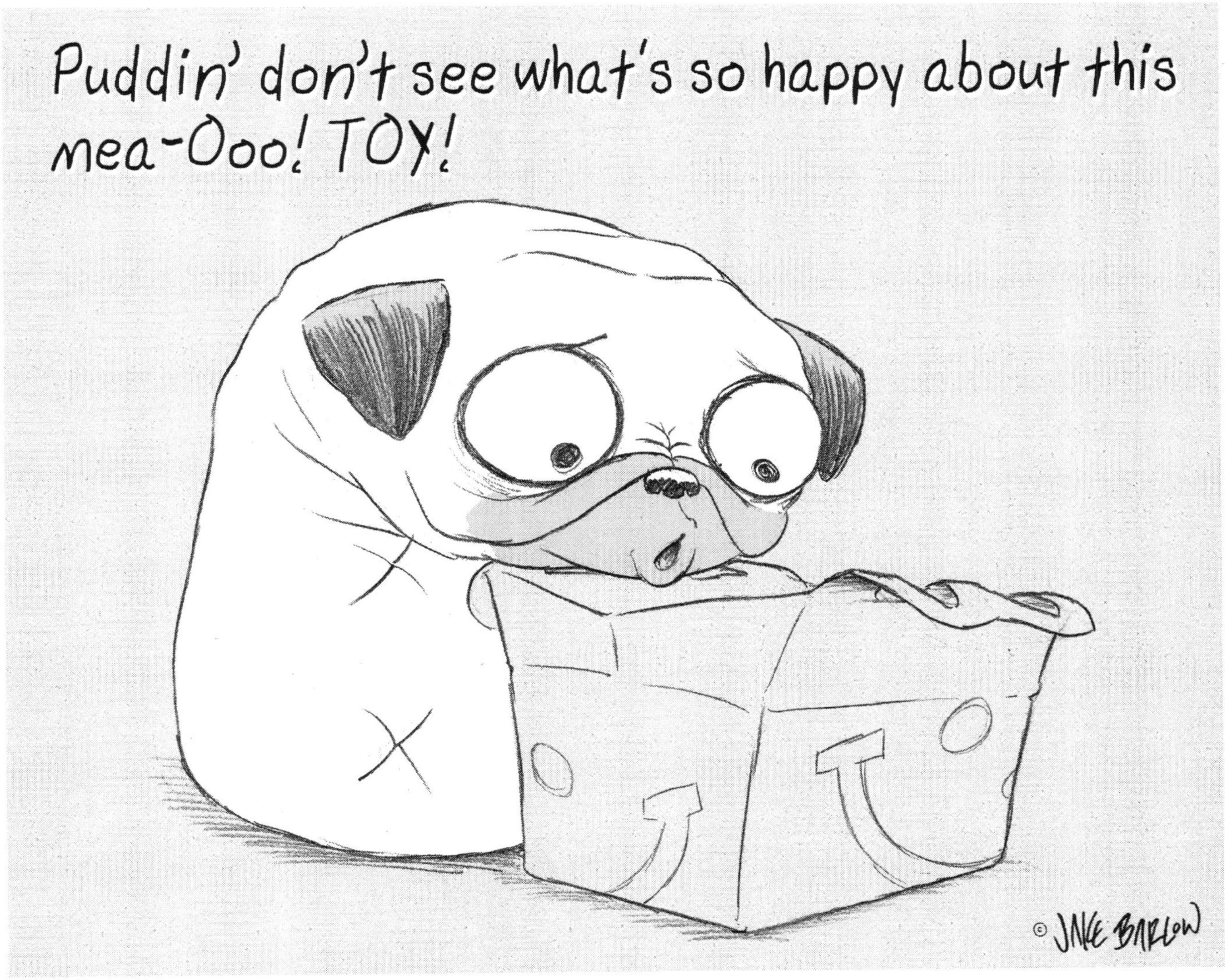
Puddin' don't see what's so happy about this mea-Ooo! TOY!
© JAKE BARLOW

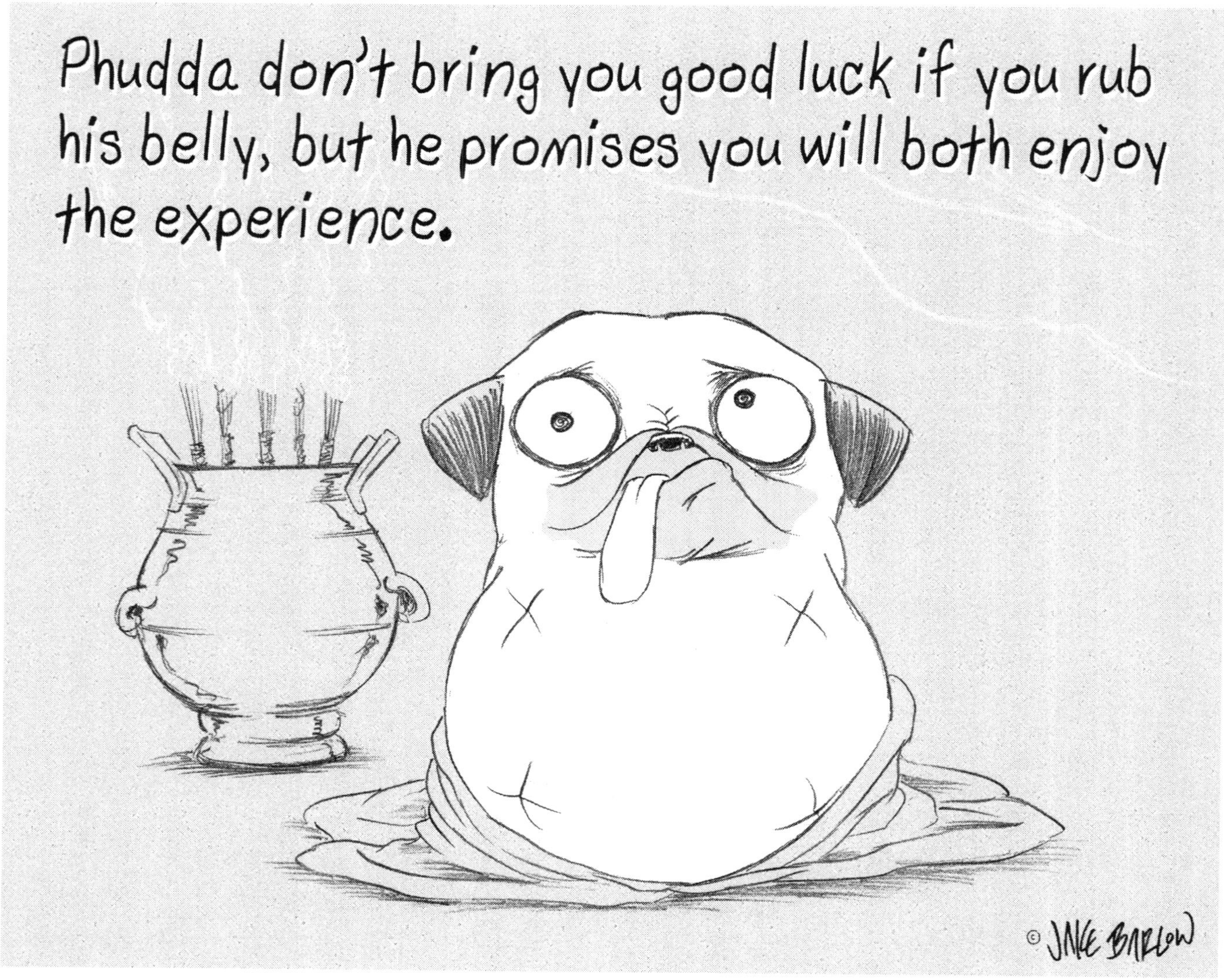
Phudda don't bring you good luck if you rub his belly, but he promises you will both enjoy the experience.
© JAKE BARLOW

Puddin' don't take the direct route, but he enjoys the ride.

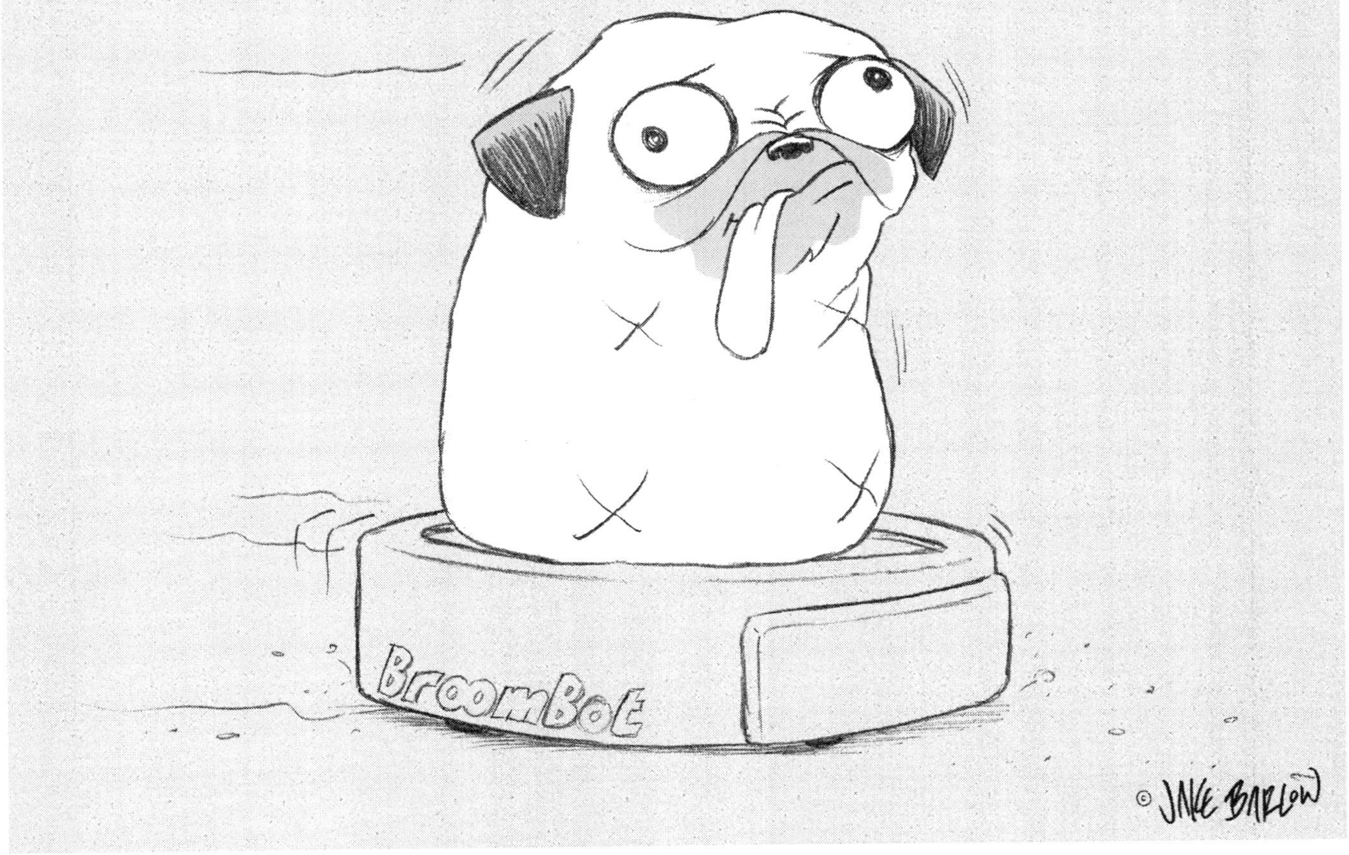
BroomBot
© JAKE BARLOW

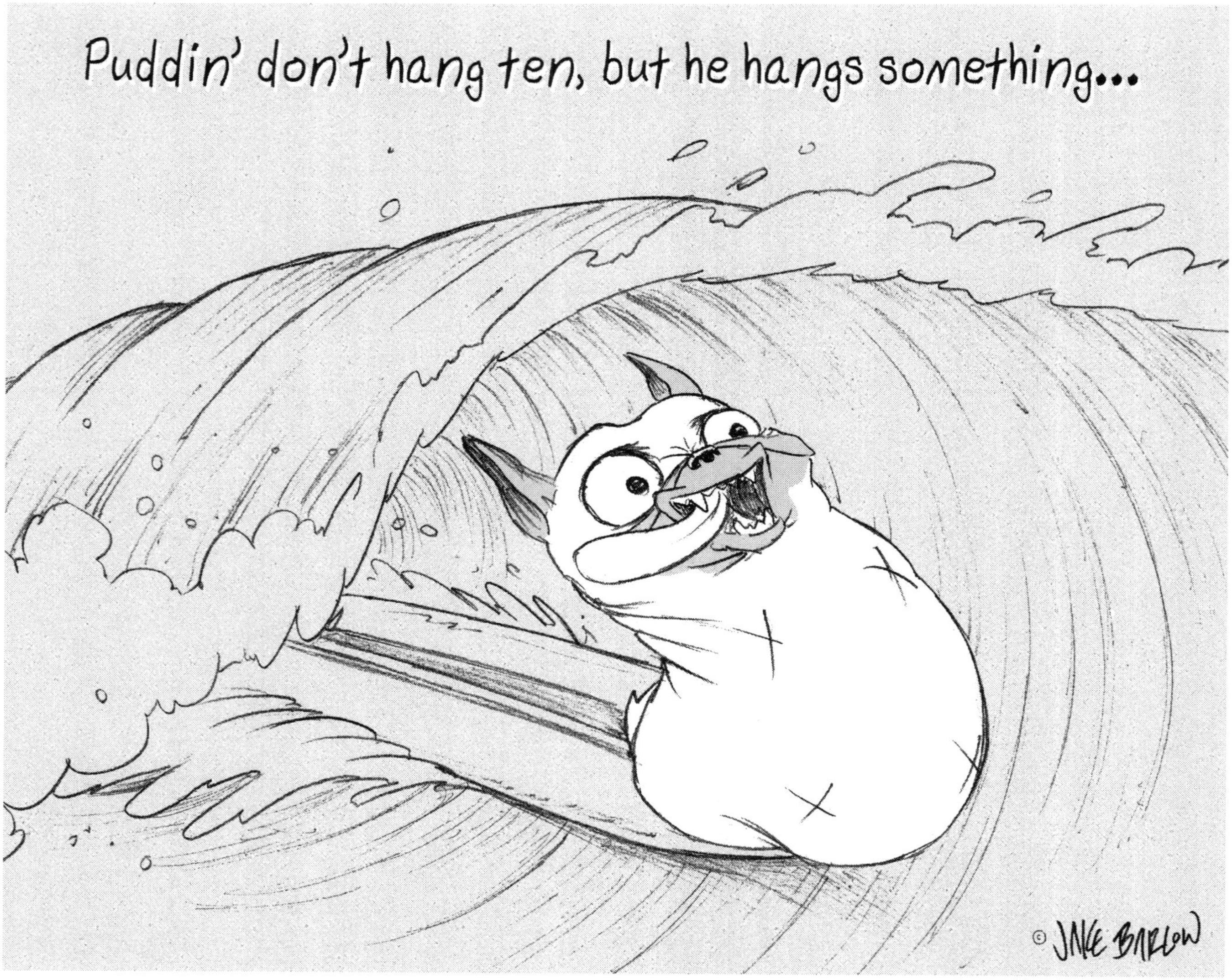

Puddin' don't hang ten, but he hangs something...
© JAKE BARLOW

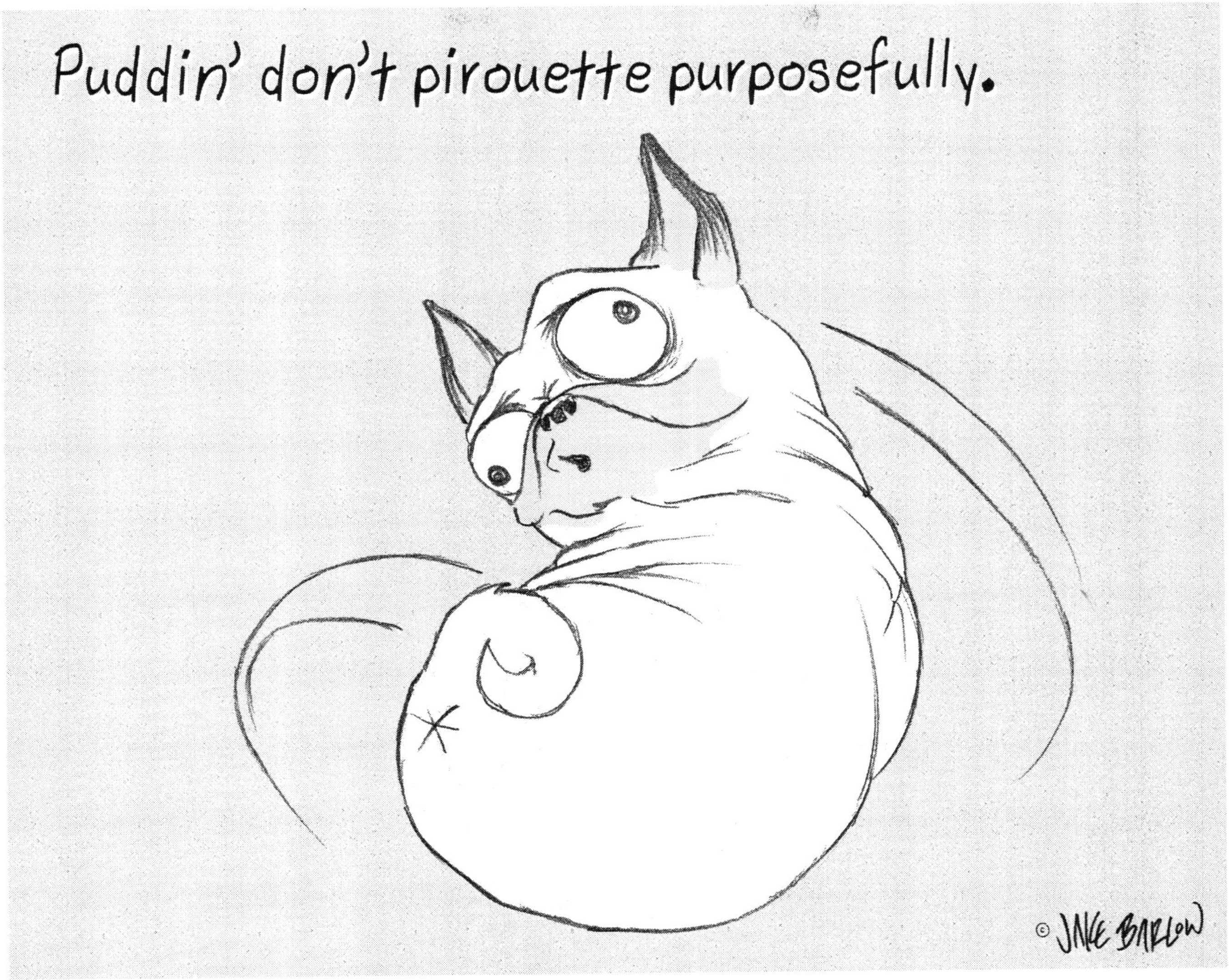
Puddin' don't pirouette purposefully.
© JAKE BARLOW

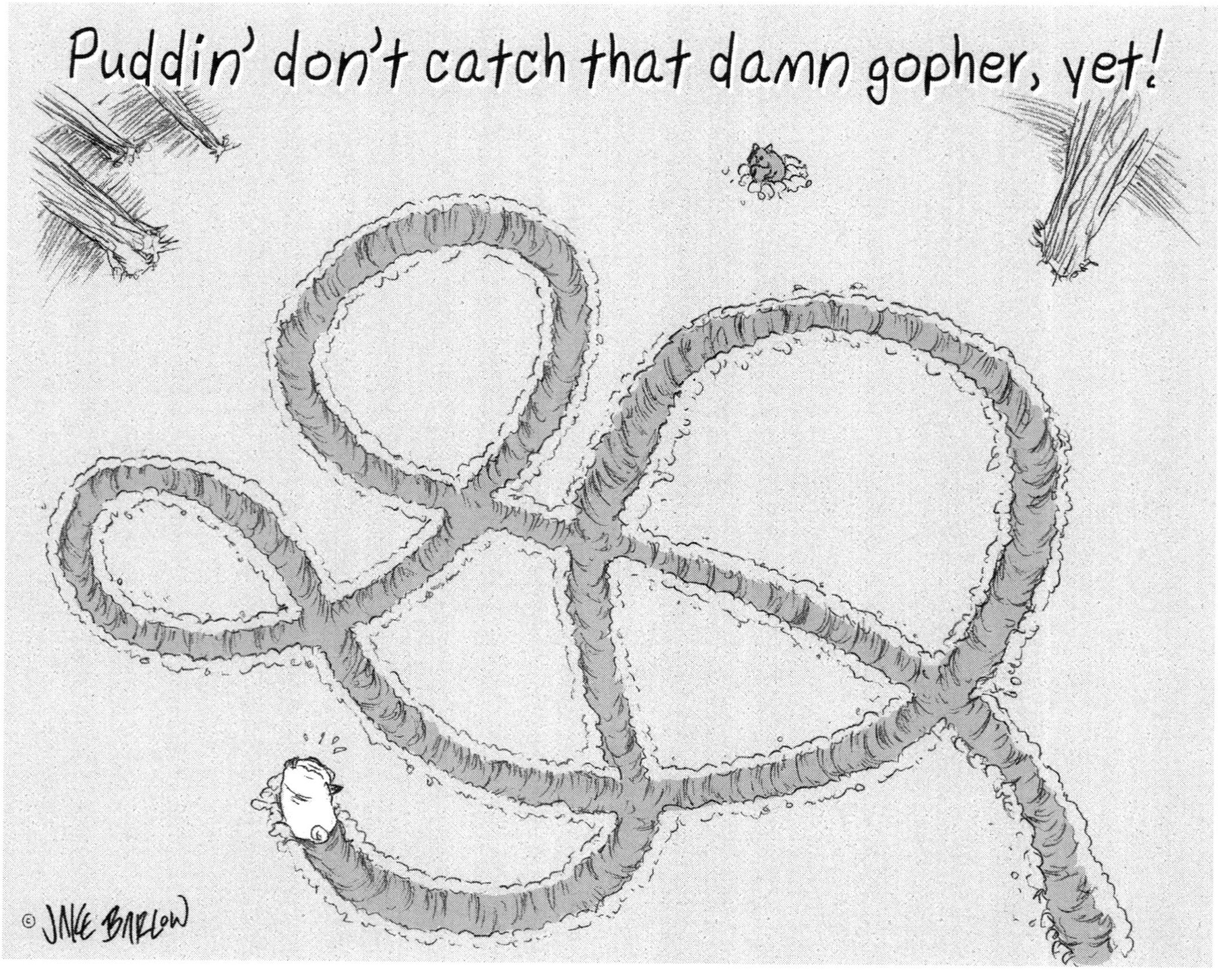
Puddin' don't catch that damn gopher, yet!
© JAKE BARLOW

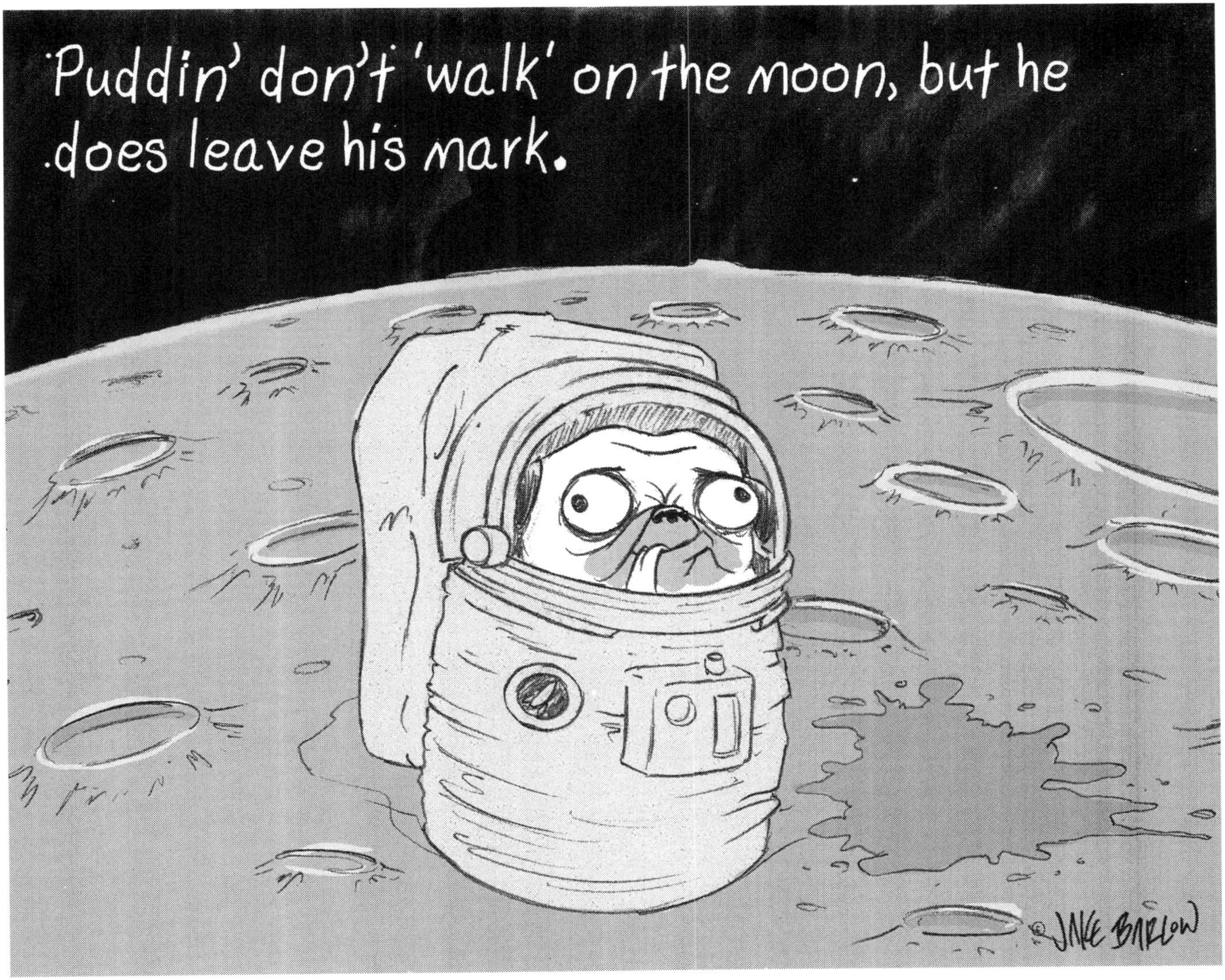
Puddin' don't 'walk' on the moon, but he does leave his mark.
©JAKE BARLOW

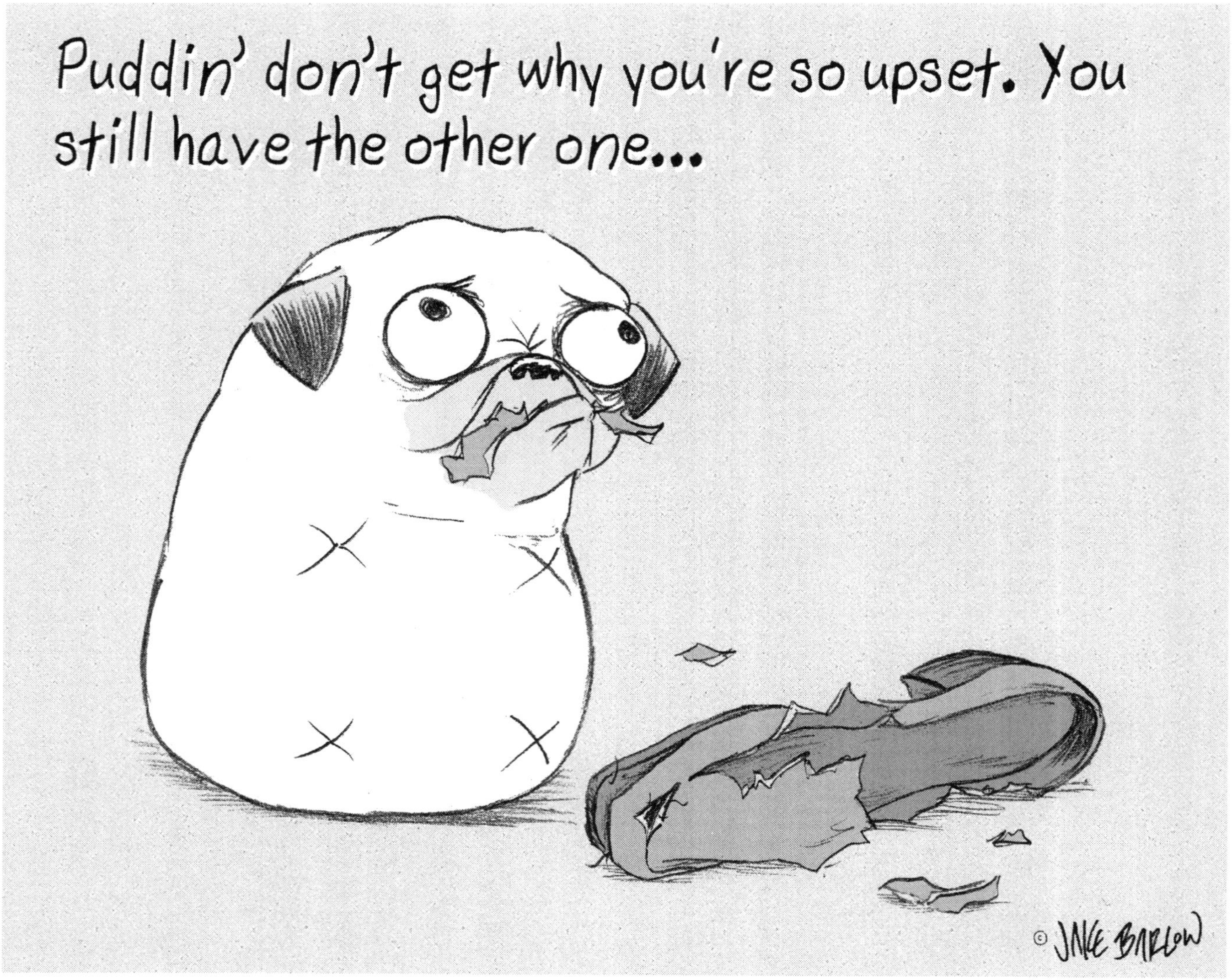
Puddin' don't get why you're so upset. You still have the other one...
© JAKE BARLOW

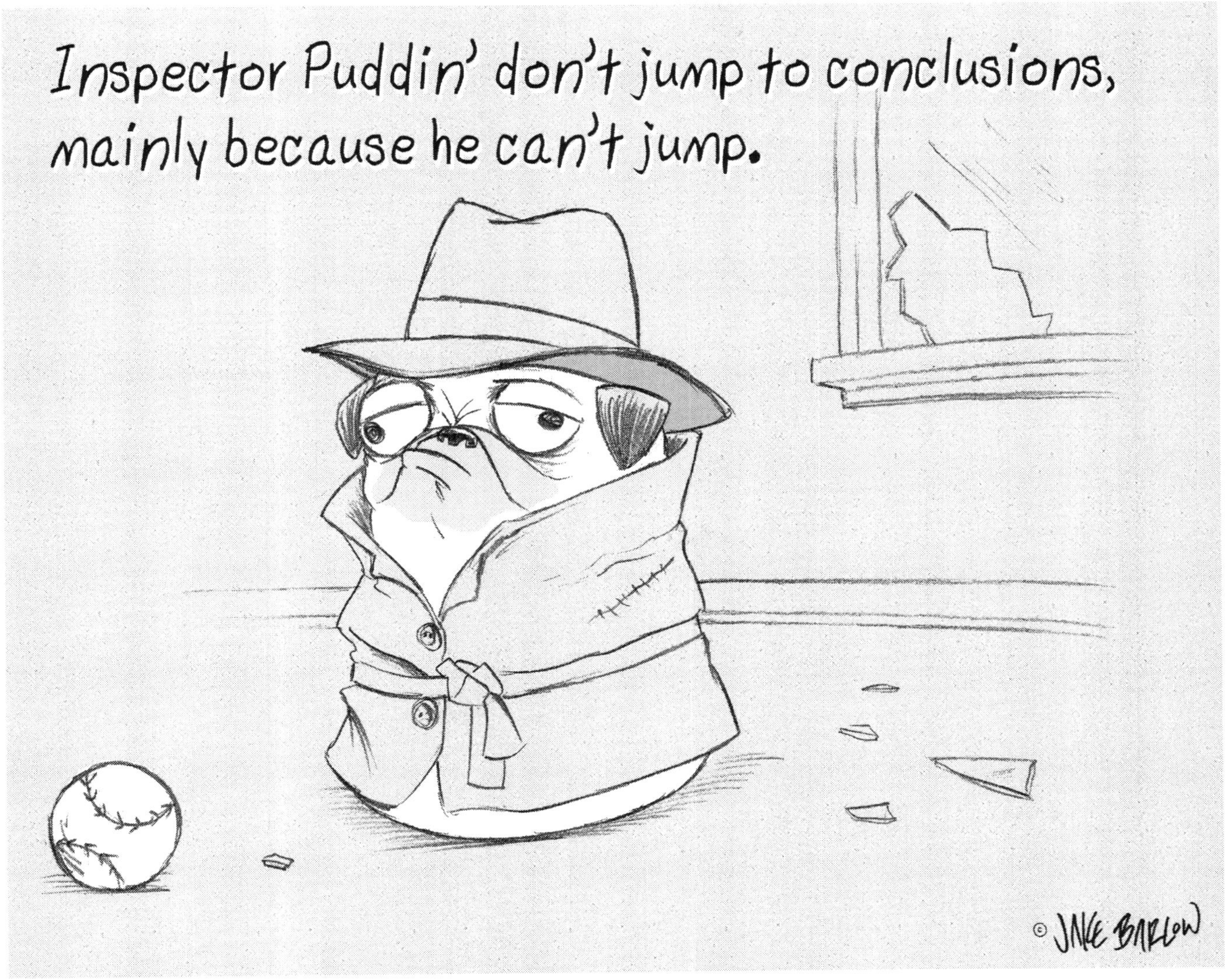
Inspector Puddin' don't jump to conclusions, mainly because he can't jump.
© JAKE BARLOW

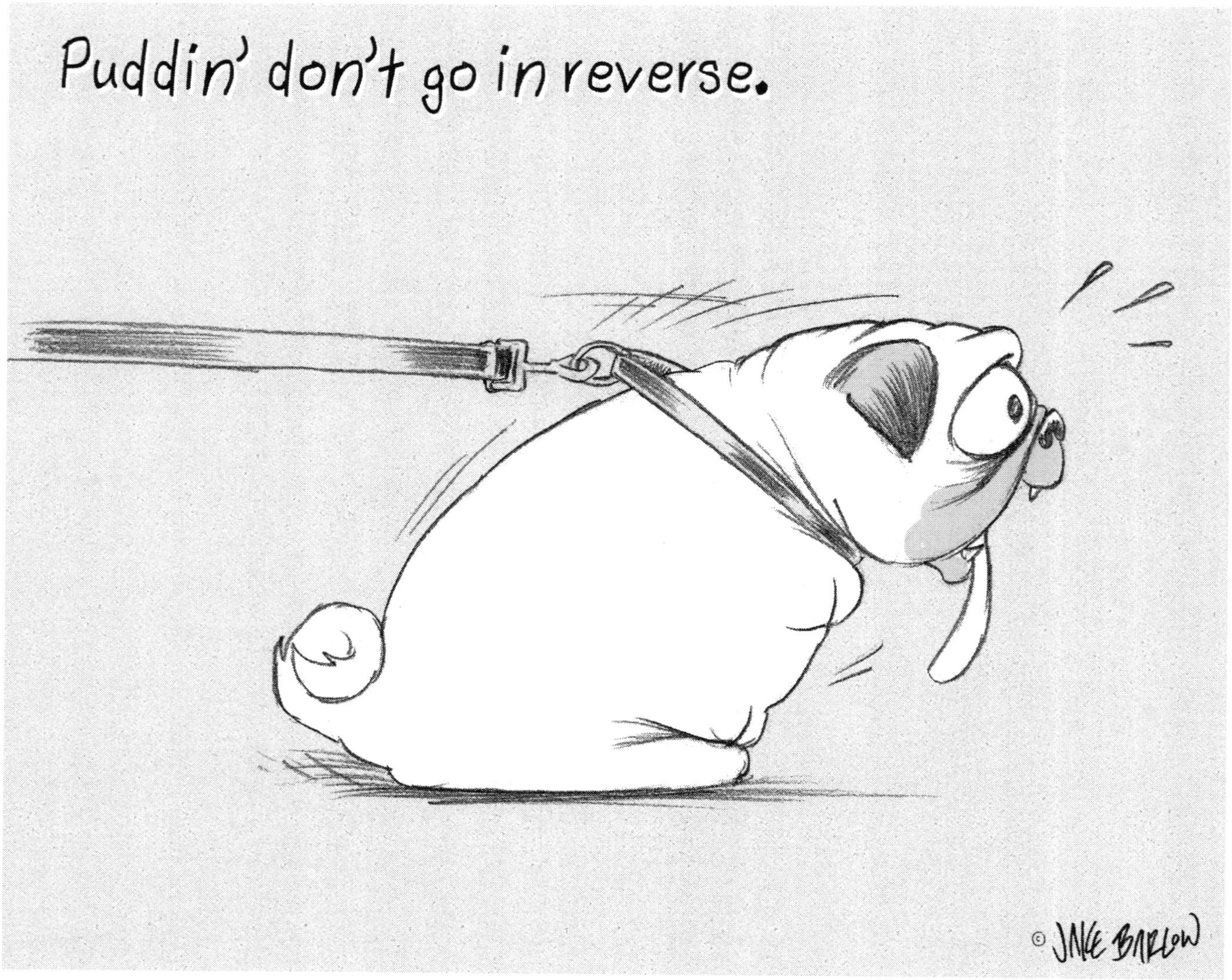
© JAKE BARLOW

Puddin' don't go in reverse.

Puddin' don't like sock puppets. Nor does he like socks, for that matter.

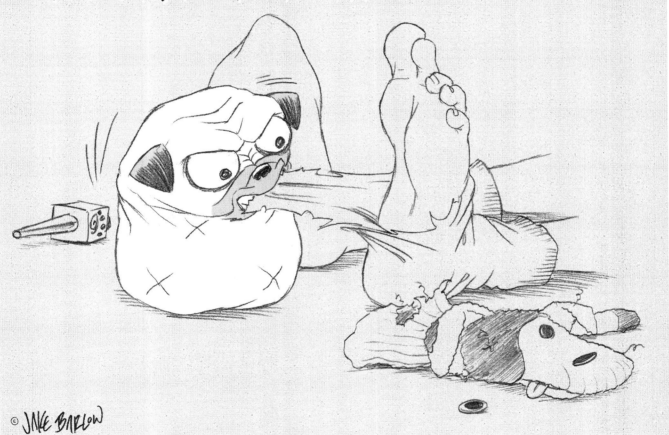

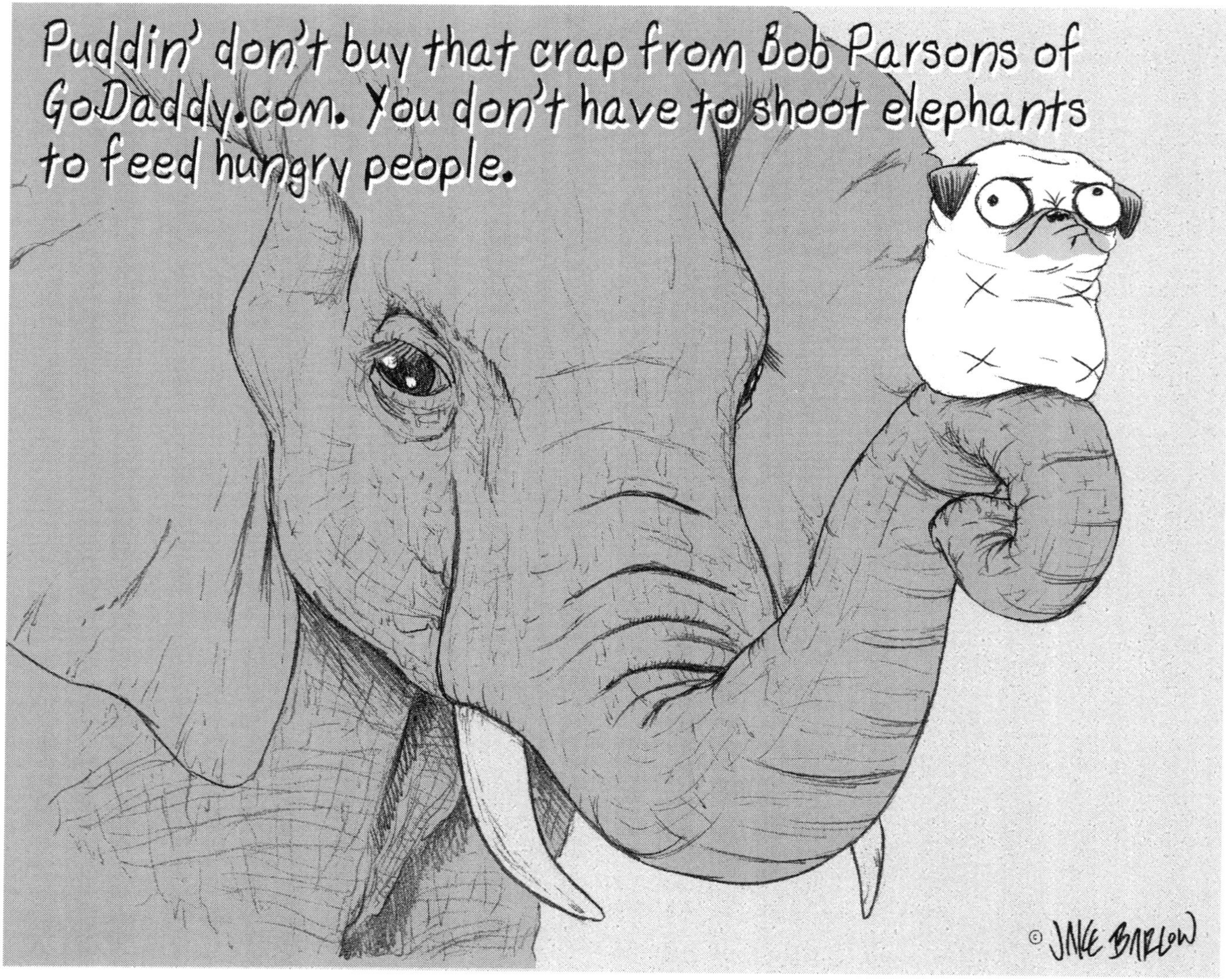
Puddin' don't buy that crap from Bob Parsons of GoDaddy.com. You don't have to shoot elephants to feed hungry people.
© JAKE BARLOW

Super Puddin' don't fight crime, among other things.

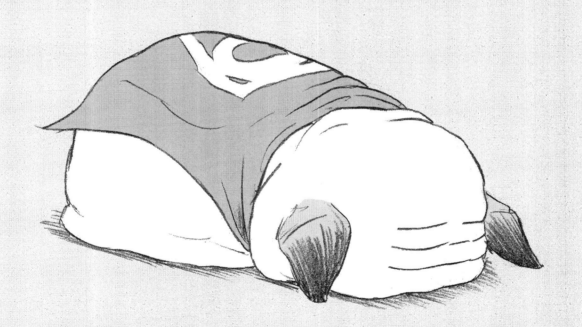

© JAKE BARLOW

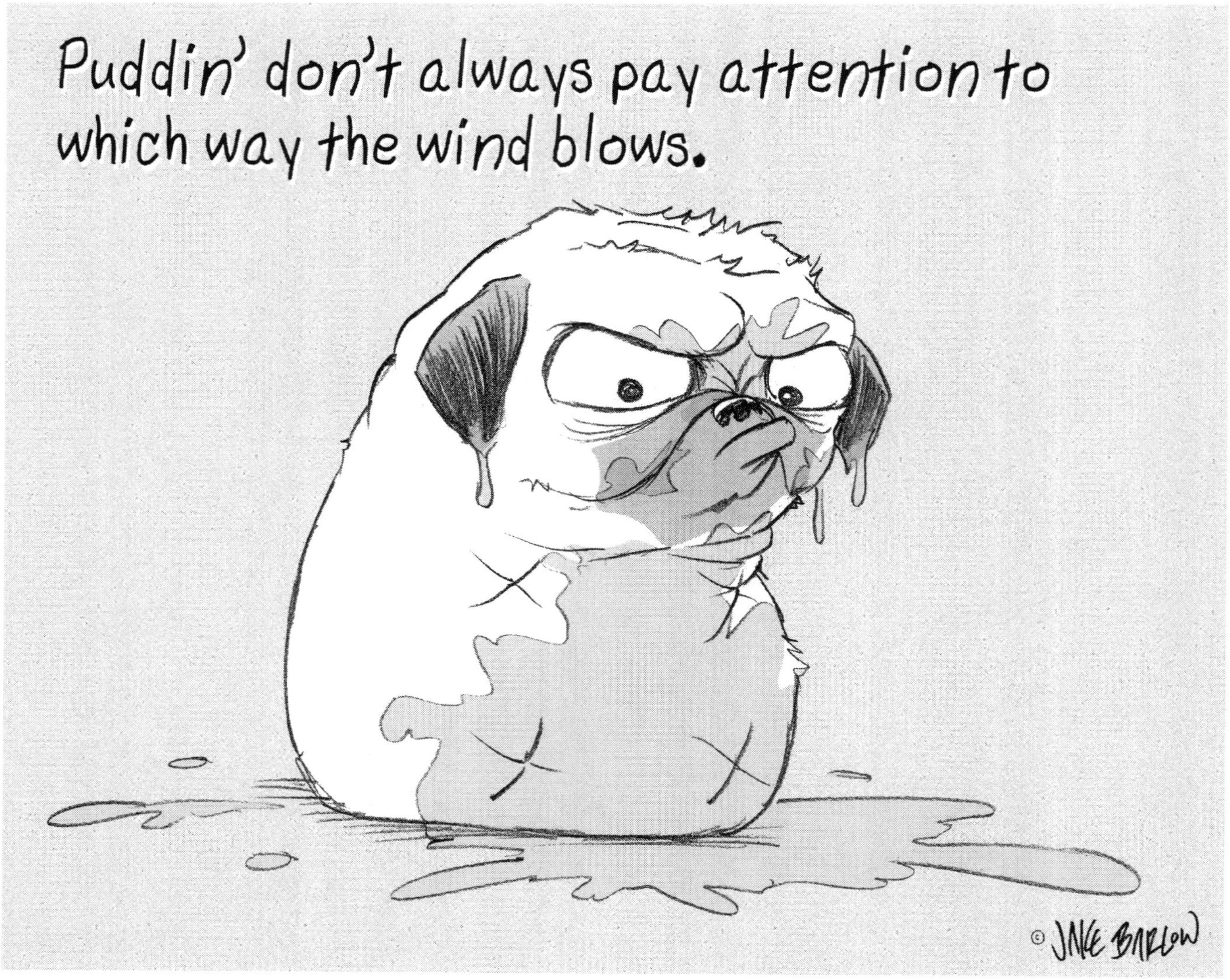
Puddin' don't always pay attention to which way the wind blows.
© JAKE BARLOW

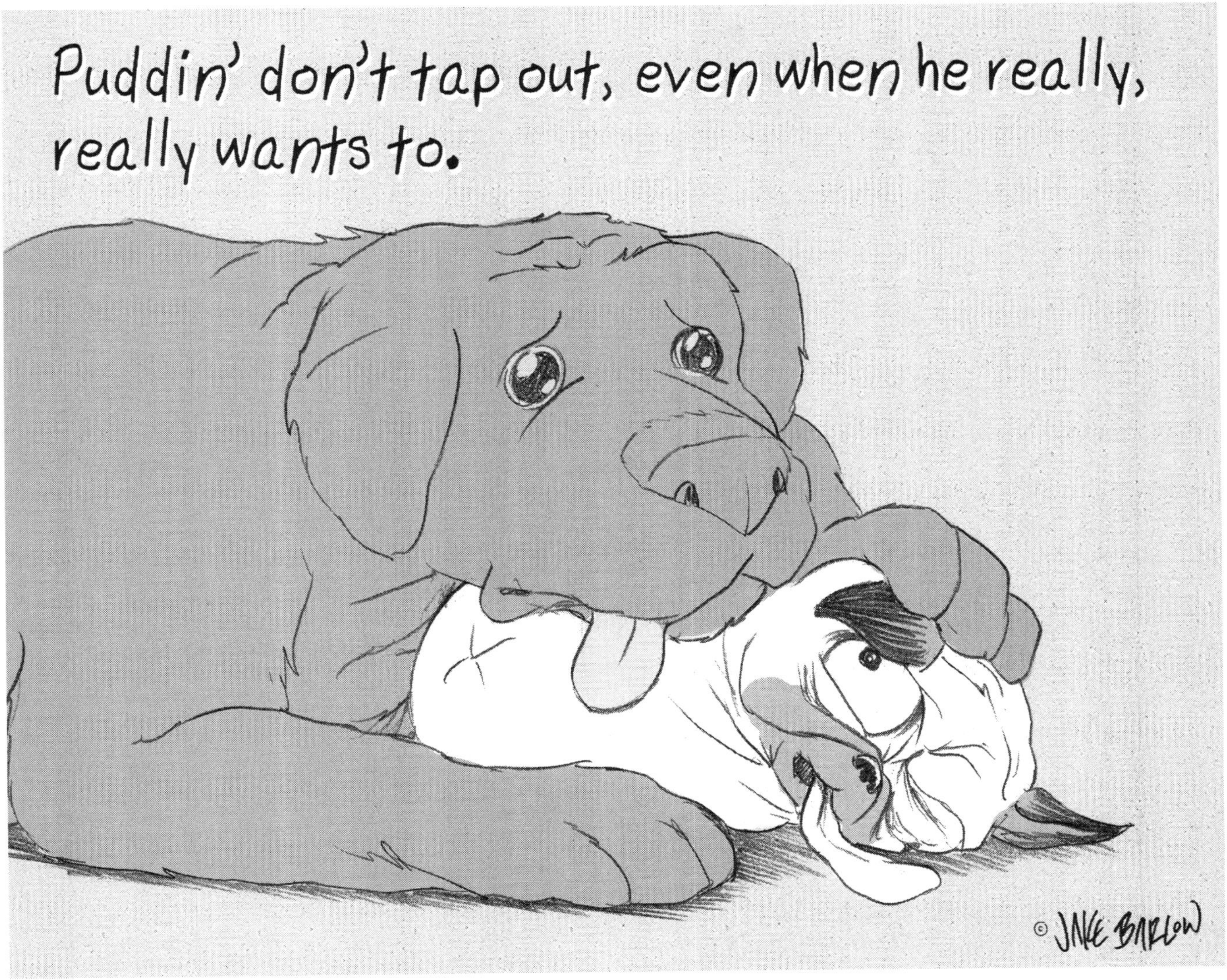
Puddin' don't tap out, even when he really, really wants to.
© JAKE BARLOW

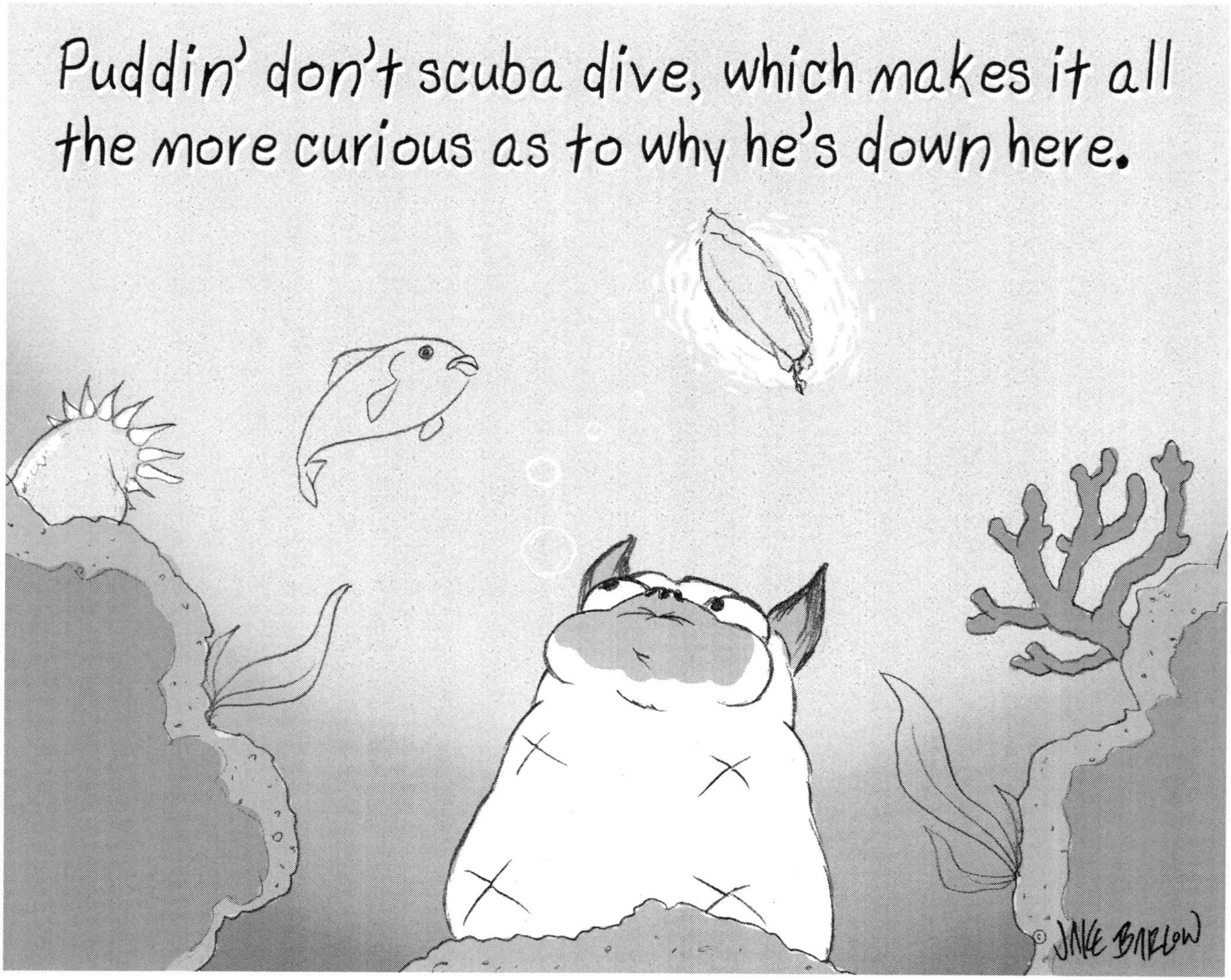
Puddin' don't scuba dive, which makes it all the more curious as to why he's down here.
© JAKE BARLOW

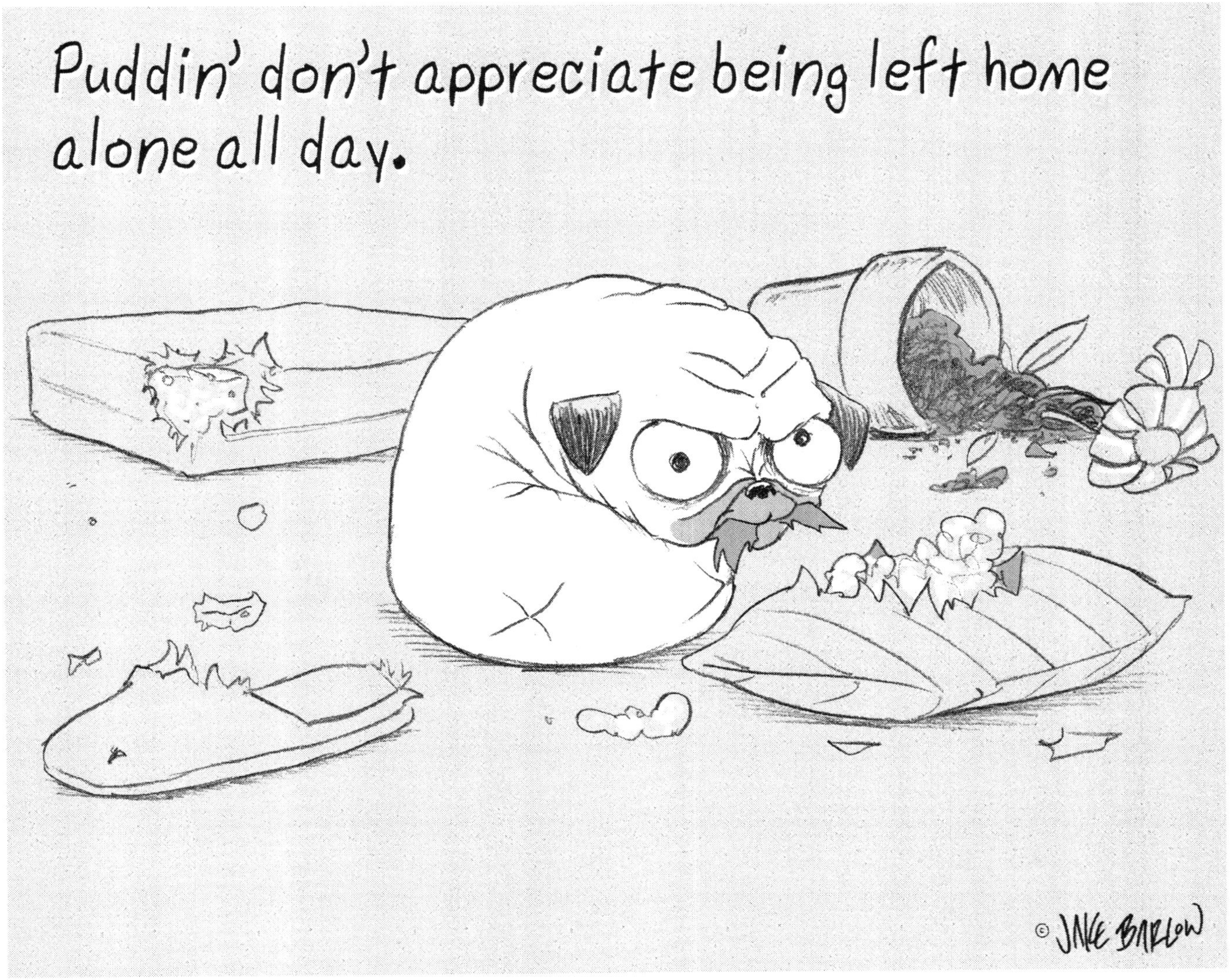
Puddin' don't appreciate being left home alone all day.
© JAKE BARLOW

Puddin' don't need a fancy ball washer.
He's got one built in.

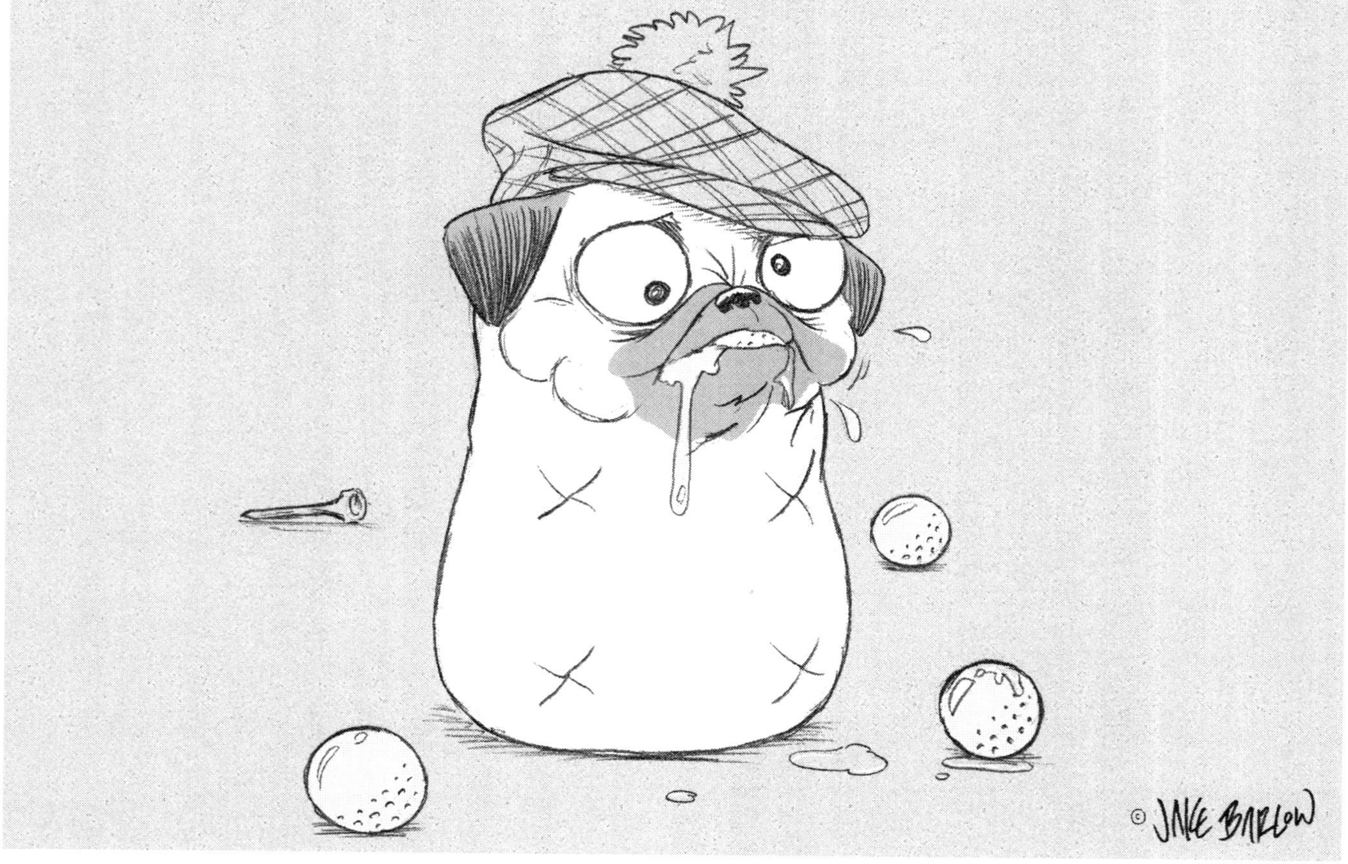
© JAKE BARLOW

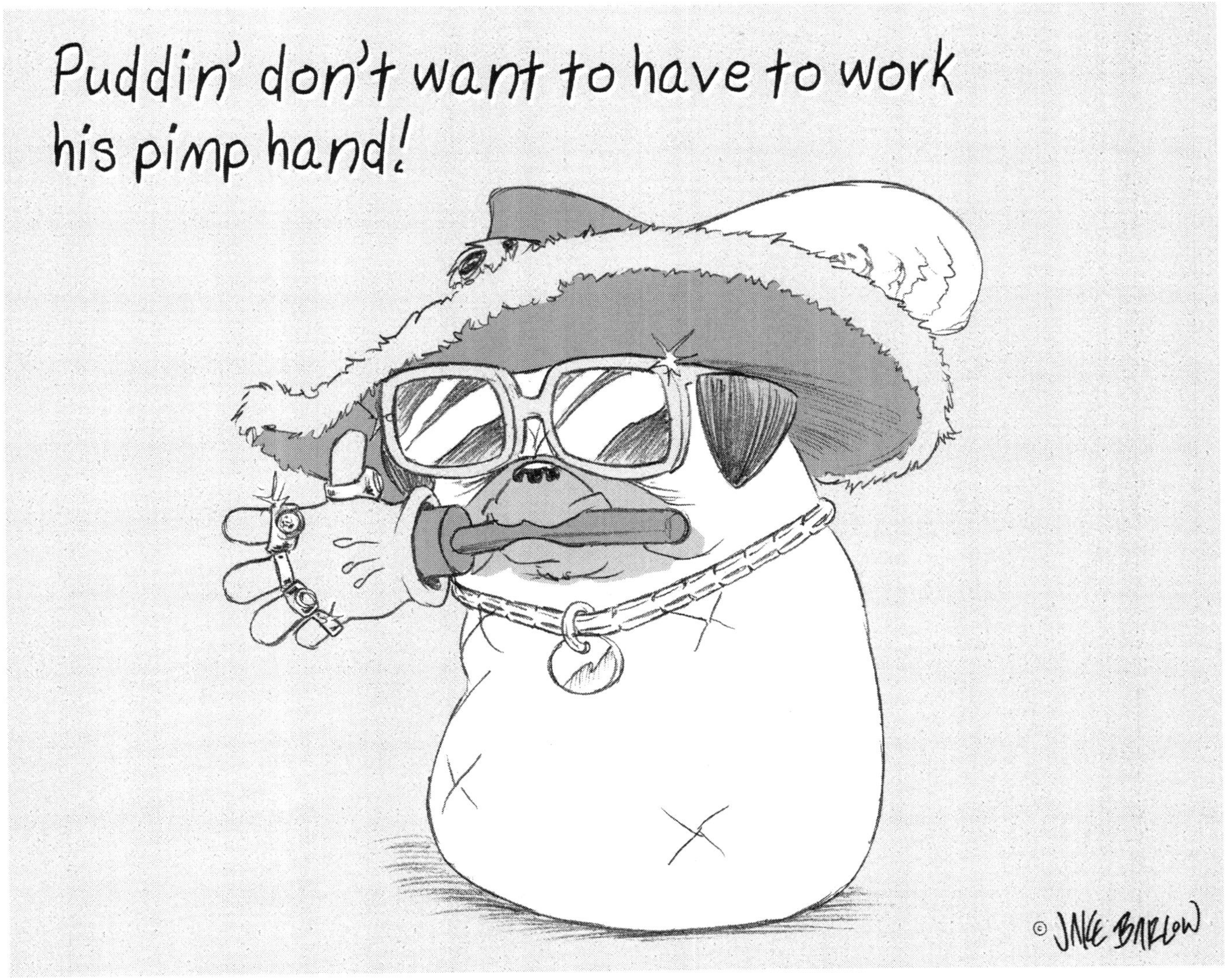
Puddin' don't want to have to work his pimp hand!
© JAKE BARLOW

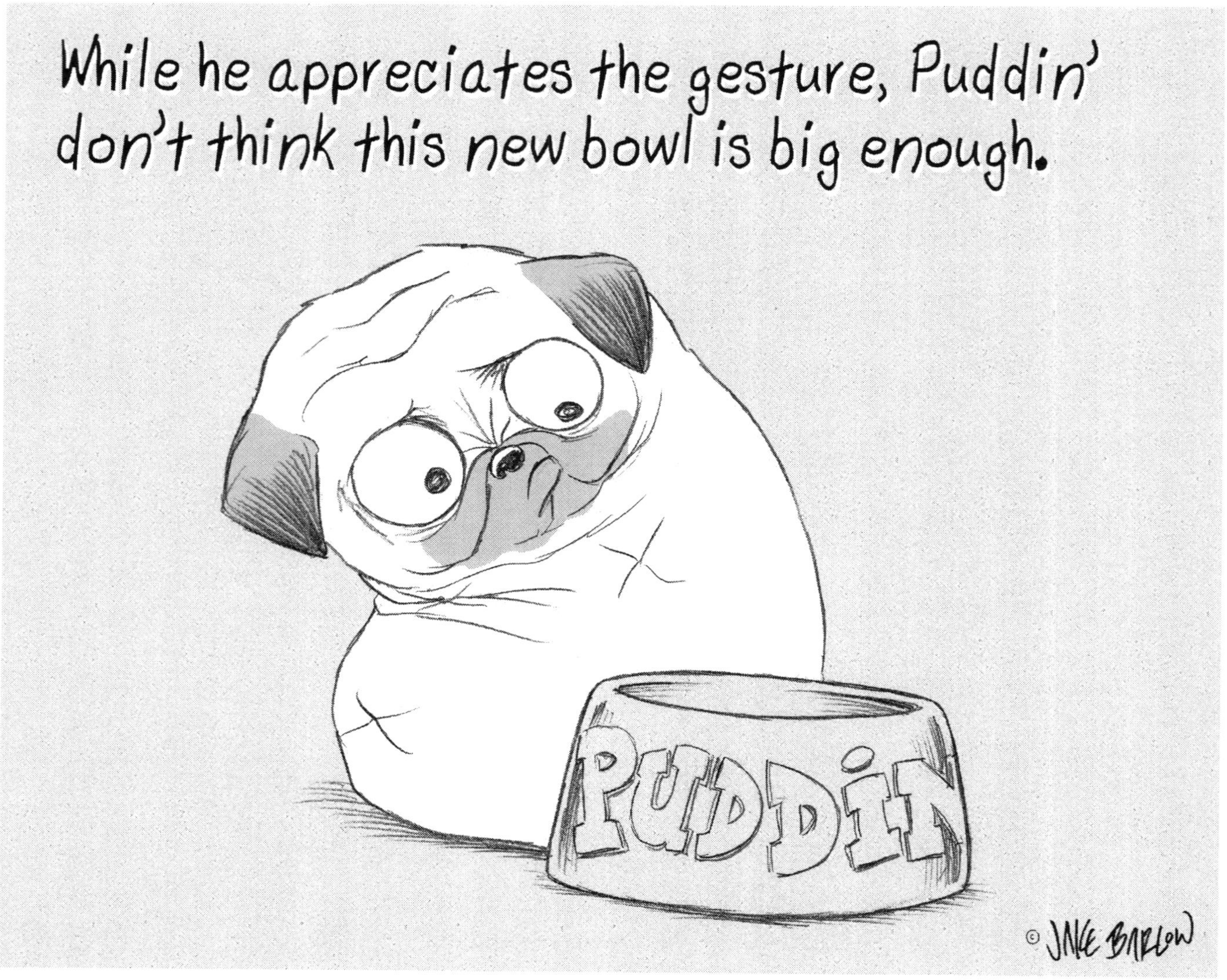
PUDDIN
© JAKE BARLOW

While he appreciates the gesture, Puddin' don't think this new bowl is big enough.

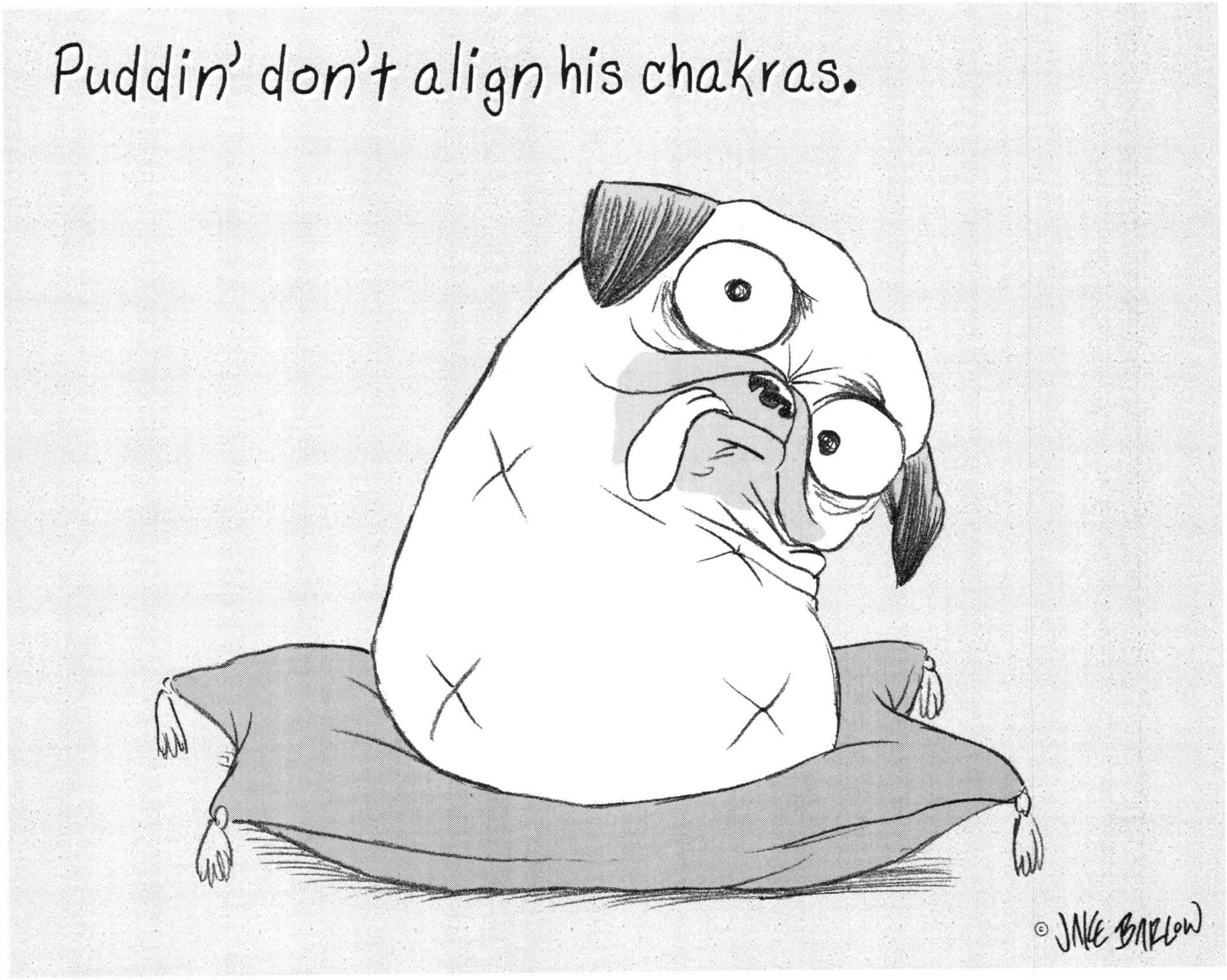
Puddin' don't align his chakras.
© JAKE BARLOW

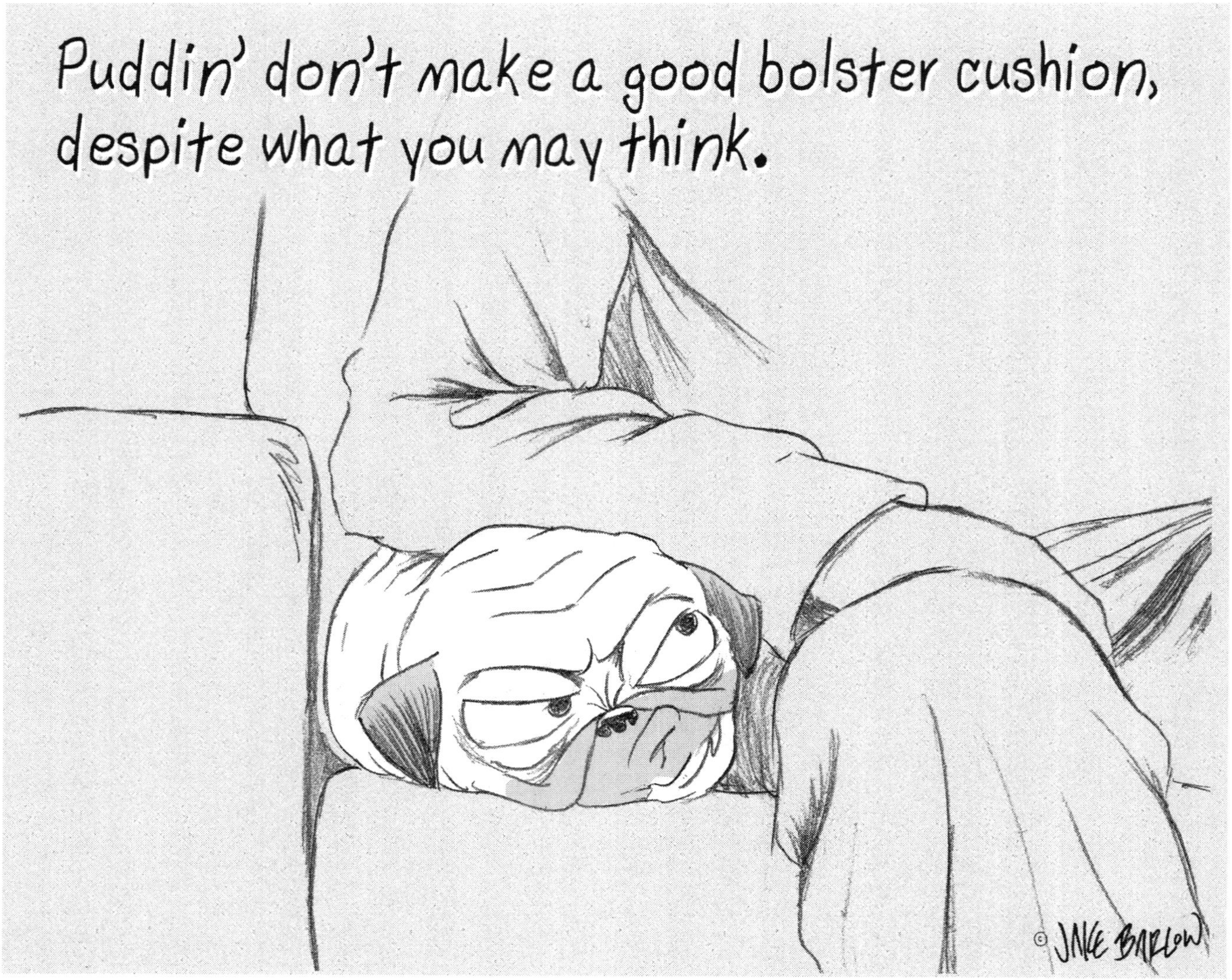
Puddin' don't make a good bolster cushion, despite what you may think.
© JAKE BARLOW

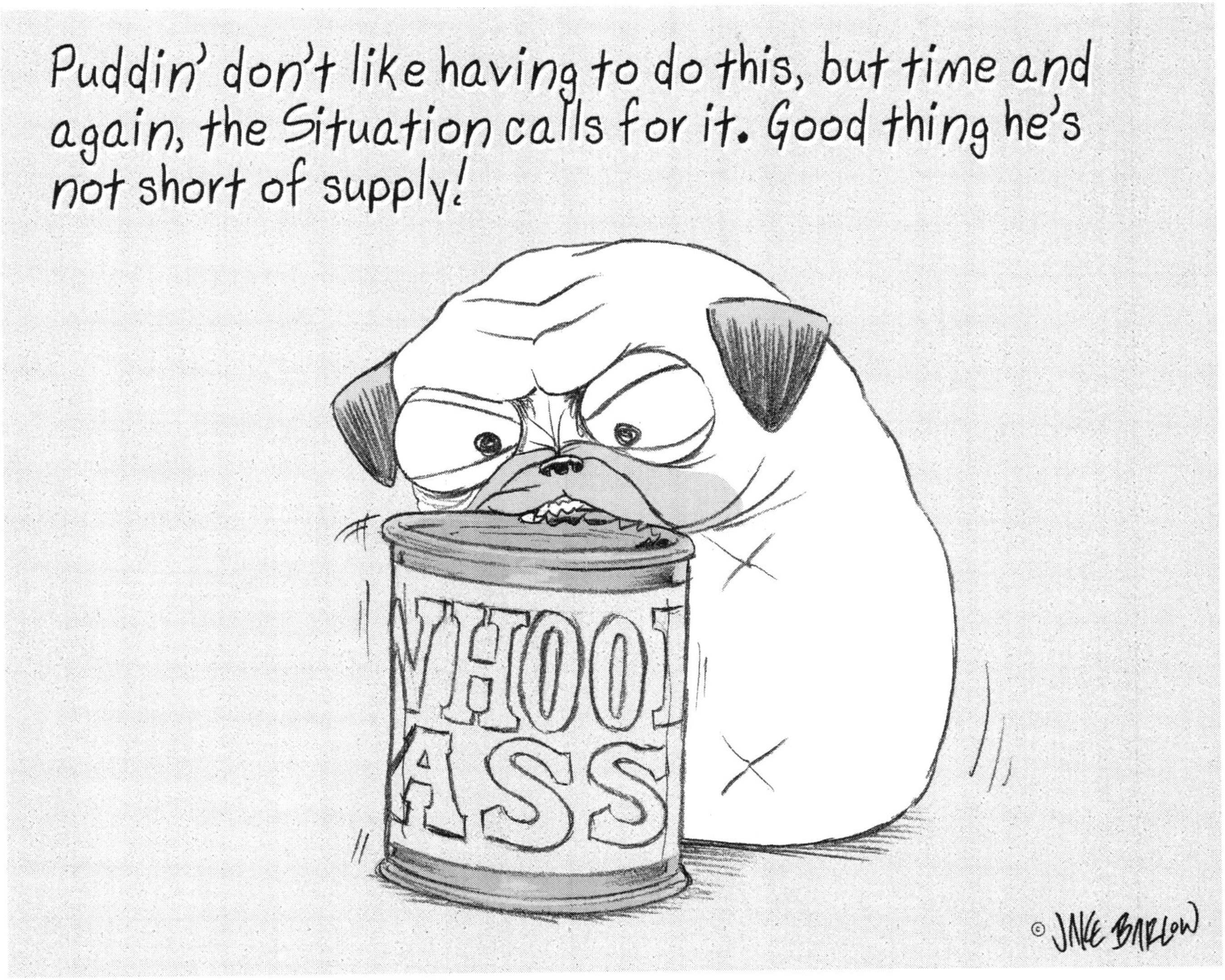
Puddin' don't like having to do this, but time and again, the Situation calls for it. Good thing he's not short of supply!
ASS
© JAKE BARLOW

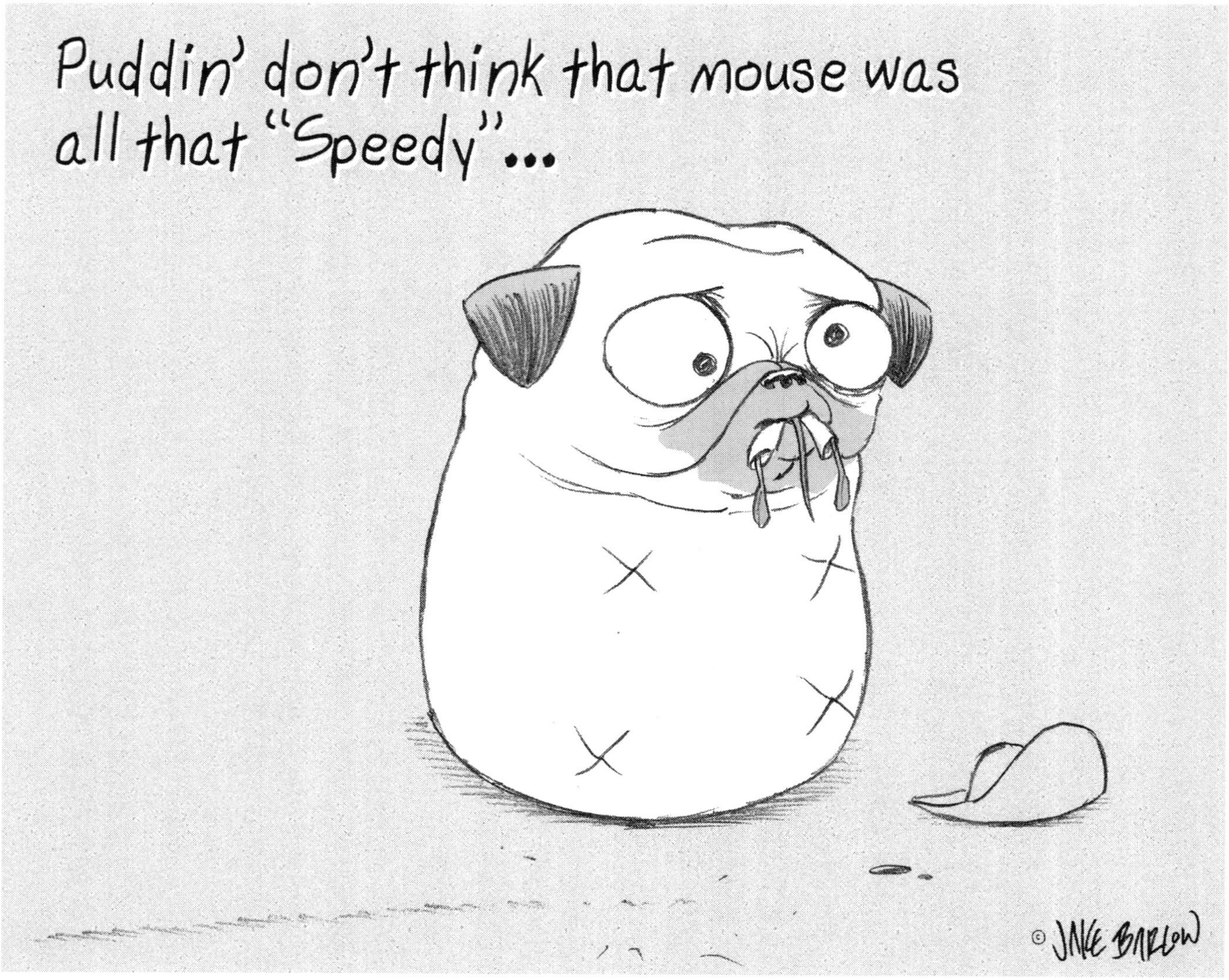
Puddin' don't think that mouse was all that "Speedy"...
© JAKE BARLOW

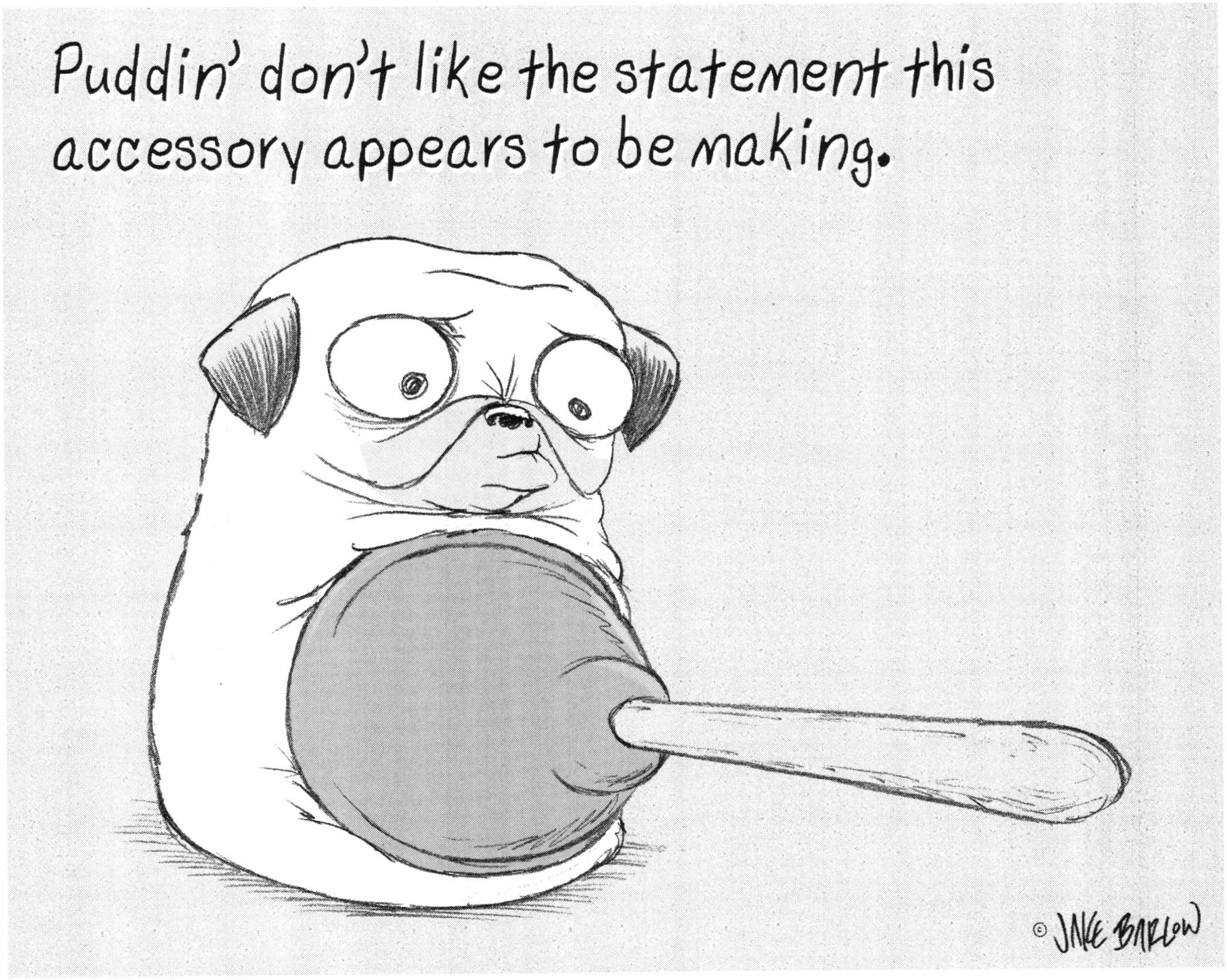
Puddin' don't like the statement this accessory appears to be making.
© JAKE BARLOW

Puddin' no comprende, amigo! Just show him the way to the margarita station!

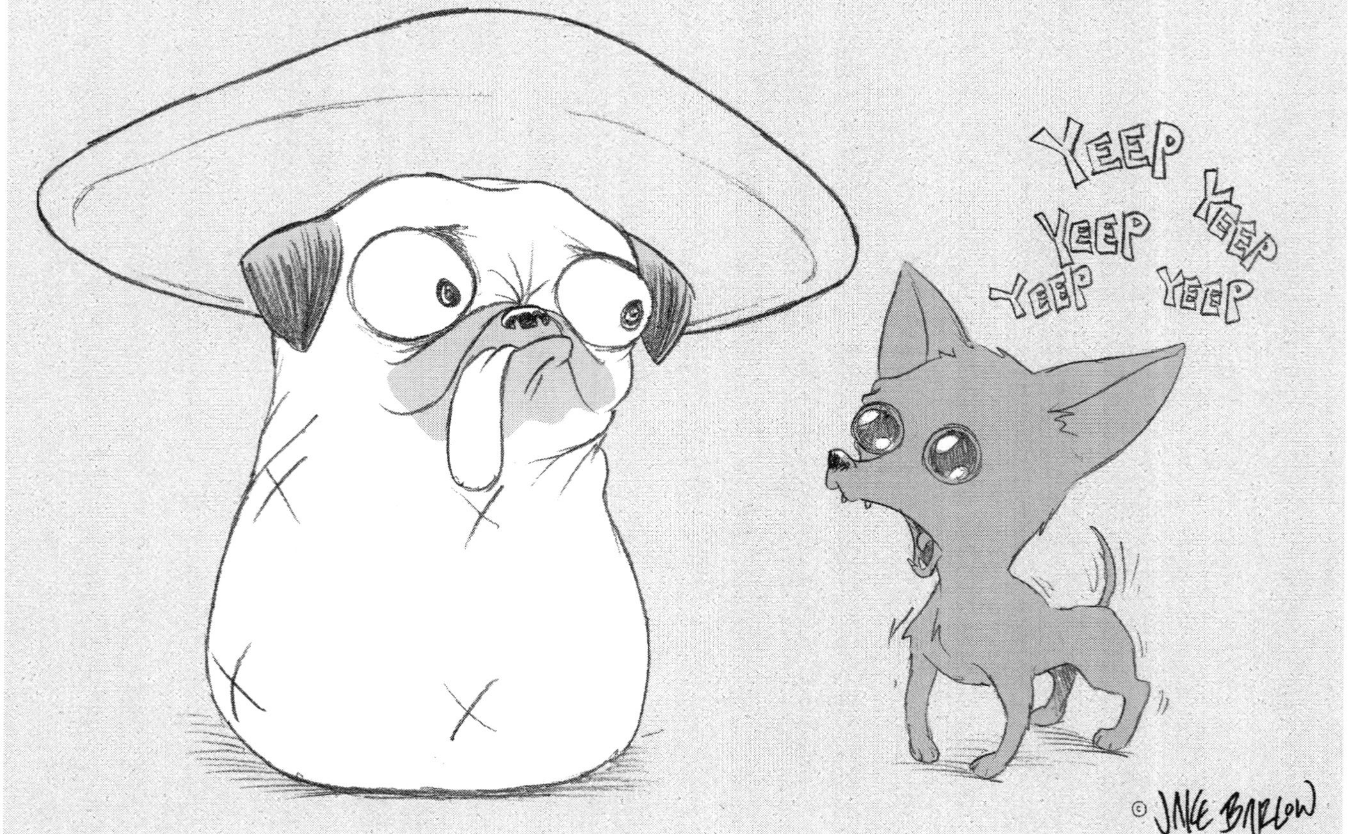
YEEP
YEEP
YEEP
YEEP
YEEP

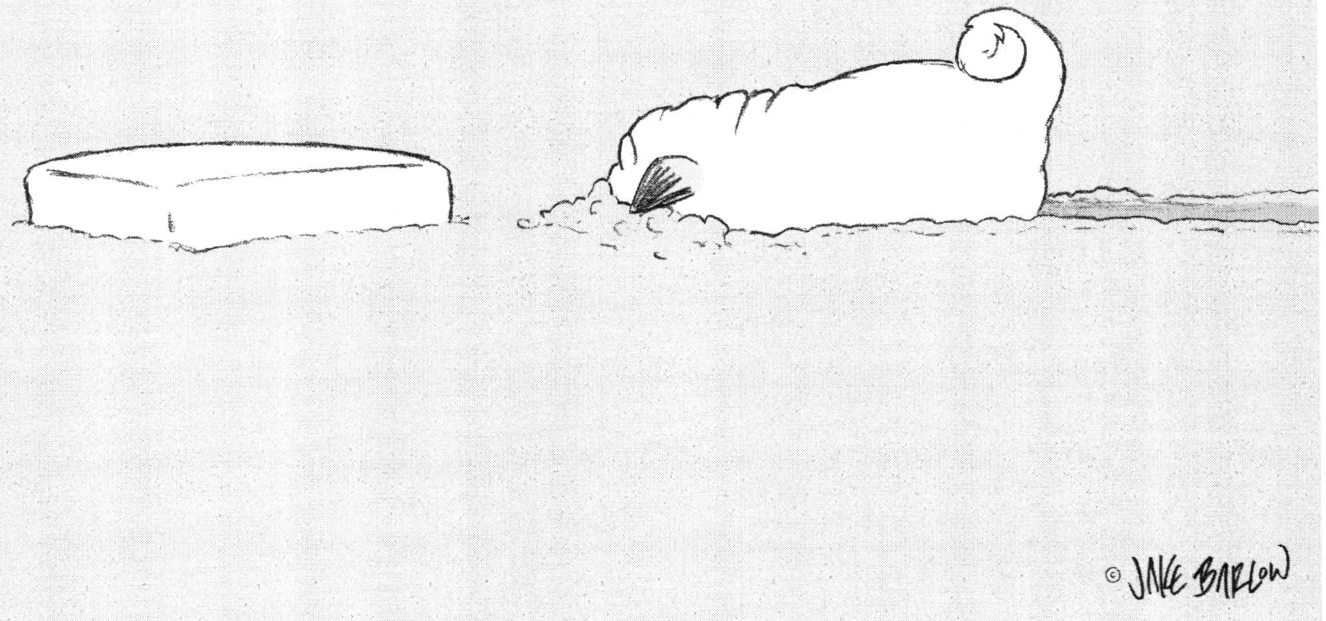
© JAKE BARLOW

Puddin' don't quite make it to second base.

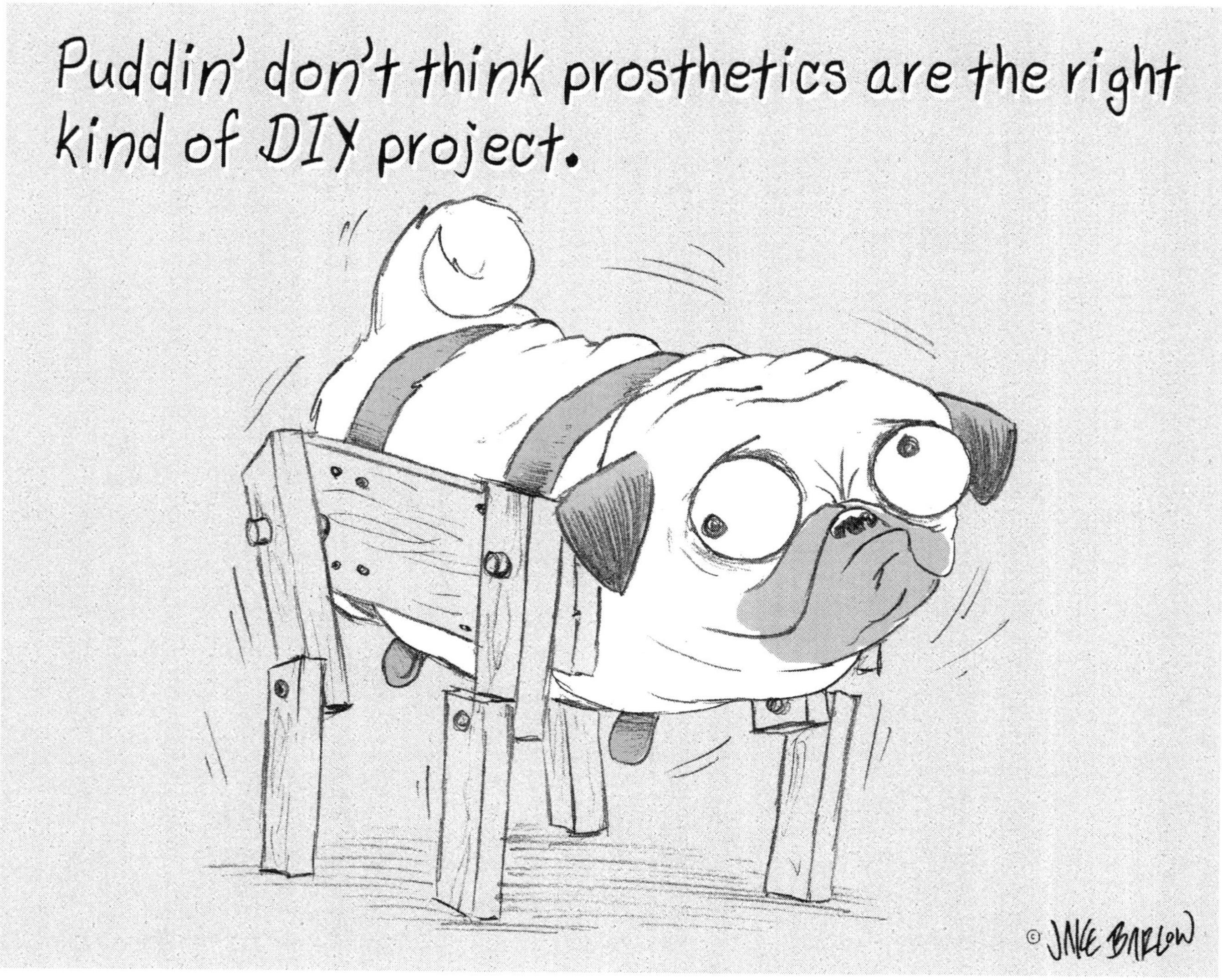
Puddin' don't think prosthetics are the right kind of DIY project.
© JAKE BARLOW

Puddin' don't "run" in circles.

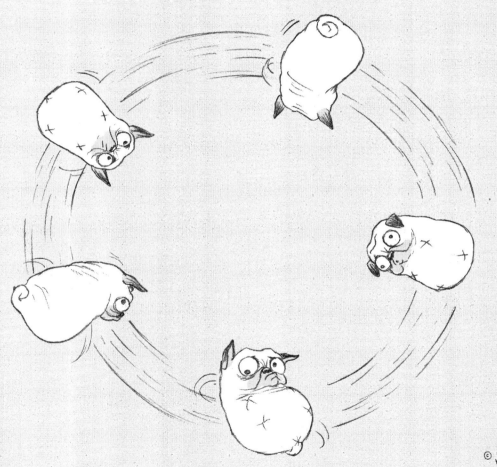

Puddin' don't know why gas prices are so high when he gives it away for free.

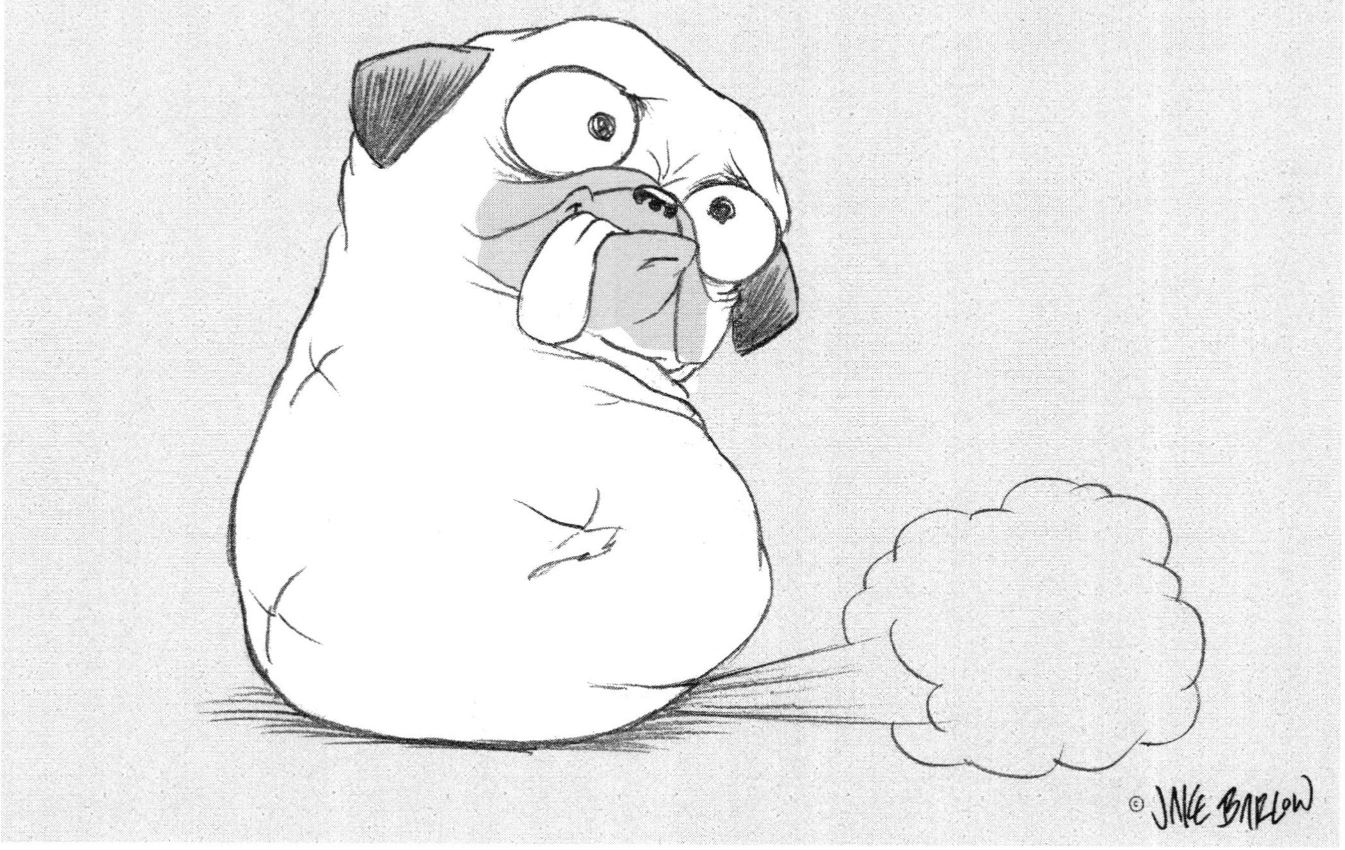
© JAKE BARLOW

Butterscotch Puddin' don't wear anything under his kilt either.

© JAKE BARLOW

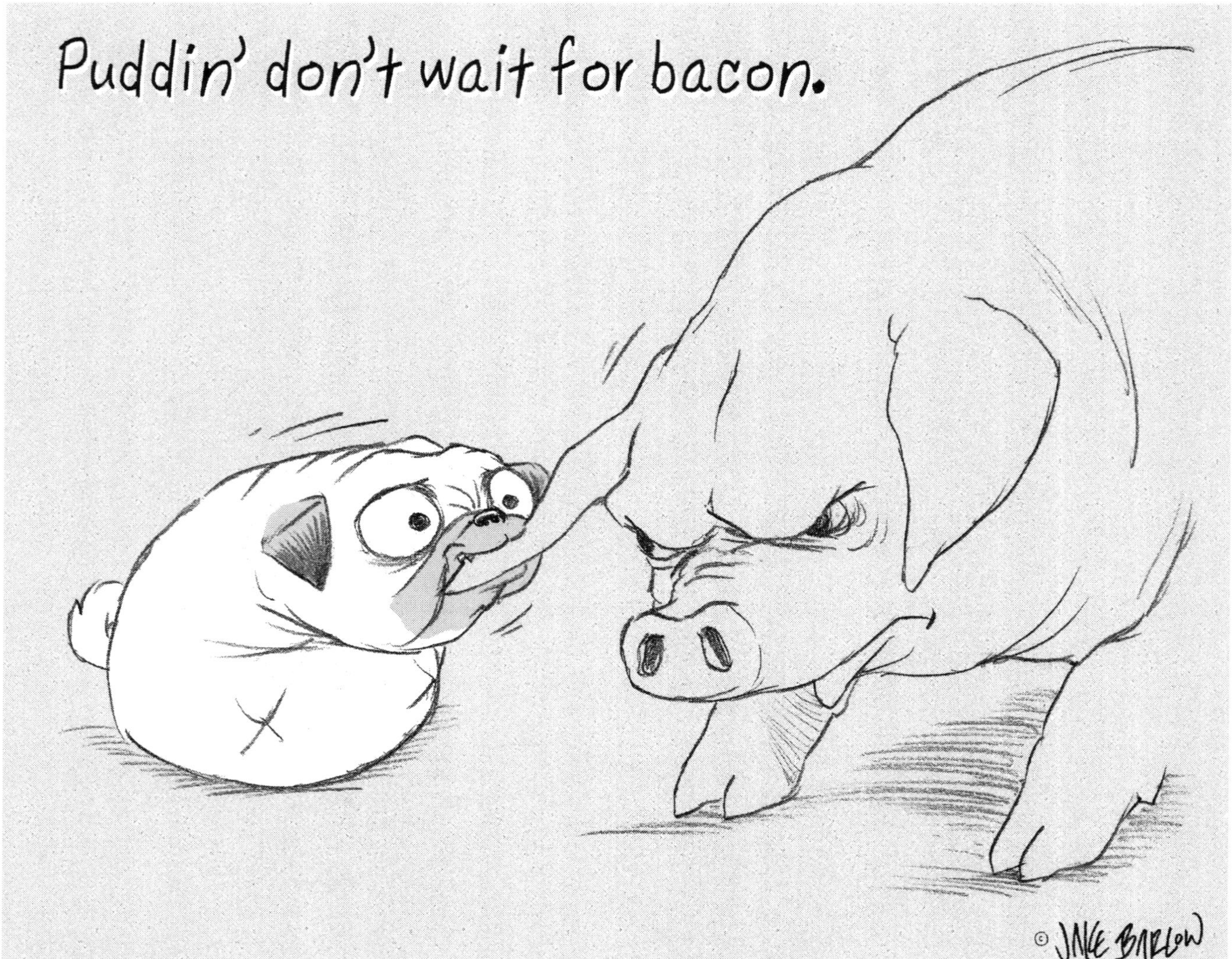
Puddin' don't wait for bacon.
© JAKE BARLOW

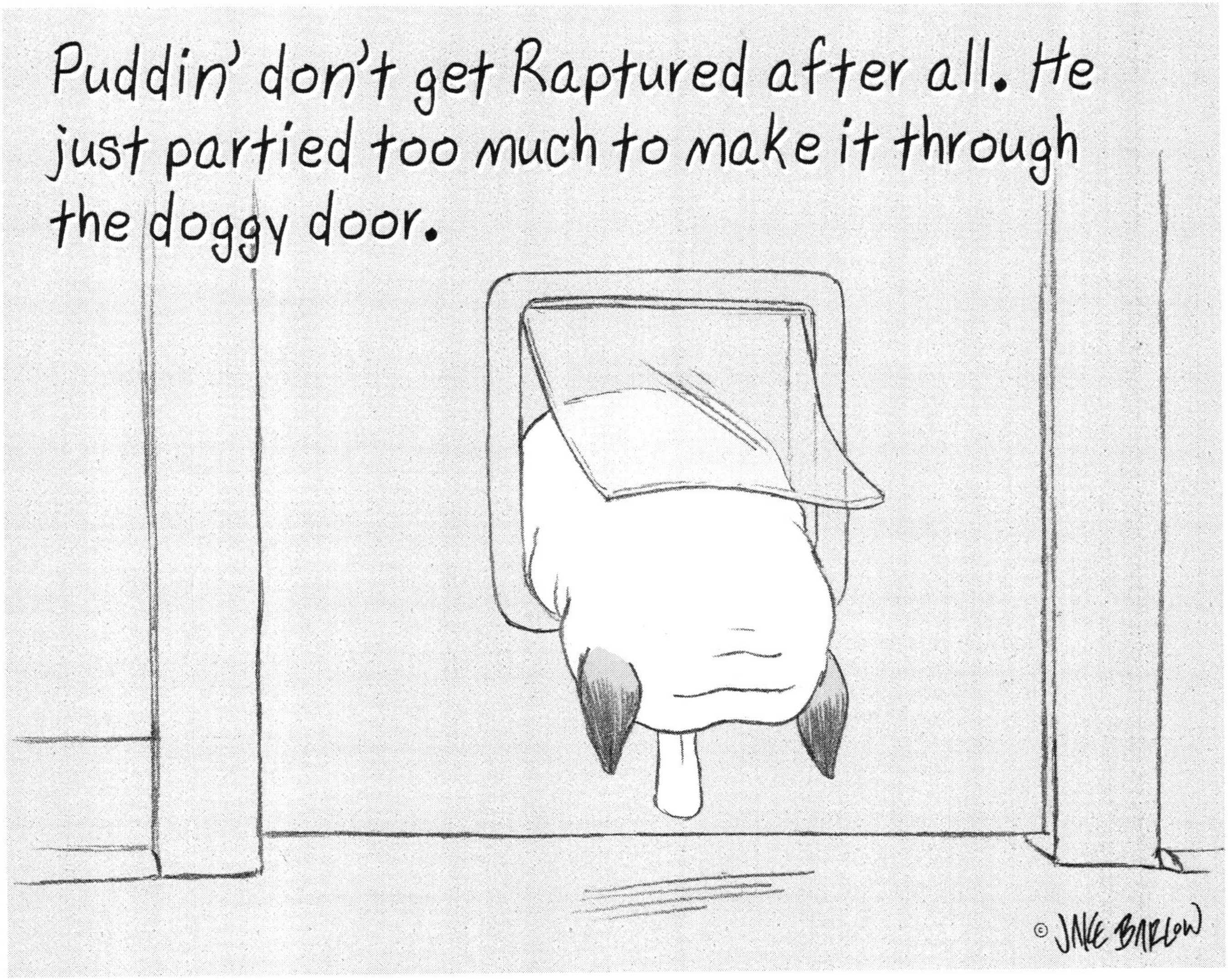
© JAKE BARLOW

Puddin' don't get Raptured after all. He just partied too much to make it through the doggy door.

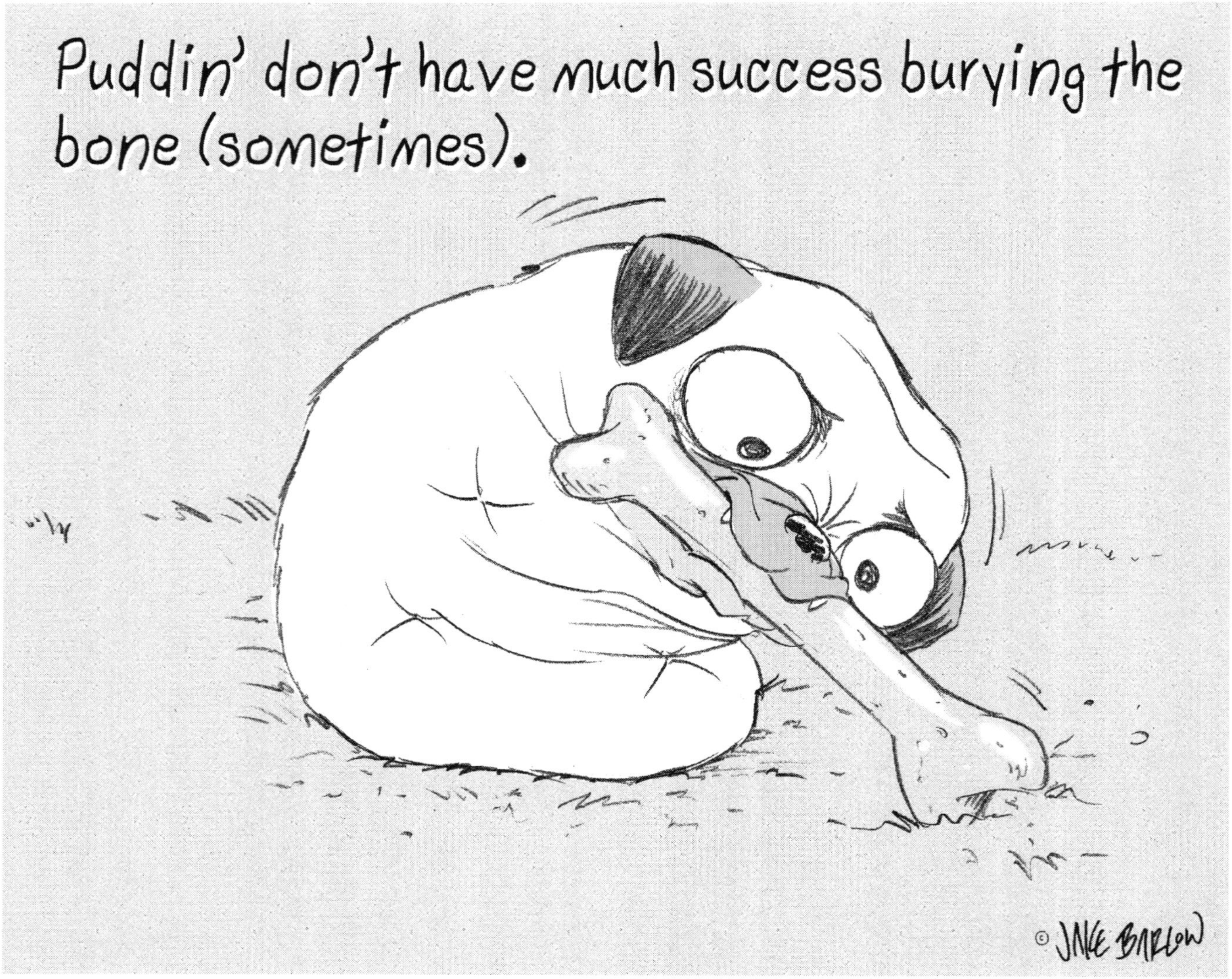
Puddin' don't have much success burying the bone (sometimes).
© JAKE BARLOW

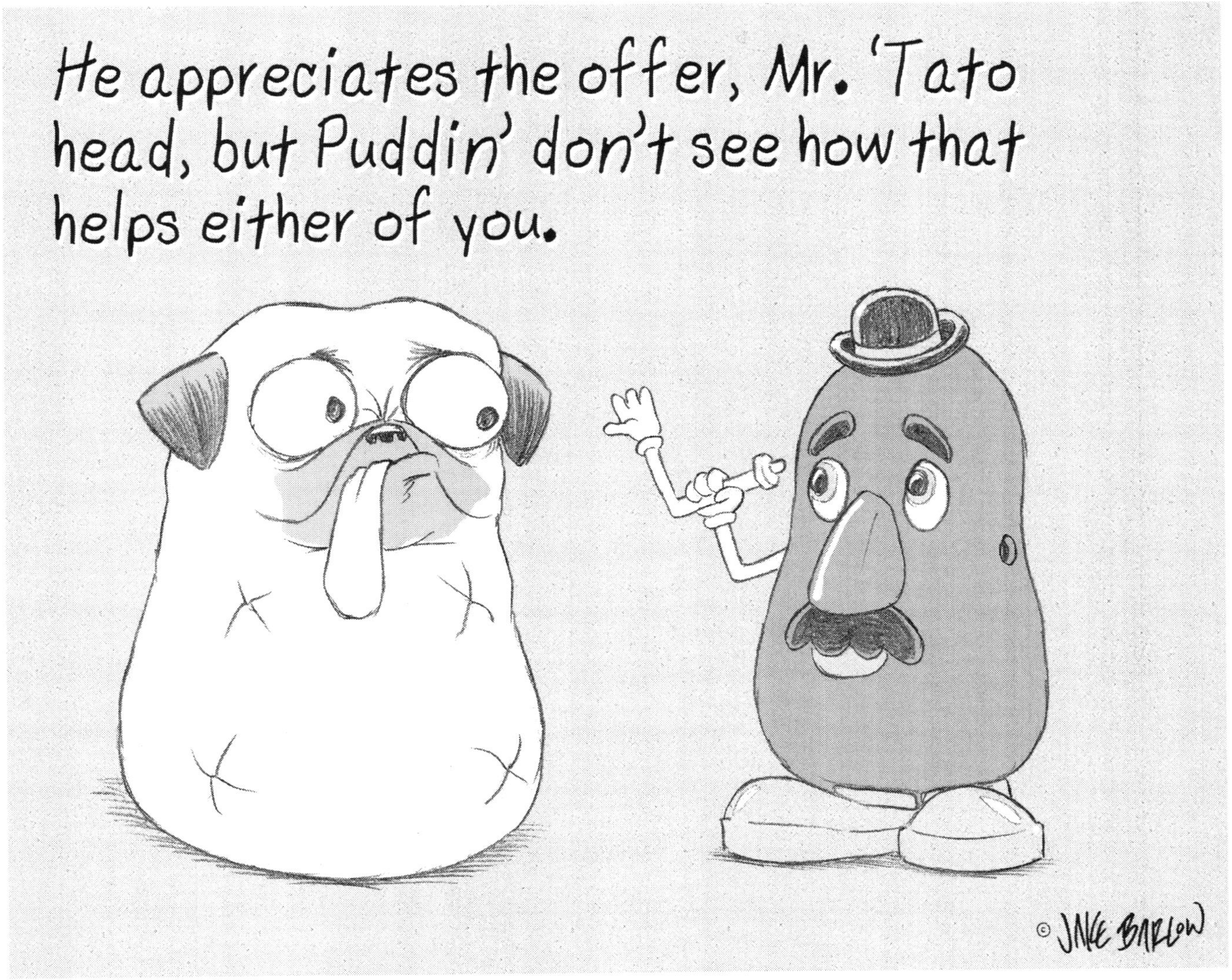
He appreciates the offer, Mr. 'Tato head, but Puddin' don't see how that helps either of you.
© JAKE BARLOW

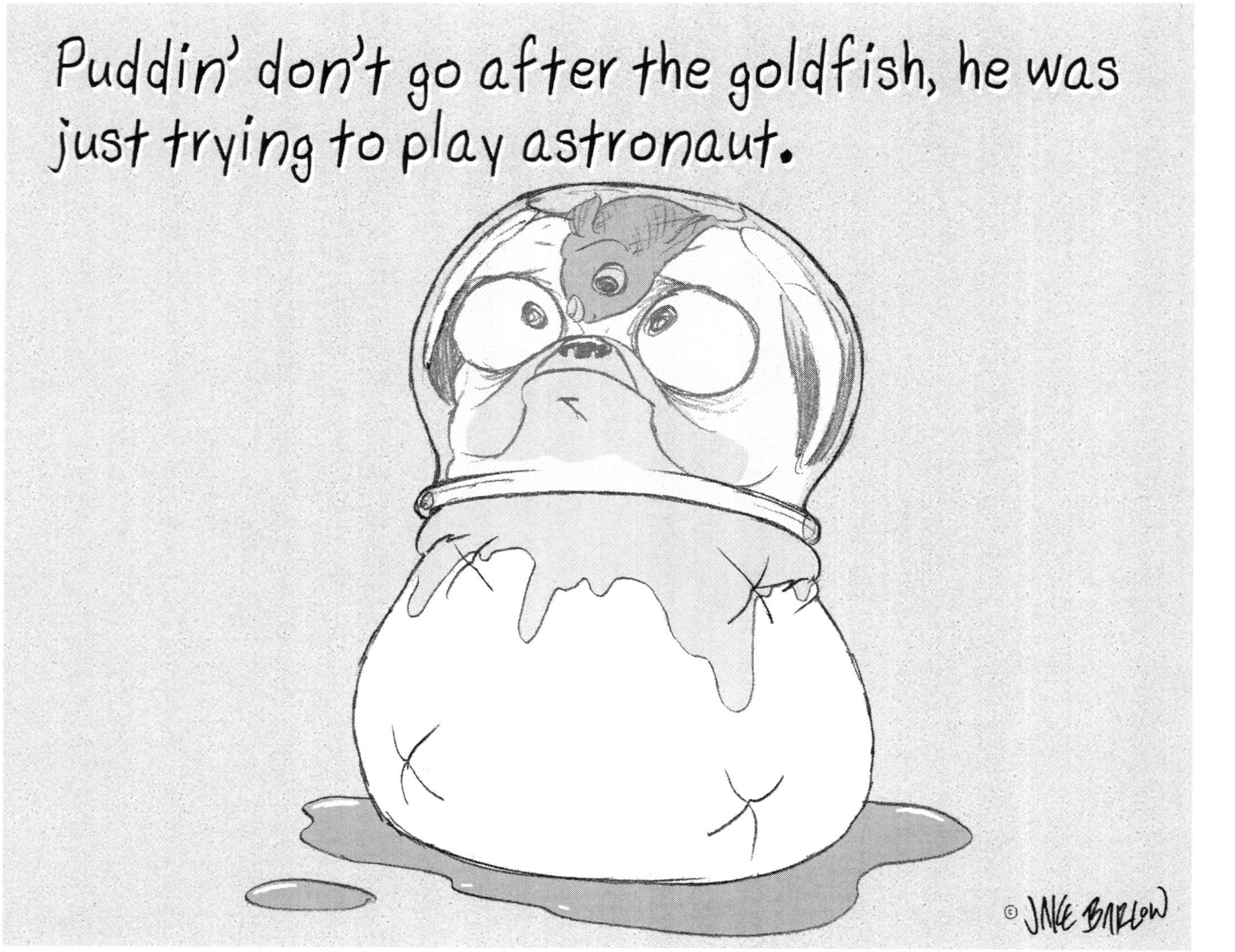
Puddin' don't go after the goldfish, he was just trying to play astronaut.
© JAKE BARLOW

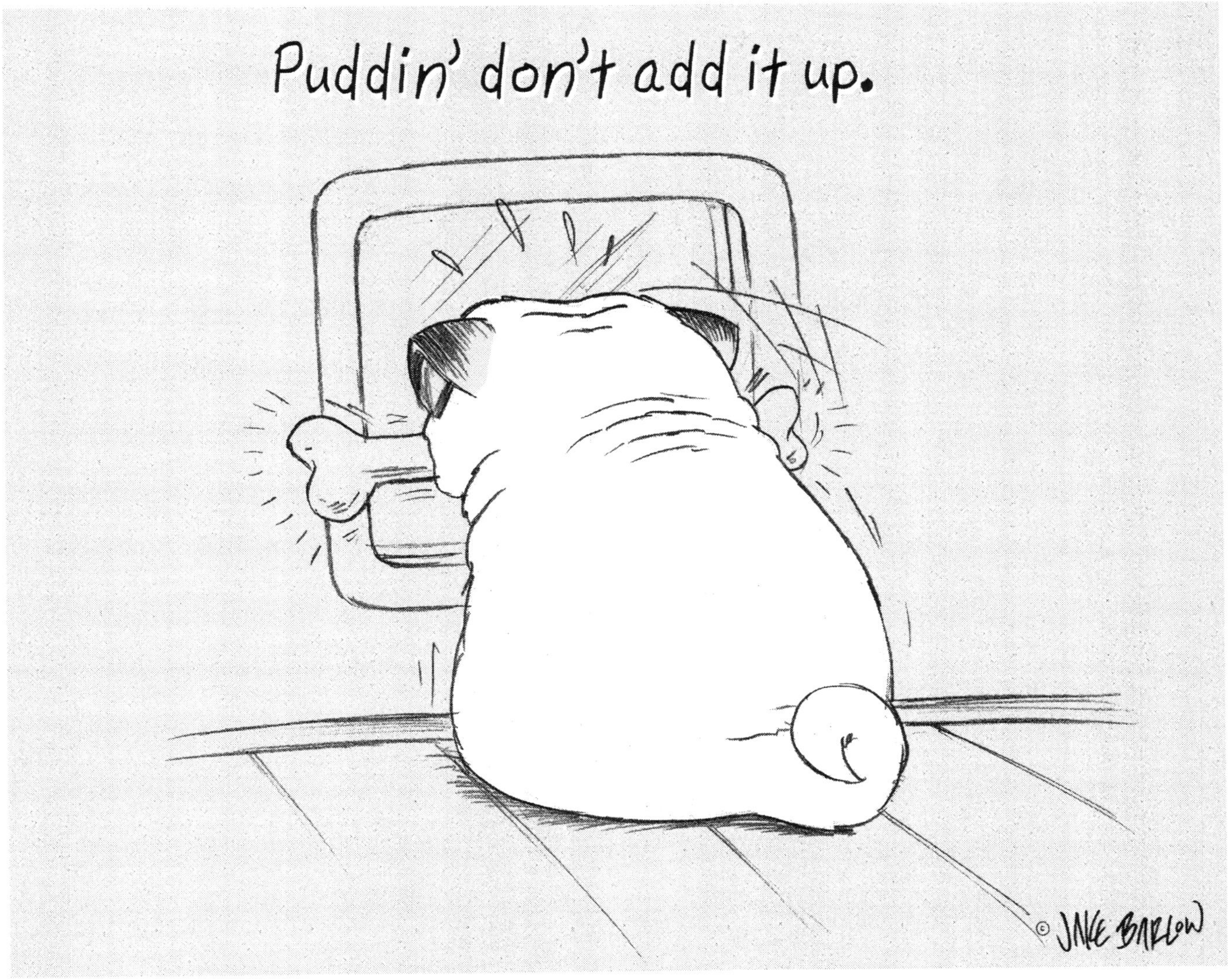
© JAKE BARLOW

Puddin' don't add it up.

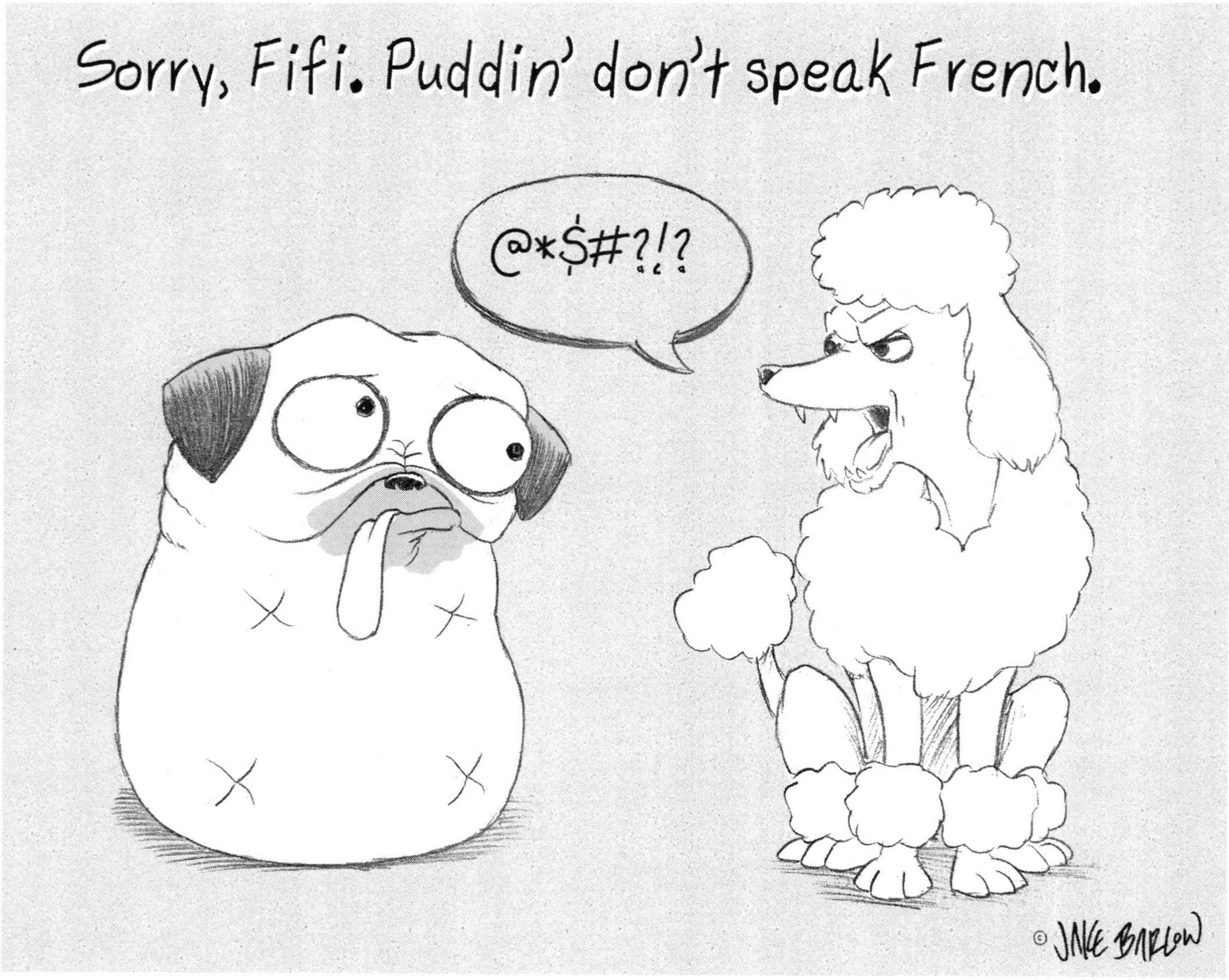
@*$#?!?
© JAKE BARLOW

Sorry, Fifi. Puddin' don't speak French.

Puddin' don't share photos of his wiener, even if it is something to be proud of.

© JAKE BARLOW

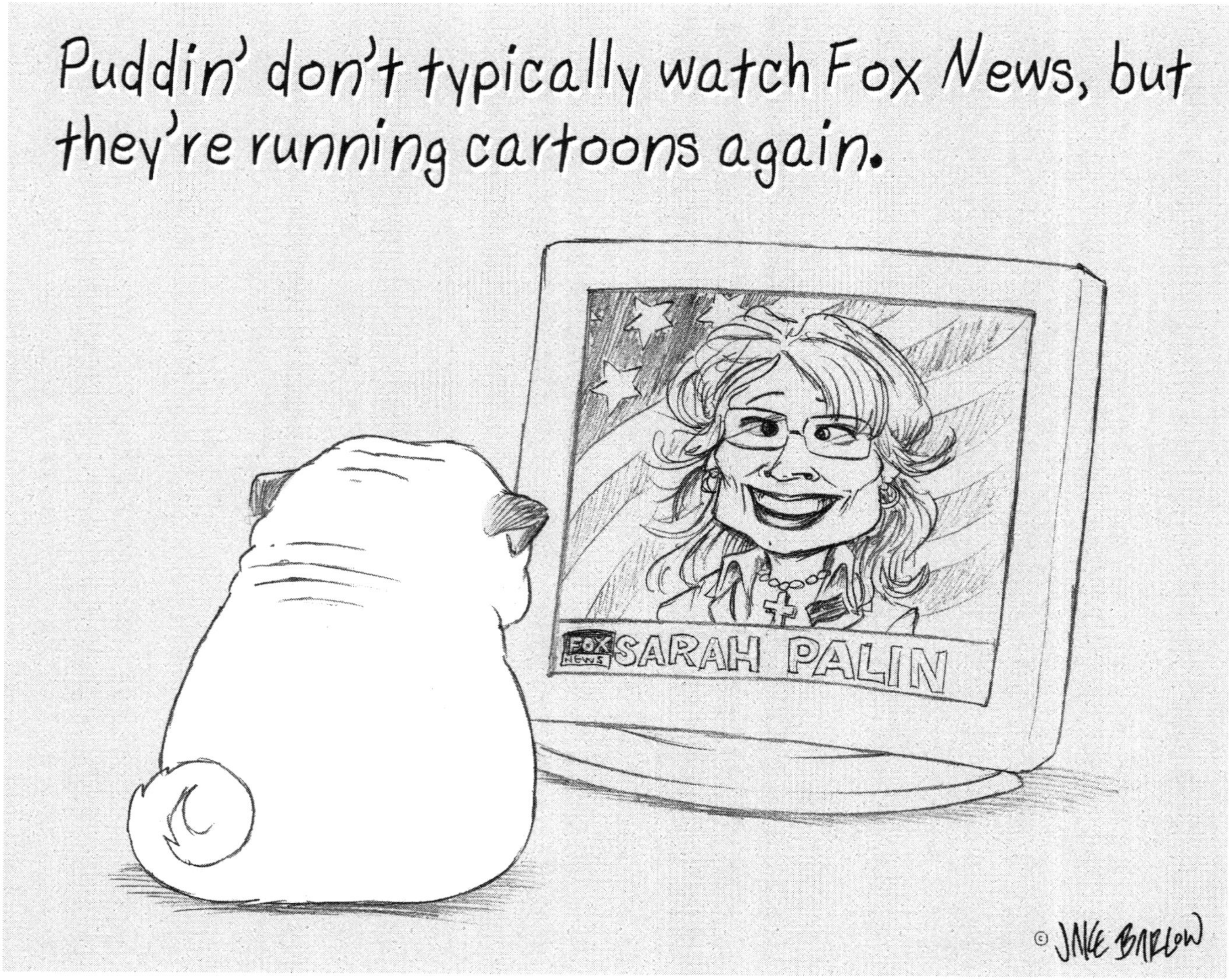
FOX NEWS SARAH PALIN
© JAKE BARLOW

Puddin' don't typically watch Fox News, but they're running cartoons again.

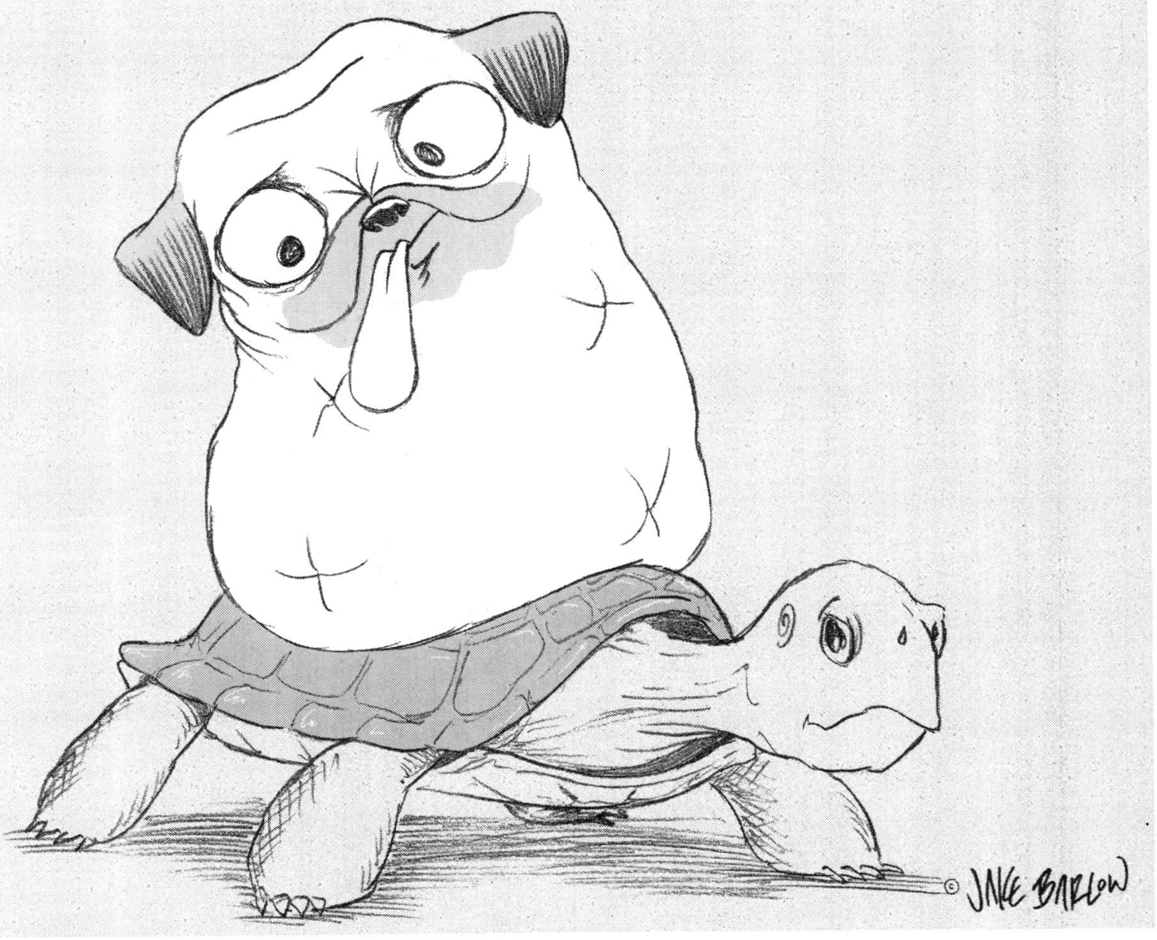
© JAKE BARLOW

Puddin' don't get there any faster.

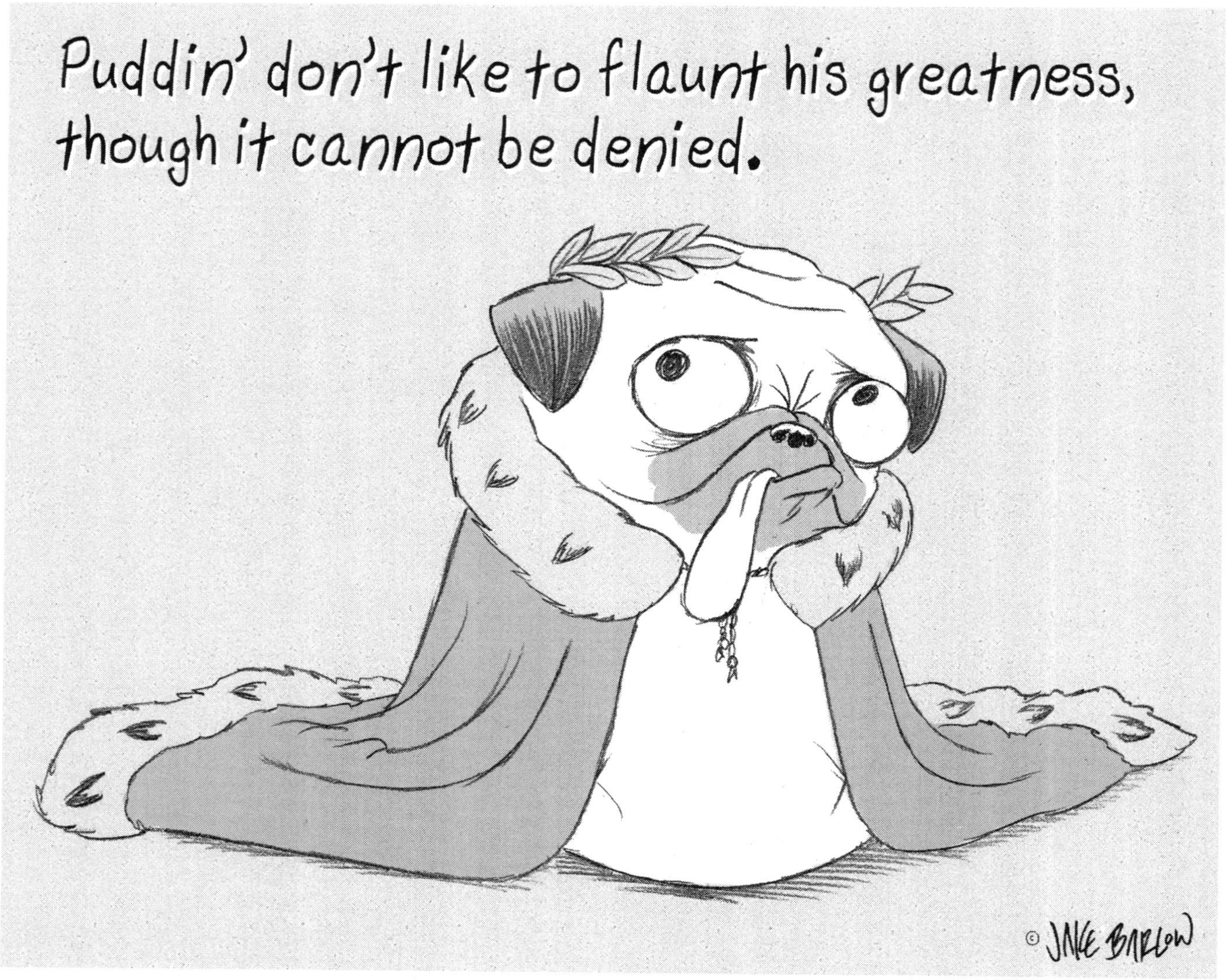
Puddin' don't like to flaunt his greatness, though it cannot be denied.
© JAKE BARLOW

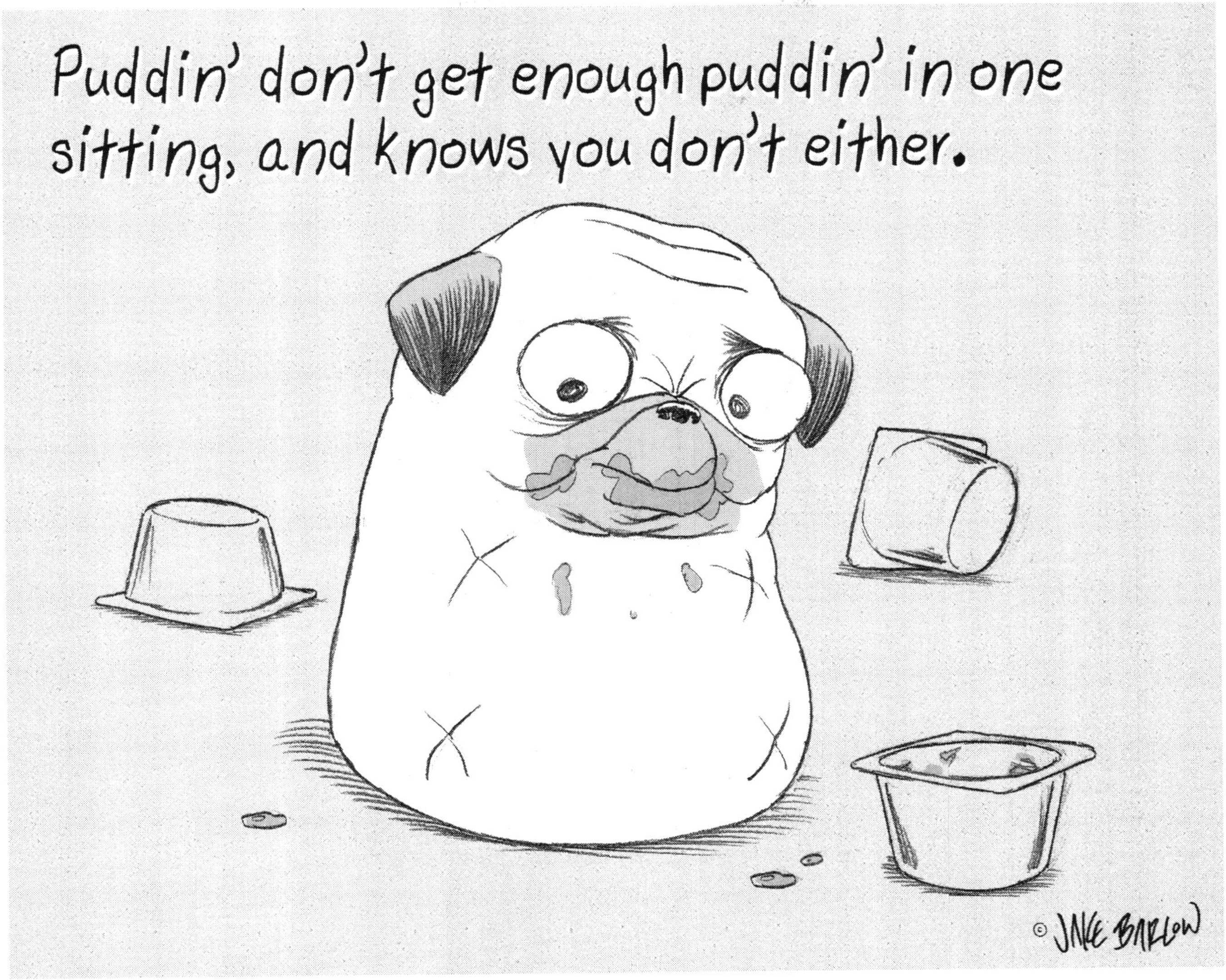
Puddin' don't get enough puddin' in one sitting, and knows you don't either.
© JAKE BARLOW

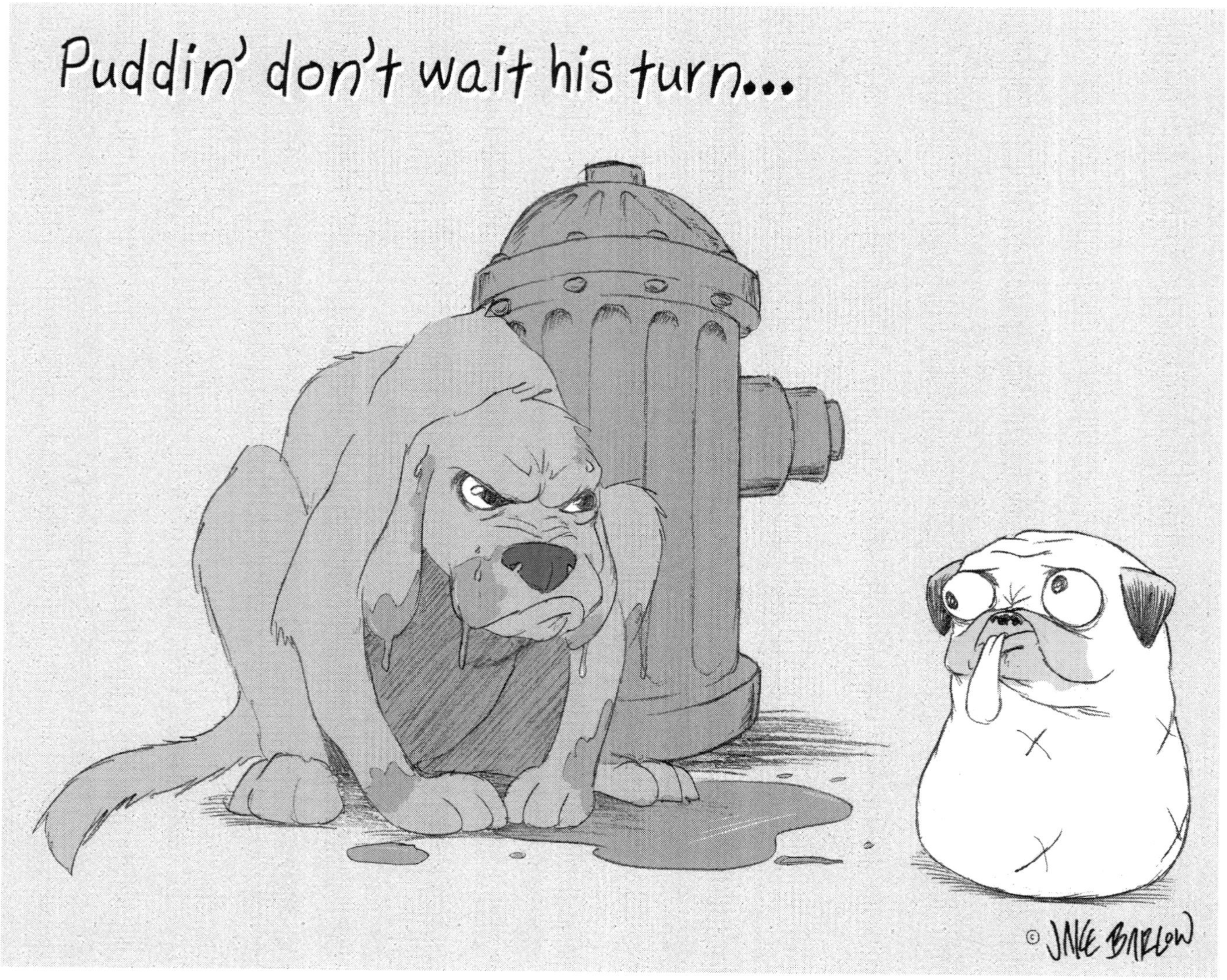
Puddin' don't wait his turn...
© JAKE BARLOW

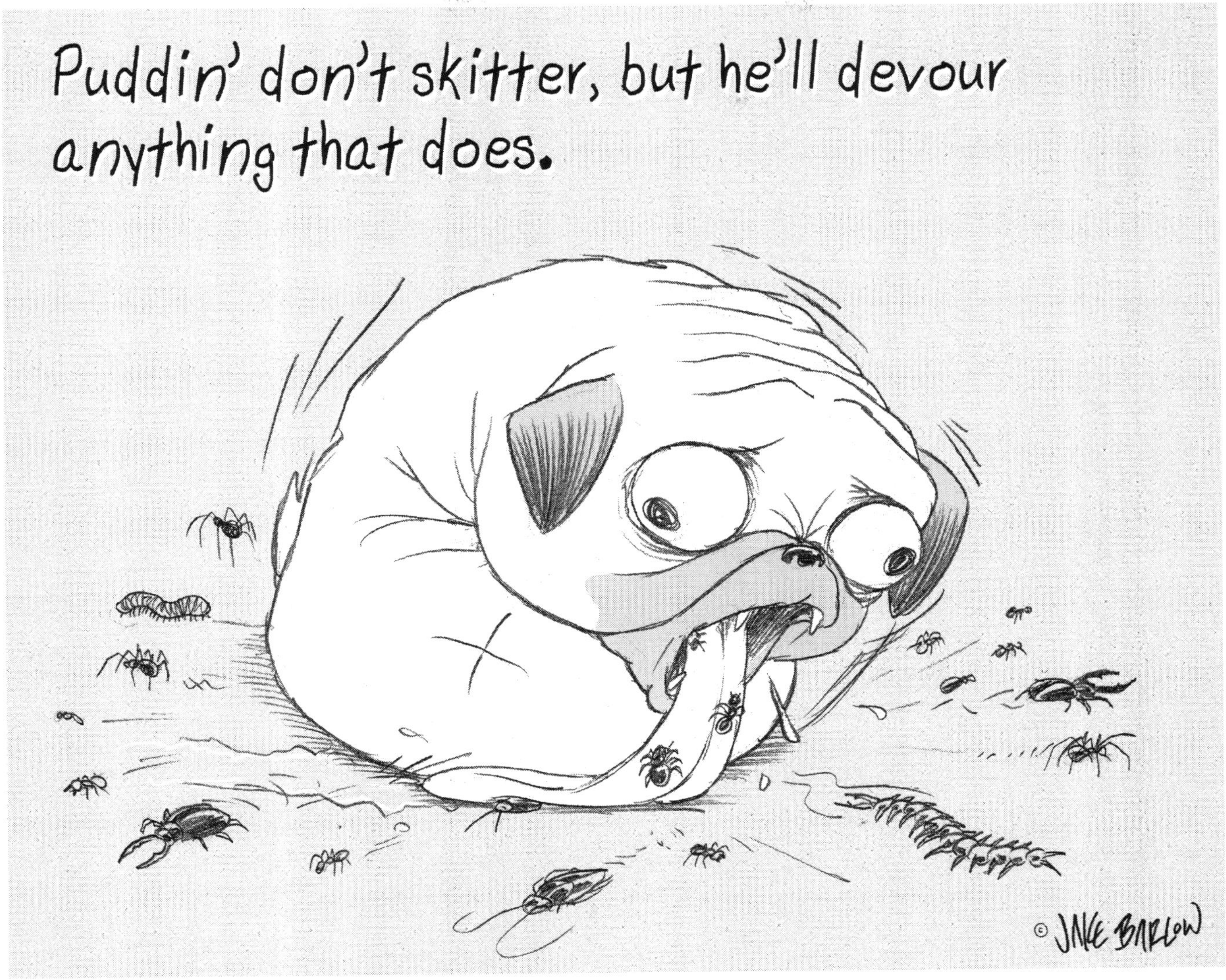
Puddin' don't skitter, but he'll devour anything that does.
© JAKE BARLOW

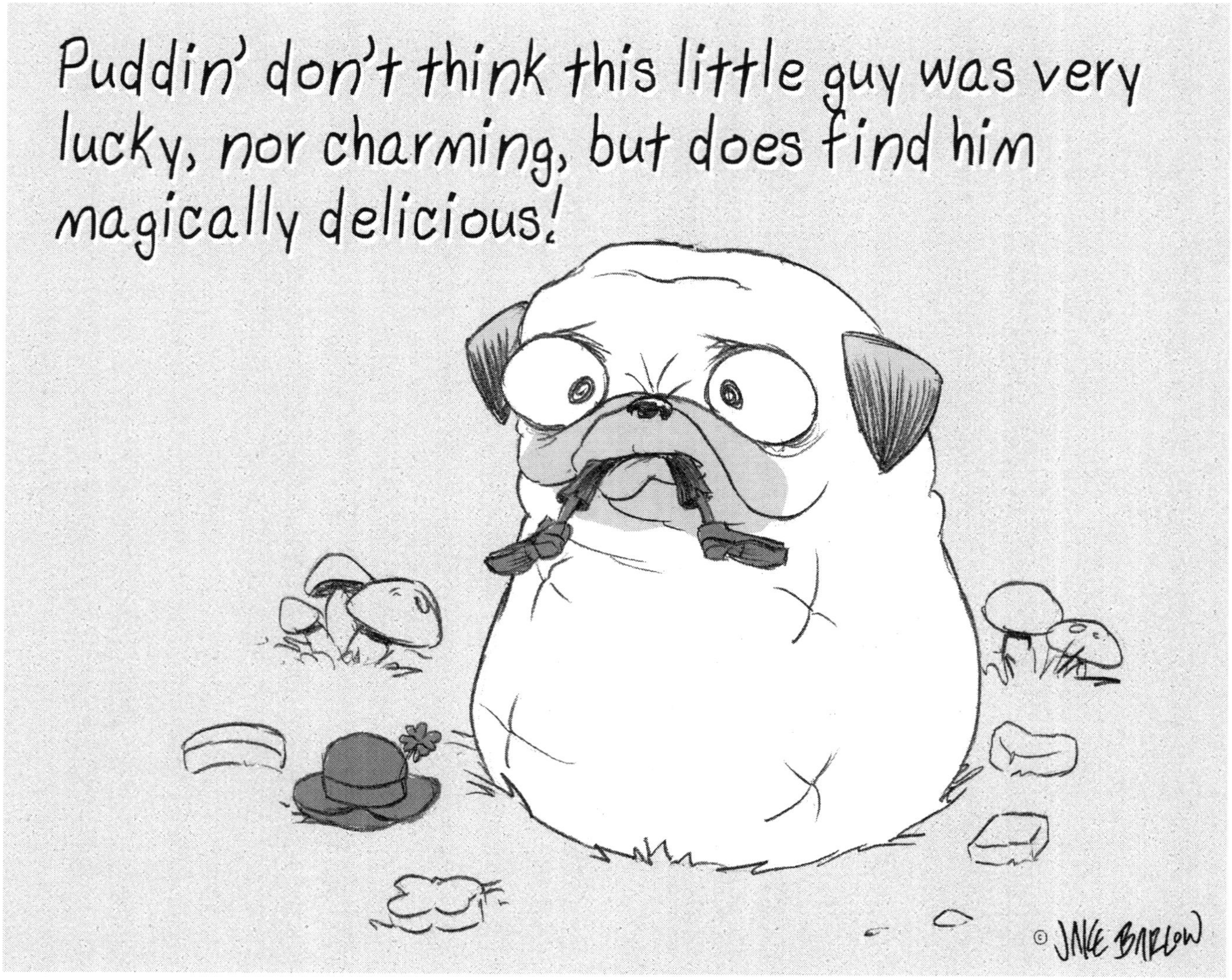
Puddin' don't think this little guy was very lucky, nor charming, but does find him magically delicious!
© JAKE BARLOW

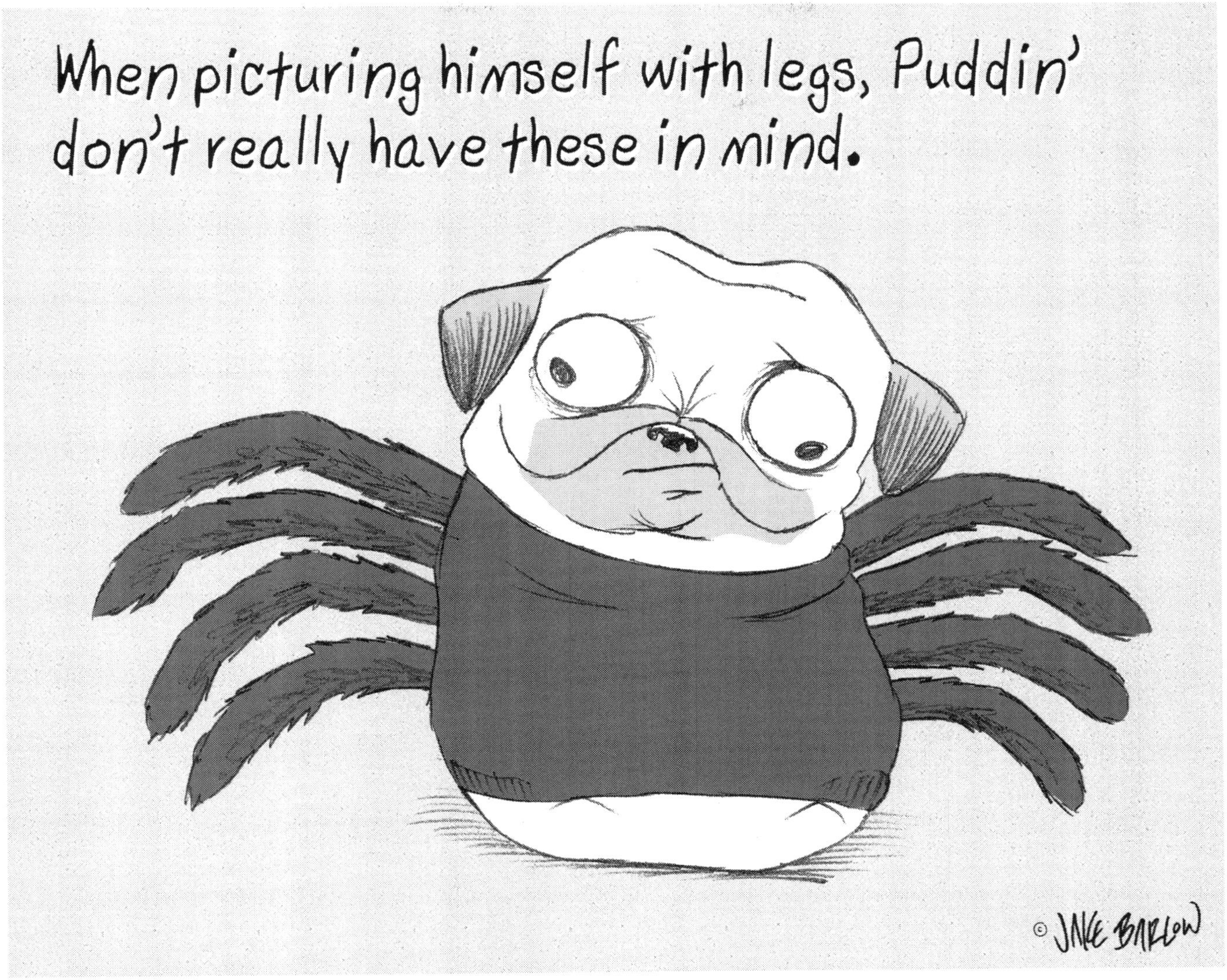
When picturing himself with legs, Puddin' don't really have these in mind.
© JAKE BARLOW

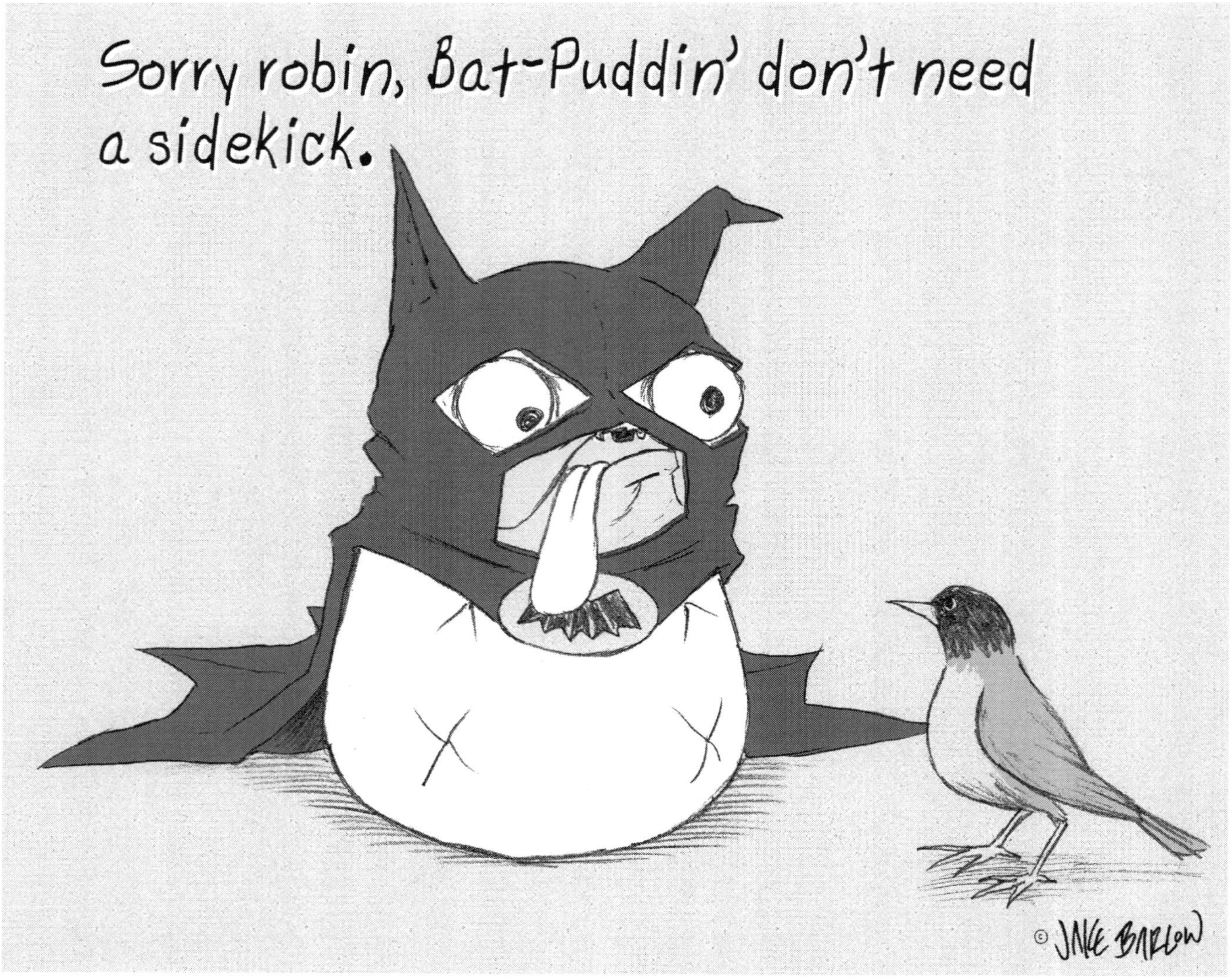
Sorry robin, Bat-Puddin' don't need a sidekick.
© JAKE BARLOW

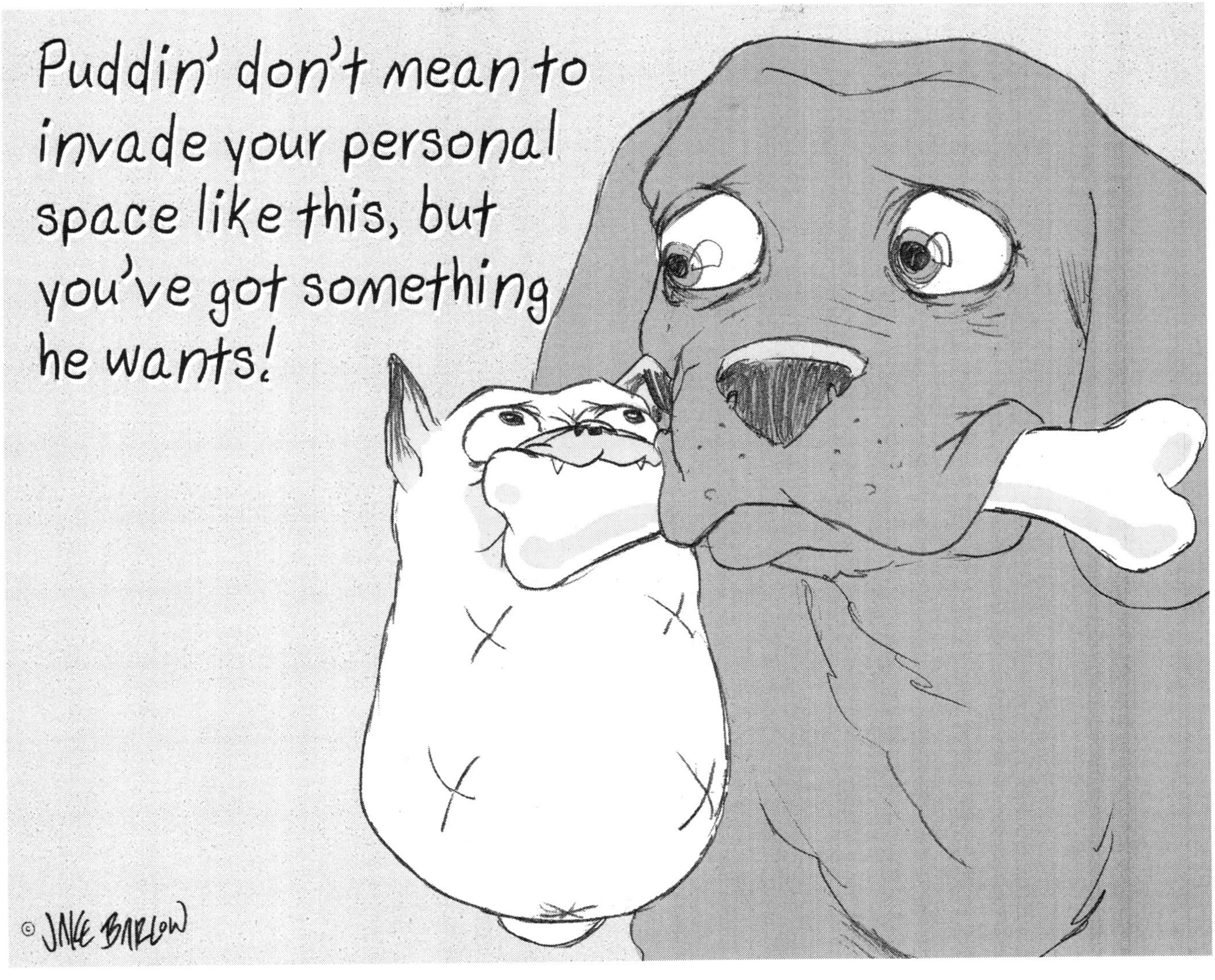
Puddin' don't mean to invade your personal space like this, but you've got something he wants!
© JAKE BARLOW

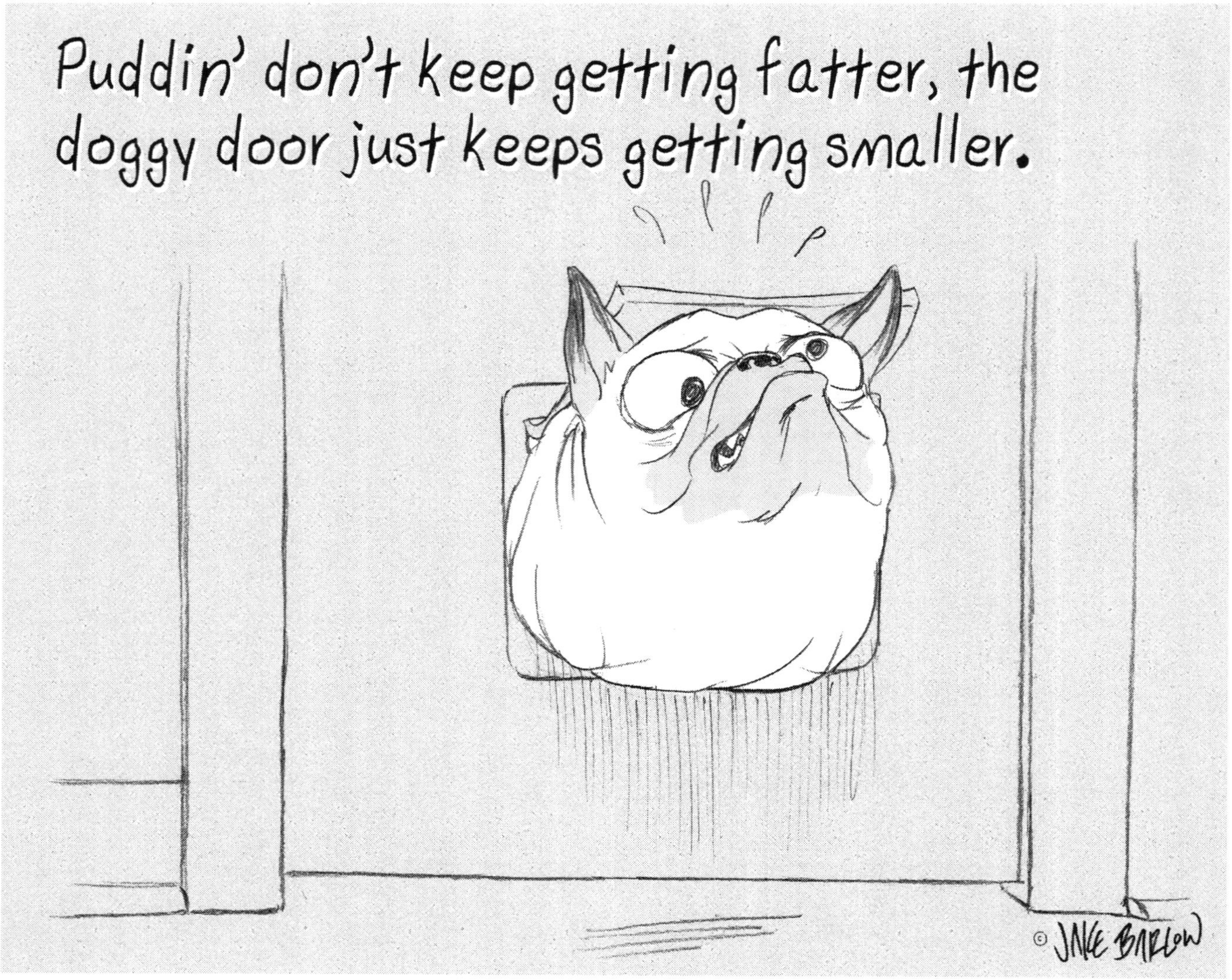
© JAKE BARLOW

Puddin' don't keep getting fatter, the doggy door just keeps getting smaller.

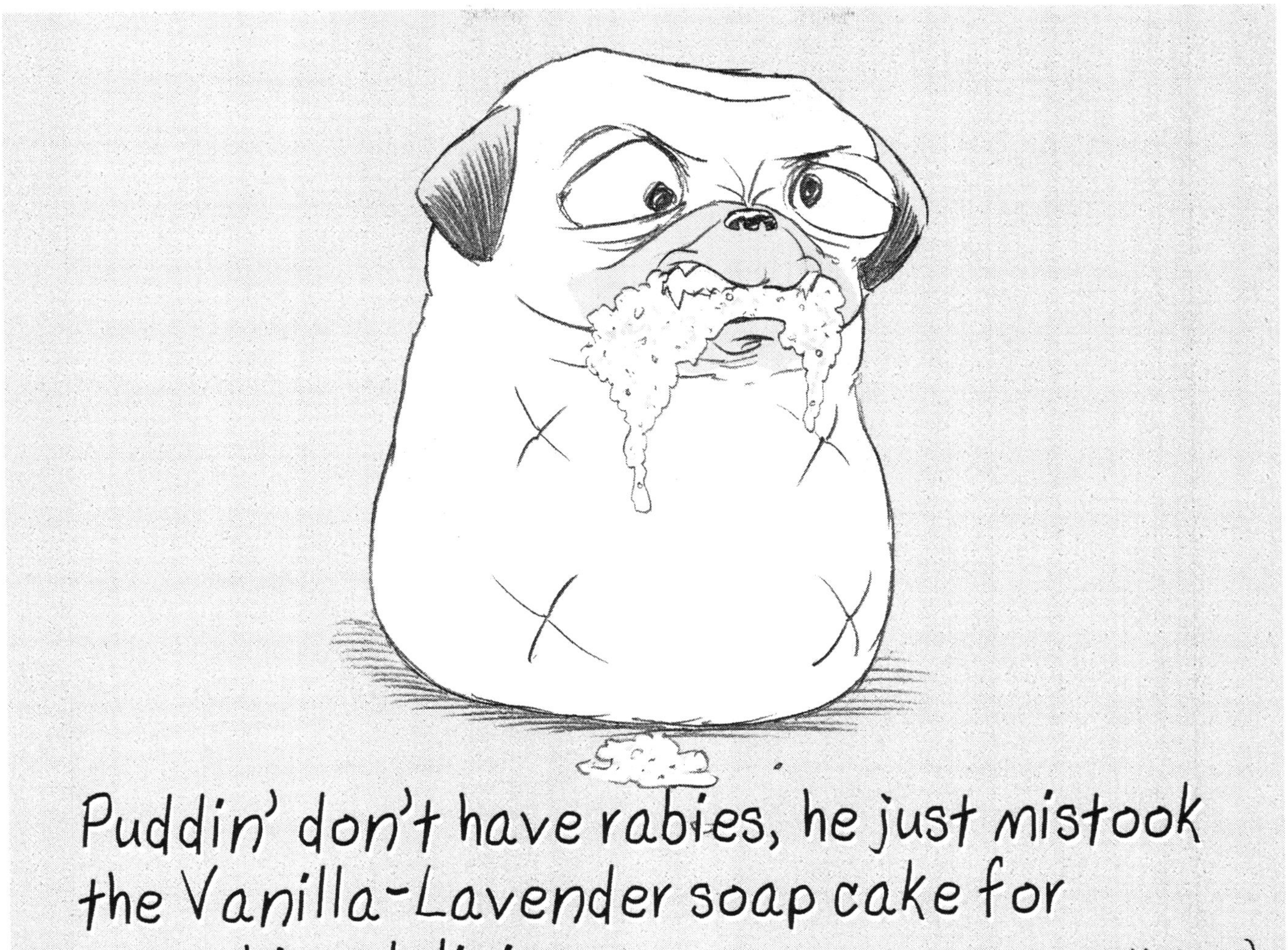
© JAKE BARLOW

Puddin' don't have rabies, he just mistook the Vanilla-Lavender soap cake for something delicious.

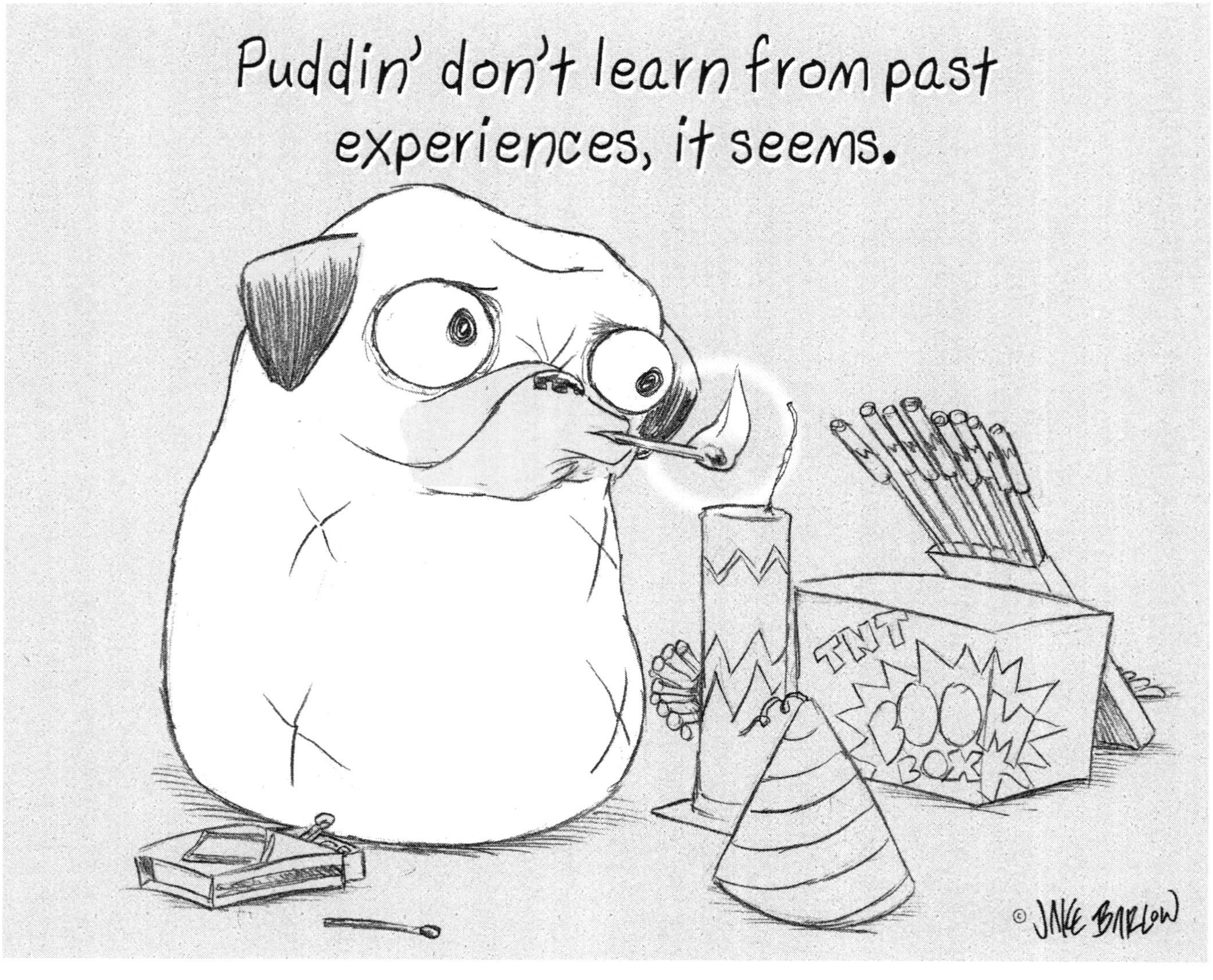
Puddin' don't learn from past experiences, it seems.
TNT
BOOM
BOX
© JAKE BARLOW

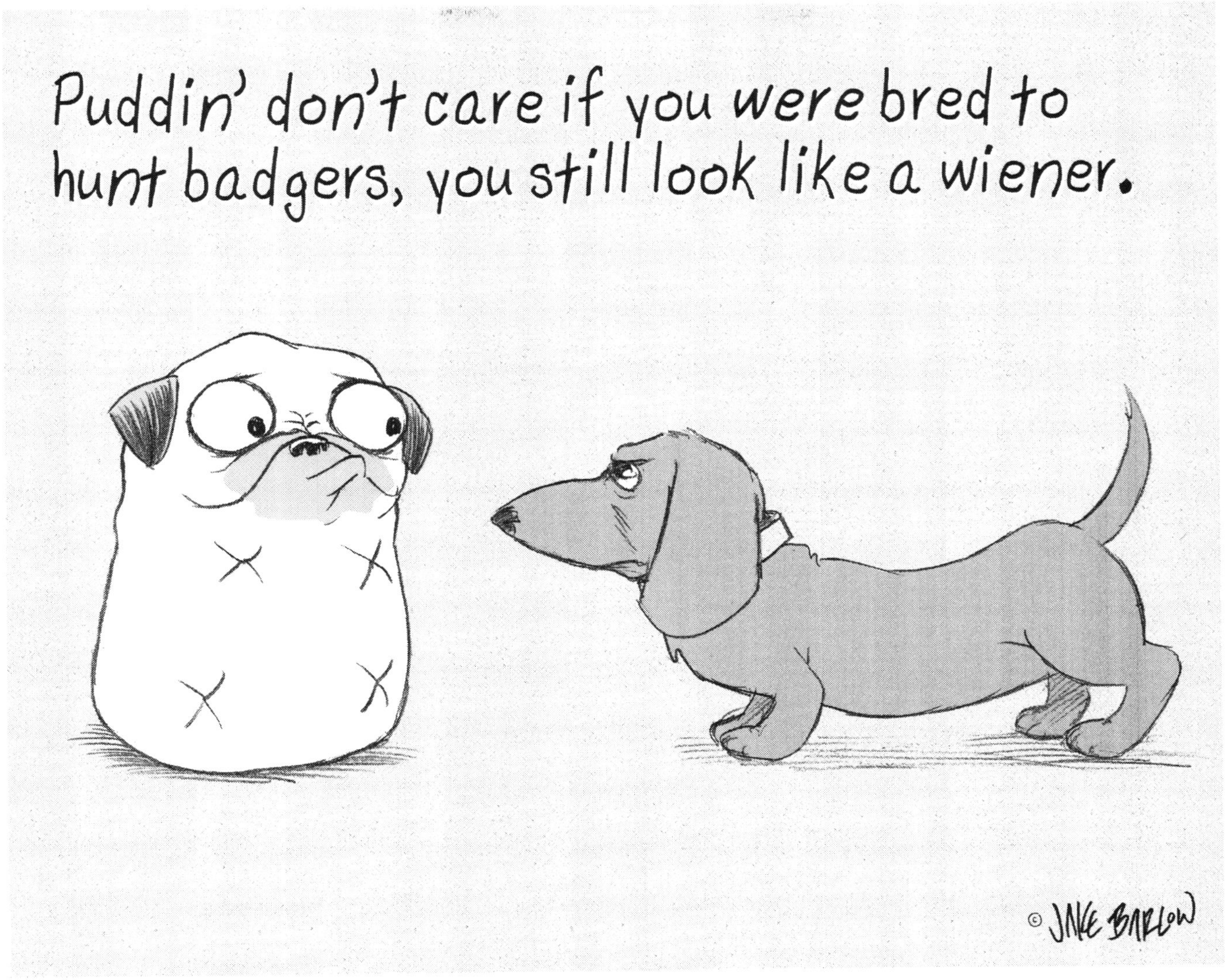
Puddin' don't care if you *were* bred to hunt badgers, you still look like a wiener.
© JAKE BARLOW

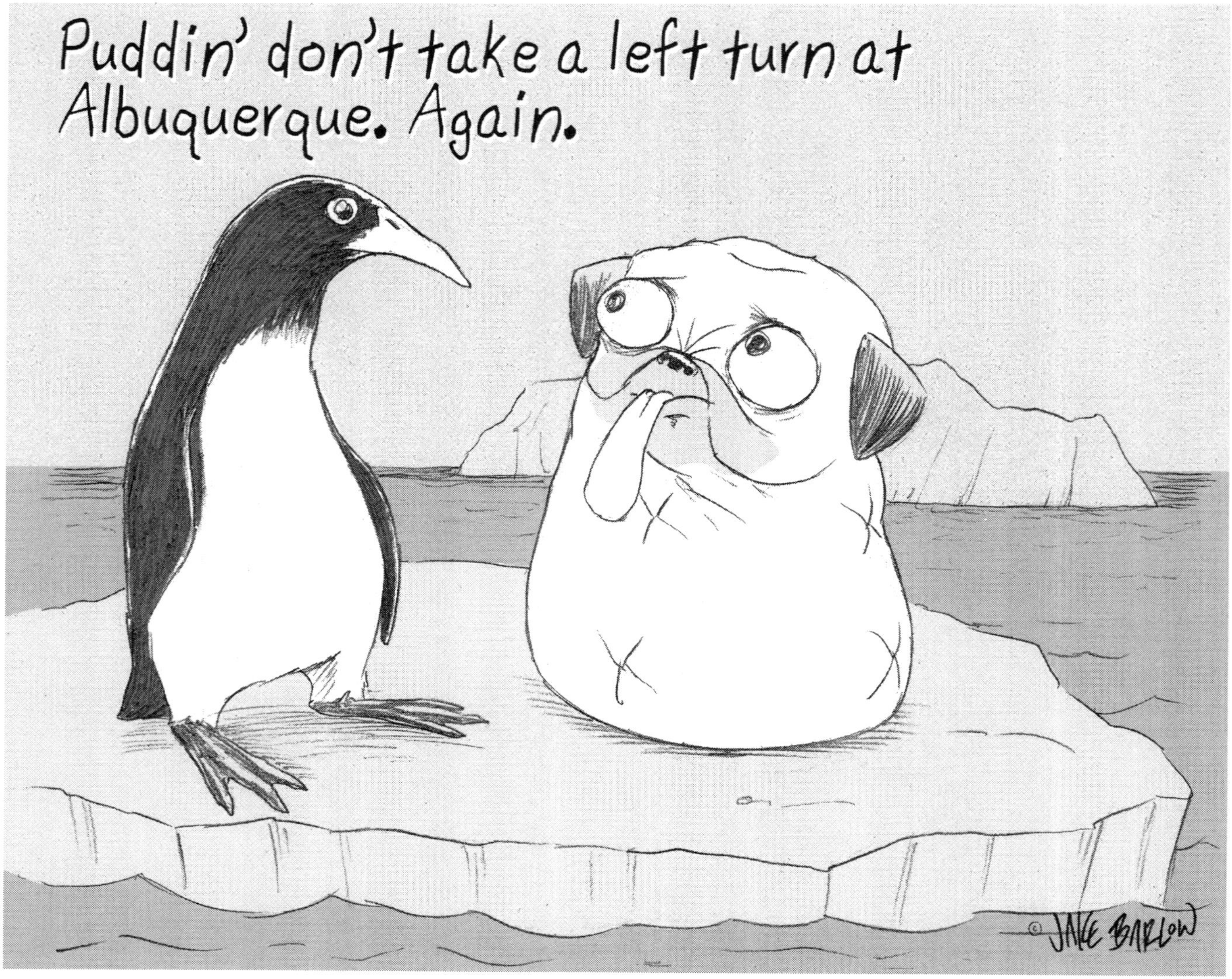
Puddin' don't take a left turn at
Albuquerque. Again.
© JAKE BARLOW

Moebius Puddin' don't begin, nor end.

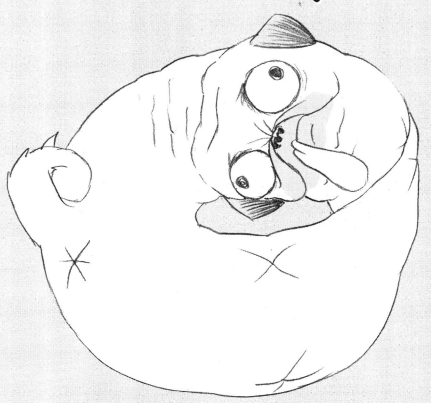

© JAKE BARLOW

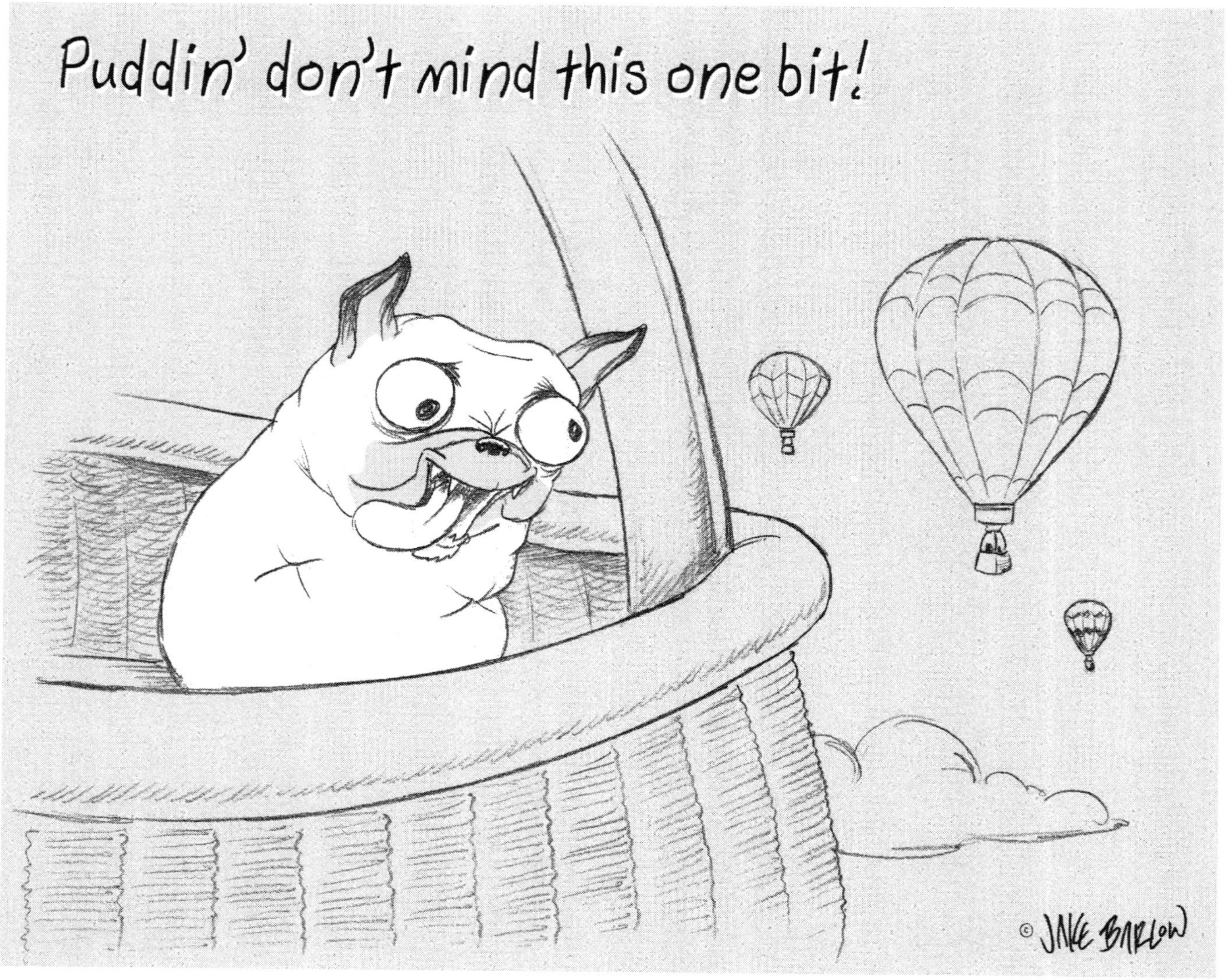
Puddin' don't mind this one bit!
© JAKE BARLOW

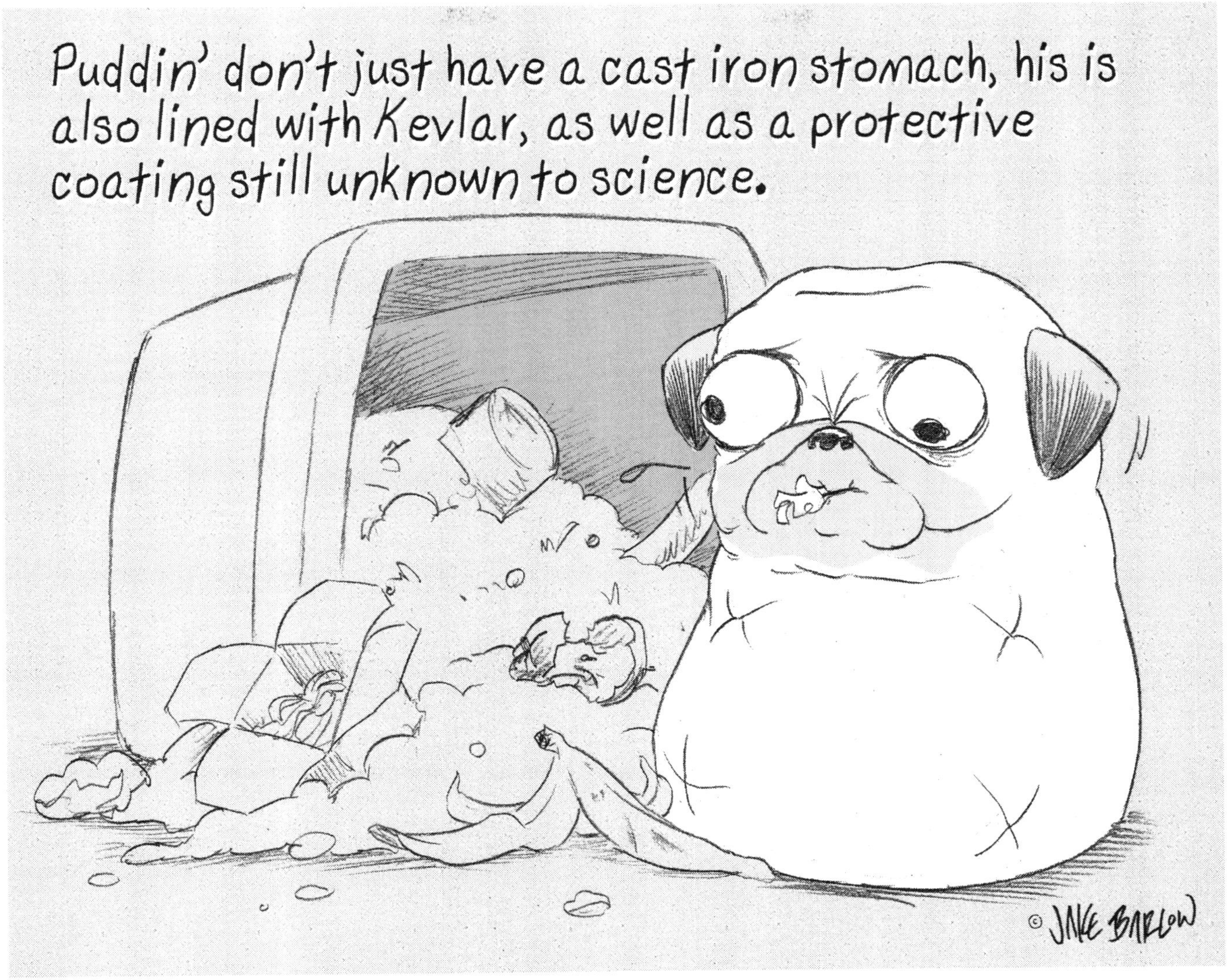
Puddin' don't just have a cast iron stomach, his is also lined with Kevlar, as well as a protective coating still unknown to science.
© JAKE BARLOW

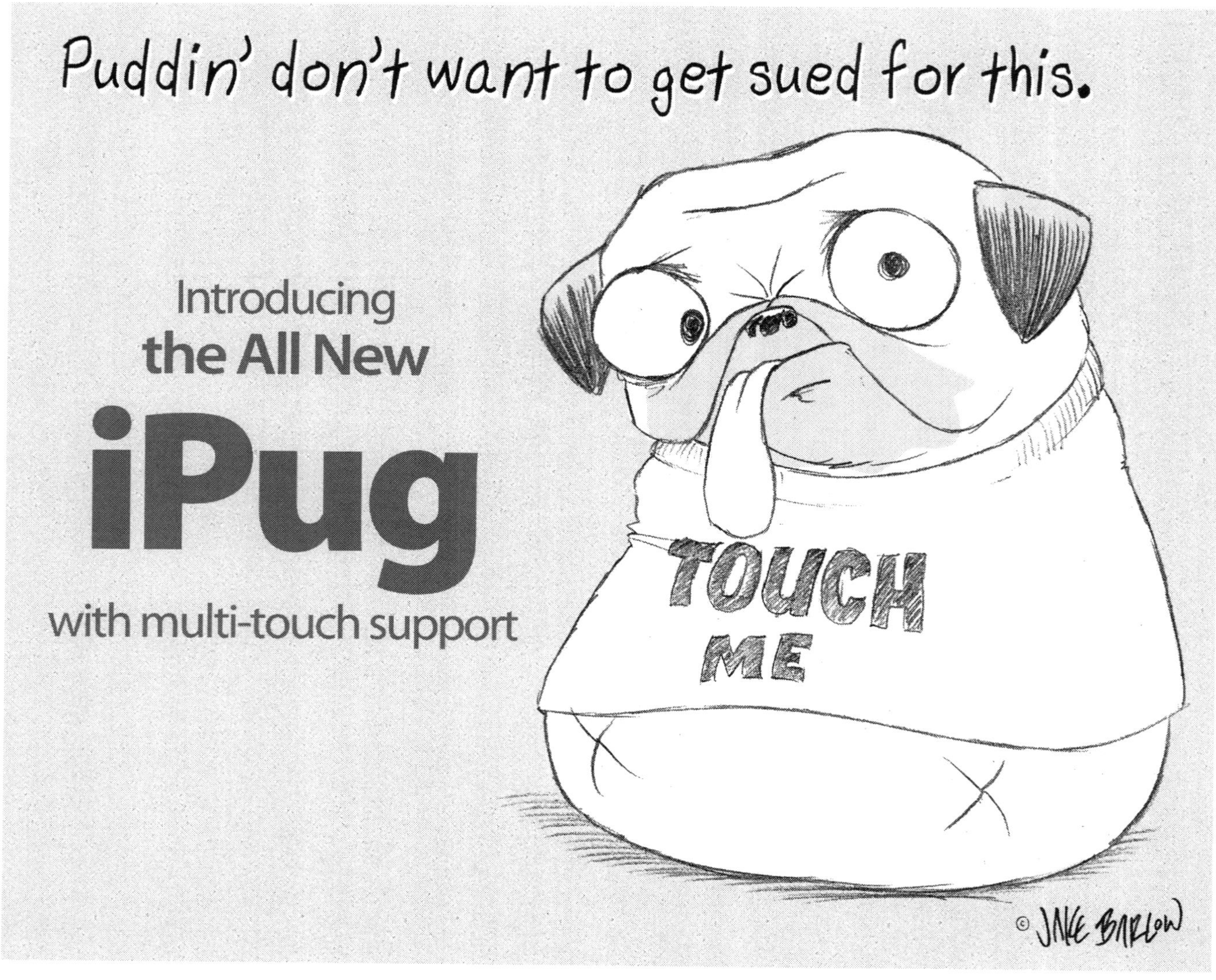
Puddin' don't want to get sued for this.
Introducing
the All New
iPug
with multi-touch support
TOUCH
ME
© JAKE BARLOW

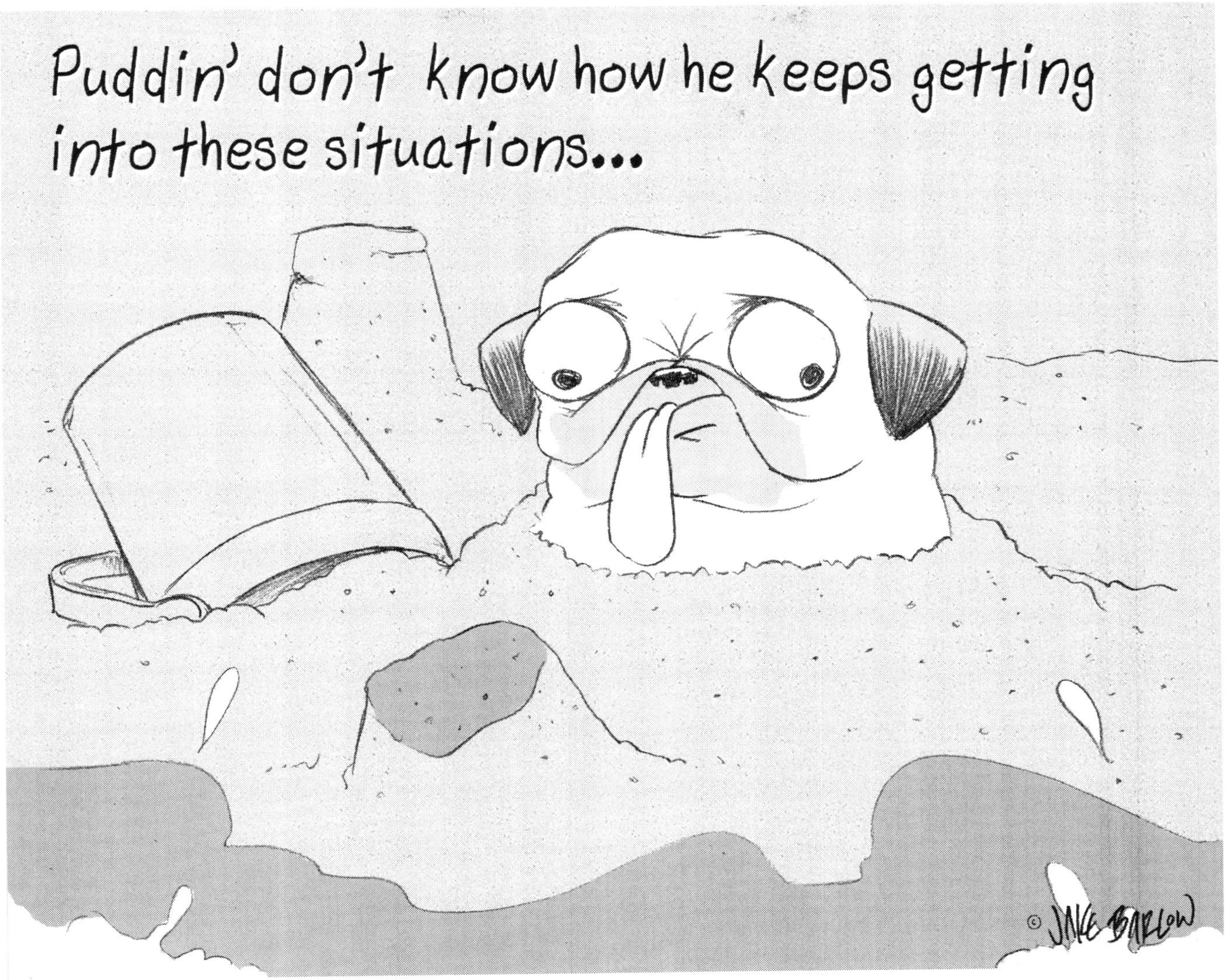
Puddin' don't know how he keeps getting into these situations...
© JAKE BARLOW

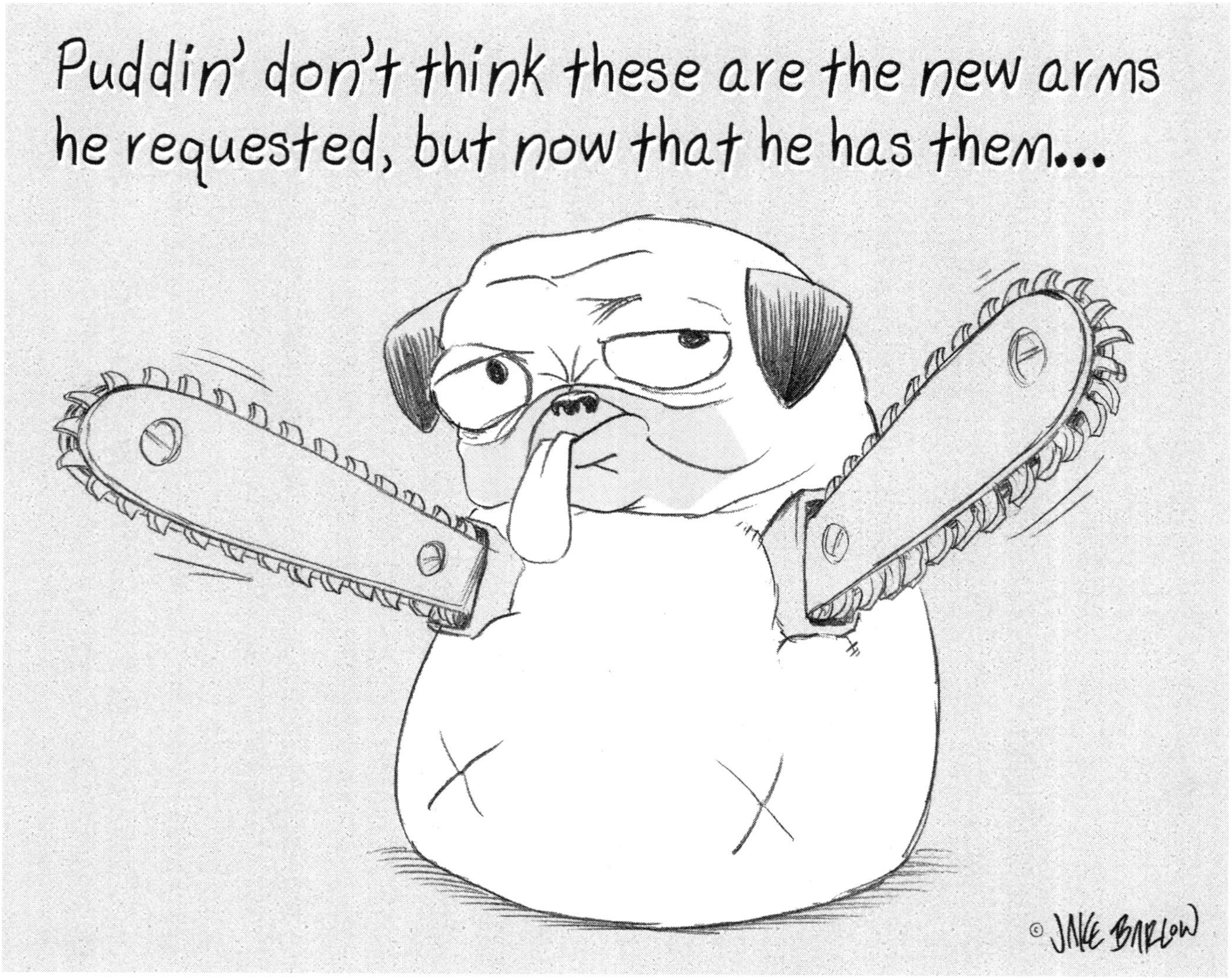
Puddin' don't think these are the new arms he requested, but now that he has them...
© JAKE BARLOW

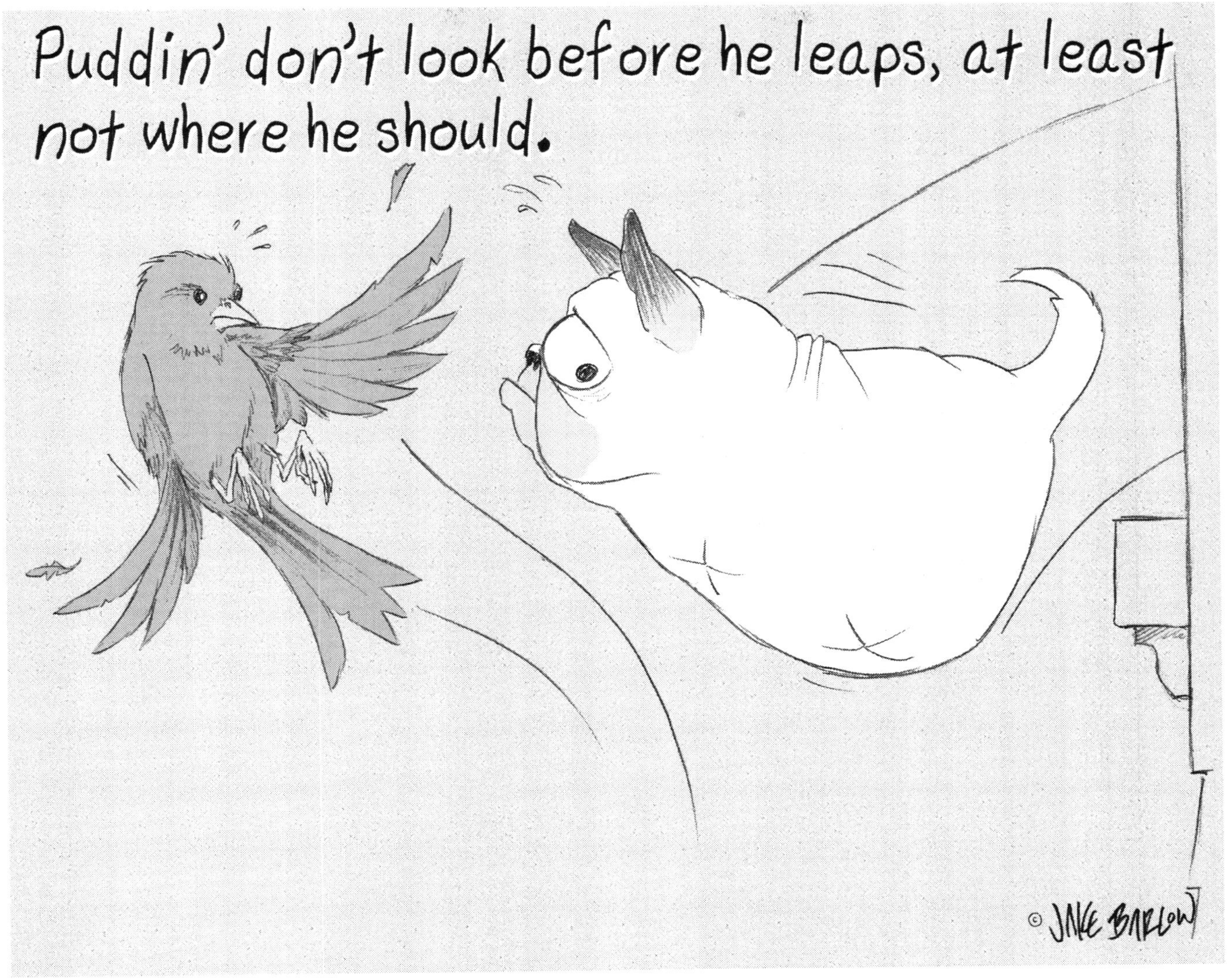
Puddin' don't look before he leaps, at least not where he should.
© JAKE BARLOW

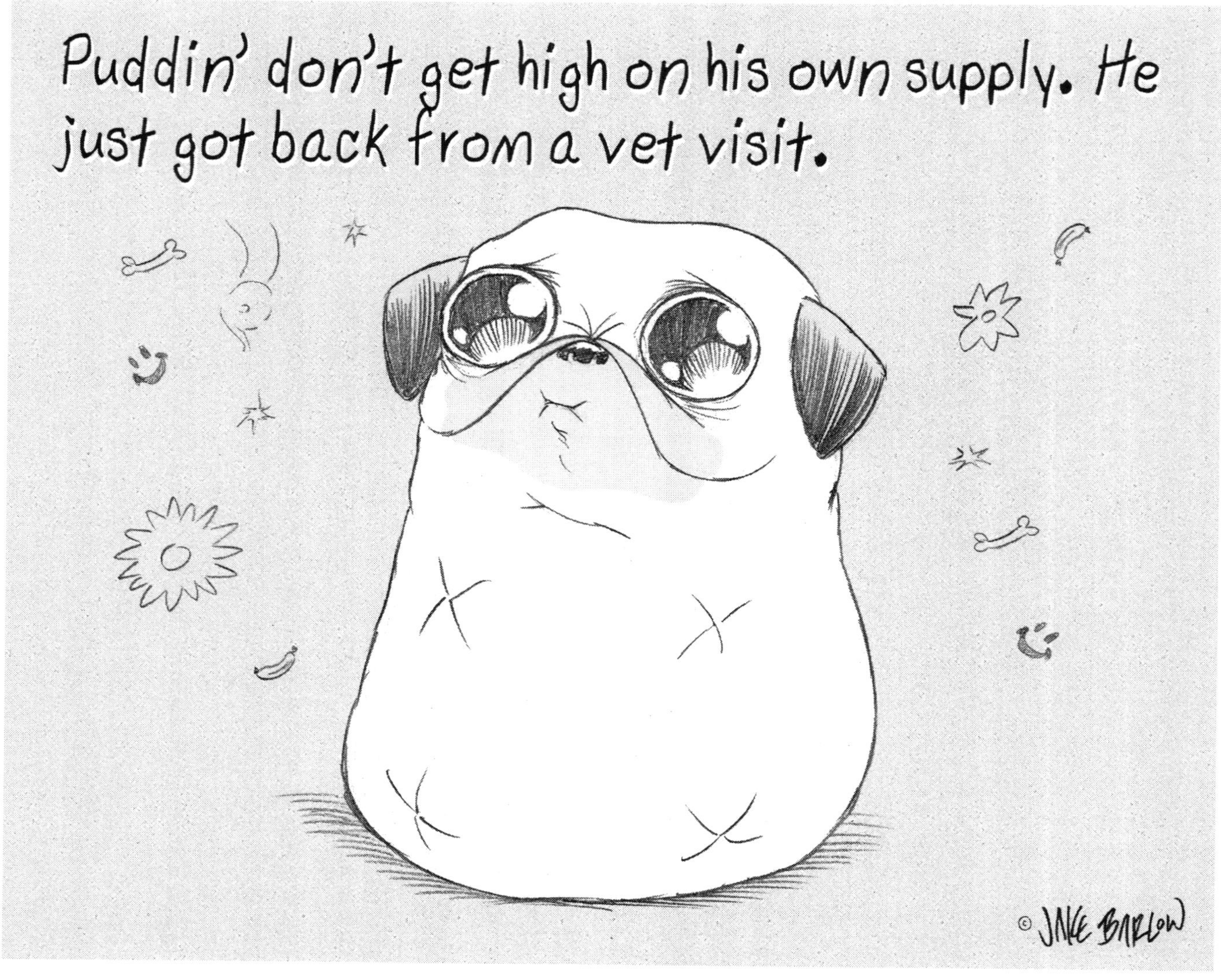
Puddin' don't get high on his own supply. He just got back from a vet visit.
© JAKE BARLOW

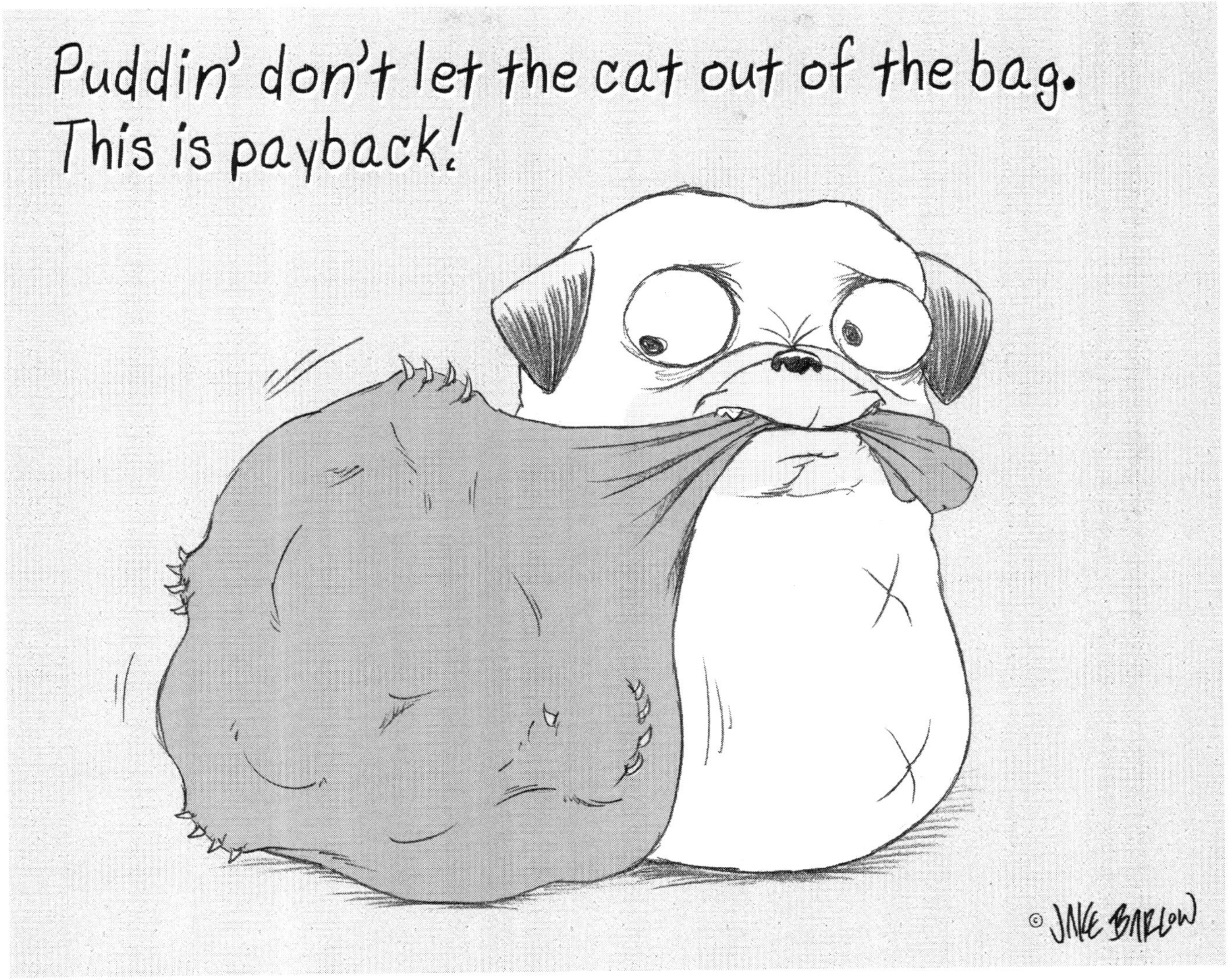
Puddin' don't let the cat out of the bag.
This is payback!
© JAKE BARLOW

Puddin' don't think handball is the sport for him.

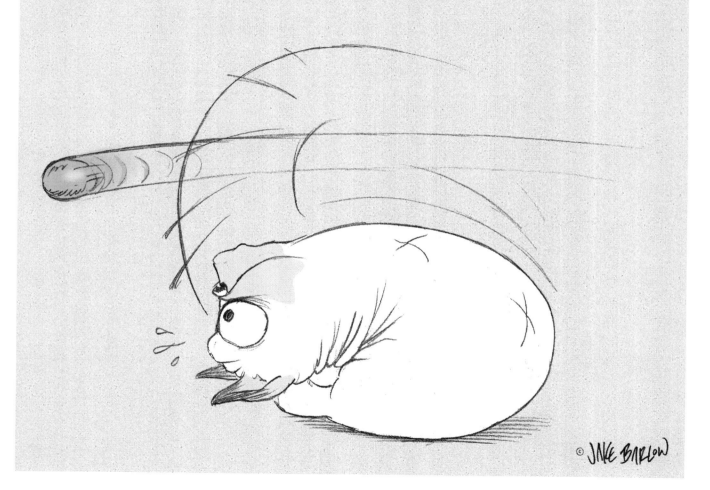

© JAKE BARLOW

Puddin' don't rise, nor shine - at least not on Mondays.

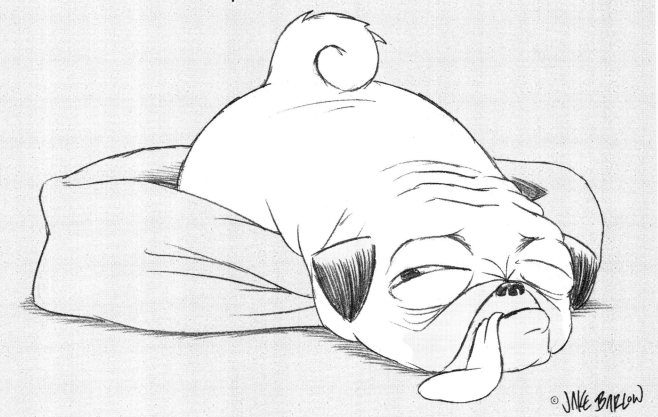

Puddin' don't know how he's gonna land this thing, but that's not really on his mind at this moment!

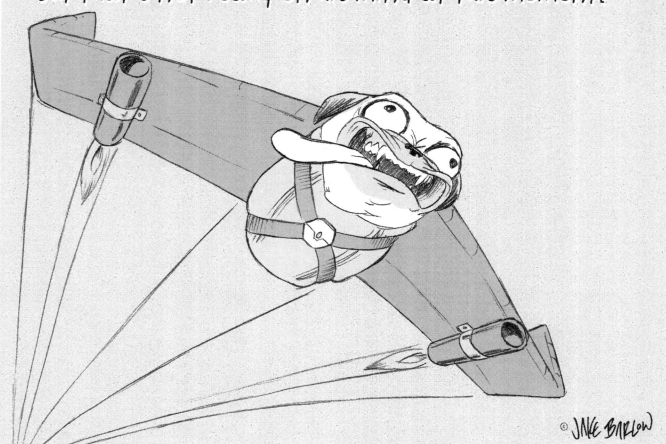

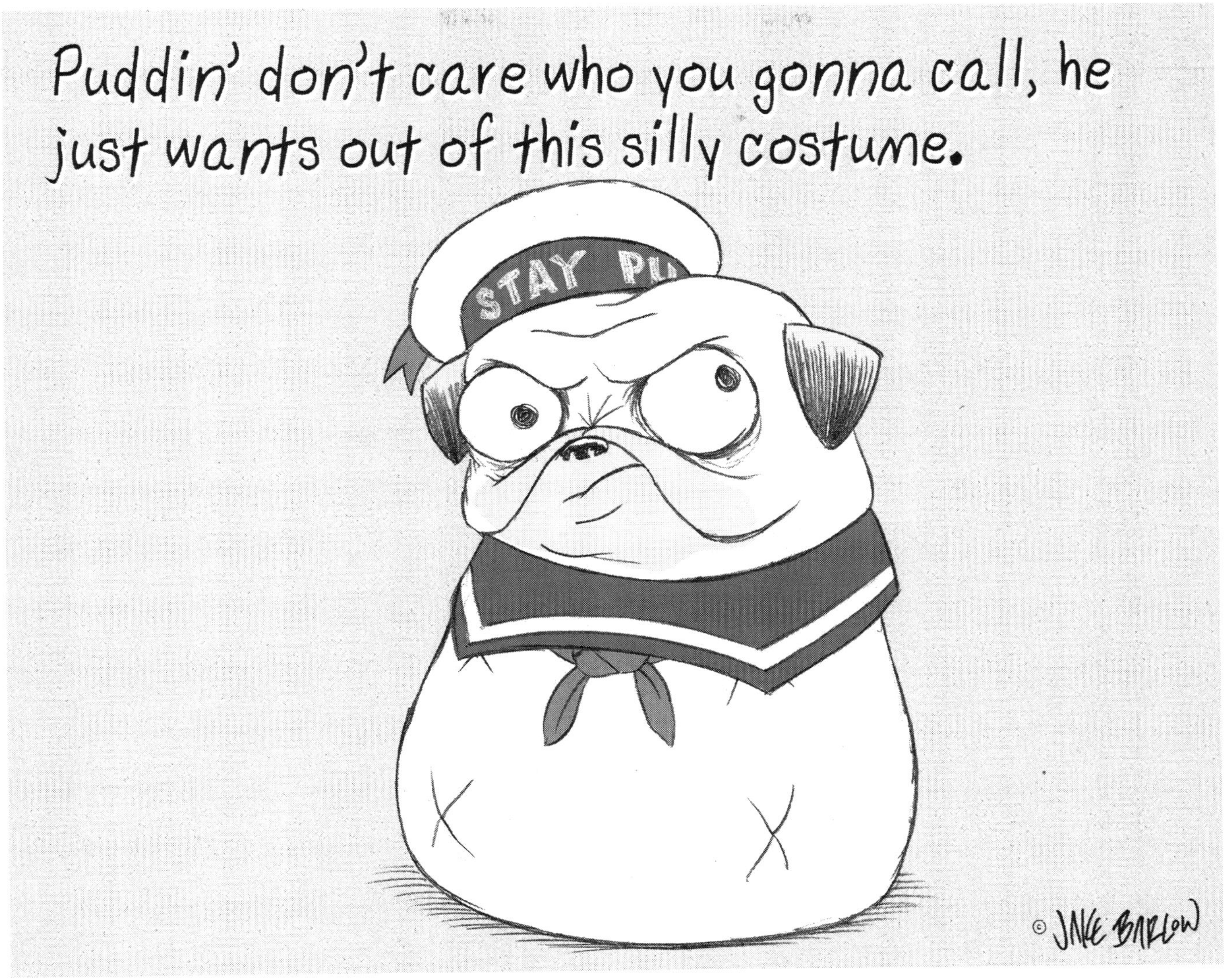
Puddin' don't care who you gonna call, he just wants out of this silly costume.
STAY PU
© JAKE BARLOW

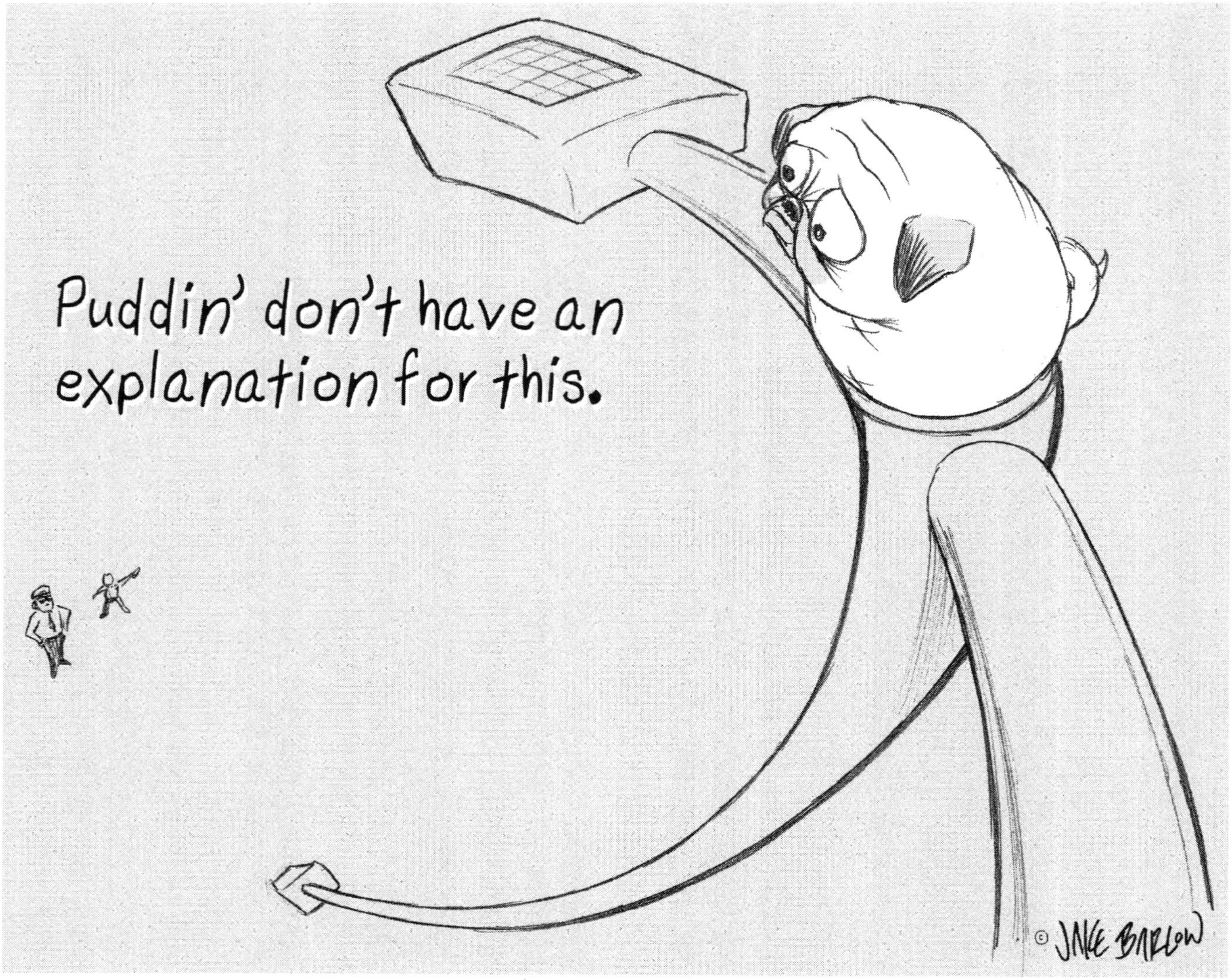
Puddin' don't have an explanation for this.
© JAKE BARLOW

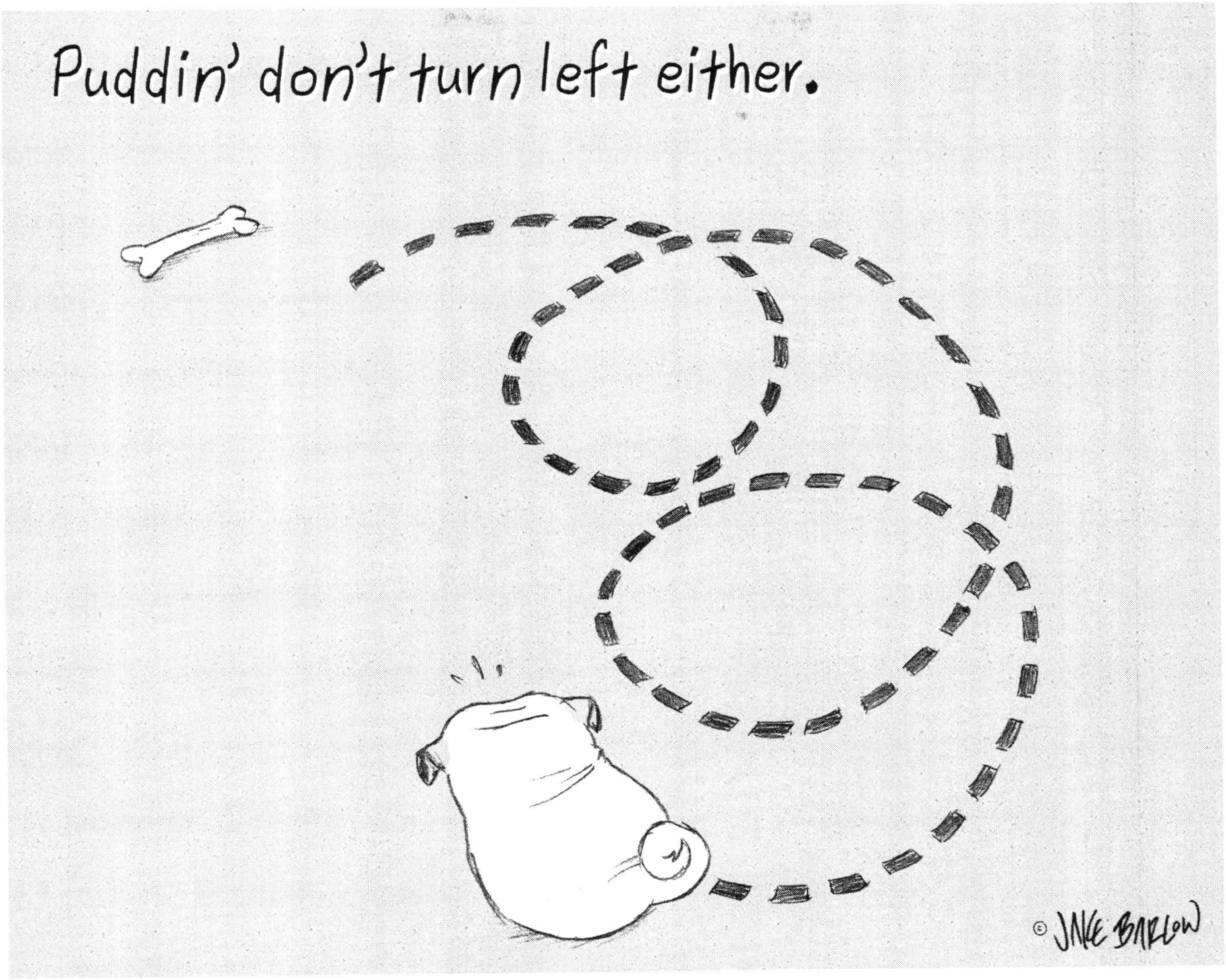

Puddin' don't turn left either.
© JAKE BARLOW

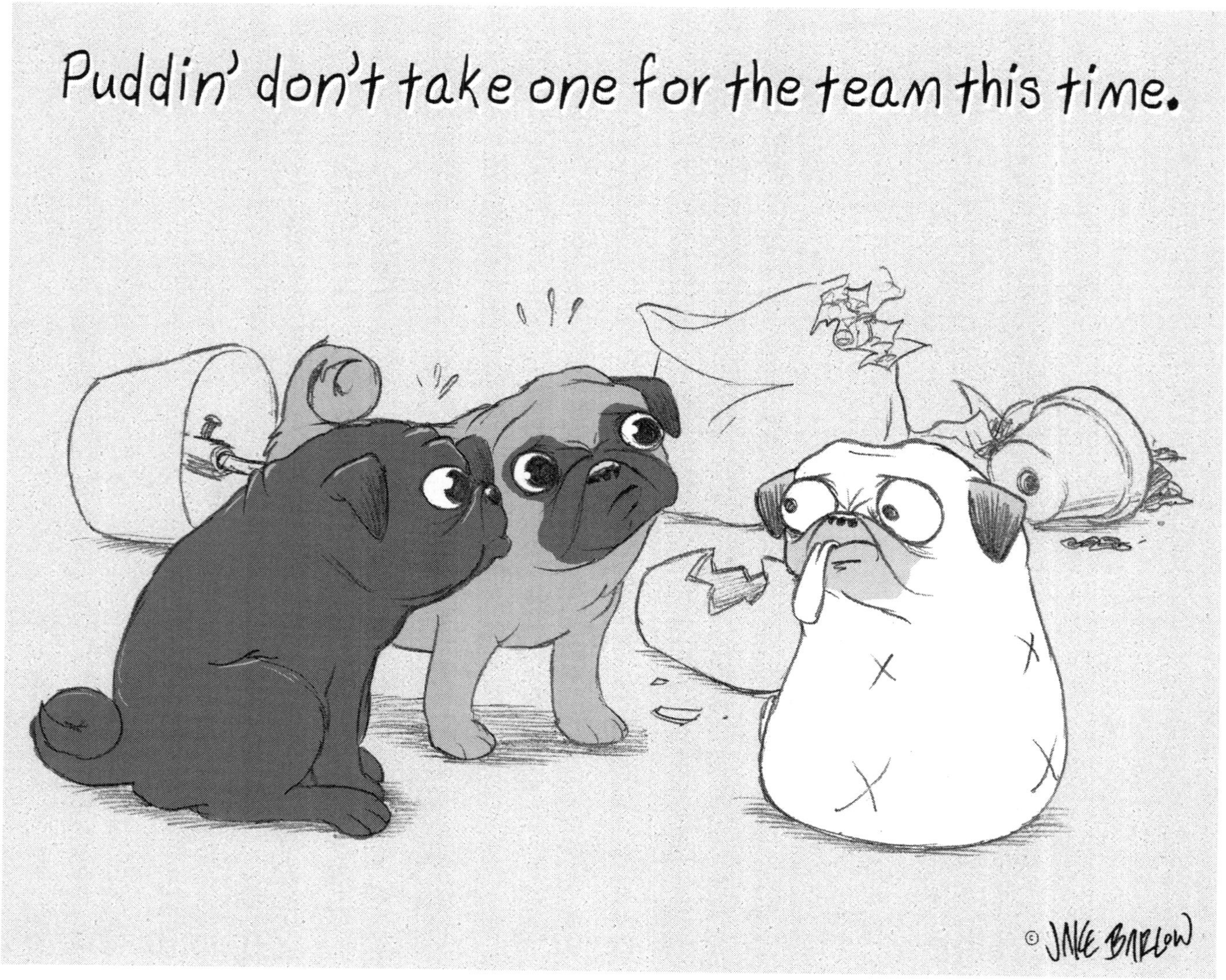
Puddin' don't take one for the team this time.
© JAKE BARLOW

Puddin' don't really know what's going on here, either.

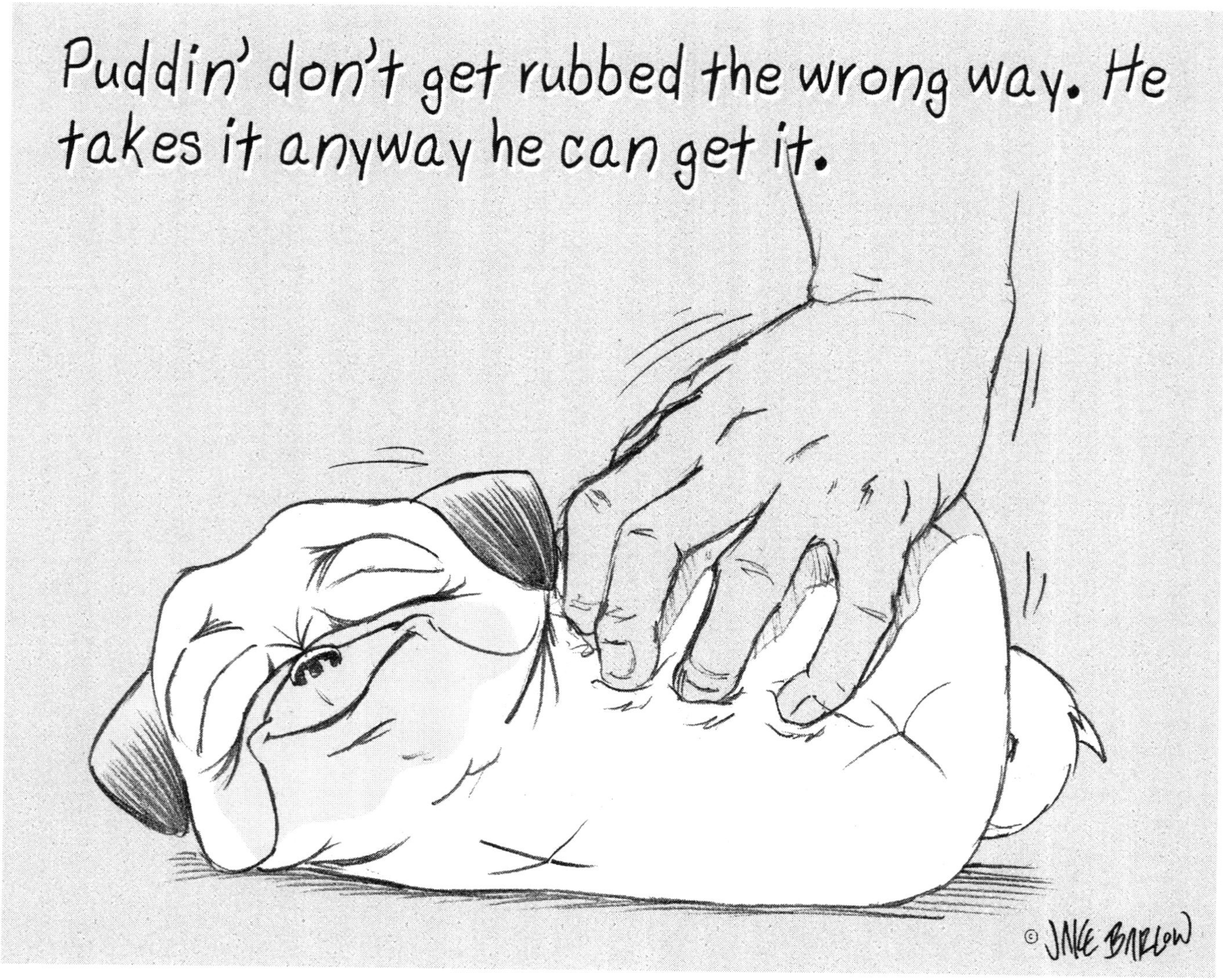
Puddin' don't get rubbed the wrong way. He takes it anyway he can get it.
© JAKE BARLOW

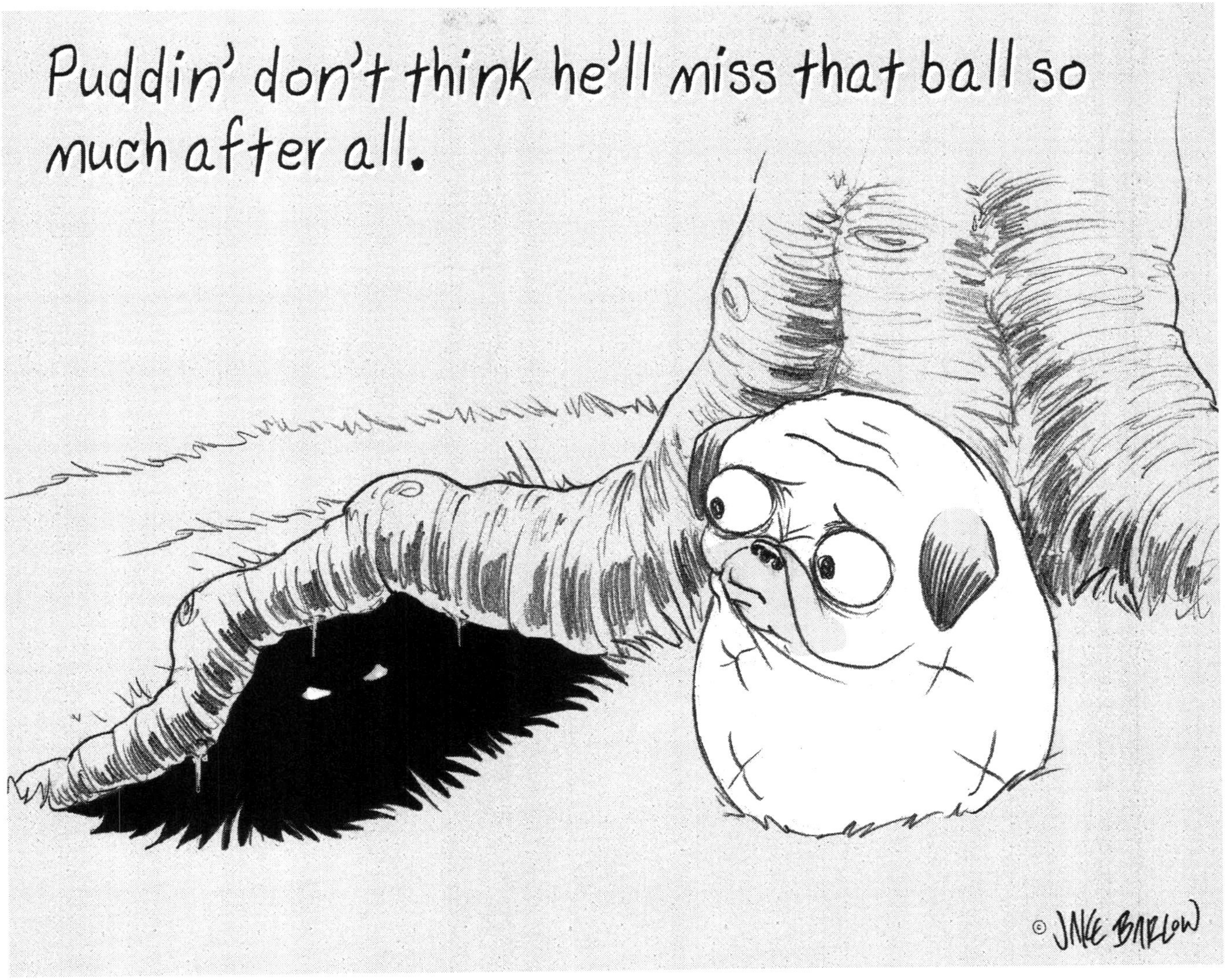
Puddin' don't think he'll miss that ball so much after all.
© JAKE BARLOW

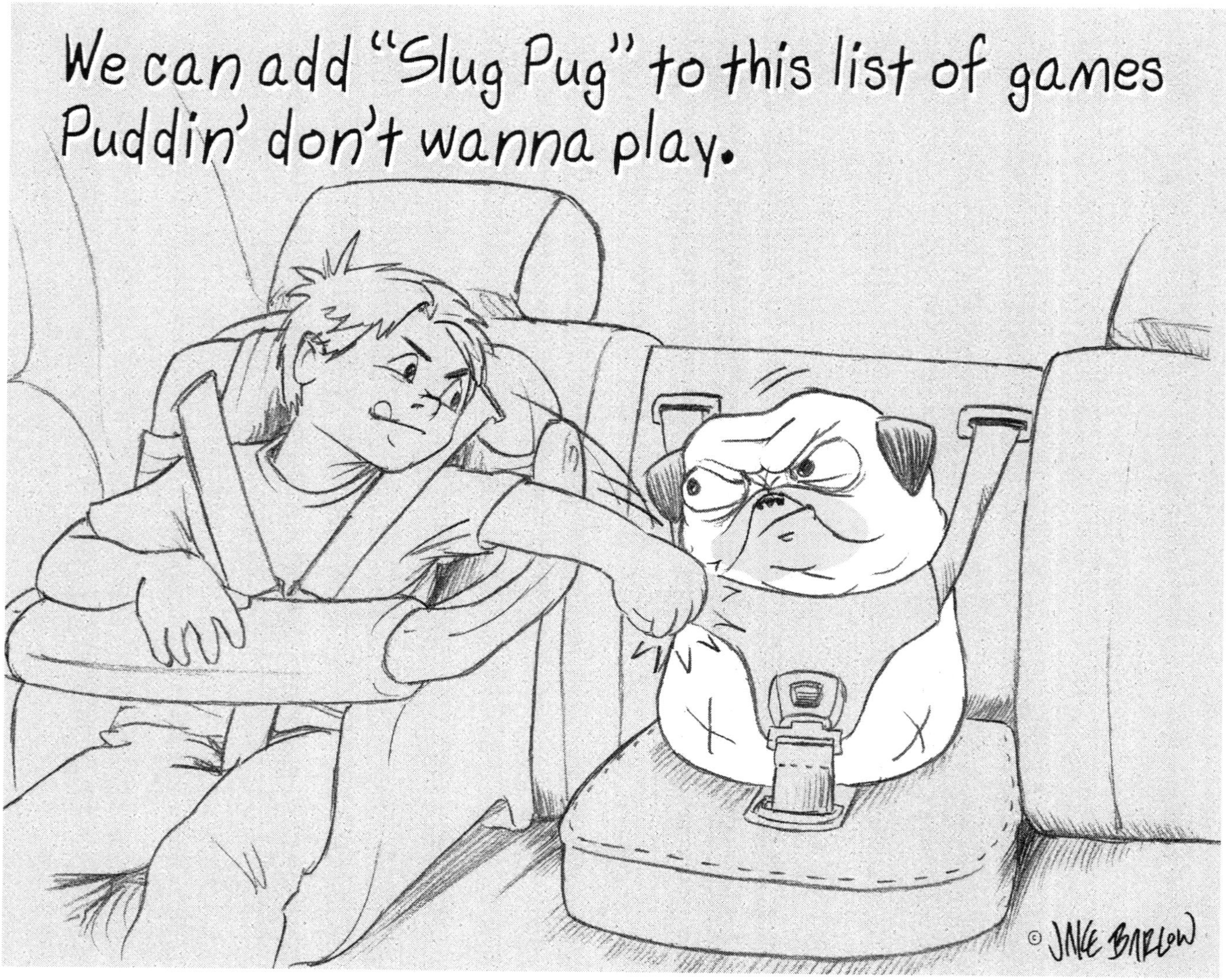
We can add "Slug Pug" to this list of games
Puddin' don't wanna play.
© JAKE BARLOW

Puddin' don't normally ride bareback...

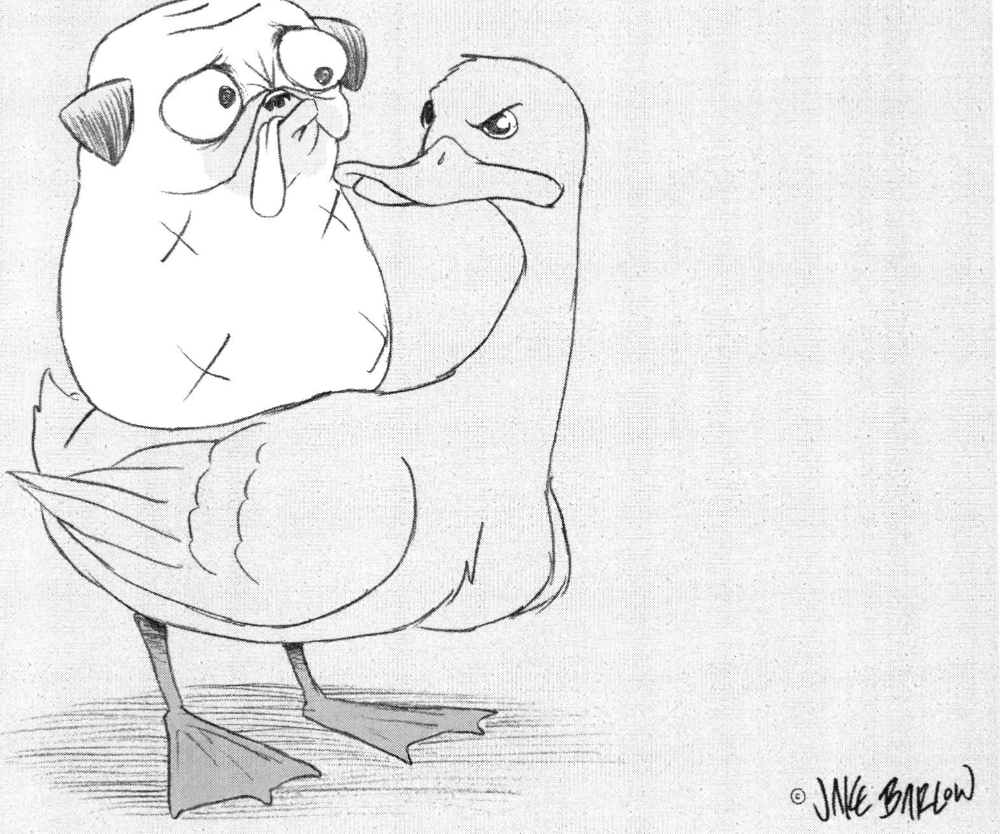
© JAKE BARLOW

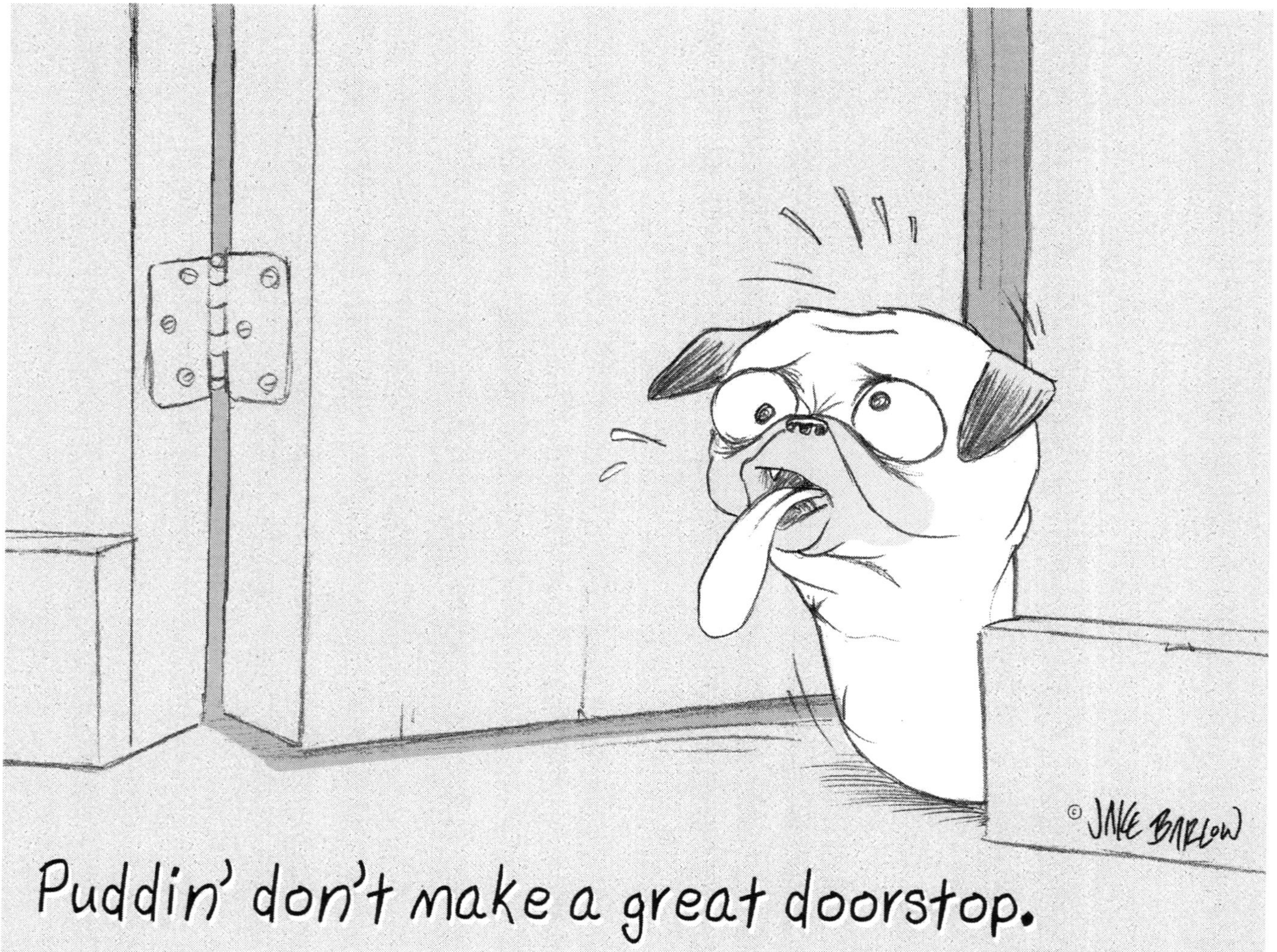
© JAKE BARLOW

Puddin' don't make a great doorstop.

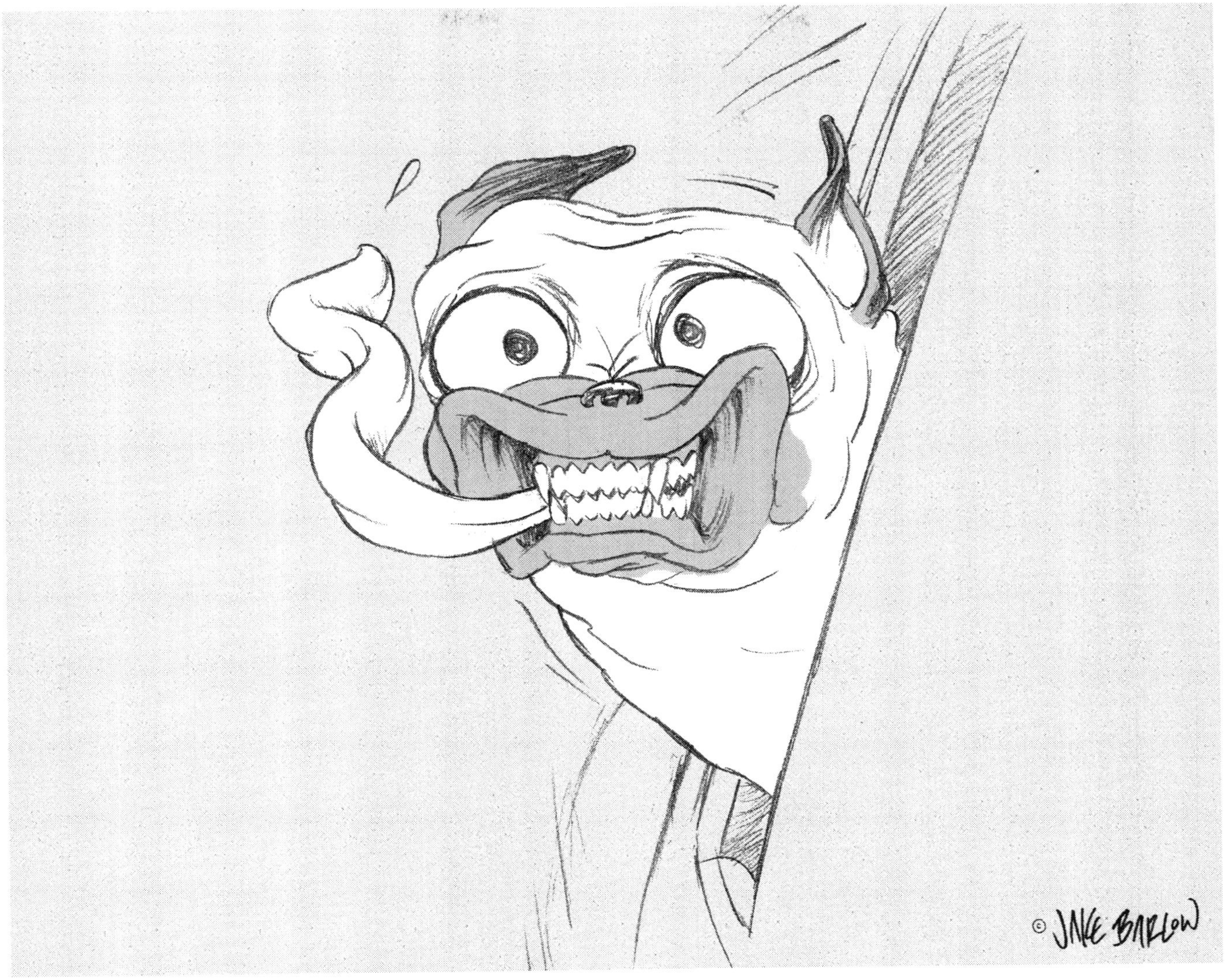
© JAKE BARLOW

Puddin' don't want to spoil this moment with words.

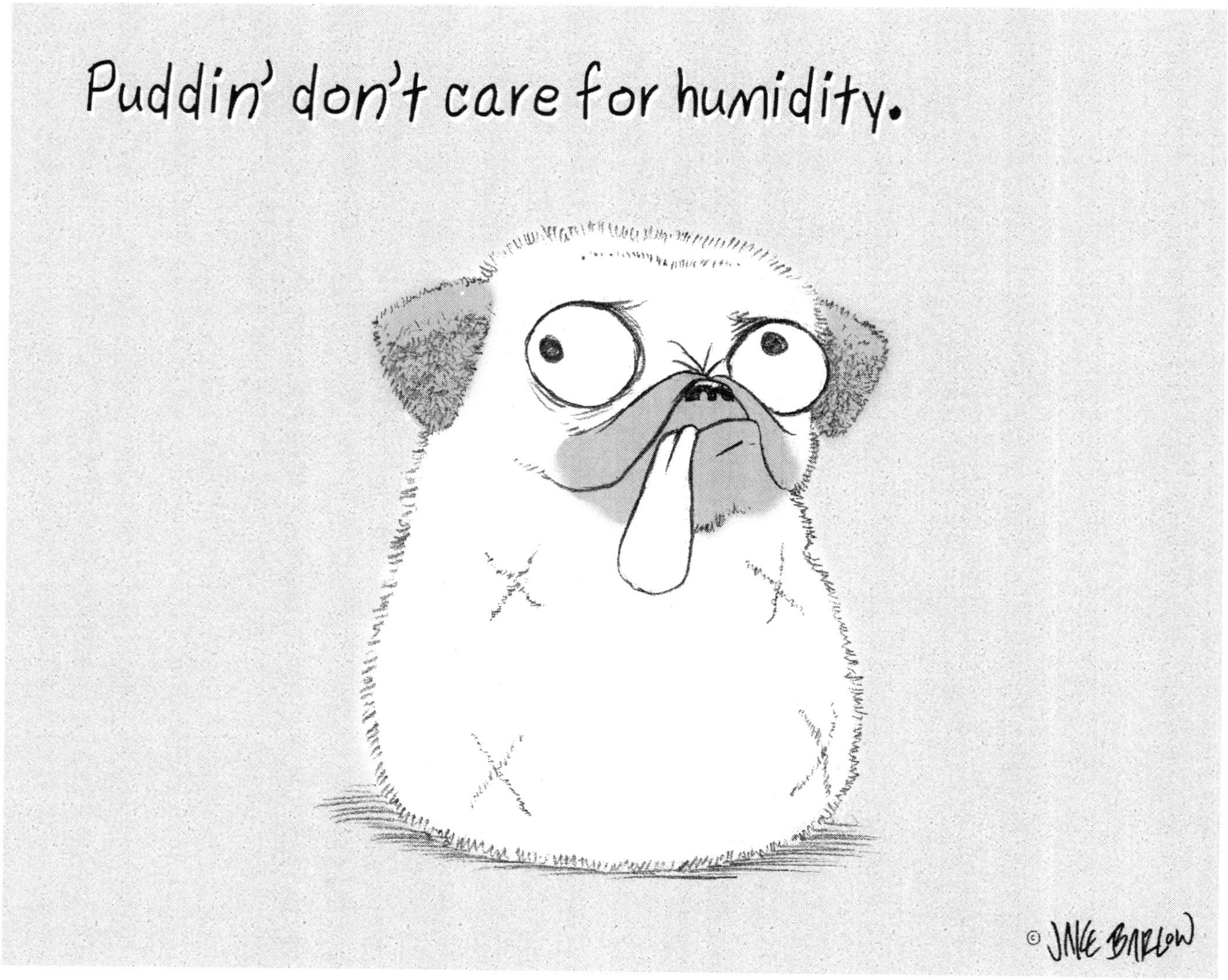
© JAKE BARLOW

Puddin' don't care for humidity.

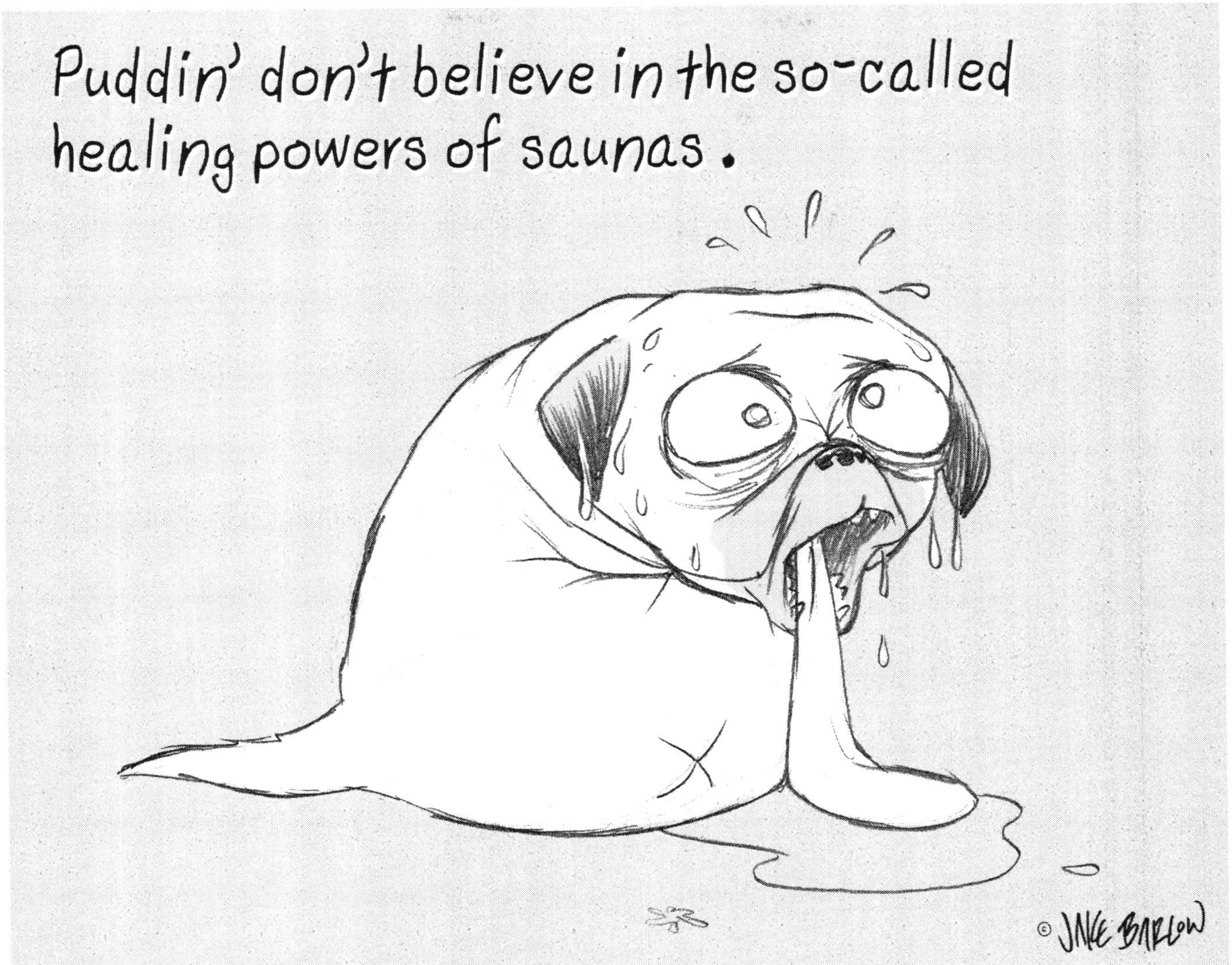
Puddin' don't believe in the so-called healing powers of saunas.
© JAKE BARLOW

In Tug of War, Puddin' don't have much game.

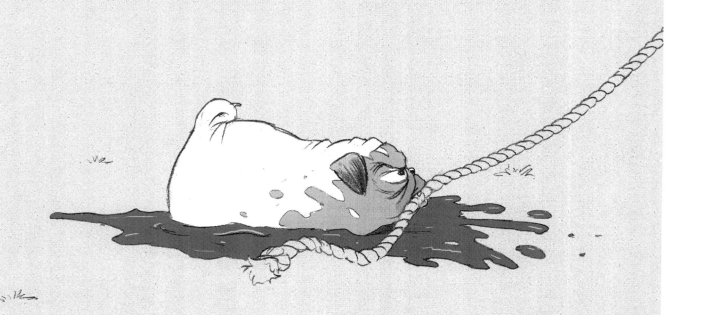

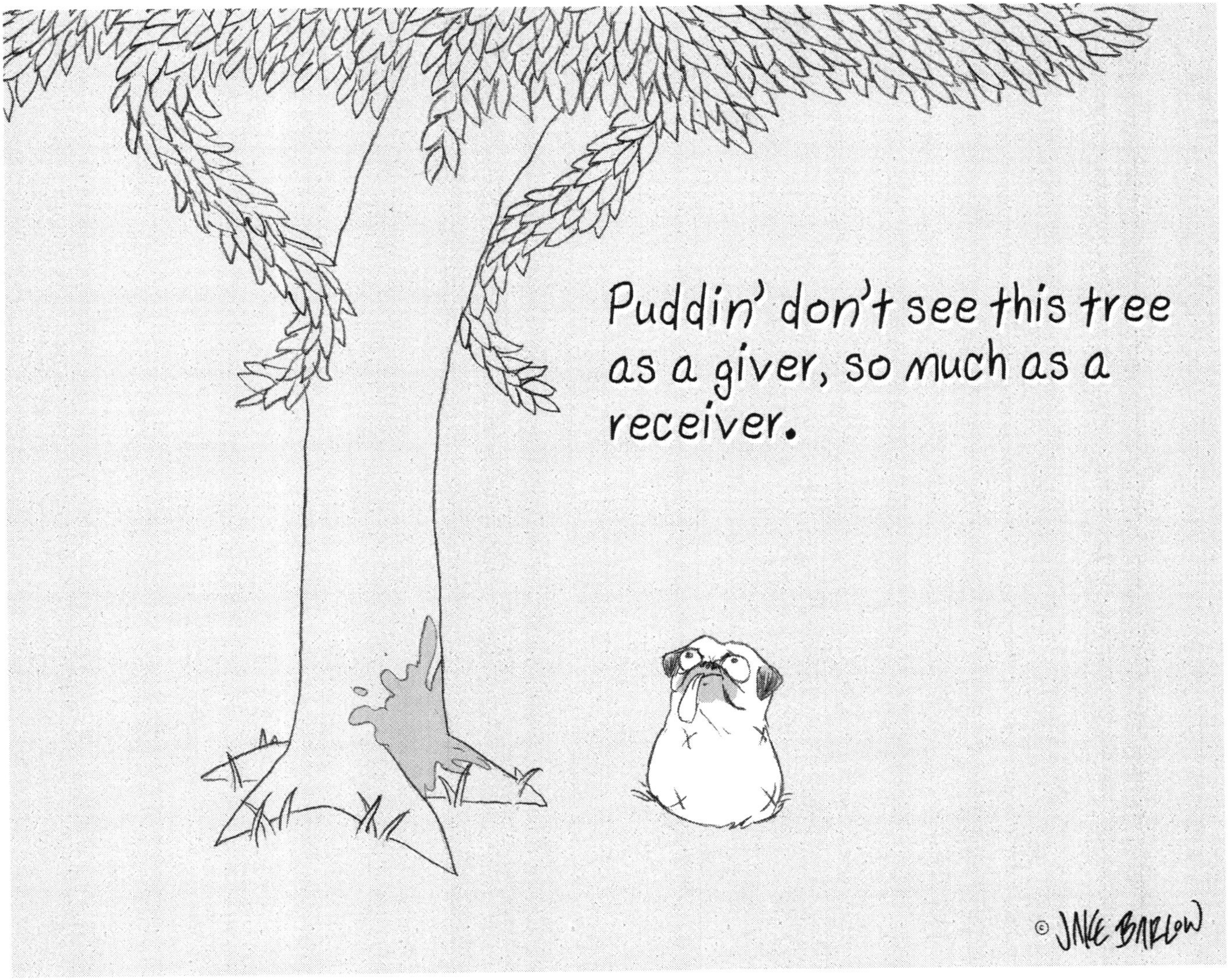
Puddin' don't see this tree as a giver, so much as a receiver.
© JAKE BARLOW

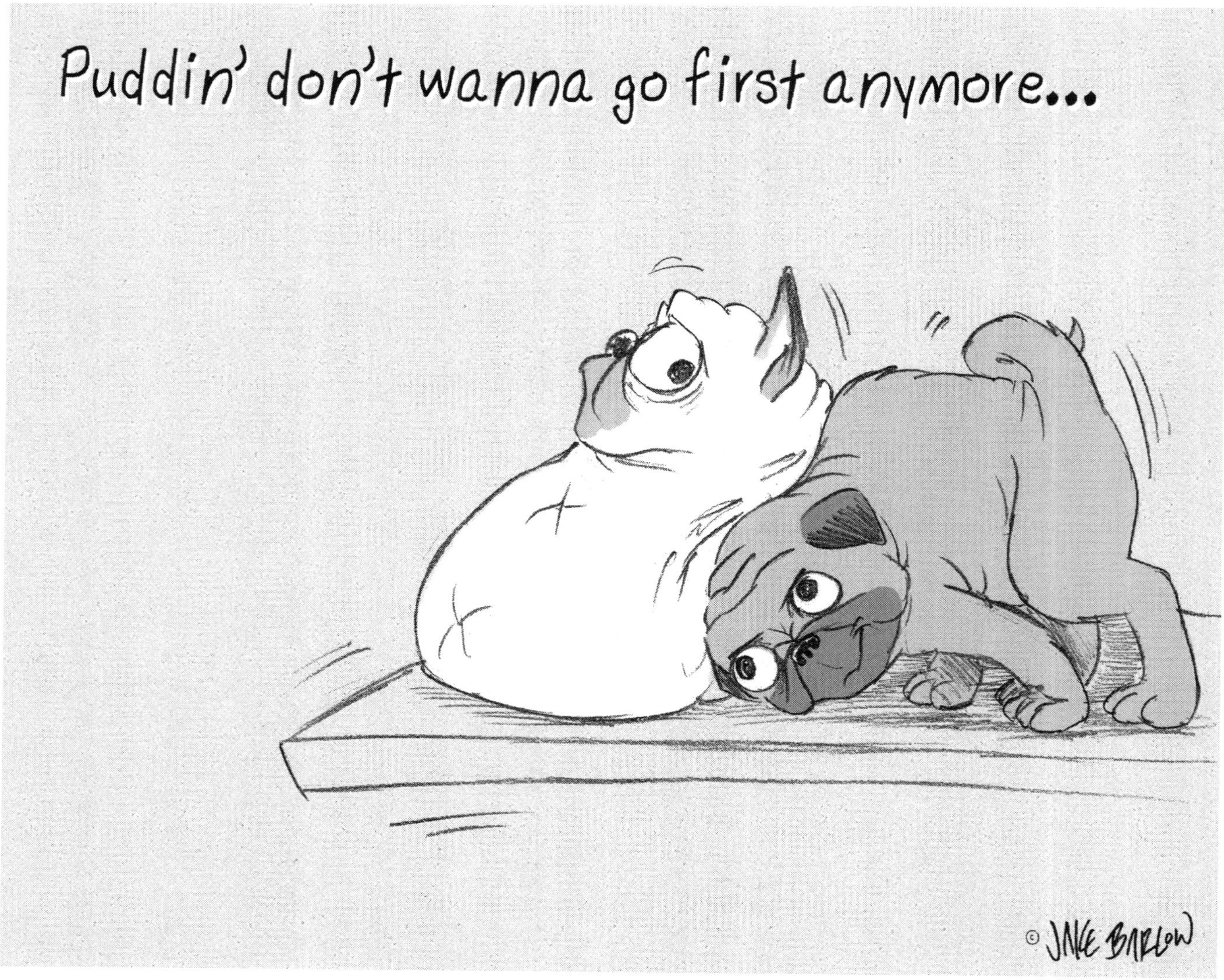
© JAKE BARLOW

Puddin' don't wanna go first anymore...

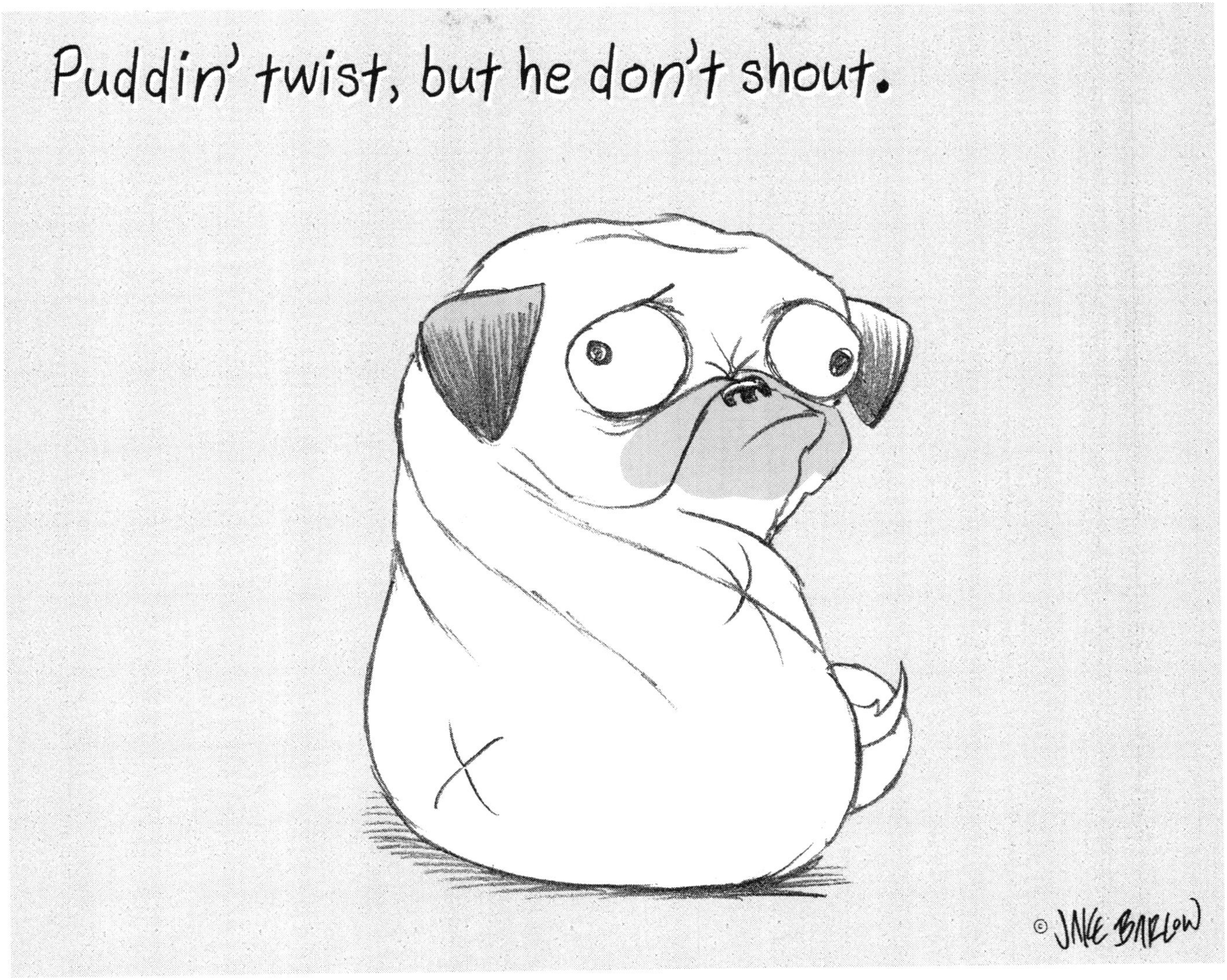
Puddin' twist, but he don't shout.
© JAKE BARLOW

The Dog Whisperer submits to him.

Honey Badger asks him for permission to not care.

He can tell everything about you when you sniff *his* butt.

He is the most interesting pug in the world.

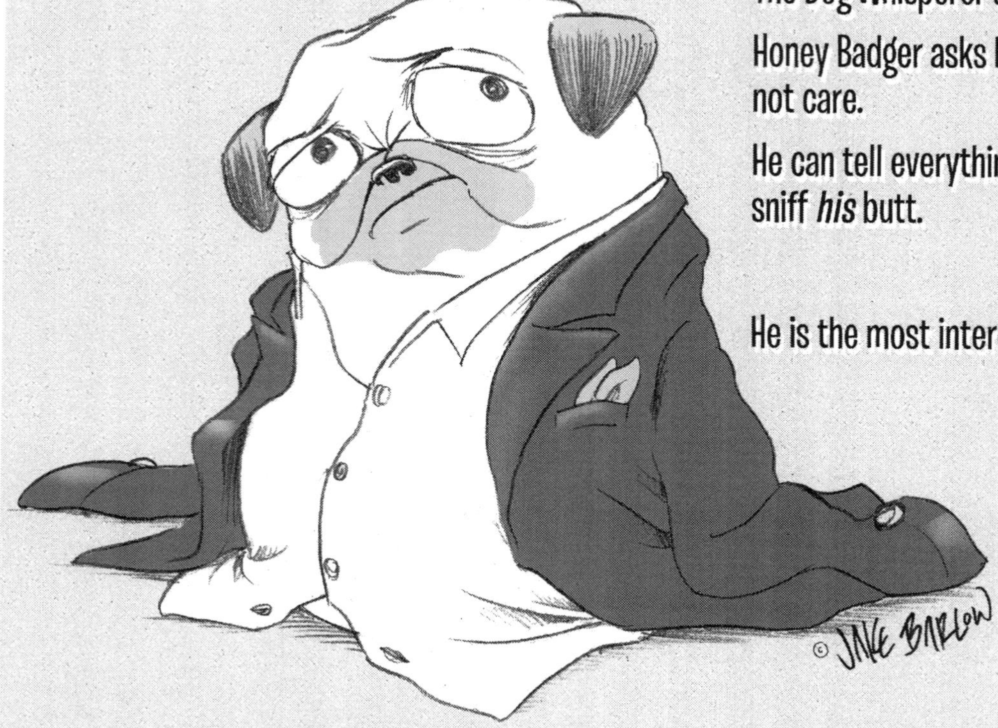
© JAKE BARLOW

Puddin' don't always drink beer, but when he does, he makes sure it doesn't taste like watered-down horse piss.

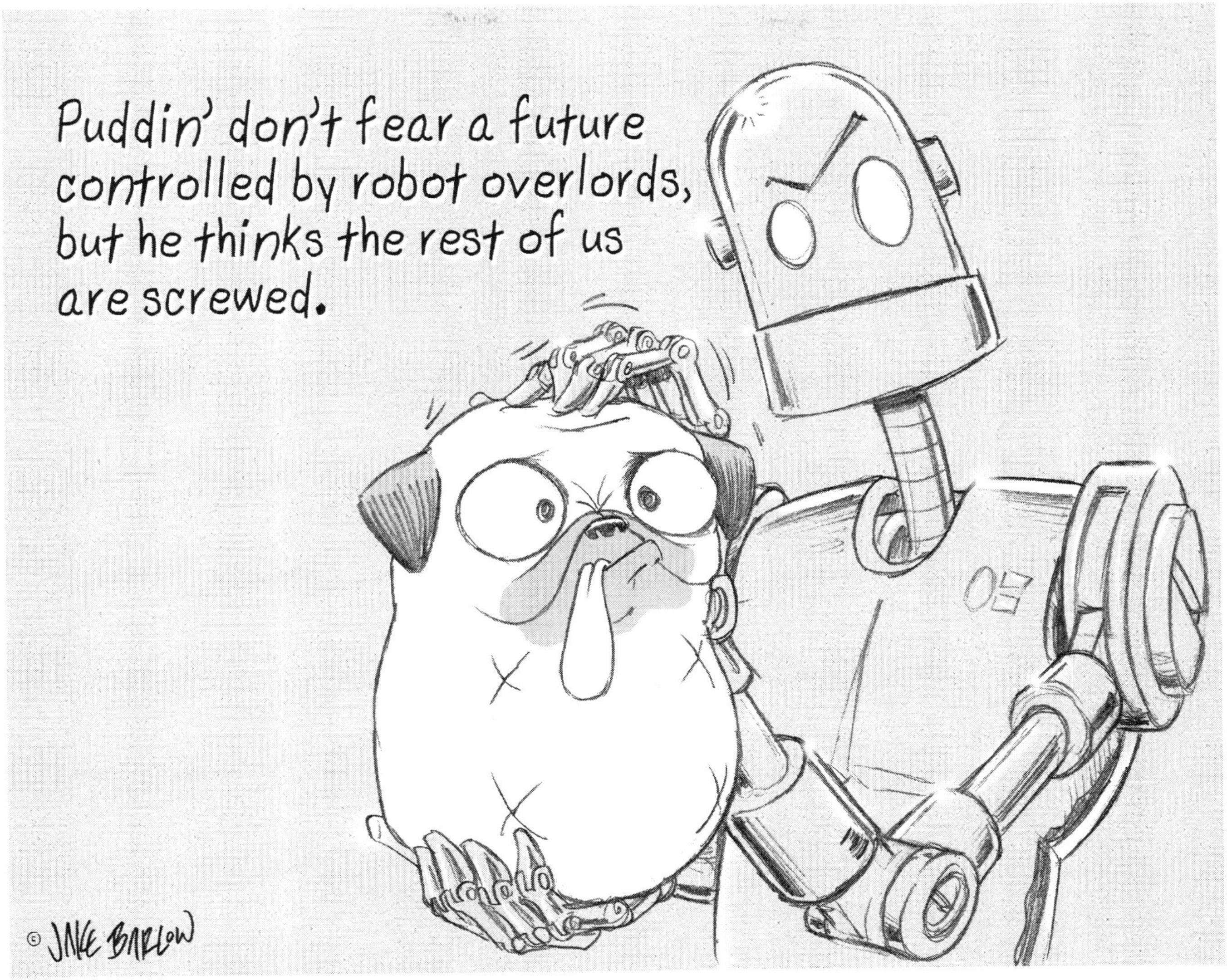
Puddin' don't fear a future controlled by robot overlords, but he thinks the rest of us are screwed.
© JAKE BARLOW

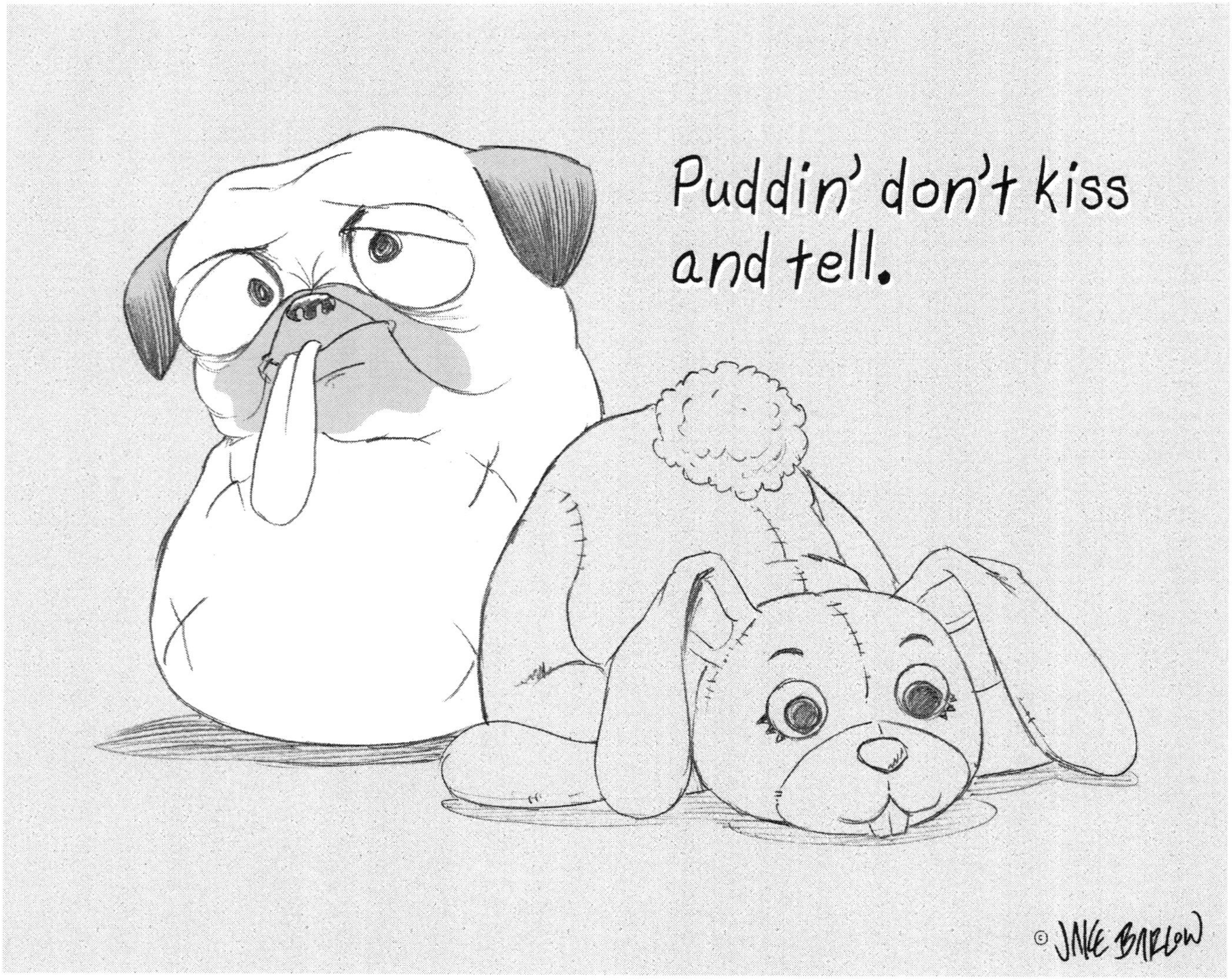
Puddin' don't kiss
and tell.
© JAKE BARLOW

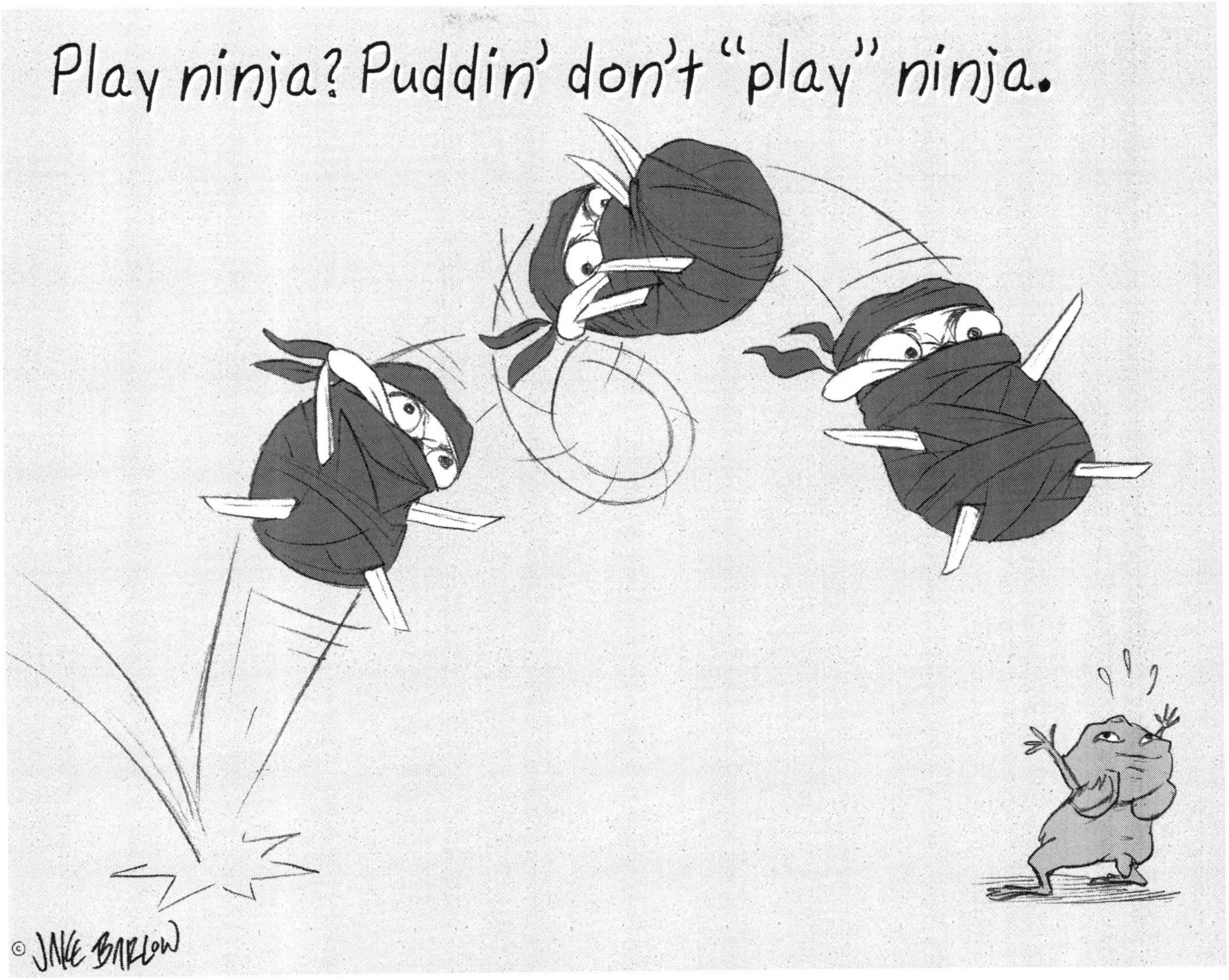
Play ninja? Puddin' don't "play" ninja.
© JAKE BARLOW

When it comes to his natural gifts, Puddin' don't give away trade secrets. Besides, this is only the half of it.

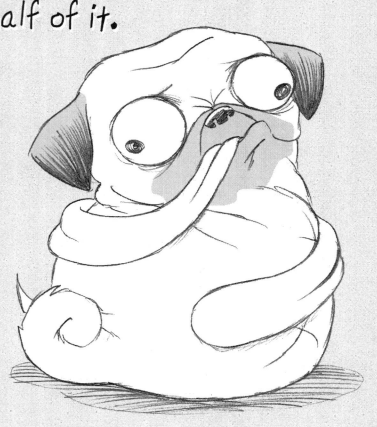

© JAKE BARLOW

Puddin' don't get off on the wrong foot, nor the right foot.

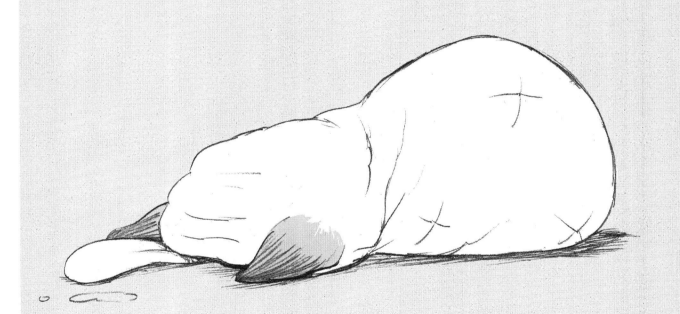

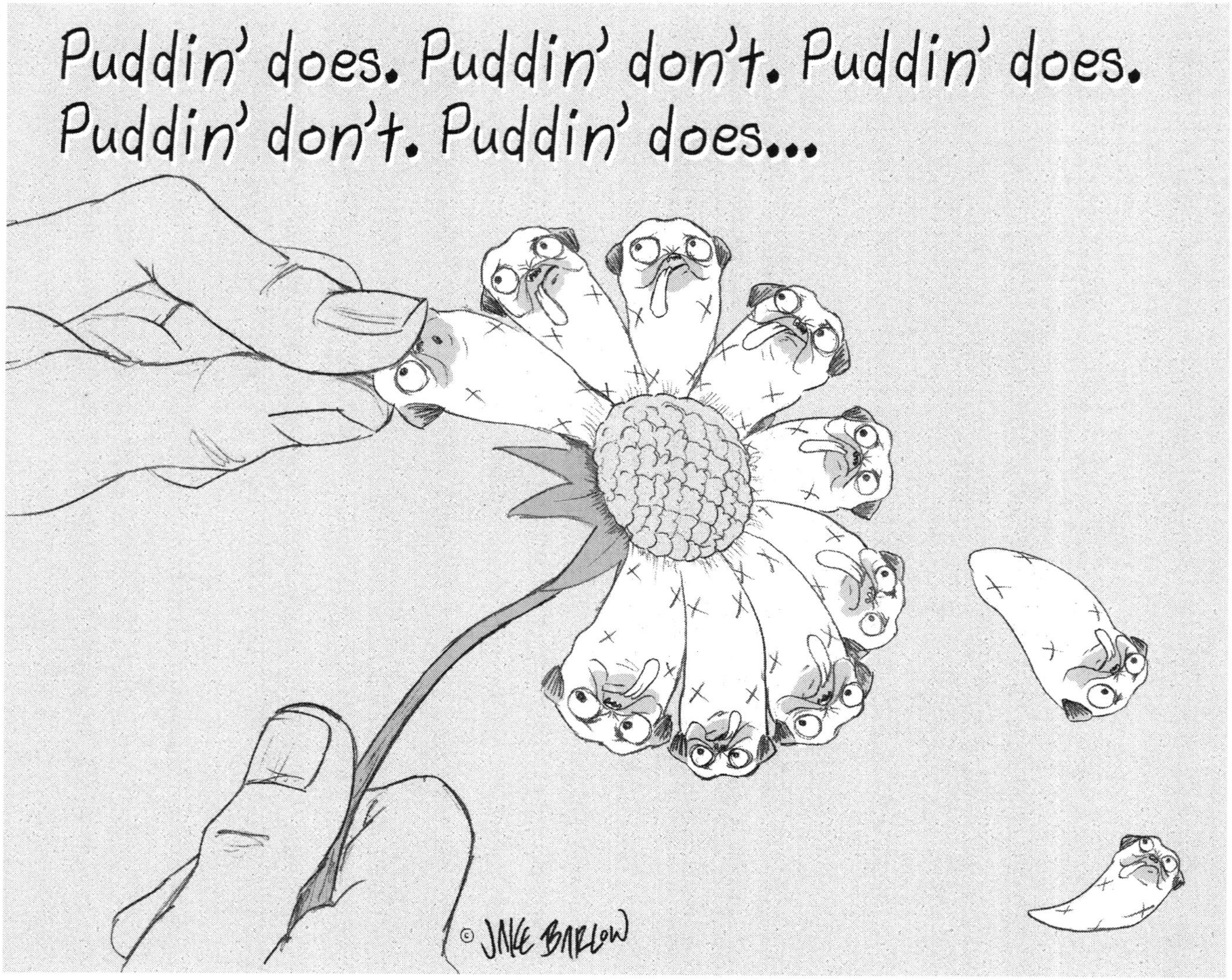
Puddin' does. Puddin' don't. Puddin' does.
Puddin' don't. Puddin' does...
© JAKE BARLOW

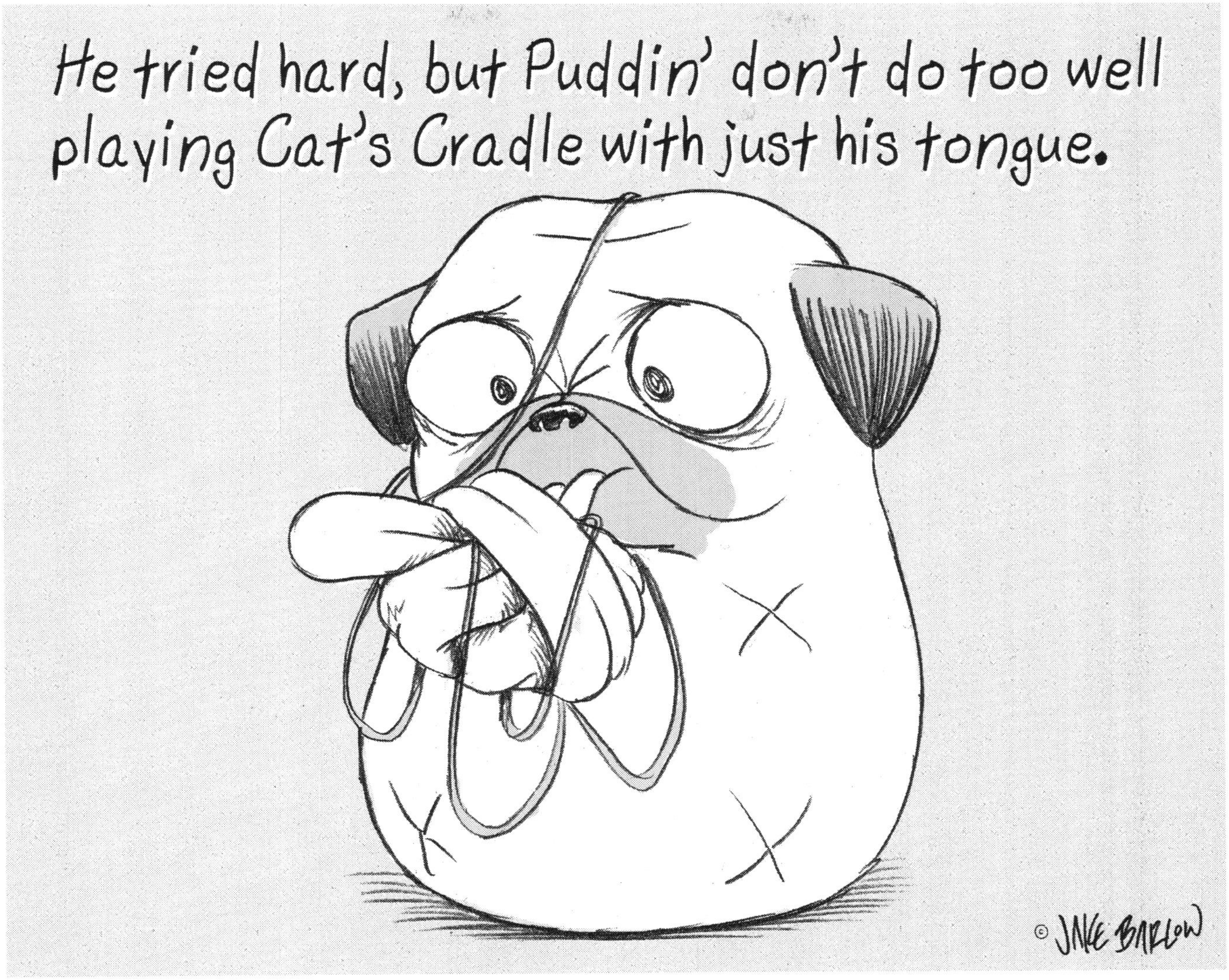
He tried hard, but Puddin' don't do too well playing Cat's Cradle with just his tongue.
© JAKE BARLOW

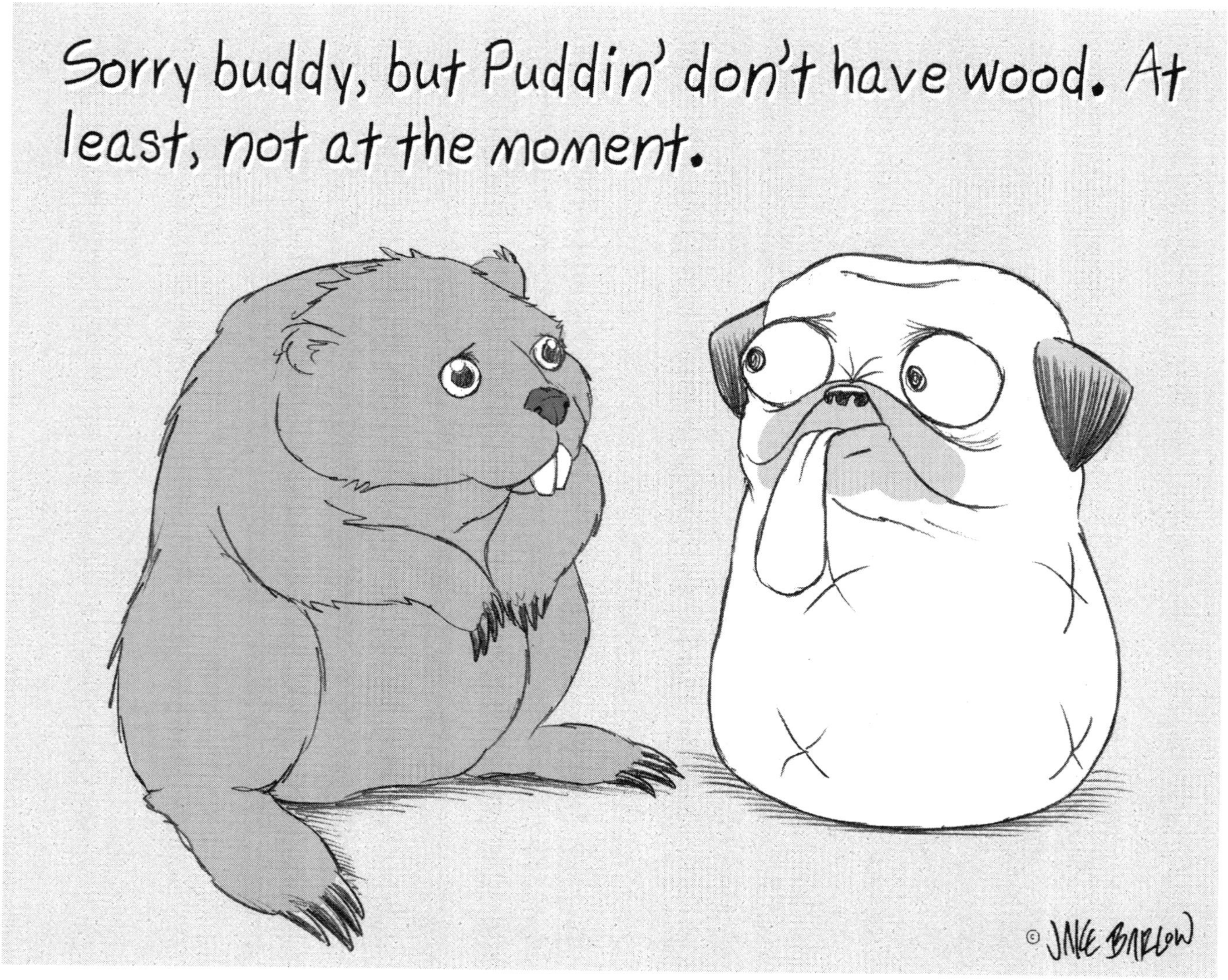
Sorry buddy, but Puddin' don't have wood. At least, not at the moment.
© JAKE BARLOW

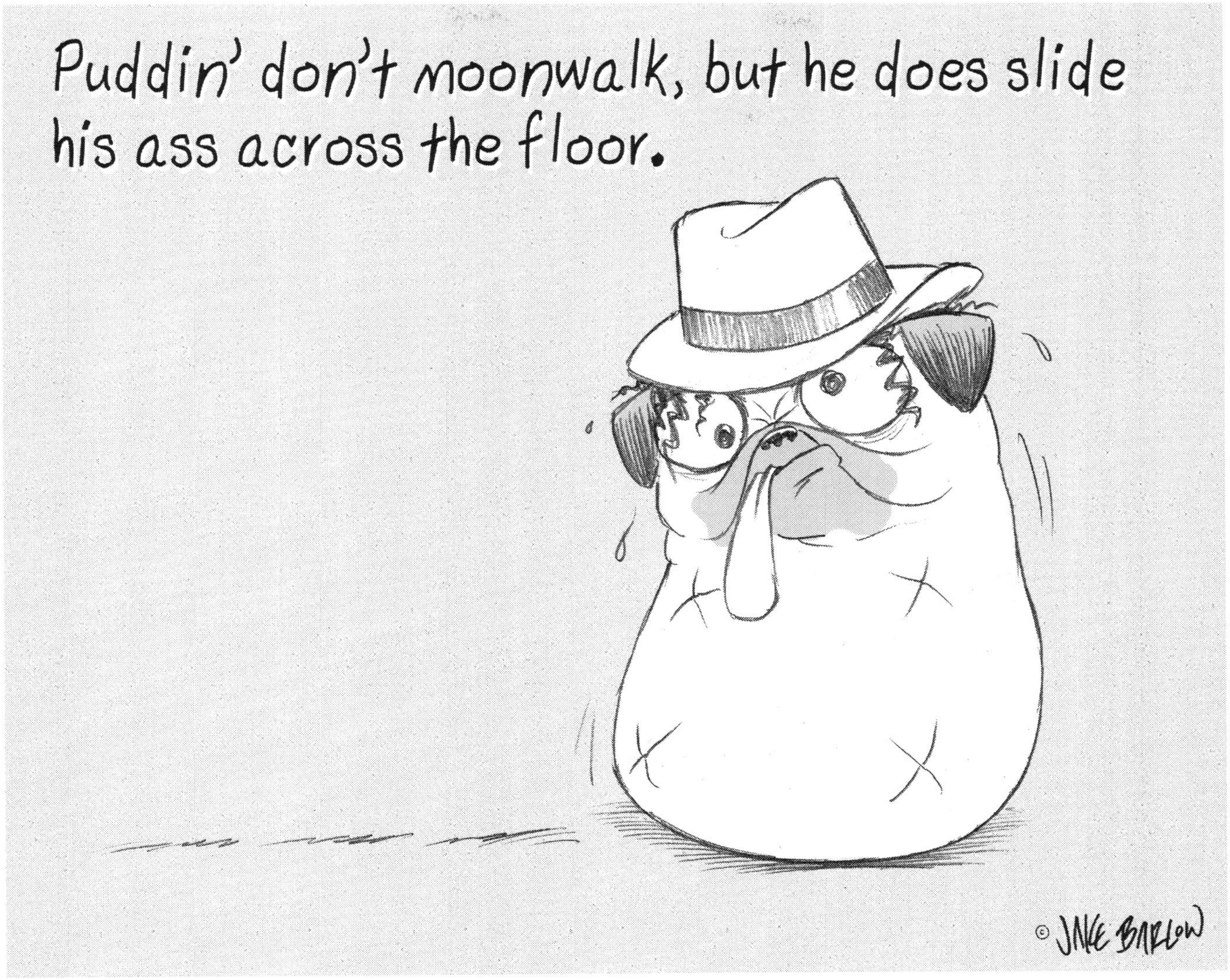
Puddin' don't moonwalk, but he does slide his ass across the floor.
© JAKE BARLOW

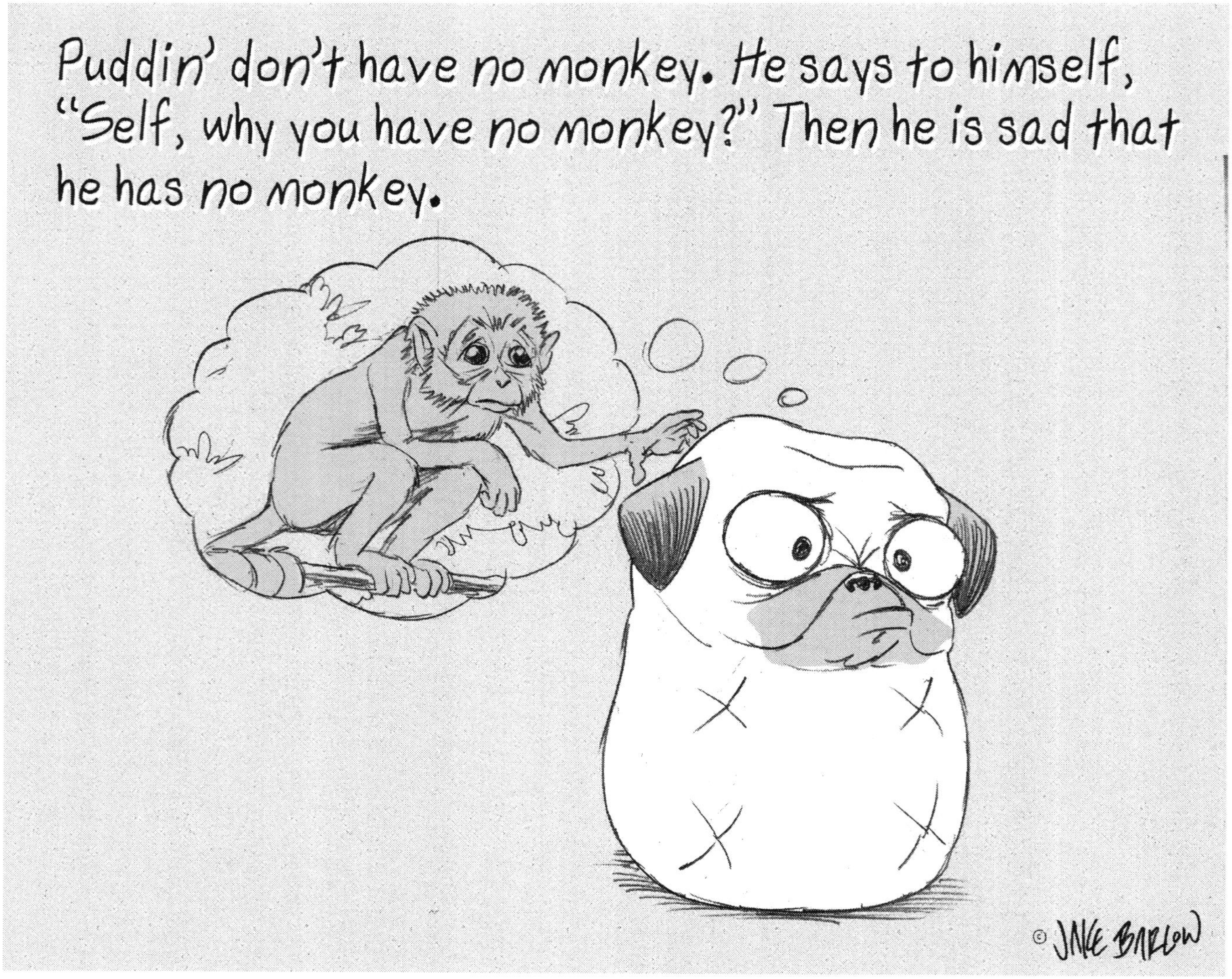
Puddin' don't have no monkey. He says to himself, "Self, why you have no monkey?" Then he is sad that he has no monkey.
© JAKE BARLOW

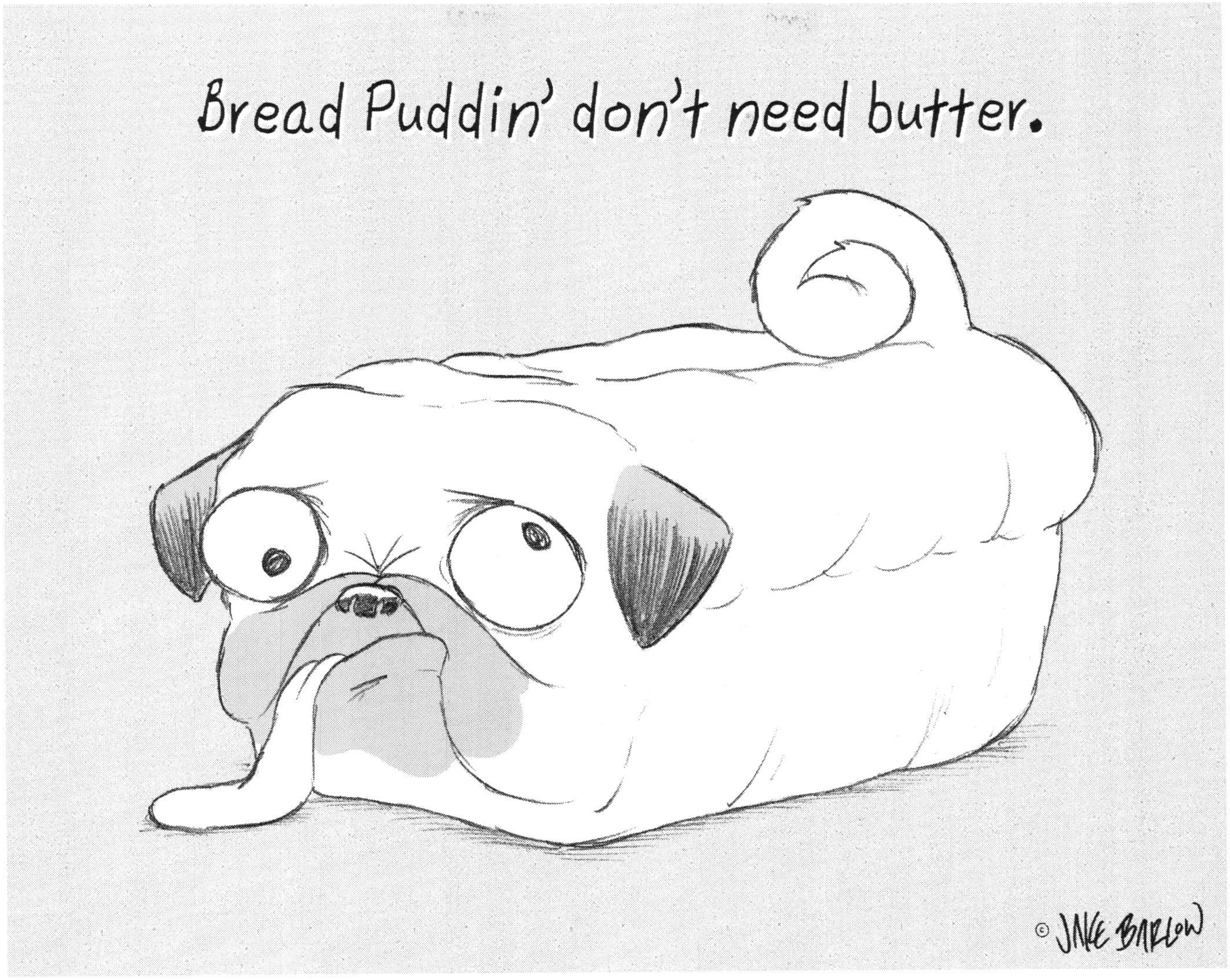
© JAKE BARLOW

Bread Puddin' don't need butter.

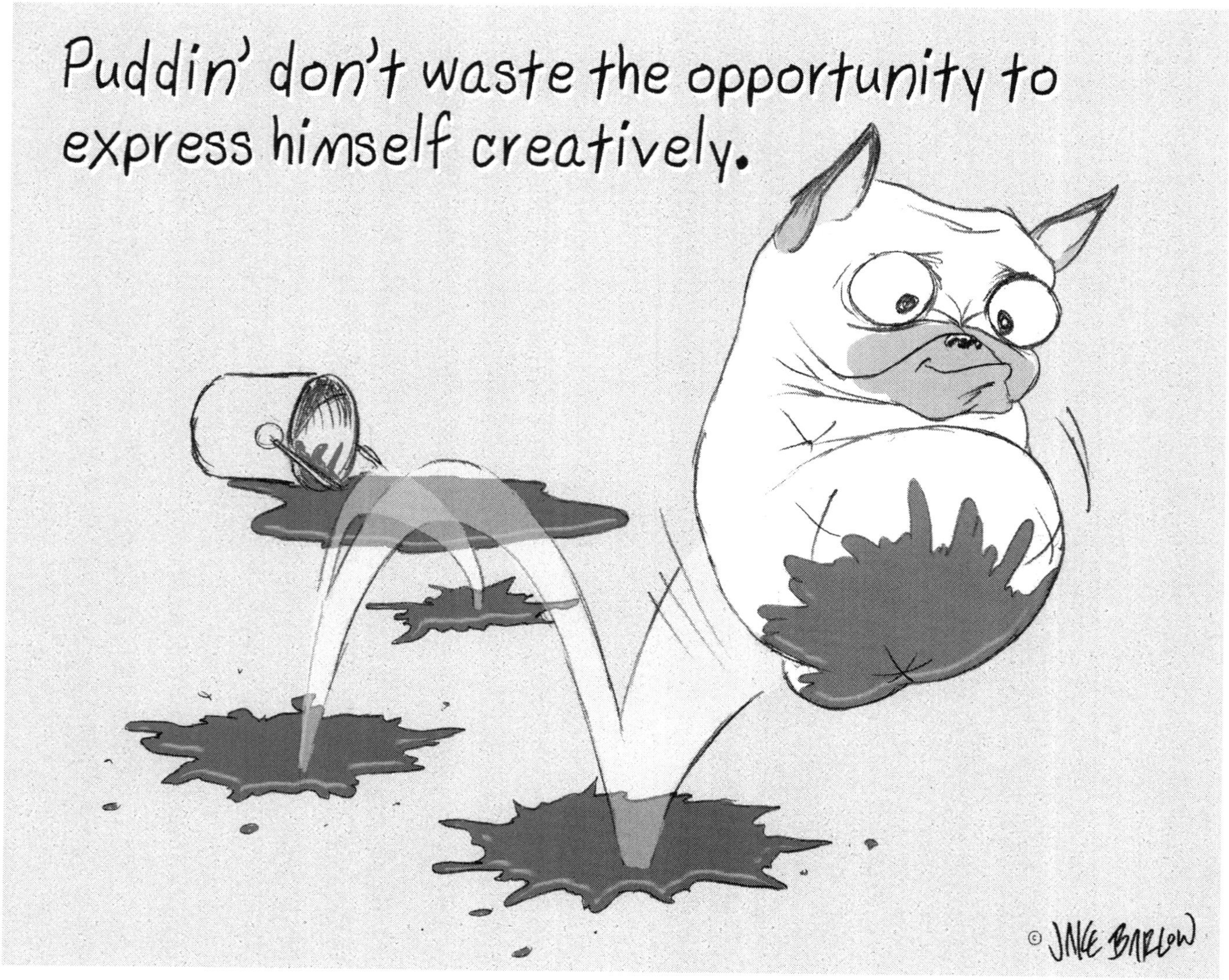
Puddin' don't waste the opportunity to express himself creatively.
© JAKE BARLOW

Puddin' don't think "Pin the Legs on Puddin'" is an acceptable party game!
© JAKE BARLOW

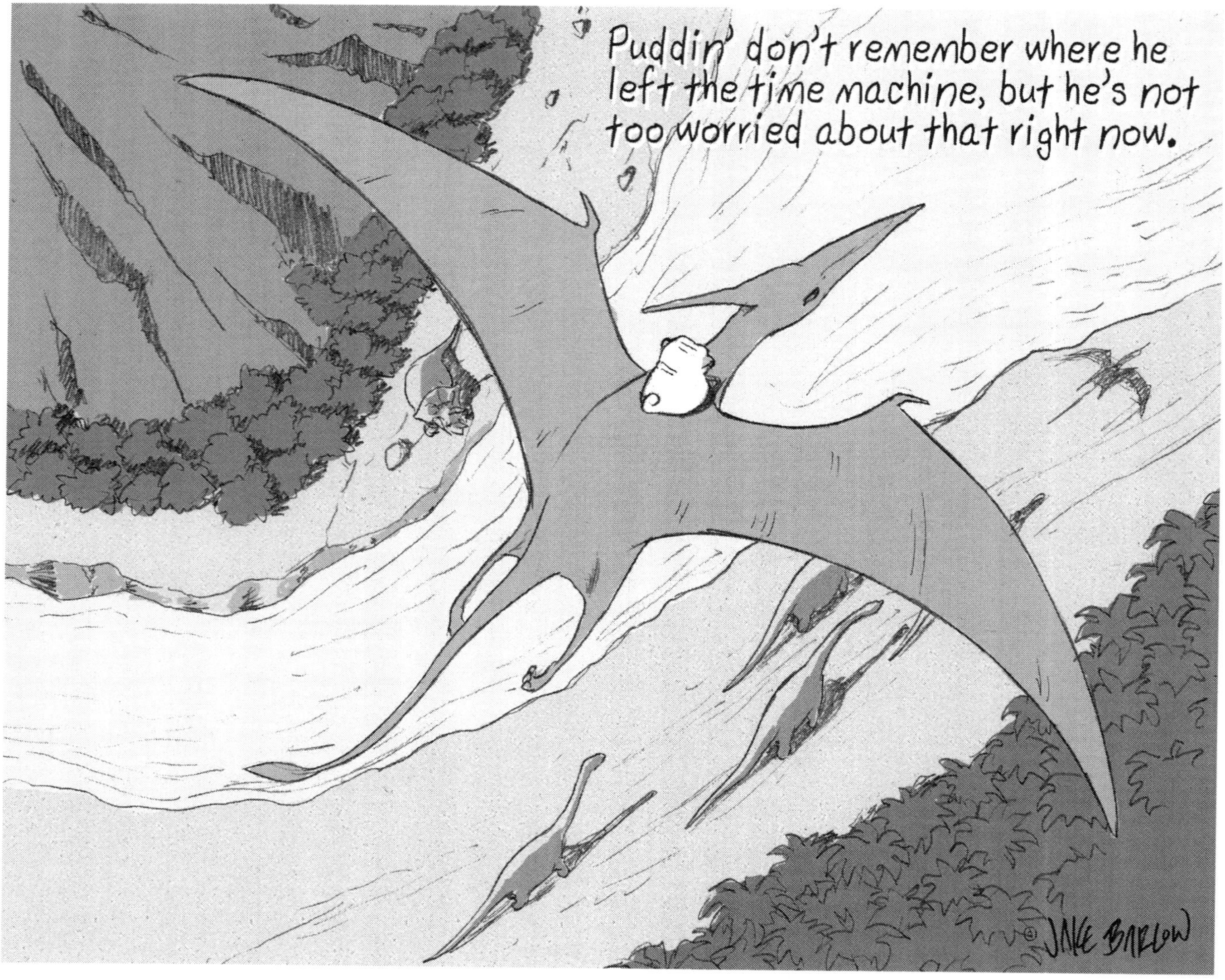
Puddin' don't remember where he left the time machine, but he's not too worried about that right now.
JAKE BARLOW

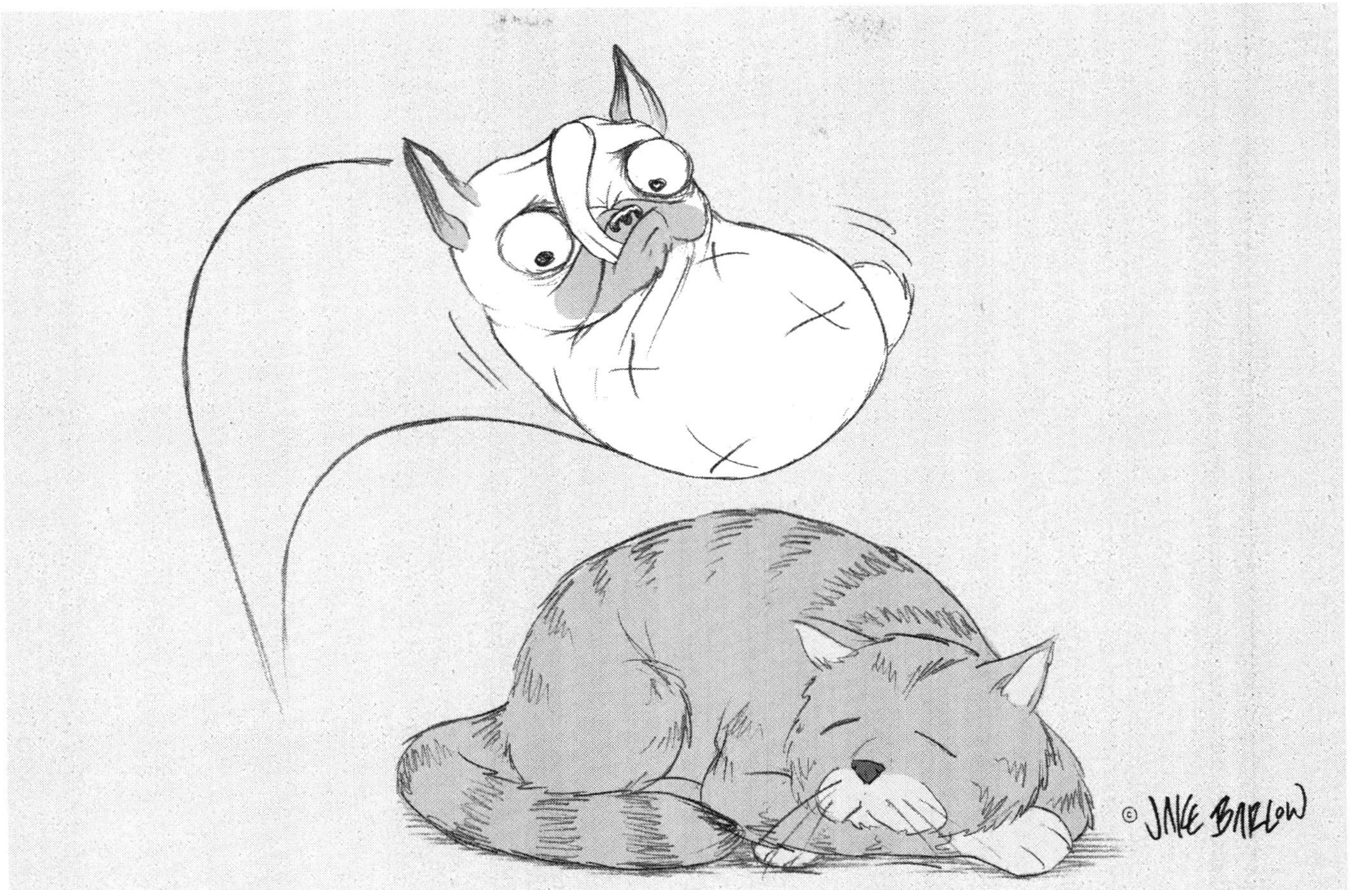
© JAKE BARLOW

Puddin' don't have elbows, so this piledriver will only be so effective, but it will be so worth it!

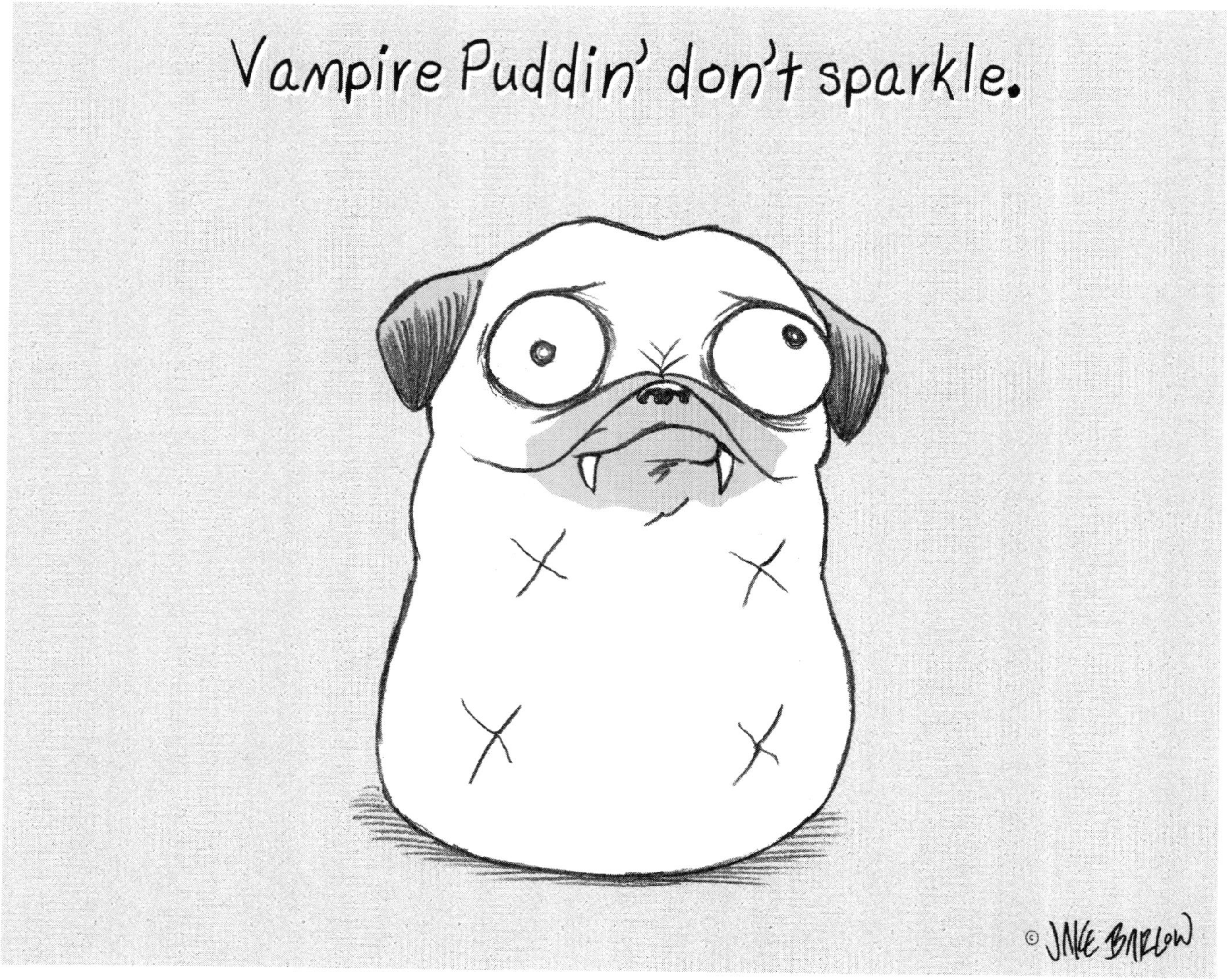
Vampire Puddin' don't sparkle.
© JAKE BARLOW

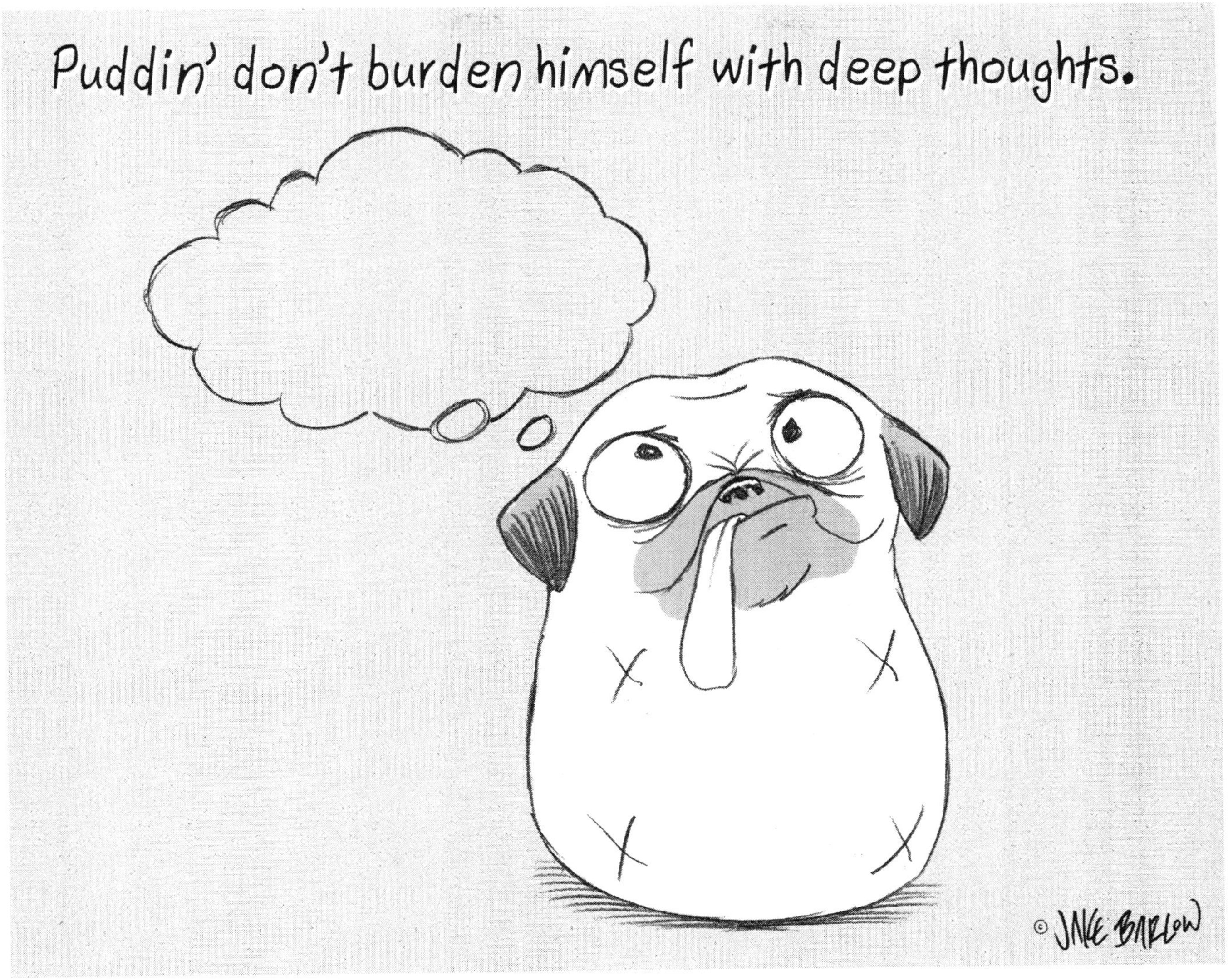
© JAKE BARLOW

Puddin' don't burden himself with deep thoughts.

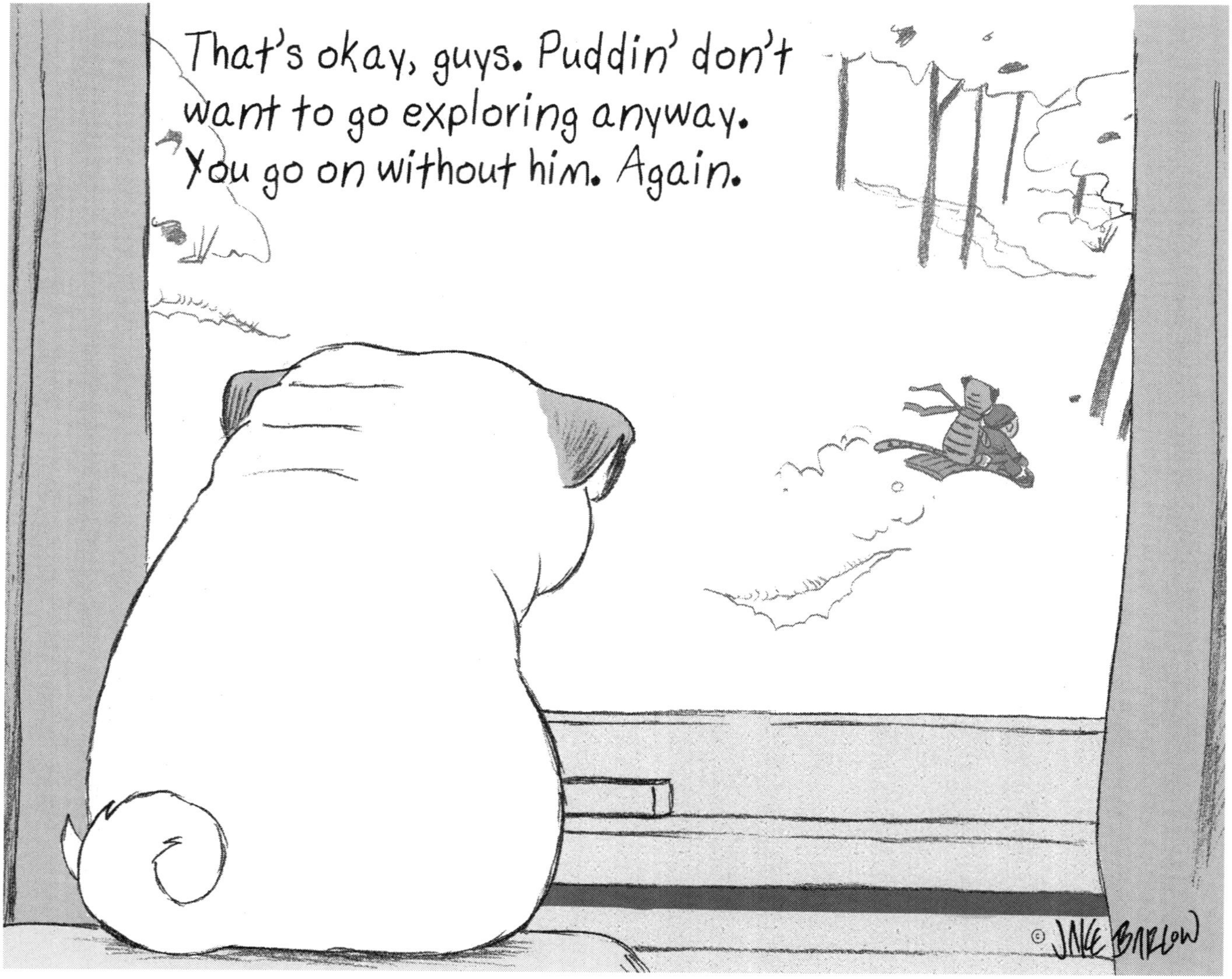
That's okay, guys. Puddin' don't want to go exploring anyway. You go on without him. Again.
© JAKE BARLOW

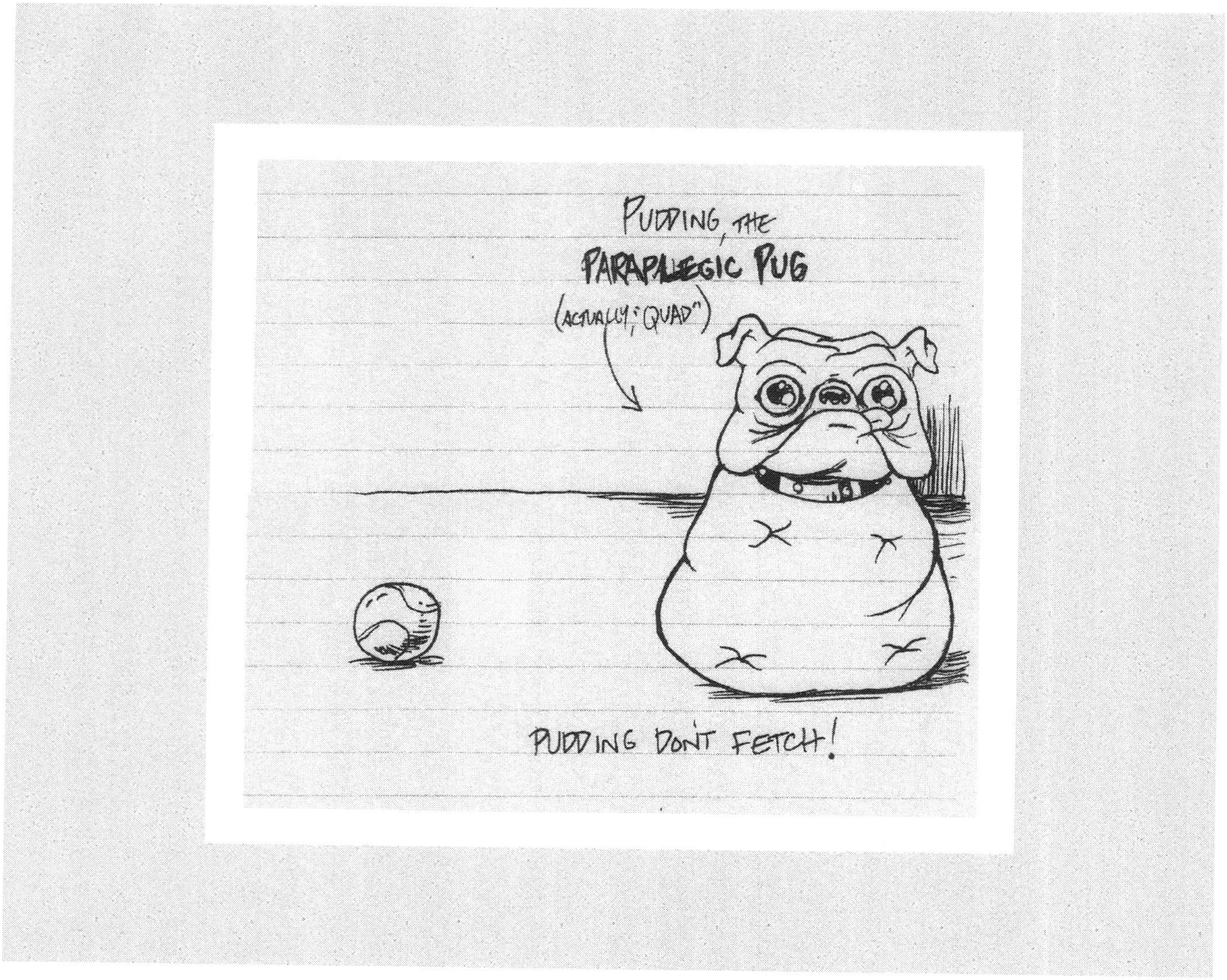
PUDDING, THE
PARAPLEGIC PUG
(ACTUALLY, "QUAD")
PUDDING DON'T FETCH!

A simple doodle, drawn while fighting off boredom. While drawing, I made a mistake I couldn't correct. Rather than finish drawing in the legs, I decided to leave them off. Then, I wondered what a legless dog might be called, and "Pudding" immediately came to mind. Pudding the Paraplegic Pug - even though he looks more Frenchie, and is actually quadraplegic. Of course, you have to wonder what a legless dog would do, and, well, he certainly don't fetch.

A personal note to fans of Puddin' Don't:

Firstly, thank you very much for being fans. If it were not for you, Puddin' may not still be here. That so many people now look forward to seeing Puddin' in their inboxes, or in the news feeds on Facebook, or on Tumblr.com, I am inspired and motivated to make sure that happens, even when it looks like I won't have enough time to make it happen.

This has been a labor of love since the beginning, and is undoubtedly the most enjoyable project I've ever worked on. While it is my dream one day to be able to make a living by drawing Puddin' cartoons, for now I still have to keep my day job. But I will keep drawing Puddin', posting the cartoons online, and will keep making and selling Puddin' merchandise to continue raising much needed funds for animal shelters and rescues, so long as Puddin' has fans.

While it is important for me to also thank my wife, Clarice, for her continued support - and patience, I must also thank all of Puddin's fans, present, past, and future, for your support!

Sincerely,

JAKE BARLOW

Sketchbook

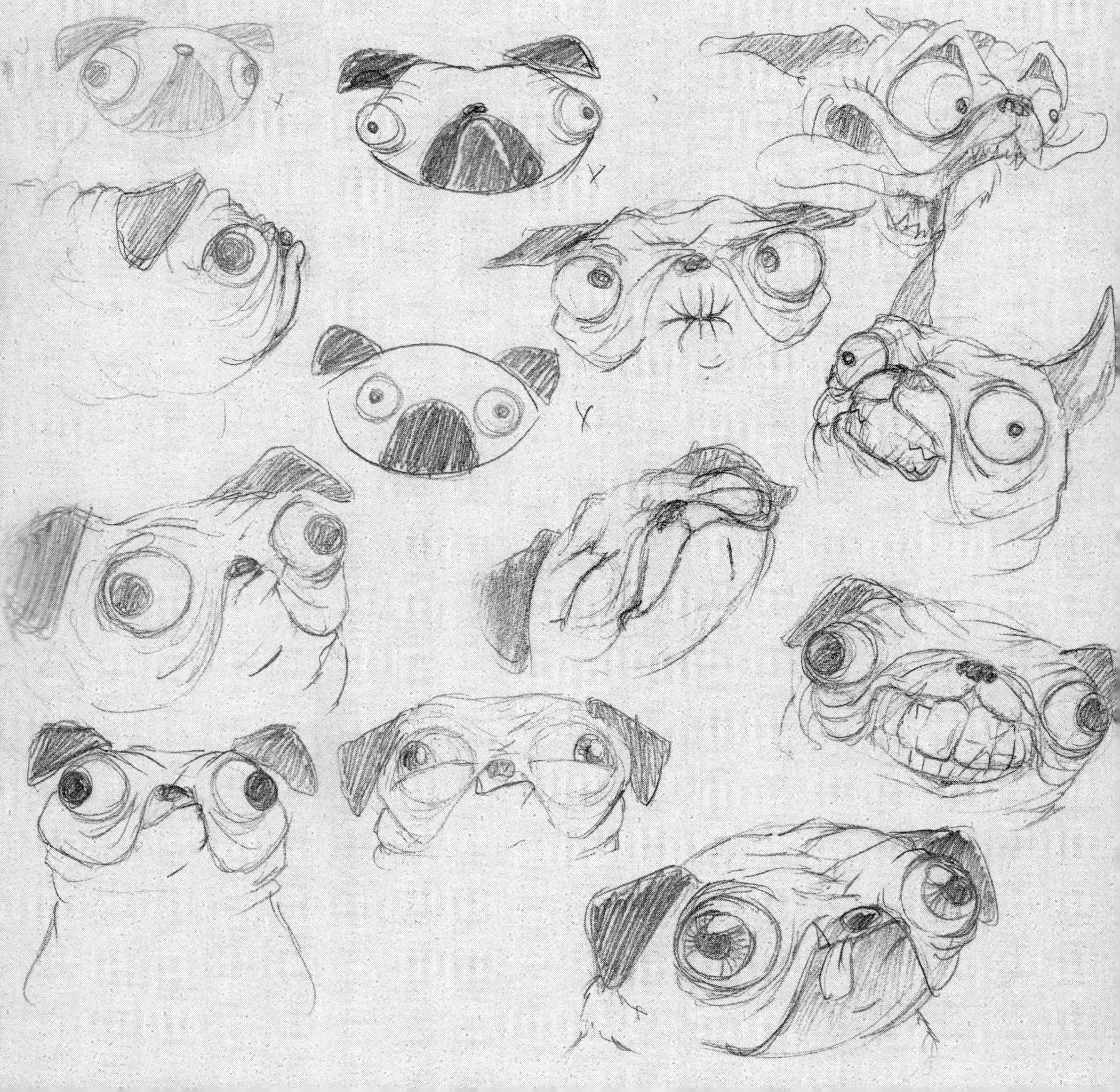

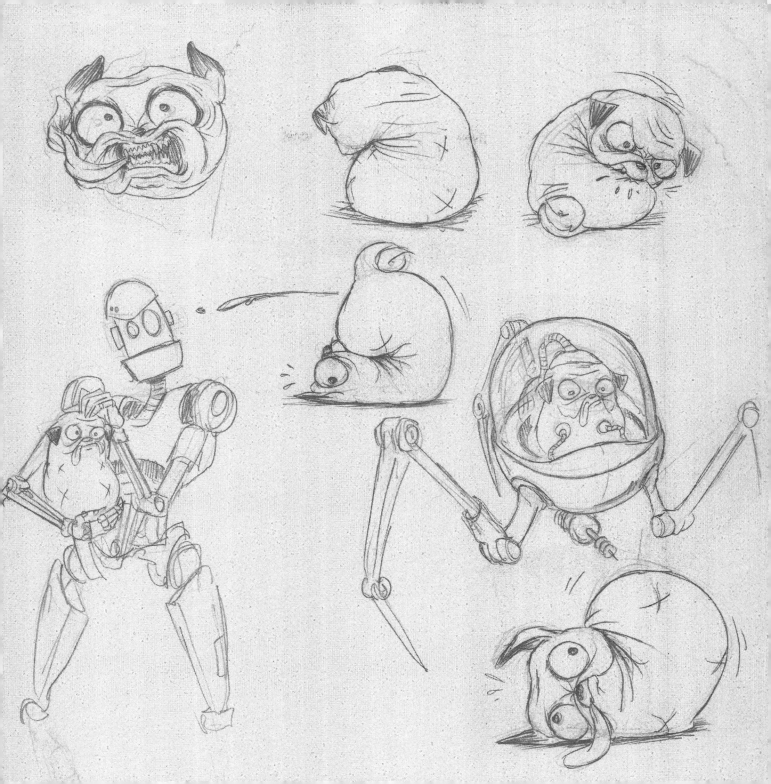

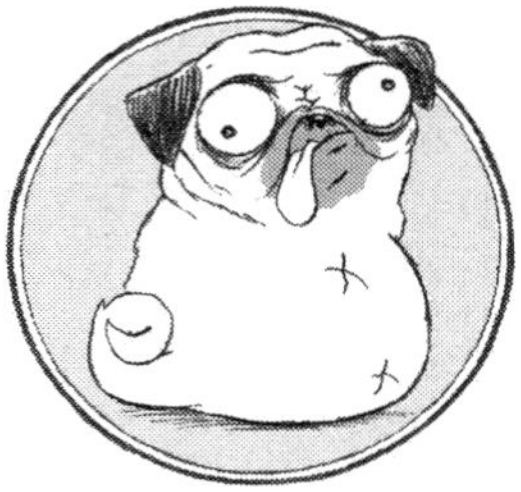

Puddin' Don't

Created by Jake Barlow

Puddin' Don't can be seen daily online at www.puddindont.com

No animals were harmed in the making of anything related to *Puddin' Don't*.
Please do not eat this book, or feed it to anyone.